Economists in Discussion

Economists in Discussion

The Correspondence between G.L.S. Shackle and Stephen F. Frowen, 1951–1992

Stephen F. Frowen

palgrave
macmillan

First published 2004 by
PALGRAVE MACMILLAN
Houndmills, Basingstoke, Hampshire RG21 6XS and
175 Fifth Avenue, New York, N. Y. 10010
Companies and representatives throughout the world.

PALGRAVE MACMILLAN is the global academic imprint of the Palgrave Macmillan division of St. Martin's Press, LLC and of Palgrave Macmillan Ltd. Macmillan® is a registered trademark in the United States, United Kingdom and other countries. Palgrave is a registered trademark in the European Union and other countries.

ISBN 0–333–77208–3

This book is printed on paper suitable for recycling and made from fully managed and sustained forest sources.

A catalogue record for this book is available from the British Library.

Library of Congress Cataloging-in-Publication Data
Economists in discussion : the correspondence between G.L.S. Shackle and Stephen F. Frowen, 1951–1992 /c Stephen F. Frowen [compiler and editor].
p. cm.
Includes bibliographical references and index.
ISBN 0-333-77208-3 (cloth)
1. Shackle, G.L.S. (George Lennox Sharman), 1903—Correspondence. 2. Frowen, Stephen F. —Correspondence. 3. Economists—Great Britain––Correspondence. 4. Economics—Philosophy. 5. Decision making. 6. Economists—Great Britain—Biography. I. Frowen, Stephen F. II. Shackle, G.L.S. (George Lennox Sharman), 1903–

HB103.S47A4 2003
330.1'092'2–dc21 2003053269

10 9 8 7 6 5 4 3 2 1
13 12 11 10 09 08 07 06 05 04

Printed and bound in Great Britain by
Antony Rowe Ltd, Chippenham and Eastbourne

This book is dedicated to the late George and Catherine Shackle in loving and eternal memory

Contents

Acknowledgements ix

Introduction xi

THE LETTERS 1

Appendices

1 The Big Flake
G.L.S Shackle 328

2 Reflections on George Shackle: Three Excerpts from the Shackle Collection 332
Stephen C. Littlechild

3 Obituary of G.L.S. Shackle 338
Stephen F. Frowen

4 In Memoriam: G.L.S. Shackle, FBA, 1903 to 1992 340
Stephen F. Frowen

5 Missing Letters Discovered in February 2004 among Paters Bequeathed by Catherine Shackle to Cambridge University Library 344

Name Index 363

Subject Index 368

Acknowledgements

My chief debt is to G.L.S. Shackle's wife Catherine Shackle, who has given me every encouragement to publish this volume. She died on 14 June 2003, just seven weeks after approving the Introduction to this correspondence in her letter of 26 April 2003. I had become her 'Other-Brother', and she became for me the sister I never had. It is my deepest wish to dedicate this volume to both the late George and Catherine Shackle.

I am particularly grateful to Mr. T.M. (Tim) Farmiloe, who as Publishing Director of Macmillan originally accepted the correspondence for publication shortly before his retirement. Our relationship over many of my books has been a very happy one and I am glad to say that our friendship grew with every new volume and continues to deepen. He also gave every encouragement in 1988 to the publication of my Festschrift, edited by Philip Arestis, *Contemporary Issues in Money and Banking* (second edition *Money and Banking: Issues for the Twenty-First Century*, 1993).

I am glad to say that my collaboration with Ms. Amanda Watkins, Senior Commissioning Editor, Palgrave Macmillan, has also been very constructive and fruitful, and I wish to express my special thanks to her for taking over this project from Tim Farmiloe and see it through to its final completion. Her assistance and support cannot be praised enough.

I must further express my gratitude to the past and present Keeper of Manuscripts at Cambridge University Library, Mr. A.E.B. Owen and Dr. Patrick Zutshi respectively, and their staff, in particular Ms. Kathleen Cann, the author of the 'Catalogue of the Shackle Papers', published in *Economics as an Art of Thought* (editors P.E. Earl and S.F. Frowen), pp. 368–418, and Mr. Godfrey Waller, Superintendent of the Manuscripts Reading Room, for their unfailing assistance in tracing letters included in this volume.

Thanks are also due to Professor Sir Brian Heap, Master of St. Edmund's College, University of Cambridge, and to Dr. The Rev. Frank McHugh, the former Director of the Von Hügel Institute Cambridge, for their general support and interest in this endeavour, to my colleague at University College London, Professor Victoria Chick, for reading and commenting on parts of the book, to Ms. Anne Usher, the Departmental Administrator at UCL, for much assistance, and to Miss Joe Piris for typing a great part of the correspondence.

Lastly, but with special emphasis, I would like to express my deepest thanks to Mr. Keith Povey, the copy-editor of this volume and many of my previous books. Our working relationship for nearly two decades has been most inspiring and I cannot recall any occasion when I did not take up his suggestions and/or approve of his editorial changes. In fact, it was my special request to Palgrave Macmillan that Keith Povey should copy-edit this volume, which is particularly close to my heart. His superb efforts on this occasion again have been greatly enhanced by the outstanding subject index prepared by Mr. Anthony Horton. 'Without an index (and an ample one)', writes George Shackle in 'The Big Flake' (page 328 of this volume), 'a book cannot *converse* with its reader.' Mr. Horton has enabled readers to do just this.

St. Edmund's College Cambridge and
University College London

STEPHEN F. FROWEN

Introduction

Amongst George Shackle's papers I found an unpublished and untitled note, which starts as follows:

> In the scholarly life, a young man is a traveller, an old man is a traffic policeman. The young man is seeking the footprints of his predecessors across a land unknown to him, or better, he is building a road across it. The old man is warning, advising and encouraging the travellers, and pointing out the mountain pass from which there will be seen, who knows what spreading landscape?

It is exactly in this latter sense that George Shackle, my senior by precisely twenty years, has been my mentor, advising, encouraging and warning me throughout my professional life from the time I had left Germany after the Second World War to settle in England until his death in 1992.

My correspondence with George Shackle extends over four decades from 1951 until 1992, the longest continuous correspondence he had with any of his students or colleagues. It therefore projects much of his life, personal and professional, and his writings. The idea of publishing this correspondence came when I re-read one of his last letters (17 September, 1989) in which he strongly endorsed my suggestion for the publication of his correspondence generally. He writes:

> I am most deeply touched indeed by your extraordinary generous kindness in proposing to arrange for a collection of my letters to be made and published. I began some years ago to have xerox copies made of my outgoing letters and perhaps these may be of service. My handwriting did not become as atrociously bad as it now is until a number of years ago. Mr. Owen's[1] interest in this plan is of course a very deep pleasure to me, and this has suggested to me a search among my papers for manuscript material that might interest him.

I thought it best to start with correspondence which covers virtually his entire postwar academic life.[2]

George Shackle was well known for his exquisite and effective use of English to convey his thoughts, of which his vast number of letters provides further proof. He had a great belief in the power of the English language, especially in the field of economics. In one of his letters in this volume (27 November 1967) he writes: 'The finest vehicle for economic thought, the one which allows all its subtleties and depth to be in some degree taken into account, is still the English Language.'

The late German philosopher Hans-Georg Gadamer, writing on one of the greatest European poets of the twentieth century, Rainer Maria Rilke, expressed the view that 'The passing of time is like a great filtering process which retains little, but this little endures for ever.'[3] While much of the vast amount of present-day economic literature is likely to date in no time, Shackle's writings, concentrating on fundamental ideas, will surely survive the passing of time and will inspire economists for generations to come.

I had the great fortune of meeting George Shackle soon after my arrival in England as a post-graduate student at Leeds University in 1951, where he had just been appointed to a Readership – his first postwar academic position. I was immediately struck by the brilliance of his lectures, each of which was meticulously prepared. In his clear and beautiful handwriting he would prepare a blackboard giving the essence of the lecture to come, which we were advised to copy beforehand. He would then ask us to put down our pens, sit back and just listen to his lecture. It was an ingenious way of getting his often complex ideas across to us. In seminars he had an encouraging response for everyone, even when interventions were somewhat off the mark. Nobody was afraid to open his mouth and seminar discussions soon became lively and interesting sessions.

Essentially, George Shackle was a very shy and withdrawn man. Once, when I had been invited to give a lecture at Liverpool University after he had already been teaching there for many years, one member of staff came up to me, apologising for asking a personal question: 'How did you manage to get into such a close relationship with Professor Shackle? We tremendously appreciate having him with us and admire him, but we feel that we don't really know him.' From the very beginning, I never had any problem on this count. To me, he was somebody I deeply admired, both as a person and a scholar, and right from the beginning he became my role model.

I was fortunate in that he responded. He instantly realised my predicament as an immigrant from a recently hostile country and wanted to help. I had graduated in economics at Bonn University in 1948, and arrived in England in 1949 newly married to Irina Minskers, a Lecturer in German at Leeds University, and by 1950 had a young child. Physically, I was not well at all, after a serious relapse of a tuberculosis contracted towards the final stages of the war. Furthermore, my command of English was rather limited at first, as my schooling had been in Greek, Latin and French. In this situation, to start a professional career in England seemed almost impossible. And yet I had to succeed. If, in the end, I did manage to make my way, it is largely due to the never-ending support and encouragement I have received from George Shackle. His friendship over four decades helped me to get over moments of crisis and despair, but it was also moments of joy and success, however modest, he so delightedly rejoiced in with me. Our personal ties tightened further when, in 1955, he became the godfather of our second child, Tatiana (called Tanya). All this, I think, clearly emerges from the correspondence in this volume.

George Shackle's letters to me are initially addressed to 'Frowein' and subsequently to 'Frowen'. The explanation is as follows: My name at birth was Horst Otto Frowein. On arrival in England, I adopted the first name of Stephen, as I intensely disliked the Nazi association with the name of 'Horst', and signed my letters 'S.H. Frowein'. I anglicized my surname by dropping the 'i' when acquiring British nationality in February 1956, thereby reverting to an early medieval version of my family name. In addition, when converting to Roman Catholicism in 1952, I was baptised again at St. Anne's Cathedral, Leeds, under the name of 'Stephen Francis' so that my name became Stephen Francis Frowen.

Until the late 1970s George Shackle used the traditional form of addressing me in his letters by my surname only. It was not until the end of 1979, after his second marriage, to Catherine, that we got on Christian names terms. This happened in quite an enchanting way on my first visit to Alde House, the beautiful mansion where George and Catherine lived in Aldeburgh, with George still using his bungalow 'Rudloe' in the Alde House estate for working purposes. When I arrived, they were both waiting for me by the front door. George beamingly greeted me with 'My dear Frowen' when Catherine jokingly pushed his arm and said: 'He is not Frowen, he is Stephen.' This was my first meeting with Catherine and at once we became, and until her death in June 2003 remained, the closest of friends. With her brother Gilbert, a pilot with the Royal Air Force, being tragically killed in action during the Second World War, I had the honour of becoming her 'Other-Brother'.

Not surprisingly, this correspondence is partly personal and partly professional – it is a correspondence between friends as well as between economists. At the personal level, there are many deeply moving letters I received from George Shackle, but the one which brought tears to my eyes was a letter he wrote on 19 January 1979, after an unusually long interval in our correspondence, in which he writes:

> The past twelve months have been an exhausting, sad and baffling time for me. Susan [his first wife] died on 10 April [1978] after a fortnight which caused me heart-breaking grief ... The months that followed were a nightmare ...

But in the same letter there was a mysterious inkling of hope, because the letter continues:

> In recent months, I have found a source of serenity and hope which has again given my life some sense of purpose.

The mystery was not solved until I received his letter of 19 June, 1979, in which he states:

> Last August, I began going once or twice a week to read aloud to a lady who, despite an abounding vitality, does not see quite well enough to find reading a pleasure. She used to give me supper, my visits were soon daily, and I found in the companionship a deep solace. At the end of January we were married.

This marriage to Catherine, lasting over 13 years until his death in March 1992, was one of the happiest I have ever known. Without Catherine, he would not have survived long after the death of his first wife, Susan, and we would have been deprived of the brilliant papers he wrote after his second marriage, later published under the title *Business, Time and Thought* (1988).

My professional collaboration with George Shackle started in January 1952, when he kindly agreed to read my translation into English of *Über Wert, Kapital und Rente* by Knut Wicksell, originally published in German in 1893. Much of the correspondence between then and 1954, when the book was published, concentrated on his involvement with this work, to which he also contributed a long introduction. In my 'Translator's Note', I wrote:

> A debt of the deepest gratitude ... I owe to Professor G.L.S. Shackle, not only for his introduction, but also for his countless valuable suggestions after most carefully reading the entire MS. Although I am solely responsible for any blemishes and mistakes, it is only fair to say that any merits which this translation may possess are in a very large degree due to his exact scholarship and to his friendly corrections of my rendering which I adopted throughout.[4]

George Shackle was quite captivated by the problems of translation. In one of his later letters (28 June, 1969), he writes: 'Translation is a most exacting and difficult art which I believe can throw much light on the ideas themselves.'

In January 1954, I was appointed Assistant Editor of *The Bankers' Magazine* and subsequently Editor upon the death of my predecessor, Dr H.C.F. Holgate. The Editorial Chair I held until 1960. This period, too, was one of intense cooperation with George Shackle, as is evident from the correspondence covering the period 1954-1960, during which he contributed two papers and three review articles, plus a Foreword to a collection of publications from *The Bankers' Magazine* called *Economic Issues*.[5]

The next stage of our collaboration was during my Senior Lectureship at Woolwich Polytechnic [now the University of Greenwich] (1962–1967), where I introduced an annual Economic Lecture and a series entitled

Woolwich Economic Papers. Two of these lectures were presented by George Shackle and published in this series.[6] A number of letters during the 1960s are concerned with these issues.

During my subsequent teaching period at the University of Surrey from 1967 to 1987, I organised a conference in honour of G.L.S. Shackle in September 1984. The proceedings were published by Macmillan in 1990.[7] There is an important letter from George Shackle in this correspondence during the period leading up to the conference, dated 10 November, 1982, in which he says:

> The idea you propounded ... of a conference on my efforts to make, as I would say, a theory of business as essentially an imaginative process, is for me gratifying in the extreme ... [I]n order to be fertile, the discussion should bear on certain questions where I have most radically discarded the received notions of the purpose, style of thought, and conceptual tools of a theory of business decision.

It then sets out in detail the ideas he would especially like critics to regard as the essence of his scheme.

The conference proceedings were dedicated to both George and Catherine. Their absolute delight, when they received an advance copy, is touchingly expressed in letters by Catherine Shackle (13 January, 1990) and George Shackle (2 April, 1990).

Much of the correspondence during the mid-1980s is also concerned with the publication of a collection of George Shackle's late essays.[8] These essays were mainly published between 1981 and 1987 when he ranged in age between 78 and 84 years. He was delighted when I proposed the idea of such a collection to him and, in a decisive way, was exceedingly helpful and cooperative in bringing this project to a happy conclusion. One of the major problems, apart from the selection of the papers and placing them in the right order, was the title. George Shackle's mind was set on *Business, Time and Thought*, and as is evident from the relevant letters in this volume (2 August and 9 August 1985), it took some effort to overcome the hesitation and objection to the proposed title on the part of the then Editorial Director of Macmillan, Mr. Tim Farmiloe. In the end, with his great charm and courtesy, he made an important concession to our views on this matter and seemed quite happy himself with the title George Shackle had insisted on.

Fitting titles for his books were always vital to George Shackle. At one time, he withdrew a manuscript from his long-standing publishers, Cambridge University Press, and had it published by Edinburgh University Press, because CUP would not agree to his proposed title *Imagination and the Nature of Choice* (1979).[9]

Business, Time and Thought was finally published in 1988,[10] bearing the dedication: 'We, the author and the editor, dedicate this work to Catherine

Shackle.' To see the joy of both, Catherine and George, when they held the first copy in their hands, was a deeply emotional experience I shall never forget.

The year 1988 also brought the publication of a *Festschrift* dedicated to myself on my 65th birthday[11] with an immensely touching but also penetrating Foreword by George Shackle and his paper 'Elasticities of Surprise in the Concept of Policy', the last one he was to publish.

Already, at the time of his retirement, George Shackle began to feel rather out of sympathy with recent trends in economics. In his letter of 20 July 1969, he writes:

> The tendency to trust in supposedly self-contained mathematical models; the belief that mere attention to 'facts' and the application to them of arbitrarily chosen, *ad hoc*, principles for their interpretation, can give us knowledge; the neglect of the history of ideas ... ; and the belief that 'facts' can exist without pre-conceived classifications or concepts; seem to me likely to lead the subject into disrepute. I am trying to get my feelings and thoughts about all this into a book, but it will be a 'groping' one.[12]

On 2 November, 1971, he again refers to the respectability economics has lost with the public 'by its over-ambition to become a mathematized exact science with absurd claims to predictive powers'.

It is hoped that scholars will select distinctive themes in George Shackle's understanding of the nature of economic thought for further research. My own theme, jointly with the Reverend Francis P. McHugh, which has already been earmarked, relates to the history of economic thought and its early foundations. From the thirteenth to the eighteenth century, 'economic' thought was a specialised branch of moral theology, particularly of casuistry. As the process of its secularisation took hold, it developed as an autonomous discipline, in mathematical exact form and with the claims to predictive power which Shackle found so unappealing. Recent debates among economists, ethicists and theologians have not been successful in any theoretical restructuring. The research project referred to will take up Shacklean ideas linked to 'unknowledge', 'risk', 'uncertainty' and 'time', which he used in an attempt to restructure economics, in order to see if economic thought in this form may stimulate theological thinking more penetrating in business and public policy.

The final years of George Shackle were overshadowed by his failing eyesight, which is first mentioned in his letter of 22 March 1985. In the end, his letters became almost illegible and he began dictating letters to his wife Catherine which she wrote in her strong and beautiful handwriting, signed by George himself. Increasingly, she also wrote letters herself on his behalf. For this reason, I have included in this collection, with Catherine

Shackle's gracious consent, some of her own letters relating to issues concerning George Shackle and myself.

It is touching and typical of the man that George Shackle was to write, in one of his last letters dated 2 December 1991 (three months before he died):

> I hope to go on working at our subject for some time yet although I am 88 years old. I feel that if I stop working I shall stop living. One must of course beware of merely repeating oneself but if I fall into this trap you and others will make me aware of it.

In any long-standing correspondence, there are obviously gaps caused partly by letters getting lost and partly by the correspondence being disrupted by illnesses and personal tragedies. On the whole, I have been fortunate in that George Shackle kept most of my letters, and I certainly kept the ones I received from him, although in moving from place to place some inevitably got lost or mislaid. However, on the whole, the correspondence is as complete as one can hope for, given that it covers more than four decades.

In his letter to me of 16 October, 1953, George Shackle writes about Professor Phelps Brown:

> Professor Phelps Brown is not only an eminent economist but ... a very splendid man and the kind of man that one would wish to be. I have met very few men of whom I would truly and sincerely say 'I should like to take him as my model'; but he is one of them.

This is exactly the way I feel about George Shackle. To me, he has always been the man I should like to take as my model – however difficult it is even to approach his greatness, combined with a gentleness and humility seldom found.

Notes

1 Mr. A.E.B. Owen, Keeper of Manuscripts, Cambridge University Library, until his retirement in 1990.

2 For an account of the Shackle Papers at Cambridge University Library (Manuscripts), see the following two chapters in P.E. Earl and S.F. Frowen (eds.) *Economics as an Art of Thought: Essays in memory of G.L.S. Shackle* (London and New York: Routledge, 2000): Kathleen Cann, 'Catalogue of the Shackle Papers' (pp. 368–418), and the authoritative study by Stephen C. Littlechild, 'Disreputable Adventures: The Shackle Papers at Cambridge' (pp. 323–367).

3 Hans-Georg Gadamer, 'Rainer Maria Rilke nach fünfzig Jahren', *Poetica. Ausgewählte Essays* (Frankfurt am Main: Insel Verlag, 1977), p. 78. The quotation in its original German version reads as follows: 'Der Gang der Zeit ist wie ein grosser Filterungsvorgang, der Weniges, and dies dauernd, zurückbehält.'

4 Knut Wicksell, *Value, Capital and Rent,* with a Foreword by Professor G.L.S. Shackle, translated by S.H. Frowein (London: George Allen & Unwin, 1954, p. 14). Reprinted 1970 by Augustus M. Kelley, New York.
5 Stephen Frowen and H.C. Hillmann (eds.) *Economic Issues – A financial and economic debate in the critical years 1954–57* (London: Waterlow & Sons, 1957).
6 The papers concerned are: 'General thought-schemes and the economist', *Woolwich Economic Papers,* no. 2, March 1963, and 'On the Nature of Profit', *Woolwich Economic Papers,* no. 13, 1967.
7 Stephen F. Frowen (ed.) *Unknowledge and Choice in Economics,* Proceedings of a conference in honour of G.L.S. Shackle (London: Macmillan, 1990). This volume also contains an enlightening biographical speech by George Shackle (pp. 192–6) and a complete 'G.L.S. Shackle Bibliography' (pp. 197–209). Stephen Frowen's bibliography is included in Jens Hölscher (ed.) *50 Years of the German Mark* (London: Palgrave, 2001), pp. 203–12.
8 *Business, Time and Thought,* edited by Stephen F. Frowen.
9 George Shackle's view was that economic theory must be based on a theory of knowledge, and such a theory must really be a theory of how we can cope with the fact that knowledge is about the past (however recent) but decision is about the future: it is about what to do in a singular, once-and-for-all situation. He held the firm view that probability does not answer the decision-maker's question. These themes he brought to a final statement in his book *Imagination and the Nature of Choice.*
10 Stephen F. Frowen (ed.), *Business, Time and Thought.* Selected Papers of G.L.S. Shackle (London: Macmillan; New York: New York University Press, 1988).
11 Philip Arestis (ed.), *Contemporary Issues in Money and Banking. Essays in Honour of Stephen Frowen,* Foreword by G.L.S. Shackle (London: Macmillan, 1988, pp. xxii, 217). Second edition *Money and Banking. Issues for the Twenty-First Century,* Foreword by Helmut Schlesinger (London: Macmillan; New York: St Martin's Press, 1993, pp. xxxiii, 319).
12 The book in question is G.L.S. Shackle, *Epistemics and Economics. A Critique of Economic Doctrines* (Cambridge: Cambridge University Press, 1972).

The Letters

1

The University
Leeds 2
23 May 1951

Dear Mr. Frowein,

Please accept this with my very best wishes.[1]

Yours sincerely,

G.L.S. Shackle

G.L.S. Shackle

1 The gift concerned was a copy of the first edition of *Expectation in Economics* by G.L.S. Shackle with the dedication reading: For Stephen Frowein with kind regards, G.L.S. Shackle.

2

8 Parkstone Avenue
West Park
Leeds 6
24 May 1951

Dear Sir,

It was extremely kind of you to send me a copy of your work on *Expectation in Economics* with your good wishes. You have given me such a great joy with your parcel, which I got so unexpectedly this morning. I want very much to express my deepest gratitude for your friendliness and kind remembrance.

I am so happy to have a copy of my own of your book with your dedication. Now, as I have more time for reading, it will be a great pleasure for me to read your book more carefully than I had the opportunity of doing during the term. I am most interested in the new theories your book contains and, I am sure, it will help me to develop and widen my knowledge of economic thinking in this country as much as all your lectures have done during the last academic session and for this I am so grateful to you.

To have so much time for general reading is, I find, the great advantage of my present illness.[1] All the time I was a bit ashamed of my poor reading knowledge of English literature. Thus I started with Jane Austen's *Pride and*

Prejudice, which I liked and enjoyed very much. At present I am reading Harrod's biography on J. M. Keynes[2] which, of course, is of great interest to me.

Due to the complete rest I have now, my health seems to improve rapidly. I feel much stronger and hope that the next X-ray photograph will be more satisfactory. Fortunately my tuberculosis is not positive, so that I can be together with my family as much as I like and don't need to miss any important step in the mental and physical development of our now 16 months old son.

Thanking you once again, dear Sir, for all you kindness towards me, I am,

Yours faithfully,

S. H. Frowein

1 The illness referred to was a relapse of the tuberculosis of the lungs caught while serving as a medical orderly in German military hospitals for infectious diseases.
2 R.F. Harrod, *The Life of John Maynard Keynes* (London: Macmillan, 1951).

3

8 Parkstone Avenue
West Park
Leeds 6
19th June 1951

Dear Dr. Shackle,

Whilst reading your book on 'Expectation in Economics' which you kindly sent me, I was struck by the idea to translate it into German, if I could get your permission.

I am quite convinced that it would be possible to find a good publisher in Germany. I have some connections in this line through my professors at Bonn University and a German friend of mine, who has recently translated Mr. Hicks's *Value and Capital* into German.

In case you have no objections to my translating your book, it would be, as far as I know, the task of the interested German publisher to get in touch with your publisher in England, the Cambridge University Press.

As I am sure that a translation of your book, which certainly is of the greatest interest to economists and students in my home country, would help to make it better known there, I would be most obliged to have your views in this matter.

With many thanks I am,

Yours sincerely,

S. H. Frowein.

S H Frowein

4

8 Parkstone Avenue
West Park
Leeds 6
21st June 1951

Dear Dr. Shackle,

I was so very happy to get your letter this morning. I could not imagine a more satisfactory task than translating your book. I only hope that my knowledge of the English language will prove adequate to bring out the finer shades of meaning and to do full justice to your work. In my present state it is a great joy for me to have found a task which gives me the prospect of so much interesting work.

I think, it would be a great help and I should be most grateful to you, if you could get in touch with the Cambridge University Press.

With many thanks and kind regards,

Yours sincerely,

Stephen Frowein.

Stephen H Frowein

5

The University
Leeds 2
26 June 1951

Dear Mr. Frowein,

I am delighted to say that the Cambridge University Press have written to tell me that there would be no difficulty on their side about the translation.[1] Their suggestion is exactly what you yourself proposed: that when a German publisher has been found, he should be asked to approach the English publisher (The Manager, Cambridge University Press, 200 Euston Road, London, N.W. 1) about the translation rights.

The Cambridge Press are thinking of printing a new edition, and I have just sent them a list of alterations, the only important ones being in the final Appendix at the end of the book. Apart from that, page 23 in Chapter II has been re-written and a new paragraph has been inserted on page 24. There are no other substantial changes. They will be sending me proofs, but I don't know when: as soon as I have them, I will send them to you.

I expect you are well provided with books, but if there is anything special that I could lend you (the journals, perhaps) or get for you, do please let me know.

With every good wish,

Yours sincerely,

G.L.S. Shackle

G.L.S. Shackle

1 This refers to a proposed translation of *Expectation in Economics* by G.L.S. Shackle.

6

8, Parkstone Avenue
West Park
Leeds 6
5th July 1951

Dear Professor Shackle,

I was so very pleased to learn from your letter that the Cambridge University Press do not make any difficulties about the translation. It was extremely kind of you to get in touch with your publishers on my behalf. I have written to my German friends and hope to find a suitable publisher soon. I intend to go to

Germany myself in about a month time for further medical treatment in the Black Forest so that it will be possible for me to take up personal contact with the publishers.

Thank you ever so much for your kind offer to lend me some of your books. At the moment I am well provided with books, but if may ask you some day for some journals, I would be very grateful.

I must confess that it was a real shock to me to read in *The Times* that you are leaving Leeds for a Liverpool chair. It will be a great loss for Leeds, but I must be grateful that I had the chance of listening to your lectures last year.

With every good wish,

Yours sincerely,

Stephen H Frowein

7
8, Parkstone Avenue
West Park
Leeds 6
20th December 1951

Dear Professor Shackle,

I am awfully sorry to be so slow in getting a German translation of your work published. The task to find a German publisher proved more difficult than I assumed it to be. Many firms were most interested in publishing your book in German, but had already taken over so many obligations that they had to refuse; others were at the moment in financial difficulties. At last I have found a publisher in Göttingen with a very good reputation – one of the oldest firms – who is considering the matter. As soon as I hear from them, I shall write to you again.

With kindest regards,

Yours sincerely,

Stephen Frowein

8

University of Liverpool
Department of Economics
11 Abercromby Square
Liverpool 7
23 December 1951

My dear Frowein,

You are doing me an immense kindness in taking so much trouble to try to get my book published in German. I should be tremendously pleased if you succeed, and I cannot thank you enough for all you are doing. Even if we do not at present find a German publisher who is willing and able to publish your translation, there will still be a hope of doing so in a year or two, and I shall always remember the very great happiness you gave me in suggesting the translation. There is some news about the book since I last wrote to you, I have received from Cambridge University Press the proofs of those pages which are being altered in the second edition, and have corrected and returned them to the Press, so that I hope soon to have a complete proof of the new edition. The changes are confined to the first Appendix and to Chapter II, pages 23 and 24, with a minor correction to some equations in Chapter IV. As soon as I receive the complete proof I will send you a copy.

The other day I had a letter from Professor Travaglini, of the University of Genoa, enquiring whether he would be allowed to have the book translated into Italian. Of course I was glad to give my own consent, and I wrote to the Cambridge University Press about it.

The term at Liverpool seemed very busy, but I think I have an excellent first-year class of whom good things may be expected.

May I thank you again for all you have done, and send you my very best wishes for your happiness and good health in the New Year.

Yours sincerely,

G.L.S. Shackle

G.L.S. Shackle

9

8, Parkstone Avenue
West Park
Leeds 6
2nd January 1952

Dear Professor Shackle,

Thank you so very much for your kind and encouraging letter. I am extremely grateful to you for giving your time to read my translation.[1] I posted the first chapter this afternoon.

This is just a short note to thank you very warmly for all your kindness.

Yours sincerely,

Stephen Frowein

Stephen Frowein

1 The English translation refers to Knut Wicksell's *Über Wert, Kapital und Rente,* published under the title *Value, Capital and Rent,* with a Foreword by Professor G.L.S. Shackle, translated by S.H. Frowein (later Stephen F. Frowen) (London: Allen & Unwin 1954).

10

The University of Liverpool
Department of Economics
11 Abercromby Square
Liverpool 7
22 April 1952

My dear Frowein,

I should be so happy if you would accept this book [*Mathematics at the Fireside*] as a future present for your little son [Michael].

With all good wishes and very kind regards,

Your sincerely,

G.L.S. Shackle

G.L.S. Shackle

11

The University of Liverpool
Department of Economics
11 Abercromby Square
Liverpool 7
1 May 1952

My dear Frowein,

It is most kind of you to let me read the MS of your translation of Wicksell in advance. May I say at once that the fluency and ease of your version are astonishing? It would scarcely be possible to tell that this was not a book originally written in English by an Englishman. The reading of your text impresses me yet again with Wicksell's greatness as an economist. He must surely be one of the dozen, or fewer, who occupy the absolute top rank. He must also have been a master of the German language, or else you have achieved a miracle.

While reading your text, I ventured to jot down a note of any point that seemed to me to offer even the slightest possibility of advantageous change, and as you will see, these points are very slight indeed, and certainly only involve fine shades of feeling. I scarcely think it worth while to enclose this page of notes, in returning your manuscript, but I will do so as evidence that I read with care and attention.

I shall look forward very much to seeing some more of the text.

With kind regards

Yours sincerely,

G.L.S. Shackle

G.L.S.Shackle

12

8 Parkstone Avenue
West Park
Leeds 6
12th May 1952

Dear Professor Shackle,

Thank you very much indeed for your letter. It was extremely kind of you to give so generously of your time, especially as I know how busy you are. I felt most encouraged by your kind words.

In accordance with your suggestions I have made a few alterations.

I am very grateful to you for allowing me to send you some more of the text and I shall forward the next chapter as soon as it reaches a readable stage.

With kindest regards,

Yours sincerely,

Stephen Frowein

13

The University of Liverpool
Department of Economics
11 Abercromby Square
Liverpool 7
23 December 1952

My dear Frowein,

I do not know how to thank you for this exquisite book [*Die Minnesänger*]. It is far the most beautiful thing that has come into our house for a long time, and my wife and I were lost in admiration of it when we opened the packet. Nothing could be more fascinating to my wife [Susan Shackle] than these pictures: she is an artist, though not in especial an illuminator.

It is a long time since I had news of you, but I heard that you were thinking of a new profession – I should be so glad to know how things are going? I wonder how your family is, your little boy.[1] My children seem to be growing up very fast, the nursery days are gone in no time, and they are the most delightful ones.

I do most warmly wish you every success in whatever line of work you may decide on – and perhaps already embarked on. I do hope you will let me know how you are getting on, and hear your news sometimes.

Do you remember John Norton? I heard he was going to Cambridge, but I have not heard from him this term. I have just had a letter from Kubinski who has obtained a research post in the Gold Coast.

With every good wish for your success and happiness, and with my wife's and my very best thanks for your gift.

Yours sincerely,

G.L.S. Shackle

G.L.S. Shackle

1 The reference concerns Stephen Frowen's son Michael Bernard James Frowen. Born on 17th January, 1950, he died tragically aged 39 on 19th October, 1989 (see 'The Michael Frowen Foundation: Michael Frowen – A Short Biography' by Stephen Frowen, *Annual Report 1993* of the Medical Council on Alcoholism, London, p.10).

14

8 Parkstone Avenue
West Park
Leeds 6
29th December 1952

Dear Professor Shackle,

I wish to thank you very warmly for your kind letter which made me so very happy and for your and Mrs. Shackle's kind wishes for Christmas and the New Year and in Michael's name for the beautiful Christmas card you sent him. He was thrilled with it and I had to 'read' the pictures with him over and over again. I shall put it away for next year so that he can open the little windows from the 1st of December onwards. This kind of Christmas card is known as 'Adventskalender' in Germany and I never hoped to find it in this country. It was a delightful surprise for us all to get it.

We had a very nice Christmas and our little boy Michael (3 years old) was very excited about everything. According to the German custom, we lit our Christmas tree at 5 o'clock on Christmas Eve for the first time and after having sung a few carols and read the Christmas story from the Bible, my father-in-law [Dr. Sam Minskers] came in, disguised as Father Christmas, bringing Michael all his toys in a big sack. Although he was first a little frightened, he soon made friends with Father Christmas and, in the end, could be persuaded to give him a kiss.

The news you heard about my thinking of a new profession were true. I nearly became untruthful to Economics due to the fact that I found it extremely difficult to get a post in this country, owing mainly to my foreign nationality.[1] And as I have always been greatly interested in medicine, especially in the treatment of tuberculosis, I applied for admission to the medical school and, after some initial difficulties, was accepted under the condition that I would first take preliminary examinations in Chemistry, Physics, Botany and Zoology.

I therefore started in September with a special course at the Leeds College of Technology. In November however, I was unexpectedly asked by the London bank Wm. Brandt's Sons & Co. Limited[2] to come for an interview – the first I have ever been invited to – and six weeks afterwards, I was offered the post. This bank has many connections with Germany and other German-speaking countries, and one of the directors was actually looking for an economist with a German background. The arrangement is now that I shall take up my work in London on January 20th for a probation period of six months. This, of course, means a separation from my family for some time, which, as you will know from your own experience, is not so desirable. But I hope that in due course, we shall all be able to settle in London. It would of course be nice for my wife to get a lectureship in one of the London colleges.[3]

At the moment I am trying to finish the translation of Wicksell's work *Über Wert, Kapital und Rente* which I have promised to finish by the end of January. I wonder whether you could kindly spare some time for reading the MS. I should be very grateful for doing me this favour. But I am afraid you will probably be too busy just now.

With many thanks once again and my wife's and my own best wishes for your and your family's health and happiness in the New Year,

I am with feelings of warm gratitude,

Yours,

Stephen Frowein

1 Stephen Frowen's nationality was German until he became a naturalised British subject in 1956.
2 The merchant bank Wm. Brandt's Sons & Co. Limited, established in 1805, was one of the twelve Accepting Houses in the City of London. It later merged with Grindlays Bank which itself was subsequently taken over by Lloyds Bank.
3 Stephen Frowen's wife, Irina Frowen, was at that time a Lecturer in German at the University of Leeds.

15

8 Parkstone Avenue
West Park
Leeds 6
30th December 1952

Dear Professor Shackle,

The enclosed calendar I intended to send together with *Die Minnesänger*. But as I only got it today from Germany, I should be so happy if you and Mrs. Shackle would accept it as a New Year's greeting from us.

Yours sincerely,

Stephen Frowein.

Stephen Frowein

16

University of Liverpool
Department of Economics
11 Abercromby Square
Liverpool 7
30 December 1952

My dear Frowein,

I am more pleased than I can say to hear of your splendid success in securing the appointment with Wm. Brandt and Sons Ltd. It would have been a pity to have to spend many years acquiring a new training, when such a post as this needs just your special combination of gifts and attainments. And I am of course delighted to think that you will still be an economist. Do please send me the MS. of your translation of Wicksell, I shall look forward very much indeed to reading it. I do hope that you will be keeping a copy, however, for I am always terribly afraid of manuscripts getting lost in the post. I am just reviewing Tinbergen's *Econometrics*; the translator has done excellently, but he has not by any means attained the level of your work on the earlier chapters of *Über Wert, Kapital und Rente*. I have been noting the cases where he uses a word which is just not the word an English author would have written: How could he tell, for instance, that 'a few' is sometimes too casual when one means 'some'? It is the subtlest nuance of idiom, but it is just enough to make the translation less than perfect. It was your complete grasp of this sort of distinction that so astonished me.

With very kind regards,

Yours sincerely,

G.L.S. Shackle

G.L.S. Shackle

17
8 Parkstone Avenue
West Park
Leeds 6
19th January 1953

Dear Professor Shackle,

I was very much distressed to hear that you have been taken ill. I hope sincerely that it is nothing serious and wish you with all my heart a speedy recovery.

It was extremely kind of you and Mrs. Shackle to think of my manuscript in all your trouble. If sending the typescript back would not inconvenience Mrs. Shackle too much, I should be grateful to have back the part you have looked at. Please do not trouble about the other part unless you are really fit. I shall ask the publishers for an extension.

With best wishes,

Yours sincerely,

Stephen Frowein

Stephen Frowein

18
The Old Vicarage
Easingwold, York
20 January 1953

My dear Frowein,

Thank you very much indeed for your kind letter. This upset has happened at a most unfortunate moment, when I had all sorts of interesting things on hand, one of which is your MS. I am enclosing 26 pages, which I have read very carefully, together with the notes I had written on them. (I thought it best not to write at all on the MS.) I hope to get started again at the end of this week, and if you can allow me say until the end of the following week I will try to finish.[1]

There is one point on which I have consulted several friends, and that is the last word of the title. Some of them say the word covers more than 'rent' as a technical term in English economics, but they do not agree on an alternative! No doubt you have given much thought to the matter, and have decided to leave 'rent' as the best practical solution.

With all best wishes,

Yours sincerely,

G.L.S. Shackle

G.L.S. Shackle

1 The notes referred to are in the Manuscripts Reading Room at the University Library, Cambridge.

19

University of Liverpool
Department of Economics
11 Abercromby Square
Liverpool 7
30 January 1953

My dear Frowein,

I am sending back to you the rest of that part of your manuscript, which you sent me, with two more pages of notes. One or two points here seem to me a little more important than mere 'drafting points'. I see that one reader of your MS. has inserted the word 'erratically' instead of your own phrase 'in discontinuous leaps'. It seems to me quite certain that you are right and he is wrong. I judge this from the context, which suggests that the contrast is with continuity in the technical sense (or what economists seem to call 'infinite divisibility').

I do hope the delay in returning this has not seriously inconvenienced you.

With all best wishes and kind regards,

Yours sincerely,

G.L.S. Shackle

G.L.S. Shackle

20
Easingwold

My dear Frowein,

How can I thank you enough for these lovely flowers, they have given intense pleasure to all of us – my wife was so delighted, and needless to say your exceedingly kind thought warmed my heart.

I cannot tell you how much I appreciate this gift and still more, the kindness, which prompted it.

Please forgive this scribble, I am nearly late for the next post.

Yours sincerely,

G.L.S. Shackle

G.L.S. Shackle

21
124 Haverstock Hill
London, N.W.3
1st February 1953

Dear Professor Shackle,

I really do not know how to thank you for the great trouble you have taken in reading my MS so carefully and for having made so many most valuable and important corrections and improvements. I only hope that it was not too great a strain to do all this work during your convalescence.

Please forgive this delay in answering your letter of January 20th. I was just setting out for London to take up my new appointment there, and I did not want to answer until I could do so at leisure and reply in detail to various points, which you had raised. Yesterday I received your letter and the second part of the MS.

It was awfully kind of you to discuss the best translation of the word 'Rente' with your friends. I think, perhaps, in view of the difficulty of finding a satisfying equivalent word in English, it might be best to keep 'rent' in the title. In the last part of the translation, I have sometimes had to qualify the word by using some such phrase as 'ground-rent'. I shall, however, be most grateful for any suggestions.

In most cases I made the suggested alterations. There were, however, one or two cases where, it seems to me, the change suggested by you would perhaps mistranslate the German. I am therefore sending you to-morrow a further instalment of the book with some alternative translations, and I should be most grateful for your comments on these. I have also noted down one or two phrases which did not make sense to you, with suggested emendations.

I hope that you have now completely recovered from your illness.

With all best wishes and kind regards,

Yours sincerely,

Stephen Frowein

Stephen Frowein

22

University of Liverpool
Department of Economics
11 Abercromby Square
Liverpool 7
1 March 1953

My dear Frowein,

Please forgive the inconsiderable time I have left this part of your MS: I have had influenza.

Reading your translation with an eye to possible improvements is a fascinating task, though the opportunity to make any suggestion occurs so rarely. My admiration of Wicksell and your handling of him continually grows.

Yours sincerely,

G.L.S. Shackle

G.L.S. Shackle

23

8, Parkstone Avenue
West Park
Leeds 6
7th March 1953

Dear Professor Shackle,

I am indeed grateful to you for reading and correcting so carefully the further portion of the MS., which I received from you on Wednesday. As before, I have incorporated practically all your improvements in the revised text, including *discontinuously* for *erratically* and *continuously* for *'at a constant rate'*. In the first case Wicksell used the phrase *sprungweise veränderlich*, and in the second case *stetig veränderliche (Grössen)*.

The kind praise which you bestow upon the translation is most encouraging, although, I fear, greatly in excess of its merits.

I was very sorry to hear that you had fallen victim to the 'flu epidemic. I do hope you are now quite well again.

I should of course like to send you the remaining part of the MS. as soon as it is ready, but I am afraid that, as a result of your two illnesses, so much of your own work may have accumulated that you may have difficulty sparing the time.

Once again, with many thanks, and kindest regards,

Yours sincerely,

Stephen Frowein

24

University of Liverpool
Department of Economics
11 Abercromby Square
Liverpool 7
17th March 1953

My dear Frowein,

Do by all means send me the rest of your manuscript. I should be very disappointed not to see it. I am gradually getting abreast of my arrears of work.

I do hope you have found your new post [at the merchant bank Wm.Brandt & Sons Ltd] to be in every way congenial and that you are very happy in it.

With all best wishes

Yours sincerely,

G.L.S. Shackle

G.L.S. Shackle

25

c/o. Dr. Gilbert
37 Eton Avenue
London N.W.3
19th May 1953

Dear Professor Shackle,

I am enclosing the last part of the translation in the hope that you can spare some time for reading it.

May I draw your attention to the following passages: page 157, line 3 and page 163, line 12, referring to 'at a constant rate' and 'at any time'. Would you be good enough to compare the translation of these passages with the original and give your verdict as to whether the sense has been correctly rendered (page 108, line 5 and page 111, line 18).

With many thanks in advance, and best wishes,

Yours sincerely,

Stephen H. Frowein

Stephen H. Frowein

26
8, Parkstone Avenue
West Park
Leeds 6
25th May 1953

Dear Professor Shackle,

A fortnight ago I sent the finished part of the translation of the Wicksell's *Value, Capital and Rent* to Allen & Unwin and was delighted to get a very appreciative letter from them.

It would make me extremely happy and I would consider it a very great honour if you could write an introduction to this translation. You have been so very kind to me in the past and given so generously of your time that I venture to ask you for this further favour. I mentioned this possibility in my letter to Allen & Unwin and they, of course, would be delighted if you could spare the time for writing this introduction and would allow six pages for it.

I do not dare to press you too much but I should be delighted to get a positive reply.

With kindest regards,

Yours sincerely,

Stephen Frowein

Stephen Frowein

My present London address is:
c/o Dr. Gilbert,
37, Eton Avenue
London, N.W.3

27
The University of Liverpool
Department of Economics
11 Abercromby Square
Liverpool 7
27 May 1953

My dear Frowein,

It is exceedingly kind of you to think of me when seeking someone to write the introduction to your translation of Wicksell. I shall of course be very happy indeed to attempt it, though I do not feel at all adequate to what will be an important event in economic publishing, the first appearance in England of this major classic. You do not say in your letter how much time I can have, would the middle of August be too long? I am extremely anxious to have ample time to do the very best I can, and until the middle of July I have rather heavy engagements.

I am so delighted that the publishers were pleased with your translation, as well they might be, for it will set a new standard.

I am working on the chapter you sent me, and hope to return it before any examination scripts descend on me this weekend.

With all best wishes and very kind regards,

Yours sincerely,

G.L.S. Shackle

G.L.S. Shackle

28

c/o Dr. Gilbert
37, Eton Avenue
London, N.W.3.
28th May 1953

Dear Professor Shackle,

Thank you so very much for your extremely kind letter and for being prepared to give so much of your precious time to writing the introduction to my translation of Wicksell. I cannot tell you how happy I am to know that it is you who will write this introduction. My only fear is that the quality of the translation might not justify an introduction by so great a scholar.

I have written to Messrs. Allen & Unwin asking them to let me know whether it will be early enough if they have the introduction by the middle of August. I shall let you have their reply as soon as possible.

With all best wishes and kindest regards,

Yours sincerely,

Stephen Frowein

Stephen Frowein

29

The University of Liverpool
Department of Economics
11 Abercromby Square
Liverpool 7
9 June 1953

My dear Frowein,

I am now returning your manuscript with the notes I have made on it. I have tried to answer your question about the passages on pages 157 and 163. You will see that I have suggested this must, according to the context, mean 'continuous variable' and it seems something of a puzzle to know why the German text gives a different rendering. Can it be that Wicksell entrusted the work, or took advice on putting it into German, from someone who misunderstood? Or is the German expression used here the regular and proper one for what English expresses as 'continuously variable'?

I hope all goes well and that you will have no trouble over this last section of your work.

With very kind regards,

Yours sincerely,

G.L.S. Shackle

G.L.S. Shackle

I am sending the book separately by registered post.

30

37 Eton Avenue
London, N.W.3.
11th June 1953

Dear Professor Shackle,

Thank you so very much for returning the last part of the translation and Wicksell's book. You have again taken so much trouble in correcting my translation that I find it difficult to express my gratitude for your kindness and invaluable help.

I asked Allen & Unwin whether it would be early enough for them to have your introduction by the middle of August. The answer was that I should be passing the proofs for press towards the end of July and that this would be the latest date by which they would like to have the introduction; otherwise the book would be held up. Do you think you could supply the introduction by this date without being hurried too much? If not, I should prefer the book to be published a little later and would try to persuade Allen & Unwin to wait another fortnight.

With many thanks once again and very kind regards,

Yours sincerely,

Stephen Frowein

31

North Bank Cottage
Circular Road
Seaview
Isle of Wight
10th July 1953

Dear Professor Shackle,

This is just to tell you that I have not yet received the final proofs of Wicksell from Allen & Unwin, although I was asked to return the proofs by the end of July. I therefore think that there is no reason for you to hurry with the introduction you kindly promised to supply.

I was very pleased to be asked by Allen & Unwin to do further translations for them and to translate a booklet and an article by W.A. Jöhr of St. Gallen which will form part of a collected volume on the "Rôle of the Economist in Official Employment" to which H.W. Singer is also contributing. Unfortunately the time-limit is very short (middle of September), considering my full-time banking job, and I shall once gain have to postpone the translation of your work for which I should like to have ample time.

My family and I are having a lovely time on the Isle of Wight where, through friends of ours, we met Professor Baykov (Birmingham University) and his family. Our two boys of the same age ($3\frac{1}{2}$) are good friends by now. We shall be here until July 20th.

With very kind regards,

Yours sincerely,

Stephen Frowein

32

The Old Vicarage
Easingwold
York
13 July 1953

My dear Frowein,

I was so pleased to have your letter, and glad to think of you having a seaside holiday with your family. I have never stayed on the Isle of Wight itself, but just opposite, at Milford.

I am working on the Introduction, but I should be very much relieved to think that I could take, say, one week into August without delaying publication of your work. One thing I considered if you would like me to do: I understand that one can obtain from the Oslo 'Institute of Economics' a complete mimeographed list of Wicksell's published works. I am writing for this, and if I get it, I will attach it to my Introduction (providing they give permission for this, which I shall ask for). The changes of fashion in economic theory are fascinating. When I was trying to write a Ph.D. thesis at LSE in the thirties, on capital theory, that subject was being intensively cultivated under Professor Hayek's influence. Now in the latest *E.J.* there is a review of Professor Schneider's text-book; while praising the book very highly, Machlup notes that capital theory is hardly mentioned. Yet elsewhere the tide seems to be turning: someone has pointed out that Leontief's system is really concerned with problems of capital theory.

Next week I have to give a lecture at Sheffield; it has been 'on my plate' for some months, and I think it must have been your work on Wicksell that gave me the idea of choosing 'Keynes and the Swedes' as a subject.

I do hope you will have good weather for your holiday. With all best wishes and very kind regards,

Yours sincerely,

G.L.S. Shackle

33

Northbank Cottage
Seaview
18th July 1953

Dear Professor Shackle

I was so very happy to have your letter and want to thank you very much for your kind thoughts. We are enjoying our stay here enormously. Seaview is a charming little place on the Isle of Wight and especially suitable for children.

You are putting so much work into the introduction to my translation and my indebtedness to you for all your kindness increases more and more.

I have not yet received any proofs from Allen & Unwin and I should think that it would be early enough if you were able to supply the introduction by the middle of August. I think it would be an excellent idea to attach to your introduction a complete list of Wicksell's published works and, I am sure, the publishers will be very pleased with this suggestion. But would it not be too much trouble for you?

I should so much have liked to listen to your lecture 'Keynes and the Swedes'! Will it be published?

With all best wishes and very kind regards,

Yours sincerely,

Stephen Frowein

Stephen Frowein

P.S. I shall have to return to London tonight.
(37, Eton Avenue, N.W.3.)

34

37 Eton Avenue
Hampstead
N.W.3.
30th July 1953

Dear Professor Shackle,

I am so happy to hear that the writing of the Introduction is well launched. I have written to Allen & Unwin asking them to send you a spare proof as soon as possible.

For the time being, however, I could send you a copy of my typescript. I shall prepare it for you over the weekend. Will this be early enough?

With many thanks for all your kindness and all best wishes,

Yours sincerely,

Stephen Frowein.

Stephen Frowein

35

Department of Economics
University of Liverpool
11 Abercromby Square
Liverpool 7
24th August 1953

My dear Frowein,

I hope all is going well. I have been a little anxious as to whether I was lagging behind your publishers' schedule, but I have now *finished* the Introduction, except for final touches for the purpose of which I hope the publishers will let me see your proofs? I finished the writing last night, and I am now copying out by hand (as I invariably do) as a means of deliberate revision. I will then have typed copies made, and send you two of them. I do hope that thus I shall have kept my promise in spirit and not delayed you!

With very kind regards and all best wishes,

Yours sincerely,

G.L.S. Shackle

G.L.S. Shackle

36
37 Eton Avenue
Hampstead
London, N.W.3
25th August 1953

Dear Professor Shackle,

I was so very happy to hear that you have now finished the Introduction. I feel quite guilty to have taken up so much of your precious time, but I am extremely happy that it was you who wrote the Introduction. You can well imagine how anxious I am to read it.

The publishers have promised to send you a copy of the proofs as soon as they are ready. As this might take some time I sent you today a copy of the typescript. I had intended to send it earlier but parts of it existed in handwriting only so that I had to have them typed which took a little longer than I had expected.

I am very grateful indeed to you for giving so much time and thought to this work.

With kindest regards and all good wishes,

Yours sincerely,

Stephen H. Frowein

37
The Old Vicarage
Easingwold
York
9th September 1953

My dear Frowein,

You have been exceedingly patient in giving me time to do this Introduction as well as I possibly could, and I am very grateful. I do hope it will please you, and that your publishers too will find it suitable and of the right length. With it I enclose a document which I requested from the Oslo University Institute of Social Economy, namely, a complete bibliography of all Wicksell's works: this bibliography has not hitherto been published, and I have a letter from the Institute giving the permission of Mr. Arne Amundsen, who prepared it, to us to publish in your translation. I suggest it should be printed as an Appendix.

I hope that in my remarks about yourself, at the end of my Introduction, I have got all the details correct?

I send you these things now in the hope that they will make you happy.

With all my best wishes and very kind regards,

Yours sincerely,

G.L.S. Shackle

G.L.S. Shackle

38

37 Eton Avenue
London, N.W.3
14th September 1953

Dear Professor Shackle,

Thank you so very much for your letter. Your penetrating Introduction to my translation of Knut Wicksell's *Value, Capital and Rent* is a real masterpiece. It provides a superb assessment of Wicksell's theoretical contributions and of the importance of this, his first book, originally published in German under the title *Über Wert, Kapital und Rente,* for an understanding of the development of his overall theoretical framework. Your Introduction will be an indispensable guide to readers of my translation.

I am glad to see you stressing the link between Böhm-Bawerk and Wicksell's concern with the theory of capital in *Value, Capital and Rent,* resulting in Wicksell's concept of the 'natural rate of interest'. Thus the explanation whether interest rates charged on bank loans are too high or too low could now thanks to Wicksell be seen in their relation to the level of the natural rate of interest. Based on this is Wicksell's explanation of the link between the quantity of money and the general price level – which you so aptly describe as Wicksell's greatest theoretical achievement. I am so glad to see you emphasizing that a large part of the route to our present understanding was in fact cleared by Wicksell's efforts.

I simply cannot express in words the gratitude I feel for what you have done for me and for the time and thought you have given to this work. I feel greatly honoured that my translation will be published with your introduction. I wished the work done by me justified this Introduction. Your praise, I fear, far exceeds my merit.

I am also very grateful for the enclosed bibliography of all Wicksell's works and for the trouble you have taken in getting it from the Oslo University Institute of Social Economy.

May I ask you in this context whether it might be possible for me to see you for a short while either in Easingwold or in Liverpool one weekend when I am in Leeds? I should like to discuss with you some personal problems in connection with my career. Should you be very busy just now, I would not like to take up any of your time. But if one day I could have your advice I should be most grateful. I shall go to Leeds this Saturday but I am normally there about twice a month.

With warmest thanks once again and very kind regards,

Yours sincerely,

Stephen Frowein

39

37 Eton Avenue
London, N.W.3
21st September 1953

Dear Professor Shackle,

It was exceedingly kind of you to come all the way from Easingwold to Leeds last Saturday to discuss with me my problems and I wish to express once again my warmest thanks for your extreme kindness. Few people would have done this for their best friends and, whether any of my wishes can be fulfilled or not, I shall always be grateful for the interest you have taken in my personal affairs.

I have spoken to my colleague, Mr. Langdale, about the book you would like to have translated from Italian into English. He should very much like to attempt the task but is naturally hesitating as he is not acquainted with Economic Theory. If you think that a translator without knowledge of Economic Theory can tackle the task, he would be pleased to prepare a specimen translation for you.

With best wishes and very kind regards,

Yours sincerely,

Stephen Frowein

Stephen Frowein

40

Department of Economics
University of Liverpool
11 Abercromby Square
Liverpool 7
25 September 1953

My dear Frowein,

I was delighted to have your letter and to hear that Mr. Langdale is willing to look at this Italian text-book, and consider whether he would like to attempt it. Undoubtedly it is technical, and not very excellent print (some sort of photographic process, but there is a second text with the author's own corrections, which I believe is better printed, but I have not yet recovered it from the previous translator). I should be very grateful to Mr. Langdale if he would have a look at it and decide whether he can do it without too much trouble, and if he would like to do it. I have consulted several people about this but have not yet heard from them. It is extremely good of you to put me in touch with a possible translator.

About yourself I have written to a number of the people on the list we drew up, including Mr. Wadsworth of the Midland Bank Intelligence Department, Professor Ford of Southampton University, Mr. Burchardt and Professor Sayers, but there has not yet been time for them to reply. I shall write some more letters to-day, and as soon as I have any replies I will let you know what they say.

Have you ever attended a meeting of the Association of University Teachers of Economics? The next annual meeting is in the first few days of January at *Sheffield*, and if you cared to join as an Associate Member, which I am sure would be possible, I could introduce you to various members of teaching staffs. This is just an idea that occurred to me. I will get in touch with the Secretary, and ask him about it. The meetings last from Friday evening to Sunday evening (just the week-end) and the time spent might be worth your while, and quite interesting. Papers on economics are read and discussed, and I believe the accommodation at Sheffield (hall of residence) is quite comfortable.

Meanwhile I am going ahead with letters.

With all best wishes and very kind regards,

Yours sincerely,

G.L.S. Shackle

41

37, Eton Avenue
Hampstead
London, N.W.3
28th September 1953

Dear Professor Shackle,

I was delighted to have your letter and to hear that you have already written to a number of people. Thank you so very much for your extreme kindness and for devoting so much of your precious time to my professional future.

I should of course very much like to attend the next annual meeting of the Association of University Teachers of Economics at Sheffield. It would be extremely kind of you enable me to attend this meeting and I am most grateful to you for having thought of it.

A few days ago I saw in *The Times* that University College advertises for an Assistant Lecturer or Lecturer in Banking. One of the lecturers in the Department whom I know told me that Professor Allen has not yet anybody in mind for this post and is waiting for the applications which must be submitted by 12th October. Do you think I might have a chance of getting this post? If you should advise me to apply, would you allow me to give your name as a referee? As a second reference I could give the name of Professor Willoughby who has been the head of the German Department at University College. If a third reference is requested I thought to ask Professor von Beckerath who has been my Professor at Bonn University.

I handed the Italian textbook to Mr. Langdale who told me today that he should very much like attempting the task if you should not succeed on finding anybody better qualified. The Italian text does not seem too difficult for him. As promised he will prepare a specimen translation for you.

With all best wishes and very kind regards,

Yours sincerely,

Stephen Frowein

42

The University of Liverpool
Department of Economics
11 Abercromby Square
Liverpool 7
30th September 1953

My dear Frowein,

I have had replies to two of the letters I wrote about your problem. Mr. Burchardt of the Institute of Statistics at Oxford says: – 'We advertised vacancies at the Institute in June and have filled all of them by now. But if another vacancy should occur I will certainly keep Frowein's name in mind and send him an application form. I would also recommend him to Blackwell's for translation jobs. They have been short of people of this kind and if there is a first-class man about for the job they certainly will make use of him. Needless to say I will also mention his name to other colleagues in the University.'

Mr. Wadsworth, the Manager of the Intelligence Department of the Midland Bank, writes as follows: – 'It is very good of you to think of this Department when looking for a more suitable opening for your highly-qualified young man. He sounds altogether exceptional, and so it is with more than the usual regret that I have to say that in the Department we have no vacancy and do not expect to have one in the near future. The proposal has been discussed with some of my colleagues, who feel that we could not suggest any prospect in the Bank generally which would represent an improvement upon those offered by Messrs. Brandt, Sons & Company.

'As you will realise, it will not be easy to find the niche which will be just right for your scholar. He has, I assume, thought of the possibility of combining academic work with business activities, though this again has its difficulties. Despite these somewhat depressing conclusions, would you like me to have a word with him? I should be quite happy to do so if you care to arrange it, being quite definite in extending the suggestion that there is no likelihood of a job here.'

I am afraid you may be a little disappointed that neither of these letters offers any immediate solution, but I feel sure that you would get a great deal of useful light on general prospects in the Banking world from Mr. Wadsworth, and I have told him that I would suggest to you that you should write to him for an appointment. I think it would be well worth your while to go and see him, even if only for a few minutes, as he probably knows as much as anyone in the country about Banking organisation and prospects. You will see from the passage I have quoted from his letter that he will be happy to see you if you write for an appointment.

I think the idea of applying for the Assistant Lectureship in Banking at University College is a most excellent one, and of course I will do everything I can to help you. By all means give my name as one of your referees. I should think the other referees you suggest will also be excellent. I do hope very much indeed that you will succeed in this attempt, but of course we must not count on it.

It is extremely kind of you to have persuaded Mr. Langdale to look at the Italian book and I shall look forward very much to hearing further about how he gets on with it.

With very kind regards,

Yours sincerely,

G.L.S. Shackle

G.L.S. Shackle

I am always so delighted to have your letters, but I fear they must take up time that you can ill spare. So don't trouble to write until you have news of your application: I will go ahead meanwhile with other letters on the list we made.

43

The University of Liverpool
Department of Economics
11 Abercromby Square
Liverpool 7
7th October 1953

My dear Frowein,

I have just had a note from Professor G.C. Allen who is Head of the Department of Political Economy at University College, Gower St., London. He mentions the Assistant Lectureship in Banking about which you spoke to me. I very much hope that you will apply for it as I think this is the sort of opening we must go for. I am sure you would like Professor Allen, and I am quite sure that you would fill such a post most admirably in case we had good luck. There will no doubt be a number of applicants but I see no reason why you should not compete with them on level terms.

Yours sincerely,

G.L.S. Shackle

G.L.S. Shackle

44

37, Eton Avenue
Hampstead
London, N.W.3
7th October 1953

Dear Professor Shackle,

I was so very happy to have your letter. It is exceedingly kind of you to do so much for me and I feel that I have already taken up far too much of your precious time.

I have written to Mr. Wadsworth[1] of Midland Bank asking for an interview and I am most grateful to you for having made this appointment possible.

In the meantime I have drafted my application for the post at University College. I have not yet posted it, as I should feel much happier if you would have a glance at it. Would it be possible for you to read through the enclosed application? Please do not write to me, as you will be terribly short of time at the beginning of the new term. If you approve of my application, just return it to me in the enclosed envelope. I am still waiting for the testimonial from my German Professor, Professor Erwin von Beckerath.

Many thanks for your kind help.

With all good wishes and very kind regards,

Yours sincerely,

Stephen Frowein

Stephen Frowein

1 J.E. Wadsworth, together with W.F. Crick, formed the outstanding economic team at the Midland Bank in the 1950s.

45

37, Eton Avenue
Hampstead
London, N.W.3
10th October 1953

Dear Professor Shackle,

You are so kind to me and in the last few days you have again done so many things for me that I do not know which to thank you for first.

It was extremely thoughtful of you to write to Professor Allen before I had applied for the Assistant Lectureship and I am also most grateful to you for reading my application. Following your advice I did mention my time at Leeds, and the section "Educational Career" now reads as follows:

> … I continued my economic studies at Leeds University where I was a member of Professor G.L.S. Shackle's group. I also attended lectures on Advanced Monetary Theory and Banking and started research connected with the German Currency Reform of 1948.

As I mentioned to you on the phone, I had a letter from Mr. Phillips, Secretary of the Economics Research Division at the London School of Economics who writes that he does not know whether he will be able to offer me a suitable position, but he will be glad to discuss the question with me on Tuesday at 6 p.m.

I should of course be delighted if one of these possibilities came true.

To know that there are certain possibilities is a tremendous encouragement to me and words fail me to express how deeply grateful I feel towards you. I know that whatever the future might have in store for me, I owe everything to you.

Yours sincerely,

Stephen Frowein

46
37, Eton Avenue
Hampstead
London, N.W.3
14th October 1953

Dear Professor Shackle,

I should just like to give you a short report about the result of the two interviews you had kindly arranged for me.

At the London School of Economics I had the opportunity last night to talk to Professor Phelps Brown, Professor Paish and Mr Phillips. Apparently Professor Phelps Brown himself is looking for a suitable research assistant who could help him in his statistical investigations. I do not know of course whether Professor Phelps Brown would think me suitable for the post. From my own point of view I would of course consider it a very great privilege to work with so eminent a scholar, and the experience I could gain in this work would certainly be most valuable for any further academic work. The only, and I am afraid rather serious, drawback for myself is the low salary of £375 per annum. If I could get this kind of post at a northern University or if my wife could get a lectureship at London University the situation would be different. But as it is, I feel that out of consideration for my family, it would be rather difficult to accept a possible offer of this kind. An Assistant Lectureship would be different, as such an appointment would enable me to spend about half the year in Leeds with my family where I could do my research and prepare my lectures. How much I would regret not to be able to accept such a tempting offer you can imagine.

The second interview at the Midland Bank, however, proved much more satisfactory than I expected. Mr. Wadsworth was extremely kind and even asked one of his research assistants to show me in detail what the work in his Department consists of. Although Mr. Wadsworth could not make any promises, my impression was that he would do everything in his power to help me. I should in fact be exceedingly happy if I could get a post like this, as the work is most interesting. Apart from this the salary and security connected with this post would enable me to settle in London with my family even if my wife should not succeed in getting a Lectureship at London University.

I am so grateful to you for your help and shall never forget your extreme kindness. Whatever appointment I will obtain in the end, I shall try to show my gratitude to you by proving worthy of your recommendations.

With best wishes and very kind regards,

Yours sincerely,

Stephen Frowein

Stephen Frowein

47

Department of Economics
University of Liverpool
11 Abercromby Square
Liverpool 7
16 October 1953

My dear Frowein,

I was so excited to know how you had been getting on at the interviews that on Wednesday I nearly sent you a telegram, but restrained myself because I thought it might worry you in business hours.

Professor Phelps Brown is not only an eminent economist but, if it is not out of place for me to say so, a very splendid man and the kind of man that one would wish to be. I have met very few men of whom I could truly and sincerely say 'I should like to take him as my model'; but he is one of them. Nevertheless, it is plainly impossible for you to consider a post where your salary would be so low. The strain and difficulty would injure your work, and I am sure Professor Phelps Brown would be the first to sympathise with this and understand it. I worked as his research assistant at Oxford for two happy years and came increasingly to admire him and to be grateful to him.

As it seems to me, one difficulty with which you may be faced is having to decide for or against one post while another is in the offing. I believe it is possible you may be asked to go for interview at University College, but no doubt the authorities at LSE would consent to wait until the result is known. If, as I gather from your letter, it is not quite impossible that something may emerge from the banking world itself, we may reasonably feel that we have set things moving satisfactorily. But we must not be too sanguine.

With all the very best possible wishes and kindest regards,

Yours sincerely,

G.L.S. Shackle

G.L.S. Shackle

48

37, Eton Avenue
Hampstead
London, N.W.3
19th October 1953

Dear Professor Shackle,

I was so very happy to find your letter this morning when I returned from Leeds. I also had a letter from Professor Allen of University College London asking me to attend for interview on Wednesday 28th October at 2.30. You may well imagine how excited I was and how impatiently I am looking forward to this date which may be decisive for my whole future. I do wish Liverpool were not so far away so that I could see you just for an hour between two lectures at the University in order to be able to discuss with you the thesis I intend to write and the article on the German Currency Reform I hope to publish, as I will probably be asked questions in this connection. I shall also try to form some clear idea about the lectures I would have to give. I stopped my translation work for the time being and I am doing as much reading as possible at present. I wish so very much to be successful in this interview.

I can well understand your admiration for Professor Phelps Brown. Although he could not spare much time for my interview, I was enormously impressed by the personality in the few moments I had the opportunity to see him. I should have considered it a very great privilege to work for a person like Professor Phelps Brown and I feel that two years with him must be invaluable for any young man – not only from the professional point of view.

I cannot thank you enough for the interest you are taking in my future and I shall never forget your kindness.

With all best wishes and very kind regards,

Yours sincerely,

Stephen Frowein

49

Department of Economics
University of Liverpool
11 Abercromby Square
Liverpool 7
21st October 1953

My dear Frowein,

All your news are splendid, and I am on tenterhooks about it all. I am sure you are wise to put your translation work aside for the moment, and concentrate on preparation for the critical interview. But do not let the thought of it make you over-anxious! No one can ever tell the outcome of such affairs in advance, there are so many factors that no one outside the selection committee can know: special requirements for a teacher of a particular type of students, prejudices regarding the kind of experience they look for, mere personal caprice even. So whatever happens, don't let it depress you if it should not come off. We shall in that case just have to resume the campaign wherever it then stands.

I am most anxious that we should have a meeting before the interview to discuss your two plans: article on monetary reform in Germany, and your proposed thesis, especially the latter. I feel it would be a good idea to go to the interview armed with an outline plan of the thesis, and if they do not happen to ask for it you could mention its existence. If I were trying to prepare such a plan, I think I might begin by listing various possible principles on which the subject would be treated; e.g. from the viewpoint of a list of the economists who have written on monetary theory and have in some degree been influenced by Wicksell; or from the viewpoint of *ideas* which can be traced to Wicksell, and the controversies in which, so to say, each side has claimed him as one of their own team. Even the mere geographical and linguistic aspect has some interest: for instance, if Wicksell had written in a different language, a different set of economists would have been influenced by him, the later Austrian School might have developed quite differently, and so on. But this is rather aside from the serious business you will be concentrating on. I have recently come to feel more and more what a wonderful book the *Treatise on Money* was in spite of, or even because of, its internal contradictions or cross-purposes. Did you ever come across the rather sharp interchanges, or debate, between Hayek and Keynes in *Economica*, etc. (Spring) 1933?

I am afraid that if you were at home last week-end you will not be coming to Leeds this coming Saturday? If you should be coming, let us meet, if you would like it, on Saturday afternoon. I would come over by the train which reaches Leeds City station at 4.30 and would meet you anywhere you like. But probably this is impossible or not convenient; if so perhaps you would care to send me a synopsis of your thesis and I will do my best to make some useful comments on it, though I am sure you will need no help in producing a highly interesting one.

Needless to say, I wish you all the good luck there is.

Yours sincerely,

G.L.S. Shackle

G.L.S. Shackle

Just send me a telegram or postcard; there is plenty of time, if you would like me to come over to Leeds on Saturday.

50

37, Eton Avenue
Hampstead
London, N.W.3
22nd October 1953

Dear Professor Shackle,

I am extremely happy to hear that you will be able to see me on Saturday. But I could not possibly accept your kind offer to come to Leeds, as this would be far too great a trouble for you. Would you not prefer me to come to Liverpool? I could take the train, which leaves Euston at 12.30 on Saturday and arrives in Liverpool at 4 p.m. Could you be so kind as to let me know what you think of this plan?

With many thanks for all your kindness and best wishes,

Yours sincerely,

Stephen Frowein

Stephen Frowein

51

37, Eton Avenue
Hampstead
London, N.W.3
29th October 1953

Dear Professor Shackle,

This morning I received the proofs of your Introduction, which I enclose herewith. The stamped proofs I shall have to return to Allen & Unwin, while the copy is meant for you. I should be very much obliged if you would kindly return to me the stamped proofs whenever this is convenient for you. There is no hurry at all as there are still quite a few proofs outstanding.

You can well imagine how impatiently I am looking forward to hear of the University College's decision. I was very impressed by the friendliness with which Professor Allen and the other members of the committee conducted the Interview. I am sure that I should be very happy indeed in Professor Allen's Department.

If I should not be appointed at University College, Professor Phelps Brown would like to see me again on Monday evening. In spite of the financial difficulties connected for me with this post, I was very happy about the news.

I do wish I could express adequately my gratitude to you and Mrs. Shackle for your generous hospitality last Saturday. I am only afraid that my visit was connected with far too great a trouble for you, especially through my missing the train at 7 o'clock.

With all good wishes and very kind regards,

Yours sincerely,

Stephen Frowein.

Stephen Frowein

I also wish to thank you for having taken the trouble to leave my umbrella in Leeds.

52

37, Eton Avenue
Hampstead
London, N.W.3
2nd November 1953

Dear Professor Shackle,

I was so happy to have your letter this morning and I wish to thank you very much for returning the proof. In my letter to Allen & Unwin I shall make a special point of the two errors you mention.

I am still without any news from Professor Allen. I suppose that the post was offered to one of two other candidates and Professor Allen will probably write to me as soon as the successful candidate has accepted. I was full of hope until Saturday but now I am almost certain to get a negative reply. But I am extremely grateful to you for all your kind help in connection with this post. Without your recommendation I should never have been short-listed.

Professor Phelps Brown would like to see me again on Wednesday evening at 6.30p.m. and I am very much looking forward to this discussion. Mr. Phillips will kindly try to find out whether there is a possibility for me to give a few German Conversation Classes at the London School of Economics with the view of increasing my salary if Professor Phelps Brown should like to appoint me. But on the whole I feel that a post with such a low salary I could only accept somewhere near Leeds.

May I write to you again as soon as I have received further news? I feel that I cannot possibly ask you to give any more thoughts to my problems as this takes up far too much of your precious time, I shall always be grateful to you for what you have done for me.

With all good wishes and very kind regards,

Yours sincerely,

Stephen Frowein

53
37, Eton Avenue
Hampstead
London, N.W.3
5th November 1953

Dear Professor Shackle,

Many thanks indeed for your kind letter, which gave me such an amount of new strength at the moment when in fact, I was in need of it.

I had a very nice letter from Professor Allen, which I enclose. I saw Professor Phelps Brown last night. He was extremely kind and advised me either to write and publish a paper or to write a thesis in order to get an English Degree. I could be accepted at the London School of Economics with my German qualifications. I am only afraid that if I overworked myself for too long, my health might fail again. But I shall discuss this question with my doctor. When I am naturalised next year I should also like to apply for an appointment with one of the international organisations. But unfortunately I cannot apply for naturalisation before June.

I am very grateful for all you have done for me and I shall never forget your kindness and all the thoughts you have given to my problems.

With very best wishes and kindest regards,

Yours sincerely,

Stephen Frowein

54

37, Eton Avenue
Hampstead
London, N.W.3
18th November 1953

Dear Professor Shackle,

In accordance with your wishes, I am now enclosing the first part of the corrected proofs as you might like to have a glance at them.

I am not quite happy about the way the printers have expressed the difference between F () and *f* () and between f () and *f*() by using the same signs F () and *f* (), only with the difference that for *f* () and *f* (), letters of F () and *f* () have been used. The disadvantage of this is clearly shown on pages 15 and 16. I have drawn Allen & Unwin's attention to this point. If their printers should not be able to use the same type as in the original text, I shall have to think of another way of making the distinction between F, *f*, f and *f* clearer.[1]

In the meantime I have had another talk with one of my directors [all members of the Brandt family at the merchant bank Wm. Brandt's Sons & Co.] and, although he would like me to stay, there is no hope for me here. The prospects of any immediate promotion are almost nil, as most of the present managers and assistant managers are relatively young and not likely to move on to other jobs for some time. For these reasons, I feel, that I cannot possibly ask my wife to give up her post, but, on the other hand, a separation for a much longer time would also be intolerable. I sometimes do not know which way to turn with the result that I got a rather disagreeable rash on both hands, which, according to a specialist I have seen, is caused by nerves and can scarcely be cured unless I solve my problems first.

But I am always happy when I think how much you have done for me and I shall never forget your kindness.

Also the fact that my translation – imperfect as it is – will be published soon gives me some satisfaction of course.

With all good wishes and very kind regards,

Yours sincerely,

Stephen Frowein

1 In the English edition the terms *f* () and *f* () were changed to *J* () and j() respectively.

55

The University of Liverpool
Department of Economics
11 Abercromby Square
Liverpool 7
29th December 1953

My dear Frowein,

My wife and I were thrilled and delighted with the wonderful illustrated book you so very kindly sent us: it is far the most exciting Christmas present that we had, of course the very thing that my wife is interested in. She used to do cloisonné enamel, and the clear brilliant colours and designs in these pictures delighted her. It is more kind of you than I can say to have spared this book for us, we do appreciate it.

I shall look forward very much to seeing you on Saturday.

Yours sincerely,

G.L.S. Shackle

I wonder if you would care to bring proofs of Wicksell.

56

37 Eton Avenue
Hampstead
London, N.W.3
6th January 1954

Dear Professor Shackle,

In the meantime you will have received my telegram saying that I have been offered the post of Assistant Editor of *The Bankers' Magazine*.[1]

I had an interview with Mr. Schwartz[2] on Monday afternoon after which he expressed his wish to appoint me. As the official appointment had to be made by the publishers, Messrs Waterlow & Son Ltd., he got in touch with the Managing Director, and this morning I received the letter with which the post was formally offered to me.

Mr. Schwartz told me during the interview that, after having read your letter to Mr. Wadsworth, he could not have done anything else but employ me! How shall I ever be able to thank you for the kindness you have shown me? I am most happy about this appointment and feel that I could not have wished for anything more suitable.

I very much enjoyed my stay in Sheffield and was particularly happy that you could spare some time for a discussion with me on Saturday night.

Many thanks once again.

With all good wishes and kindest regards,

Yours sincerely,

Stephen Frowein

1 *The Bankers' Magazine* was founded in 1844. One of the earlier editors and contributor until his death in 1919 was Sir Inglis Palgrave, the eminent economist, close friend of Walter Bagehot and Joint Editor of *The Economist* from 1877–1883. A new Edition of his famous *Dictionary of Political Economy* was published by Macmillan as the *New Palgrave* in 1996. In 1983, *The Bankers' Magazine* was merged with the *Journal of the Institute of Bankers* and became *Banking World*. Further changes led to the title being changed again, first to *The Chartered Banker* and, in 1998, to *Financial World*.

2 George Schwartz, Editor of *The Bankers' Magazine* 1946–1954, was also the Deputy City Editor of *The Sunday Times*.

57

Liverpool

6 January 1954

Telegram from G.L.S. Shackle to S.H. Frowein:

Tremendously pleased at wonderful news. Very best congratulations.

Shackle

58

37 Eton Avenue
Hampstead
London, N.W.3
12th January 1954

Dear Professor Shackle,

Thank you so very much for your telegram. Your kind thoughts made me very happy indeed.

Although it is quite impossible to express my gratitude for all you have done for me in connection with the translation of Wicksell, I have made an attempt in this direction as you will see from the enclosed Translator's Preface to which, I hope, you will not object.

I did not express any thanks to Mr. Amundsen as you have already done this in your Introduction, or would you advise me to express my thanks as well? I was very pleased to hear from Allen & Unwin that they are preparing a final estimate to see whether they can afford to include the complete bibliography prepared by Mr. Amundsen.

With all best wishes,

Yours sincerely,

Stephen Frowein

59

37, Eton Avenue
Hampstead
London N.W.3
14th January 1954

Dear Professor Shackle,

I am enclosing a revised Translator's Preface, which I prefer to the previous one.

With all best wishes and kindest regards,

Yours sincerely,

Stephen Frowein

Translator's Note as it appeared in Knut Wicksell, *Value, Capital and Rent*, p.14

I wish to take this opportunity of thanking Professor A.J. Brown for having first drawn my attention to the need for an English Translation of Wicksell's *Über Wert, Kapital und Rente.*

I also desire to acknowledge the generous help of my friend Mr. H.G. Tupper, who gave unstintingly of his time and expert knowledge of the English Language and without whose assistance it would scarcely have been possible for me to undertake this task.

A debt of the deepest gratitude which I cannot well express I owe to Professor G.L.S. Shackle, not only for his introduction, but also for his countless valuable suggestions after most carefully reading the entire MS. Although I am solely responsible for blemishes and mistakes, it is only fair to say that any merit which this translation may possess are in a very large degree due to his exact scholarship and to his friendly corrections of my rendering which I adopted throughout.

S.H.F.

60

The University of Liverpool
Department of Economics
11 Abrcromby Square
Liverpool 7
14th January 1954

My dear Frowein,

Your splendid success was a tremendous thrill and happiness for me, but it is the reward of your own courage, determination, and enterprise. I do hope you will be extremely happy in this appointment, but I am sure you will. You have now established yourself in the kind of world where your gifts will be appreciated and will lead on to who knows what success. I am so pleased.

Your *Translator's Preface* gives me the greatest happiness, though I cannot feel I have deserved your extremely kind remarks. But I shall be very proud to show the book to my friends.

With all very best wishes and kind regards,

Yours sincerely,

G.L.S. Shackle

G.L.S. Shackle

Any news from Mr. Langdale and his experience with Fossaki, I wonder?

61

The Bankers' Magazine
85 & 86 London Wall
London E.C.2
9th February 1954

Dear Professor Shackle,

I enclose the first part of the page proofs of Wicksell and hope that there are no printing mistakes left in your introduction.

I should be very grateful, if, without inconveniencing yourself in any way, you could let me have back the galleys which I have handed to you in Sheffield, I quite forgot that these are my only means of checking the page proofs. There is, however, no hurry as I have to prepare the index before I can return the page proofs to Allen & Unwin.

I am so pleased with my new job, which I started yesterday, and cannot thank you enough for all you have done for me.

As regards *The Bankers' Magazine*, I think it would be an enormous asset for us if we were able to publish an article of yours and, what is more important, such an article would, I am sure, be of the greatest benefit to our readers. Would you perhaps like to contribute something on, say, the problem of uncertainty – the way bankers are affected by and react to uncertainty. But any other article in connection with banking would be greatly welcome. There is, in my opinion, far too little co-operation between economists and the business and banking world and it might be a good idea to try to bring these two – occasionally opponent – forces together. I should be so grateful and happy if you would consider my suggestion. There is, of course, no hurry. But if you would be good enough to let me have your views on this, I could then discuss the matter with the Editor.

With all best wishes and kindest regards,

Yours sincerely,

Stephen Frowein

62

The Bankers Magazine
85 & 86 London Wall
London E.C.2
18th February 1954

Dear Professor Shackle,

This is just to thank you for your kind letter and for the time you have again devoted to the translation.

I hope you will forgive me for postponing my proper reply to your letter. My first number of *The Bankers' Magazine* has to go to press at the beginning of next week, and I am working 16 hours every day. But I shall be less busy after Wednesday next. Amongst other things, I shall then have to review Prof. Harrod's book *The Dollar*.

It was extremely kind of you to talk to Prof. Paish about the thesis I intend to write. I shall certainly try to get in touch with Mr. Hutchinson as soon as I possibly can.

I am very happy indeed that you are considering my suggestion to contribute something to *The Bankers' Magazine*. At the beginning of March I shall have a discussion with the Editor in connection with our May and June numbers. I should be very pleased if I could then suggest a contribution from you.

I am completely happy in my new work and there are no words which can express how grateful I am to you.

With all best wishes and kind regards,

Yours sincerely,

Stephen Frowein

63

The Bankers' Magazine
85 & 86 London Wall
London E.C.2
9th March 1954

Dear Professor Shackle,

I have just received the review copy from the University Press of Liverpool and I must tell you how pleased I am to see that it is a book co-edited by you on your Theory of Expectation.[1] I shall of course attempt to review it myself unless you could think of a better-qualified person. This is the right type of book for us to review. I am really happy to see that you and your contributors have made further explorations of this most difficult territory.

With my sincere congratulations, best wishes and kind regards,

Yours sincerely,

Stephen Frowein

1 The review by Stephen Frowein of *Uncertainty and Business Decisions*, edited by C.F. Carter, G.P. Meredith and G.L.S. Shackle, appeared in *The Bankers' Magazine*, vol. 177, no. 1322, May 1954, pp. 483–4.

64

The University of Liverpool
Department of Economics
11 Abercromby Square
Liverpool 7
14th March 1954

My dear Frowein,

The sheer rush of events has been such that I have now two or even three of your letters to answer. I can see from everything you say, that you have taken over the new job with a masterly hand, I shall look forward very much to reading your article on the bank balance-sheet picture in Western Germany. This is a fascinating subject, forming part of a larger picture which will inevitably be of the most intense interest and concern to economists in a few years' time, as an object-lesson in a high-investment free enterprise economy, sharply contrasting with that of the UK in some respects. This reminds me that on Wednesday night (as part of the 'rush of events' which I have blamed for my delay) I heard a lecture by Professor Sayers on the last fifty years of banking in England. He was speaking to the Manchester Statistical Society.

It was a great pleasure to have the OEEC book for review, but after careful consideration it seemed to me that one of my colleagues, who has made a special study of the subject, would do the review much better than I could: I wonder if you would allow me to pass the book on to him?

I am sending in this letter all the page proofs of Wicksell (except those of the introduction which you have) and am delighted that the full bibliography is to be published: this makes the book complete and I feel sure will be valued by many users.

It is exceedingly good of you to undertake the review of *Business Decisions* yourself; the editors' task was a quite formal one of seeing that the papers were correctly printed and explaining in their foreword how the symposium came to be held. Nothing was altered in the papers, they are word-for-word as delivered. I did not feel justified in suggesting changes or omissions.

With kindest regards,

G.L.S. Shackle

G.L.S. Shackle

As it is Sunday, I cannot register this letter as I would have done, but I think you would not want the proofs further delayed. These are all I still have, do let me know if you still had any. I feel sure I have only these, viz. pp. 17–96 and 161–174.

Thank you ever so much for telling me about the article in the Kiel journal; I must try to get a copy of the journal.

65

The Bankers' Magazine
85 & 86 London Wall
London E.C.2
15th March 1954

Dear Professor Shackle,

Thank you so much for your kind letter. I feel very guilty indeed for having taken up so much of your precious time with my letters and queries. I hope you will forgive me.

I should be very grateful indeed if you would be so kind as to pass the review copy of the OEEC book on to your colleague. If I could have this review at the latest by April 14th, it would be published in our May issue. (Our rates are £4.4.0 per 1000 words, and in special cases £5.5.0 per 1000 words. I shall regard this review as a special case of course.) Many thanks for your kind help.

I am glad to know that you will soon have the opportunity to recover from the very strenuous weeks you have had.

With kindest regards,

Yours sincerely,

Stephen Frowein.

Stephen Frowein

(All page proofs [of Wicksell] are now in my possession.)

66

Department of Economics
University of Liverpool
11 Abercromby Square
Liverpool 7
14th April 1954

My dear Frowein,

Your exceedingly kind review of *Uncertainty and Business Decisions* will give the utmost pleasure and gratification to all the contributors; for myself I feel you are being much too kind, but I can't help feeling delighted just the same. Thank you ever so much.

We were extremely distressed to read in your letter about the disturbing time you have been through, I do indeed hope all is well. My wife and I both send to you and Mrs. Frowein our very best wishes and kindest regards.

Yours sincerely,

G.L.S. Shackle

67

The University of Liverpool
Department of Economics
11 Abercromby Square
Liverpool 7
7 May 1954

My dear Frowein,

This is in every way a most exciting number of *The Bankers' Magazine*: do I understand you are now in sole charge of the editor's desk? You know, I am sure, what an immense happiness to me your success has been (this sounds almost as though I were taking credit for it: but of course I am not). Under your direction I am sure *The Bankers' Magazine* will go on increasing in importance.

I do hope all is well with your family. It is true I am very busy indeed just now, having 'two of everything' to write (2 articles, 2 chapters of a book, 2 reviews, 2 comments on other people's articles). But I really would like to accept your kind invitation to contribute, and I will try to find a subject which might be appropriate to your journal, and on which I might be able to say something.

I was of course very thrilled to see your review of our symposium book, in print, and it gave very great pleasure also to the staff of our University Press, who have been responsible for producing the book.

With all best wishes and warmest congratulations,

Yours sincerely,

G.L.S. Shackle

68

The Bankers' Magazine
85 & 86 London Wall
London E.C.2
14th May 1954

Dear Professor Shackle,

I was delighted to have your letter. Many thanks indeed for your kind words. I am so glad and happy that you liked our May issue.

I have received a rejoinder from Ralph Hawtrey to Mr. Martin's review[1] of Professor Hawtrey's recent book *Towards the Rescue of Sterling*, which he has kindly allowed us to publish in our June issue. I shall also get an article from Prof. Hawtrey on "The relative Strength of Sterling and the Dollar"[2] for our July number.

As the Bank Rate was reduced yesterday to 3 per cent, I should have liked to publish a short article in our June issue giving the theoretical background of the problems involved. For this task I could not think of a more eminent scholar than yourself, but unfortunately you are far too busy just now and I should hate the idea of you being overburdened with work due to my fault. But you may be able to suggest a specialist in this field who might be able to do it. I should have the MS. not later than 20th May. But don't inconvenience yourself in any way, please.[3]

I shall be going to Germany on behalf of this Journal in two weeks' time. My task will be to take up contacts with German banks. I have not been in Germany for three years and you can well imagine how much I am looking forward to this journey. But I shall never forget that all my success now is only due to your kindness and I shall never cease being deeply grateful to you.

With all best wishes,

Yours sincerely,

Stephen Frowein

Stephen Frowein

I shall be in Leeds over the weekend. My telephone number is LEEDS 52872.

1 K. Martin's review of *Towards the Rescue of Sterling* by R.G Hawtrey was published in *The Bankers' Magazine*, vol. CLXXVII, no.1322, May 1954, p. 482, with a rejoinder by Hawtrey appearing in the June 1954 issue of The *Bankers' Magazine*, pp. 562–3.

2 See R.G. Hawtrey, 'Relative Strength of the Pound and the Dollar', *The Bankers' Magazine*, vol. CLXXVIII, no, 1324, July 1954, pp. 1–8.
3 G.L.S. Shackle agreed to contribute a paper on Bank Rate which appeared under the title 'Bank Rate and the Modernisation of Industry' in *The Bankers' Magazine*, vol. CLXXVII, no. 1323, June 1954, pp. 553–6.

69

The Bankers' Magazine
85 & 86 London Wall
London E.C.2
16th May 1954

Dear Professor Shackle,

I really don't know how to thank you for your extreme kindness to write this article for *The Bankers' Magazine*. You must have felt how much it means to me to have an article from you. But I would never have dared to hope that this would materialise so quickly knowing how busy you are. Many thanks indeed for the happiness you have given me and for the trouble you have taken in ringing twice.

With best wishes and kindest regards,

Yours sincerely,

Stephen Frowein

70

Telegram from G.L.S. Shackle to S.H. Frowein

Chester Rail

17 May 1954

Suggested title 'Bank Rate and the Modernisation of Industry'.[1]

Shackle

1 This paper by G.L.S. Shackle on 'Bank Rate and the Modernisation of Industry' was published in *The Bankers' Magazine*, vol. 177, no. 1323, June 1954, pp. 553–6.

71
The Bankers' Magazine
85 & 86 London Wall
London E.C.2
18th May 1954

Dear Professor Shackle,

It was exceedingly kind of you to let me know by telegram the title of your article 'Bank Rate and the Modernisation of Industry', which sounds very exciting indeed. I am so much looking forward to reading your contribution.

Please, don't trouble to shorten your article if the number of words should exceed 2500 words. I have quoted this number as a guidance only. If your article should be much longer, I could easily postpone the publication of one of the other articles.

With best wishes and many thanks for all your kindness,

Yours sincerely,

Stephen Frowein

Stephen Frowein

P.S. This morning I had a long rejoinder from Professor Hawtrey to Mr. Martin's review of his recent book.

72
The Bankers' Magazine
85 & 86 London Wall
London E.C.2
19th May 1954

Dear Professor Shackle,

I was so pleasantly surprised this morning when I received your article 'Bank Rate and the Modernisation of Industry'. I had not expected to get it before Thursday. It was exceedingly kind of you to write this article at such short notice in spite of being overburdened already. I really don't know how to thank you and I feel quite guilty for having asked you knowing how busy you are. But on the other hand I could not think of a more eminent scholar to deal with this subject and I wanted so much to present our readers with the best. Apart from this, it gives me a great personal happiness to see your name in this journal, which during the last few months has become so much part of myself.

Unfortunately I could only have a glance at your article after which I had to send it to our printers. The beginning is wonderful! I am looking forward to reading it carefully when I get the proofs.

Would you like me to send the proofs to your private address (which, unfortunately, I have forgotten)? I hope to get them on Friday morning and should be grateful if I could have them back by Monday. You can make any amendments you like as long as the length is not changed to a considerable extent.

Many thanks again. With all best wishes and kindest regards,

Yours sincerely,

Stephen Frowein

Stephen Frowein

73

The Bankers' Magazine
85 & 86 London Wall
London E.C.2
21st May 1954

Dear Professor Shackle,

I am sorry that I was not in the office when you phoned. Fortunately I had not yet posted the proofs and will now send them to your University address. Owing to a delay in our printing department, I shall not get the page proofs before Tuesday morning and it will therefore be early enough if I have these proofs back on Tuesday morning.

With many thanks for all the trouble you are taking and all best wishes,

Yours sincerely,

Stephen Frowein

Stephen Frowein

The City is greatly looking forward to reading your article!

74
4, Eldon Grove
Hampstead
London N.W.3
4th July 1954

Dear Professor Shackle,

I trust that in the meantime you will have received the offprints of your article 'Bank Rate and the Modernisation of Industry' from Waterlows, the printers of our journal. May I thank you once again for having been so exceedingly kind in writing this article, although you were overburdened with work already.

A few days ago I saw in *The Times* that the Economics Department of Liverpool University advertised for an Assistant Lecturer. If I had the slightest chance of getting this post, I should very much like to apply. I am still as happy as I could possibly be in my present work, and the only reason for this wish to apply is caused by the fact that my salary here does not enable me to settle down in London with my family. And as it is a fixed salary with no yearly increase at all, we could in fact only settle down here if my wife could find a lectureship at London University, which seems rather unlikely, mainly because of lack of vacancies. On the other hand, if I could get this post at Liverpool University, all our problems would be solved as in this case, we could have our permanent home in Leeds and my wife could go on lecturing there, where she is so happy professionally. I myself should be very glad indeed to have a teaching post, but most of all it would make me exceeding happy to have the privilege of working with you.

But the Head of your department may already have some particular person in mind for this post or you may already have got so many excellent applications from very suitable Englishmen that the chances for me would be rather remote. In this case, it would probably be wiser if I did not apply. I should be so grateful if you could spare the time to let me have your advice to which I owe so much already.

With best wishes and very kind regards,

Yours sincerely,

Stephen Frowein

Stephen Frowein

75

The University of Liverpool
Department of Economics
11 Abercromby Square
Liverpool 7
7 July 1954

My dear Frowein,

I do sympathise most intensely with your need to re-unite yourself with your family. You know well that I will do anything I possibly can to help you to do this: but I feel sure after looking at the matter from all points of view that our vacancy does not offer you a solution. Your plan would be, I gather from your letter, to spend the week-ends in Leeds and to stay in Liverpool from, say, midday on Monday to Friday afternoon. But the expense of this, with the great reduction of salary which would unavoidably be involved (we have no control over this matter, the University regulations prescribe the salary with hardly any discretion for us) and would continue for many years (it would I think take you five or six years to get back to your present salary unless there is a large upward revision in all scales) would leave you surely worse off than at present? Let me say at once what a very great delight it would be to me to have you on our staff if we could offer you a suitable post with pay reasonably commensurate with your qualifications. But those qualifications, which have so remarkably developed through your own really splendid efforts, lie in a different direction to the actual needs here at present. Those needs would have been properly stated in *The Times* if I could alter the way things are done here, but there is no shifting the habits of the administration. Our need is for a mathematician to re-organise discretely the statistical side of our department while devoting himself mainly to lecturing on the newer aspects of mathematical economics, such as Arnold Tustin's book on *The Mechanism of Economic Systems*, and the recent work of Goodwin and Chipman on the multiplier. I only wish our vacancy was in the history of economic doctrine or in banking theory, where your really first-rate qualifications would make it possible for us to put up a case (these things have positively to be fought for tooth and nail) for filling the post at the Lecturer level (instead of Assistant Lecturer). We are compelled in all ordinary cases to fill vacancies with very young men who can be offered £ 450 – [per annum]. In your case such a figure is so absurd that it is quite out of the question. You are now (already, in this wonderfully short time) entirely through your own superlative determination and enterprise, an established figure in business journalism, and my own conviction is that this is where your immediate future lies. There are other openings and related possibilities, and if I were you I would look ahead to an improvement there rather then start afresh in the academic line until there is some possibility of doing so in a way that would reward you properly.

You are making a first-rate job on *The Bankers' Magazine*: the fact that you are doing so will get about, your reputation will grow rapidly, and you will not have to be content with your present salary indefinitely. Editors are powerful men. I feel certain you have a great future, and the right academic job may come along.

I have just received from Allen & Unwin an advance copy of Wicksell: it is most beautifully printed and produced, and should really make a stir amongst those interested in translations of classical works. I am looking forward to showing it to the Swedes if I get to Uppsala for the Econometric Society meeting.

I do hope something may arise that will enable your family to join you – I have tried to think how this could be done but even in Liverpool you would be no nearer to them during the week.

With all the very best wishes for a happy outcome of this, and kindest regards,

Yours sincerely,

G.L.S. Shackle

G.L.S. Shackle

76
4, Eldon Grove
Hampstead
London N.W.3
14th July 1954

Dear Professor Shackle,

I was so moved by your letter and the time and thoughts you have given to my problems. Thank you very much indeed for your extreme kindness. I am always so grateful for your most valuable advice. If I had known that the post at Liverpool required a mathematician, I would never have troubled you. You are right in all the other points, too, which would have spoken against my applying for this post, apart from the fact that the privilege of working in your department would have more than justified a sacrifice in other respects. But, of course, to be re-united with my family is now my first and most important aim. And when, the other day, I saw another advertisement of Liverpool University for the post of Secretary to the Liverpool University Press, I started thinking again. I have now got some experience in the production of books and journals and I have also some knowledge of accountancy. I understand that these two qualifications are considered most important. The post itself seems to offer a lot of scope and initiative and would attract me very much indeed. In addition, it would perhaps not be so difficult for my wife to get a lectureship at Liverpool University, as the new Head of the German Department there is one of our best friends (Prof. David Williams from Oxford) with whom my wife has worked together for a long time at Leeds University.

Today I received my advance copy of Wicksell. The printing could really not be improved. When I looked at this volume, my first thoughts went to you in deep gratitude for all you have done to make this translation a success.

If I am not mistaken, today or tomorrow must be your birthday and I should be so happy if you would accept my very best wishes for your future happiness.

With kindest regards and many thanks, once again,

Yours sincerely,

Stephen Frowein

77

4, Eldon Grove
Hamspstead
London, N.W.3
25th August 1954

Dear Professor Shackle,

I am enclosing a review by Mr. Hillmann of *Value, Capital and Rent*, which I should like you to see before it appears in the September issue of *The Bankers' Magazine*. If there are any alterations or additions you think advisable, Mr. Hillmann would only be too pleased to incorporate them in his review.[1]

I was very happy to receive an article from Mr. Please [a member of G.L.S. Shackle's Department at Liverpool University] on 'Investment by the Nationalised Industries' which he was kind enough to submit to *The Bankers' Magazine* for publication. It will appear in our October issue.[2]

You must have had a most interesting time in Sweden and I wished I could hear from you personally about it.

With all good wishes and very kind regards,

Yours sincerely,

Stephen Frowein

1 H.C. Hillmann's review of the English translation of Knut Wicksell, *Value, Capital and Rent* was published in the *The Bankers' Magazine*, vol. CLXXIII, no. 1326, September 1954, pp. 262–3.
2 See S. Please, 'Investment by the Nationalised Industries', *The Bankers' Magazine*, vol. CLXXVIII, November 1954, pp. 408–11.

78

The Bankers' Magazine
85 & 86 London Wall
London E.C.2
25th October 1954

Dear Professor Shackle,

I was thrilled to receive your review this morning. It is so perfect that I feel we must publish it as a review *article*. In our section 'Book Reviews' it would perhaps not find the attention it deserves. Which title would you suggest?[1]

It was exceedingly kind of you to do this review for us and I am especially grateful to you for sending your MS so early.

Our November issue will contain an article by D.J. Morgan of the London School of Economics on 'G.A.T.T at the Cross-Roads'.[2] There is also a letter from Professor Hawtrey commenting on Mr. Harrod's article on Convertibility Problems.[3] A rejoinder from Mr. Harrod reached me too late and will be published in December.[4]

Did you see that review of *Value, Capital and Rent* in last week's *Economist*?

Today I had a letter from Professor Crispino F Meru of Manila saying: '... there are excellent contributions in your back numbers, for instance an article by G.L.S. Shackle on "Bank Rate" etc. which I read several times. I should like to convey my sincerest thanks and gratitude to *The Bankers' Magazine* and to Professor Shackle for forwarding this article. I hope that I will be honoured with the pleasure of communicating with Professor Shackle in the future.'

Once again many thanks. With all good wishes and kindest regards,

Yours sincerely,

Stephen Frowein

Stephen Frowein

1 Shackle's review article of Lionel Robbins's book *The Economist in the Twentieth Century* appeared under the title 'The Liberal Tradition in Economics', *The Bankers' Magazine*, vol. 178, no. 1329, December 1954, pp. 479–82.
2 D.J. Morgan, 'G.A.T.T. at the Cross-Roads', *The Bankers' Magazine*, vol. CLXXVIII, no. 1328, November 1954, pp. 385–92.
3 R.G. Hawtrey, Letter to the Editor on Roy Harrod's article on 'Convertibility Problems', *The Bankers' Magazine*, vol. CLXXVIII, no, 1328, November 1954, pp. 393–4.
4 For Roy Harrod's reply to R.G. Hawtrey, see *The Bankers' Magazine*, vol. CLXXVIII, no. 1329, December 1954, pp. 482–4.

79

The University of Liverpool
Department of Economics
11 Abercromby Square
Liverpool 7
29th October 1954

My dear Frowein,

Your letter made me really happy. I would rather leave the title for you to decide, but I wonder whether 'The Liberal Tradition in Economics' would suggest the background and the character of Professor Robbins's book?[1] But I would much rather leave it to you.

What a tremendous improvement you have made in *The Bankers' Magazine*: a debate between Harrod and Hawtrey is a really important event; this is a real 'scoop', if such an expression is not out of place in this connection. Hawtrey is a wonderfully clear and fluent extempore lecturer: I remember a meeting of the Economic Club at LSE where the proper speaker failed to arrive, and we persuaded Hawtrey to speak on 'Cheap Money'. It was just as though he had carefully prepared a lecture.

I have put together some off-prints which I thought might interest Professor Crispino F. Meru whose letter you so kindly quoted. I have taken the liberty of addressing them to him 'c/o *The Bankers' Magazine*' and I wondered if you would be so kind as to re-address them to him?

Did I tell you that I gave my advance copy of Wicksell to Professor Lindahl, who I think was Wicksell's pupil or at any rate knew him; and he was extremely interested. I also met Mr. Arne Amundsen. He seemed very shy, that no doubt is why we only heard from him indirectly.

With all best wishes and kindest regards, and very best thanks for your letter and all that was in it, which came to cheer me up on a rather black day.

Yours sincerely,

G.L.S. Shackle

G.L.S. Shackle

1 This article entitled 'The Liberal Tradition in Economics' appeared in *The Bankers' Magazine*, vol. 178, no. 1329, December 1954, pp. 479–82.

80

The Bankers' Magazine
85 & 86 London Wall
London E.C.2
30th November 1954

Dear Professor Shackle,

Many thanks indeed for your kind letter and the corrected proof. Your review article ['The Liberal Tradition in Economics'] will be the leading article in our December issue. I shall send a complimentary copy to Professor Lionel Robbins and to the publishers. Please don't hesitate to supply me with further addresses if there are any friends or colleagues you would like to receive a copy of this issue.

I am very sorry indeed for the delay in answering your letter. I was rather busy preparing the December issue, especially as the Editor fell ill. I am afraid he is suffering from lung cancer and will have to undergo surgery on Thursday. This means of course that even in the best case he will be away for many months. Fortunately he has a very good heart and his consultants seem to be quite hopeful.

Professor G.C. Allen (who almost appointed me last year) is writing an article for us on Japanese Industrial and Monetary Problems. He spent some time in Japan and the USA this summer and is, I think, the best expert on this subject. Mr. J.S.G. Wilson of the London School of Economics has promised to write a review article of Mr. Newlyn's book *Banking in British Colonial Africa* and Mr. Nove of the Foreign Office will review a Russian book on *Business Finance*. I think far too little is known about the Russian economy and publications in Russia generally, although some of these are probably of great importance. An article on Canadian economic trends is also on my list of forthcoming publications in *The Bankers' Magazine*. These will be followed by a really first class article on the USA but I don't know yet who would be best person to approach in the United States. Could you suggest anyone?

Thank you for allowing me to send you a copy of Wicksell. I posted it yesterday. The enclosed advertisement, which will appear on our December issue, may interest you.

I shall be in Leeds from the 25th December until 2nd January and during that time we intend to visit friends in Liverpool (Professor Williams, the newly appointed Head of the German Department). I should be so happy if during our stay (one day only) we could arrange a short meeting. But I can well imagine that you have a full time-table and are far too busy to meet anyone.

With all best wishes and kindest regards,

Yours sincerely,

Stephen Frowein

P.S. The discussion between Hawtrey and Harrod will continue in our January issue. I have received two more letters, one from Professor Hawtrey and a final rejoinder from Mr. Harrod.

I am particularly proud and happy to have your review article for our December issue. It gives the final touch to quite an eventful year in the life of the *Magazine*.

81

Department of Economics
University of Liverpool
11 Abercromby Square
Liverpool 7
6th December 1954

My dear Frowein,

I had such a happy day in consequence of your letter and of the inscription in your gift of 'Wicksell': this will stand always to me for one of the great satisfactions of life, a very happy thing.

Your achievement in your first 10 months of administering *The Bankers' Magazine* is astounding. The list of contributions is thrilling. I always knew you would make a success of what you undertook, but this is a revelation of what imagination and enthusiasm can do.

I had thought of sending an off-print to Professor Robbins, but it will be much better if he receives the Magazine itself from you. I think that if I receive some off-prints I can send them to all those who might care to see this review, amongst my friends. In regard to the article which you have in mind on the USA economy, I understand that Lawrence Klein is now working in Oxford for three years, I suppose at Nuffield College, and I wonder if he would be a suitable author for it?

I am delighted that you are coming to Liverpool and we can meet: any day, any time you would like, just let me know and say whether you would have lunch or tea with me. Perhaps it will be in the week following Christmas? I shall look forward immensely to hearing all your news.

With kindest regards,

Yours sincerely,

G.L.S. Shackle

G.L.S. Shackle

82

The University of Liverpool
Department of Economics
11 Abercromby Square
Liverpool 7
31st December 1954

My dear Frowein,

I rang up Mr. Edey immediately after our conversation and he will be delighted to see you at the lectures. I had been looking forward very much indeed to having you as my lunch guest at our Staff House, but we shall have plenty of time for exchange of all news in London. I gather that Professor and Mrs. Williams have been away over Christmas and until yesterday afternoon. I rang up their house on Tuesday and got a message from someone which I misunderstood as meaning that you would be coming over here on Thursday. No doubt you will be coming one day to see Professor and Mrs. Williams and so we shall have further opportunities to meet.

Yesterday I had a letter from Professor Meru. He apparently intends writing a text book for his students on money and banking and is looking out for someone to collaborate with him. It just occurred to me that you might possibly know of someone who would be suitable and willing to engage in a rather strange long distance collaboration. I suppose it would have to be someone who is an expert on banking and yet not too senior so that he would be willing to have a half share in writing a book suitable for a rather special localised readership. However, I have no doubt he has consulted you before now.

I am delighted to hear Lawrence Klein has undertaken to write the article which you have planned on the United States economy, and I am sure he will do it admirably. I must congratulate you on the *Manchester Guardian*'s review of Wicksell – though very short it is just the kind of notice which should do as much as anything to bring the book to potential readers' notice. But above all I was delighted to see that the reviewer called the translation excellent. There are many more things to discuss but as we are going to have plenty of time for talk I will not put any more in this letter.

With all best wishes for the New Year and very kind regards,

Yours sincerely,

G.L.S. Shackle

G.L.S. Shackle

83

The University of Liverpool
Department of Economics
11 Abercromby Square
Liverpool 7
3rd January 1955

My dear Frowein,

It is extremely kind of you to propose to meet me, but you will have all sorts of things to attend to and I could not think of letting you come all the way to Euston. It is a most considerate and kind thought, but I shall simply take a taxi. Indeed, I may change my plan and come by an earlier train, there is a meeting which I might attend if I get confirmation that it is really being held, and if so I should come on from there. So please do not worry about my movements, I shall be perfectly all right and will do my best to arrive in good time.

With all best wishes,

Yours sincerely,

G.L.S. Shackle

G.L.S. Shackle

84

The University of Liverpool
Department of Economics
11 Abercromby Square
Liverpool 7
3rd March 1955

My dear Frowein,

I am delighted to hear that you are coming to Liverpool to visit Professor Williams and very much hope that we may have lunch or tea together on the Saturday. Of course Professor Williams will expect to be given most of your time but I will consult him as to whether we could all have lunch together or something like that.

With all best wishes and kindest regards,

Yours sincerely,

G.L.S. Shackle

G.L.S. Shackle

85

Deepdene
Pier Avenue
Southwold
Suffolk
11th April 1955

My dear Frowein,

It is most splendid news that your family is to be with you in London – what a relief this will be from anxiety. It is a strain and worry to have one's home far away. What a very trying and worrying time you have had in these last weeks, with Michael's illness and your having to do your editorial work away from your office, and run your home at the same time. I can well realise what sort of nightmare this is: I was very disappointed indeed that you couldn't come to Liverpool, it was extremely good of you to have the idea of sending the telegram. (My little girl was delighted with the 'Greetings' form). I hope you are now enjoying this sunshine and the seaside.

We are also by the sea, in Suffolk, it was in our case a lucky accident. We have acquired a house in West Kirby (close to Liverpool) but cannot get possession, so had to take a furnished house for 3 weeks, and we chanced upon this bungalow at

Southwold. A very nice old town with many Georgian houses and charming little 'greens' with quaint cottages set round them. There was a naval battle here, in 1672; the British fleet was commanded by the Duke of York who afterwards, as James II, was turned out by Parliament in favour of William III (Dutch William). As the naval battle was against the Dutch, it is all a strange illustration of the fickleness of history, I suppose.

Just this morning I received the April *Bankers' Magazine*, and was most excited to see your splendid article.[1] May I say that it really is first-rate: a most ingenious and subtle piece of realistic analysis with, behind it, a real background of economic insight. How refreshing after the queer mixtures of out-of-date theory and ritual incantations we so often read in the City columns of some of the newspapers. What a pity they cannot all have City editors like Sir Oscar Hobson. Anyway, I was most delighted with your article, and especially with your incisive and clear advice to investors.

With all best wishes and kindest regards,

Yours sincerely,

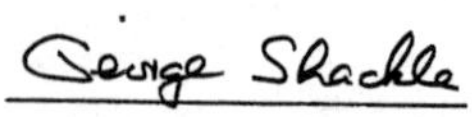

George Shackle

1 The article concerned is: S.H. Frowein, 'Monetary Policy and Investors', *The Bankers' Magazine*, vol. 179, no. 1333, April 1955, pp. 341–3.

86

The University of Liverpool
Department of Economics
11 Abercromby Square
Liverpool 7
30th September 1955

My dear Frowein,

I cannot tell you how much your kindness in suggesting that I should stand god-father to your daughter has touched me. Nothing would give me a greater pleasure. If you would tell me what date you have arranged, I will make my plans so that I can come. Perhaps you could give me some idea of the time when you will have the ceremony. Of course, all these details will not be arranged just yet, no doubt you will not know for a few weeks what the date and time will be.

I am extremely sorry to hear about the lectureship, but I hope you won't let this worry you too much: surely something will solve the problem during the year. Certainly it would be unbearable to go back to the old arrangement.

You must have had an overwhelming strenuous and anxious time, I hope things will be easy from now on.

With kindest regards, and every good wish,

Yours sincerely,

George Shackle

87

The University of Liverpool
Department of Economics
11 Abercromby Square
Liverpool 7
28th December 1955

My dear Frowein,

Just to make sure our plans are concerted, is it correct that the ceremony will be on the Friday, 6th January, at 2.45, and I am to be at your house at about 2.15?

I expect you may have written, and our letters will cross: if so, please don't trouble to write. If the above is correct, I will be there, barring some quite unforeseeable accident.

With all best wishes and kindest regards,

Yours sincerely,

G.L.S Shackle

88

The University of Liverpool
Department of Economics
11 Abercromby Square
Liverpool 7
15th March 1956

My dear Frowen[1],

I have been meaning to write to you for many weeks past, but have waited until I could send this review of the book by Professor Jöhr and Dr. Singer. A great deal has happened since I was with you in January. I hope all your family are well and as happy as you all were on the Christening day: it was a really delightful occasion, and I did feel it a great privilege to be present.

Since then you have become full Editor of *The Bankers' Magazine*: I am so very happy that this has come about, for your achievement in revolutionising the *Magazine* is really wonderful. It is something to be proud of for always, your enterprise, imagination and hard work (it must have been an intense effort over these last few months) have effected a truly remarkable transformation of the *Magazine* into something which readers can look forward to with the greatest interest. You always have someone who really knows about the topical point at issue, and something fresh every time.

You have continued to send me the *Magazine*, and I know that I ought to send a subscription, would you ask them to send me an account?

On Tuesday last I found a review of your Wicksell in *Kyklos*, vol. VIII Fas 4. Among the many reviews I have seen, all of them extremely appreciative of your translation, this one specially pleased me. It says:

> … this translation of *Über Wert, Kapital und Rente* is excellent, true both to the spirit and the letter of the original …
>
> It would be fortunate indeed for all the rounding-out of Wicksell's theoretical heritage to the English-speaking posterity of Mr. Frowein, or someone with comparable linguistic and literary talents, might be persuaded or induced to produce as felicitous a translation of the theoretical chapters of *Finanztheoretische Untersuchungen* as he has done of *Über Wert, Kapital und Rente.*

I do hope all goes well.

With very kind regards,

Yours sincerely,

G.L.S. Shackle

G.L.S. Shackle

1 When acquiring British nationality on 3rd February 1956, the surname of Frowein was anglicized by dropping the 'i' and changing it to 'Frowen', thereby reverting to the early-medieval version of the family name.

89

The Bankers' Magazine
85 & 86 London Wall
London E.C.2
22nd March 1956

Dear Professor Shackle,

Your letter has given me the greatest possible happiness. I wanted to write to you a long time ago to thank you for all you have done for me. I shall never forget that without your most generous and exceedingly kind help. I should never have succeeded in obtaining my present post. Although words fail me to express my gratitude adequately, I hope you will nevertheless be aware of the extent of my gratitude. I could not be happier in my present work and professionally there is nothing more I could wish for – except further improvements in *The Bankers' Magazine*.

I was delighted to receive your most interesting review. As it would be a pity to publish it amongst other book reviews, I have taken the liberty of placing it in the form of an article to which, I hope, you will agree. If you prefer, we could publish it under a different title and say simply "By G.L.S Shackle", as in the case of your review of Lionel Robbins' book. It would be quite simple for us to make these alterations. I should be grateful if you would kindly return one proof as soon as possible.

I was of course delighted to hear of the excellent review of the Wicksell translation in *Kyklos*. Thank you so much for drawing my attention to it. I shall try to get a copy of this issue.

With all best wishes and, once again, many thanks,

Yours sincerely,

Stephen Frowen

90

The Bankers' Magazine
85 & 86 London Wall
London E.C.2
25th July 1956

Dear Professor Shackle,

I must apologise for the delay in sending you a print of one of the photographs taken when Tanya was christened some months ago. I have now ordered a few more prints of the other photographs, which, I hope, will be ready shortly; but the enclosed snap is no doubt the best. Tanya is developing into a most lively, pretty and, I think, intelligent girl who gives us the greatest possible happiness, which is shared by Michael who adores his little sister.

We intend to take the children to the Isle of Wight next Saturday for a two weeks' holiday and shall move to our new house in the Hampstead Garden Suburb towards the end of August. We should be exceedingly happy if you could spare the time to visit us there during one of your brief visits to London.

I am just preparing a reprint of articles which appeared in *The Bankers' Magazine* since the beginning of 1954, and I should be delighted if you would allow me to include your three contributions to our journal in this collection. I enclose a list of articles which, I thought, might be worth reprinting in book form. Some of them will of course have to be brought up to date. The book will be edited by Hal Hillmann and myself and we intend to write a general introduction. I should be most happy if you could spare the time to contribute a brief Foreword to this volume. I am still trying to find a suitable title (I am thinking of 'Contemporary Economic Discussion, 1954–56'), which should be as short as possible (something like 'Economic Commentaries' which is the title of Sir Dennis Robertson's latest collection). I should be most grateful for any suggestions you may be able to make in connection with this reprint.[1]

With all best wishes and kindest regards,

Yours sincerely,

Stephen Frowen

1 The publication details of this collection are as follows: Stephen Frowen and H.C. Hillmann (eds), *Economic Issues: A Financial and Economic Debate in the Critical Years*, 1954–7. Foreword by G.L.S. Shackle (London: Waterlow and Sons Limited, 1957, pp. xi and 231).

91

The University of Liverpool
Department of Economics
11 Abercromby Square
Liverpool 7
27th July 1956

My dear Frowen,

I am delighted to hear all your good news, and especially about Tanya: what a tremendous thrill it is to have children growing up: a nursery is source of fresh life and vitality for grown-ups, they seem to give one fresh courage. Ours are almost out of the nursery stage but the school stage has its own fascination: School reports! What anxiety and excitement. My oldest boy[1] is second in his form. This sounds grand, but it appears that he only beat the next two boys by a small fraction of a percentage point. It is good to hear you are moving to a house.

The project for a collection of articles is most exciting; I realised you had got together a really remarkable collection of contributors, but even so the actual list is astonishing: you have positively given The Bankers' Magazine an altogether new lease of life: it is extraordinarily impressive, it is wonderful. Of course I will be most delighted to have my contributions reprinted.

All very best wishes for your holiday in the Isle of Wight, I have never been there.

Wth kindest regards,

Yours sincerely,

G.L.S. Shackle

G.L.S. Shackle

I was thrilled the other day to see The Bankers' Magazine quoted in The Times' City column.

1 Robert Shackle.

92

40 Gurney Drive
Hampstead Garden Suburb
London, N.2
21st September 1956

Dear Professor Shackle,

I wished you could have seen the tremendous joy you have given to Tanya with your really wonderful present. It was a great success. She hugged her pink Teddy again and again and it is still her favourite toy, the only one that she takes to her bed. It was very, very kind of you to remember her birthday and my wife and I thank you sincerely for the happiness you have given to Tanya with this present.

She really enjoyed her birthday and was most appreciative of everything.

We are now happily settled in our new house and only wish you could visit us here very soon. Our house is small but very cosy and the children seem to be happy here. Michael is still going to a small private school in Hampstead (St. Mary's Town & Country School) but as we hope to get him accepted at The Hall, a Preparatory School in Hampstead of which Professor Paish is one of the Governors, as Michael's best friend (the son of C.T. Saunders of the Central Statistical Office) will go there too. Later we hope to get him accepted at University College School, Highgate Public School or St. Paul's. About Tanya we don't know yet, but we may have to put down her name too at one or two suitable schools.

The publication of my collection of articles from *The Bankers' Magazine* is making good progress but the book will probably not be ready before February. It will consist of 240 pages and the price will be 18s. All the authors seem to be pleased to have their articles included. I am particularly happy to know that your articles and reviews will also be contained in this volume. I am still trying to find a suitable title. I was thinking of 'Economic Appraisals', but then I thought, 'Economic Fragments – Contemporary British Discussions 1954–56' sounds perhaps more modest and less pretentious. But would this title do justice to some of the excellent papers the volume will contain? I should be very grateful to have your views on this point, as there is nobody I know of who has this perfect feeling for language which stands out so clearly in all your publications.

Irene[1] joins me in sending you our kindest regards. With all best wishes,

Yours gratefully,

Stephen Frowen

1 Later Irina Frowen, Stephen's wife.

93

The University of Liverpool
Department of Economics
11 Abercromby Square
Liverpool 7
4th November 1956

My dear Frowen,

I was so pleased to have your letter, with its good news about your family. Thank you very much for sending me the galley proofs of the three articles, which you are including in your book. They have been extremely well set, the only corrections I have found are a few commas and one capital letter. Do you think it would be possible for me to have a complete set of galleys some time in order to write the Foreword, which you kindly suggested I should do? The proof would give a more unified picture than re-reading the articles in *The Bankers' Magazine*. I think you only want a page or two?

My main concern will be to point out the renaissance and the resurgence of the Magazine.

With all best wishes and kindest regards,

Yours sincerely,

G.L.S. Shackle

G.L.S. Shackle

94

The University of Liverpool
Department of Economics
11 Abercromby Square
Liverpool 7
8th December 1956

My dear Frowen,

I see with dismay that it is three weeks since I received the galley proof of your book. I have had a draft of my Foreword in existence for most of that time, but have not felt quite satisfied with it. Now I have revised and finished it; I am sorry that it is in handwriting, this is because I have no typist on Saturday, and I copied out this as clearly as I could in the hope that your printer will be able to read it.

In writing the Foreword, I had it in mind that your book will find many of its readers among bankers and their staffs, and so have tried to hint that the book is meant largely for them. It will certainly also find a place in all academic libraries, and is the ideal basis for a course on applied monetary economics. Mr. Clayton, one of my colleagues in this Department, makes very great use of the *Magazine* (that is, the recent volumes) and has borrowed the whole file, which you so kindly sent me. He is our specialist on monetary theory, and greatly admires the wonderful transformation you have wrought in the *Magazine*.

I am returning the galley proofs separately by registered post.

I have been trying to think of suggestions for the title, probably it is now too late. I did wonder whether something on these lines would do:

<u>Money and History</u>
An economic debate in the critical years

If you could bring in on the title page the names of Harrod, Hawtrey & Colin Clark I think it might show that the book is really on the highest academic level.

With all very best wishes and kindest regards,

Yours sincerely,

G.L.S. Shackle

G.L.S. Shackle

95

The Bankers' Magazine
85 & 86 London Wall
London E.C.2
11th December 1956

Dear Professor Shackle,

Your two letters arrived yesterday afternoon and have given me the greatest possible happiness. Your Foreword is wonderful but I fear it is far too kind and pays far too much credit to my very modest efforts. It could not possibly be improved by a single word. I was also glad to see that you have emphasised that the book is meant largely for bankers and I am convinced that your Foreword will help to interest bankers in the book. I am only afraid that you have spent far too much time over this and I just cannot find words which might express adequately how extremely grateful I am to you for all the thoughts and endless time you have given to this book. To describe the personal happiness which I have derived from your letter and your Foreword would be an impossible task.

I am also very grateful to you for suggesting this title. 'Money and History' would have been an excellent solution if the book did not contain articles on National Income, G.A.T.T., etc. In view of this fact, I have very regretfully decided not to use 'Money and History'* but have adopted your sub-title so that the title of the book will now be

ECONOMIC ISSUES
An economic debate in the critical years
1954–56

The title 'Economic Issues' is not without shortcomings but seems to me to be a slight improvement on 'Economic Fragments'.

I shall also mention the names of the better known contributors on the title page. This is an excellent idea for which I am also greatly indebted to you.

With all best wishes and kindest regards,

Yours gratefully,

Stephen Frowen

*Merely because reviewers might attack this title on these grounds, although most articles are obviously devoted to 'Money'.

96

The University of Liverpool
Department of Economics
11 Abercromby Square
Liverpool 7
10th January 1957

My dear Frowen,

No present could have given us more pleasure than the exquisite and intensely interesting book which you sent us. My wife and I were both enchanted with it; I as a mere admirer of such beautiful pictures, she as something of an expert in ecclesiastical art, though of a different kind, having been a silversmith and at one time made a pair of church candlesticks. Nowadays of course she has no time or facilities for such work.

I was so pleased also to receive your postcard from Switzerland. I hope (but I am sure) that your business visits were a great success.

At Bristol last weekend I saw Hal Hillmann who told me of the progress of the book. We had an excellent conference and splendid weather, almost like spring.

With all best wishes and kindest regards,

Yours sincerely,

G.L.S. Shackle

G.L.S. Shackle

97

The Bankers' Magazine
85 & 86 London Wall
London E.C.2
13th February 1957

Dear Professor Shackle,

I must apologise for the delay in thanking you for your very kind letter.

I have only just received a second page proof of your Foreword, which I enclose.[1] It is now absolutely perfect, although the passage referring to my modest efforts is still far too kind. I am so happy about this Foreword and can't thank you enough for the time and thought you have given to it.

Mr. Harrod has now added a second postscript to his article on "Convertibility Problems". If everything goes well, the book ought to be out before the end of March.

With all best wishes and kindest regards,

Yours sincerely,

Stephen Frowen

1 This refers to G.L.S. Shackle's Foreword to *Economic Issues: A Financial and Economic Debate in the Critical Years 1954–57*, edited by Stephen Frowen and H.C. Hillmann (London: Waterlow & Sons, 1957).

98

The University of Liverpool
Department of Economics
11 Abercromby Square
Liverpool 7
14 February 1957

My dear Frowen,

Thank you very much indeed for the page-proof, which I am assuming I can keep? There is nothing to correct so it seemed that you would not need it back. It is splendid to have the prospect of publication next month, this will put most publishers to shame, for nowadays it seems to take years, literally, between acceptance of a manuscript and its appearance in print.

This is a grand enterprise of yours and something that anyone would be proud indeed to have accomplished.

Yours with kindest regards, and best congratulations,

G.L.S. Shackle

99

40 Gurney Drive
Hampstead Garden Suburb
London, N.2
8th April 1957

Dear Professor Shackle,

Your greeting telegram, which I received this afternoon, has made me exceedingly happy. It is a document I shall treasure and I am most grateful for your very kind thought.

I am of course particularly glad to know that you approve of the book. This means more to me than any favourable reviews which might appear later on. I cannot thank you enough not only for your own contributions to this book, including the very kind – or better far too kind – Foreword, but also for all you have done for me. Without your initial help, I should never have joined *The Bankers' Magazine*. *Economic Issues* is therefore more your book than mine and any credit which may be due to this volume should really go to you.

I hope of course that university teachers will find it justified recommending the book to students.

With many thanks once again and with all best wishes for a Happy Easter,

Yours sincerely,

Stephen Frowen

100

The University of Liverpool
Department of Economics
11 Abercromby Square
Liverpool 7
15 July 1957

My dear Frowen,

It was most delightfully kind of you and Mrs. Frowen to think of my birthday. I was very much touched to receive your greetings telegram this morning. My wife and I were talking of Tanya only last week when something reminded us.

I have been looking out for reviews of *Economic Issues*, but so far have seen only the one in *The Bankers' Magazine* itself. I sent a copy to my own Bank Manager, partly to see whether he would recognise himself in the portrait I tried to draw of the typical banker and partly because he is himself the author of books on bank practice and has had some part in Lloyds Bank's education scheme.

I do hope all goes well with you and your family, and with the book and the Magazine. I wonder where you will go for this summer's holiday? I am supposed to go to New York in September, it is not a trip I would have sought, since it means months away from home, but it seems to be a thing one must do once in a lifetime. So I hope to get it over. (Columbia University)

With all kindest regards and best wishes, and warmest thanks,

Yours sincerely,

G.L.S. Shackle

G.L.S. Shackle

101

Columbia University in the City of New York
New York 27, N.Y.
Department of Economics
17 December 1957

My dear Frowen,

How delighted I was to have your letter, and the sweet photograph of Tanya. How quickly the time flies, it seems only the other day that she was being christened and now she looks so self-possessed and capable!

I was tremendously interested to hear of the offer made to you by the owner of the publishing house. You must have been sadly torn between such an opportunity and the environment of success which you have built up in England. The fact that the offer was made shows how splendid that success has been.

I was also *extremely* glad to hear that *Economic Issues* has been a great success. I must track down the reviews – I spent two afternoons in the library here for that purpose, but was distracted by other things.

I hope to fly home direct to Manchester at the end of January and go home from there, so I am afraid I will not be in London on that occasion. But I would like very much indeed to come and have tea with you one day and see Tanya. No doubt I will be in London someday during the spring.

I do hope this parcel will arrive in time for Christmas. I had a wonderfully happy afternoon choosing the dolly from amongst so many.

With all the very best wishes for Christmas and the New Year, to yourself and Tanya and all your family, and with very kind regards,

Yours sincerely,

G.L.S. Shackle

G.L.S. Shackle

102

Columbia University in the City of New York
New York 27, N.Y.
Department of Economics
17th December 1957

My dear Frowen,

This is just to say that a parcel in on its way to Tanya, with a letter enclosed for yourself: the parcel is of course addressed to you and answers the letter, which I was so delighted to receive yesterday. I have sent it to the address you gave – G P O Box 92, 26 Gt. Winchester Street. I hope it will reach you safely.

I am a little distrustful of the Christmas mail, so I sent this as well.

All the very warmest wishes to you and all of your family,

Yours sincerely,

G.L.S. Shackle

G.L.S. Shackle

103

The University of Liverpool
Department of Economics
11 Abercromby Square
Liverpool 7
20th July 1958

My dear Frowen,

It is a long time since I enjoyed anything so much as our little 'party' on Friday. I am ashamed of having delayed your lunch and expended your afternoon, and only hope I did not entirely wreck your schedule of work for the weekend. But I would not for anything have missed our talk together. From the merely practical viewpoint I was delighted to get you to clear up my ideas about 'special deposits' and to re-assure me about my failure to understand the *Economist* article.

It is an extraordinarily kind thought of yours to plan a review-article in the Magazine; this will be for me a source of very great happiness. The book we spoke of, enclosed, is the record of a conference at Pittsburgh, which swept in most of the American economists who are especially interested in expectational economics. The organiser was Mary Jean Bowman, who edits this volume and is herself right in the front rank on this subject. She invited Professor Meredith of Leeds, whom you may remember, to contribute, and afterwards somehow got hold of the lectures I gave in Uppsala and Stockholm in 1955, and put in a sort of combined version of two of these. Meredith's paper and mine were read at the conference, but of course we did not go.

I was extremely interested to see the reviews of *Economic Issues*, and delighted that Graham Hutton had been so appreciative.

Would you please remember me to all your family, and would you please give my love to Tanya?

With kindest regards,

Yours sincerely,

George Shackle

George Shackle

104

40 Gurney Drive
Hampstead Garden Suburb
London N.2.
21st September 1958

Dear Professor Shackle,

We were all speechless when an enormous parcel arrived on Saturday morning and out came a magnificent doll's house for Tanya's birthday.

I wished you could have been present to see Tanya's reaction. It took some time before she dared play with it because she could not believe that it was really hers. It now stands in her nursery opposite her bed and she has already given much thought to the problem of how to furnish it. It is a most exquisite gift, which we enjoyed at least as much as Tanya. You are spoiling her far too much and I do not know how to thank you for this imaginative and precious gift. I only wished you could spare the time to see her playing with all your toys next time you are in London. Thank you so much for the great joy you have given to all of us.

We had a most enjoyable time in Italy and managed to do quite a bit of sightseeing. We were most impressed with Lucca, Pisa, Florence and Perugia, but the place I liked best was no doubt Assisi, where, unfortunately, we did not have more than $1\frac{1}{2}$ days at our disposal; however, thanks to the guidance of a most charming American Franciscan Friar we managed to see quite bit of Assisi and its art treasures despite the short time at our disposal. Michael of course was most impressed when he saw the Leaning Tower of Pisa!

I was so happy about your last letter which arrived shortly before our departure and Tanya was most delighted to receive your message. She studied your letter for a long time before I was allowed to read it out to her!

Michael has just started to read your book *Mathematics at the Fireside*, which you kindly sent him a few years ago. He is very proud that he received this copy from the author of the book and carefully keeps the message which accompanied the book when you sent it to him.[1] He does very well at his new school and was given the first prize at the end of his first year. He is especially interested in mathematics.

Did I mention to you that I received a review copy of your book, which was published some weeks ago by the Liverpool University Press? It will be reviewed by Lawrence Klein who, as you probably know, is now back in America (University of Pennsylvania).[2]

I should of course be very glad to be given an opportunity of seeing your chapter on Special Deposits, which will appear in your introduction to economic theory.

As soon as the October issue of *The Bankers' Magazine* is ready, I shall concentrate on my review article on some of your recent publications, which, I hope, will be ready in time for publication in November or December.

With all very best wishes from all of us and kindest regards,

Yours sincerely,

Stephen Frowen

1 The message of 22 April 1952 reads: 'My dear Frowein, I should be happy if you would accept this book as a future present for your little son. With all good wishes and very kind regards, Yours sincerely, G.L.S. Shackle.'

2 L.R. Klein's review of *A New Prospect of Economics*, edited and contributed to by G.L.S. Shackle (Liverpool: Liverpool University Press, 1958), appeared in *The Bankers' Magazine*, vol. CLXXXVI, no. 1377, December 1958. pp. 491–2.

105

40 Gurney Drive
Hampstead Garden Suburb
London N.2
1st January 1959

Dear Professor Shackle,

I just cannot find the words which could really express the joy which Tanya derived from your far too generous present. It certainly took a little while before she dared to touch this precious gift. We were all quite overwhelmed when we opened your big parcel on Christmas Day. I have never seen such a beautiful doll. How can we thank you adequately for the great happiness, which you have given to all of us! It was most kind of you to send this delightful present. You are certainly spoiling Tanya far too much and I am sure that in her mind Godfather and Father Christmas must be more or less alike for both are connected with presents and both are unknown to her in person! However, I have told her that you might visit her sometime this year and she is very much looking forward to this great event.

I wanted to write to you much earlier but I have only just been able to put the January issue to bed. The number was more or less ready when sterling was made convertible and the whole issue had to be brought up to date. I even managed to include a seven-page article by W.M. Scammell of the University College of North Wales on 'First Thoughts on Convertibility'.[1] Did I mention to you that the Joint Economic Committee of the Congress of the United States intends to reprint one of our articles in one of their official reports? I was of course delighted when I received this request from the Congress of the U.S.

I hope you and your family had a happy Christmas. Your children must be quite grown up now!

With all best wishes for a happy New Year to you and your family, and with many thanks for the great kindness which you have shown not only to me but also to my whole family over the last few years, I am always

Yours sincerely,

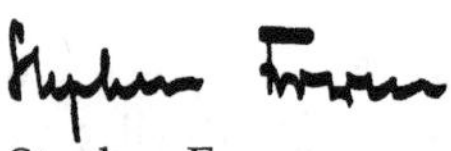

Stephen Frowen

1 See W.M. Scammell, 'First Thoughts on Convertibility', *The Bankers' Magazine*, vol. CLXXXVII, no. 1378, January 1959, pp. 13–19.

106

Garden House Hotel
Cambridge
6th January 1959

My dear Frowen,

It was the kindest possible thought of yours to send me this extremely elegant and ingenious desk calendar. I do most warmly appreciate your having thought of me, and greatly admire the compact and handsome gift itself.

I was most thrilled and delighted with the pictures of Tanya. The beauty of children is like nothing else on earth, no wonder the poet thought there was something of heaven in it. Please give her my love and my very best thanks for her message. (I hope my Christmas gift arrived intact: it was to have been sent in one of the firm's own vans, but these dolls look so fragile).

I am now enclosing my review of *The Life of Wicksell*, which you kindly gave me.[1] It is strange that Schumpeter (in his huge history of economic thought) should have been so mistaken in his idea of the character of Wicksell's career.

With warmest good wishes (please forgive me if a letter from you has crossed this one: I have been away from home for a week) and kindest regards,

Yours sincerely,

George Shackle

George Shackle

1 See G.L.S. Shackle, 'The Life of Knut Wicksell', *The Bankers' Magazine*, vol. CLXXXVII, no. 1380, March 1959, pp. 259–61 (a review article of Torsten Gårdlund, *The Life of Knut Wicksell*).

107

The Bankers' Magazine
85 & 86 London Wall
London E.C.2
14th January 1959

Dear Professor Shackle,

I was delighted to receive your very kind letter and the review of *The Life of Knut Wicksell*. I am now able to enclose a galley proof of your article and should be obliged if you would kindly return *one* of the two enclosed proofs. I am sure that after reading your review article many of our readers will wish to study the book. I am always amazed how many thoughts you manage to squeeze into a short article without affecting its readability. In fact your articles are so crystal-clear that an intelligent reader should have no difficulties in grasping what you are trying to get across. I wished I could learn this art!

As your review will appear as a review *article* you may wish to change the title. Our printers could easily do this at this stage.

I also enclose the last issue of *The Accountant*, which contains a review of A *New Prospect of Economics*.[1] I feel like writing a letter of protest to the editor!

With warmest wishes and kindest regards,

Yours sincerely,

Stephen Frowen

Stephen Frowen

1 *A New Prospect In Economics* is a textbook written by members of the Economics Department of the University of Liverpool, with the first three chapters by G.L.S. Shackle, and edited by F.E. Hyde and G.L.S. Shackle. It was reviewed by L.R. Klein in *The Bankers' Magazine*, vol. CLXXXVI, no. 1377, December, 1958, pp. 491–2.

108

The University of Liverpool
Department of Economics
11 Abercromby Square
Liverpool 7
16th January 1959.

My dear Frowen,

I was so pleased by your extremely kind remarks about my review. I would not claim anything except to take pains, but any amount of trouble is worth while when you are so appreciative. I do also most warmly appreciate your decision to make it a review article. I have very carefully checked the proof and now return it.

How kind of you to send this copy of *The Accountant* with a review of the textbook. I feel that this is quite a favourable one on the whole, but am delighted by your marginal comment. Teaching requirements, methods, tastes and the qualities of students are so diverse that no one textbook can please everybody. So far we have sold a little over 1,100, and with some good reviews I think all the contributors are content and some have heaved sighs of relief. While we were writing it, I often felt impatient at their lack of faith in their own efforts.

With all warmest good wishes and kindest regards,

Yours sincerely,

George Shackle

George Shackle

109

Università Degli Studi di Genova
Genova – via A. Bertani, 1
6th April 1959

My dear Frowen,

I am very much distressed to be only now replying to your extremely kind letter inviting me to take part in the Conference of the Business Economists Group. I should have been most thrilled to come, but I was in Genoa until Friday night, and will not be back in England, at earliest, until late on Saturday evening, so I am afraid it is impossible. I am so sorry. Thank you very much indeed for your very kind thought, I shall look forward to some opportunity of asking you to tell me about the proceedings.

I have been giving a short course of lectures here and at the same time seeing something of this dramatic city of sea and mountain scenery and streets, which plunge through tunnels in the sides of the hills. Yesterday I went out to Nervi and got a glimpse of the Italian Riviera in spring sunshine. It is of course exquisite in spite of the development (hotels and motor roads) along the coast. We saw the 'Cristofero Colombo' come into harbour. It is no doubt the pride of Genoa. I don't know whether it excites quite such passionate feelings as the 'Nieuwe Amsterdam' does in Rotterdam, where the departure of this ship is almost a national occasion.

With all my warmest thanks for your great kindness in writing to invite me, and kindest regards,

Yours sincerely,

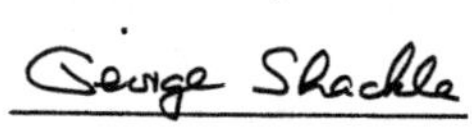

George Shackle

110

The Bankers' Magazine
85 & 86 London Wall
London E.C.2
2nd October 1959

Dear Professor Shackle,

It is difficult to describe the tremendous joy which Tanya derived from your birthday parcel. Always anxious to imitate her big brother she was very proud to get so many books. Her favourite so far is the beautiful edition of *Alice in Wonderland*

and *Peter Rabbit*, which we have to read to her again and again. It was exceedingly kind of you to send her these generous gifts, and it would certainly have been difficult to find a present which could have given her greater joy. You must have devoted no end of time and thought over choosing these books and I cannot thank you enough for your very great kindness and thoughtfulness.

Tanya has now started going to a Kindergarten, which she dearly loves. She settled down to her new routine surprisingly well and she seems to be very popular with the other children. I wished you could spare the time to visit her during one of your visits to London.

Last month I was invited to apply for a position of Economic Adviser to the Industrial and Commercial Finance Corporation of which Lord Piercy is the Chairman. The post was also advertised last week in *The Economist* as Lord Piercy was anxious to place the names of two or three candidates before the Board of Directors. I shall probably know before the end of this month.

Last month I was elected Secretary of the Ashburn Group. This is a very small group of industrial economists. It meets on Thursdays once a month at present at the National Liberal Club at 6.30 p.m. for about one hour and a half. We were discussing our programme the other night and there was considerable enthusiasm for the idea that I should presume on your friendship and ask you if you would like to come along and open a discussion on Expectations and Business Behaviour. We should not want a very heavily prepared paper, the Group is much too informal for that and I hope this invitation would not involve you in a lot of work. Sir Robert Shone of the Iron and Steel Board has kindly agreed to open a discussion on the long-term prospects, particularly of demand, in the steel industry on Thursday, 3rd December. We should be delighted if you could spare the time to address us on Thursday, 7th January, or on any other day more convenient to you.

I am just reading, with great delight, your *Economics for Pleasure*, which I am reviewing for our next issue. It is a book which I feel everybody interested in economics and finance ought to read. It is not too simple for advanced students, who will no doubt greatly benefit from reading it, and not too difficult for beginners. It is, in my view, one of the best textbooks in the market and I sincerely hope that it will also be put on the recommended reading list of the Institute of Bankers. It is indeed a book one can read 'for pleasure'.

With many thanks once again for all your kindness, and with all best wishes and warmest regards.

Yours sincerely,

Stephen Frowen

Stephen Frowen

111

The University of Liverpool
Department of Economics
11 Abercromby Square
Liverpool 7
9th October 1959

My dear Frowen,

Your letter is so full of exciting news, that I don't know which part of it to refer to first. It is wonderful to think that Tanya goes to school already. I am sure that when her serious schoolwork begins, the other children will find themselves 'left at the post'. My own little girl showed the same intense desire to keep up with her two elder brothers. It no doubt makes for an incisive attitude to life, but must be rather a strain!

Your own news is terrific. If you get this splendid post, it will only be your just reward for an astonishing performance in your present sphere. If I had a hat, I would throw it in the air.

It is exceedingly kind of you to invite me to address the Ashburn Group. It will be a great happiness to me. I am sure I used to know Sir Robert Shone at LSE (or am I off the rails in this?).

How long should my paper be? I would like to accept provisionally for 7th January, and will confirm, if I may, in a few weeks when I see how the preparation of the paper is going.

What good fortune for me that my book has fallen into your own hands. I am tremendously pleased at what you say about it in your letter. One reviewer said, ' It was perhaps more fun to write than to read'. It *was* fun to write, but I hope it is not such stiff going as some reviewers have said.

With all my very best wishes and very kind regards,

Yours sincerely,

George Shackle

George Shackle

112
The Bankers' Magazine
85 & 86 London Wall
London E.C.2
12th October 1959

Dear Professor Shackle,

Your letter has been a source of great happiness. I did not dare to hope for so prompt an answer. You must be frightfully busy just now, and it was most kind of you to reply so quickly.

I was of course delighted to hear that in principle you are willing to address the Ashburn Group and I have informed our Chairman that you have accepted provisionally for 7th January. Our usual practice is to allow about 30 minutes to the speaker who opens the discussion so that one hour can to be devoted to the actual discussion. It is needless to say how much we are all looking forward to this evening.

Irene and I should be very glad if you would be our guest to dinner after the meeting. I am sure Tanya would be allowed to stay up to wait for your arrival. She is very anxious to meet the mysterious godfather who sends her those wonderful presents. (Her favourite companion is still the pink teddy bear you sent her many years ago. Not only does he sleep in her bed, but he also accompanies her to school!).

With all best wishes and warmest regards,

Yours sincerely,

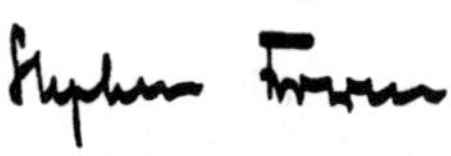

Stephen Frowen

113
40 Gurney Drive
London, N.2
10th January 1960

Dear Professor Shackle,

In the name of the members of the Ashburn Group I should like to thank you once again for the most interesting evening we were privileged to spend in your company. I had telephone calls from a number of our members who told me how much they had learnt from your paper and from the discussion which followed. They are happy to know that your paper will be published in the March issue of *The Bankers' Magazine*.[1]

There are no words which could express my gratitude for your exceedingly kind remarks about my work as editor of the *Magazine*. I was deeply moved but fear my modest efforts do not deserve so much praise.

My family and I greatly appreciated that despite your many commitments during your short stay in London, you did make it possible to squeeze in a visit to meet Tanya and the rest of the family. I only hope that the rush it meant for you did not put too great a strain on you. If I had known of all your other commitments, I would not have dared to suggest this visit to our home.

Michael was very sad that you are not *his* godfather. He was most impressed by your explanations and asked when you will be able to visit us again.

At Euston Station I rushed to Platform 13 and discovered too late that the train to Liverpool left from Platform 14. When I arrived there the train was just leaving and thus to my great distress, I was prevented from saying "good bye" properly.

Whenever I have the fortune of meeting you I feel more strongly what a privilege it is to know you and I cannot thank you enough for the personal interest you have taken in me since we first met in Leeds. It is, if anything, an understatement to say that it has transformed my whole life in more than one ways.

With all my very best wishes and kindest regards,

Yours sincerely,

Stephen Frowen

1 See G.L.S. Shackle, 'Business and Uncertainty', *The Bankers' Magazine*, vol. CLXXXIX, no. 1392, March 1960, pp. 209–13. Reprinted in G.L.S. Shackle, *The Nature of Economic Thought*, 1966.

114

Department of Economics
11 Abercromby Square
Liverpool 7
12th January 1960

My dear Frowen,

How can I tell you what admiration I was filled with by your marvellous family. Both Michael and Tanya seem to me the ideal of what children should be. Michael is quite evidently destined for great things, and Tanya is so exquisitely pretty and so beautiful in her manner and poise (for four years old, miraculously self-possessed) that I am a proud man to be her godfather.

What a wonderful evening I had with your Ashburn Group! It was astonishing how everything came together as if some dramatist has previously written out the list of characters and the play. It was so fortunate that Philip Andrews came, as I could fall back on his knowledge of the OERG [Oxford Economists' Research Group] and its doings and on his own investigation, and could 'introduce' him as if I was a television interviewer. I was so delighted also to meet, at last, the mysterious bearer of the initials J.R.C., and to find him, as I had expected, such an exceedingly delightful and charming man. Mr. Wadsworth of course is an old friend to both of us, and Sir Robert Shone I used to know in the Hayek seminar at LSE. The whole experience, for me, was magical and nostalgic in an extraordinary degree.

As to your own triumphal progress, I am over-awed by it.

I am enclosing a fair copy of my address to your Group, and should be exceedingly happy to think of it being published in *The Bankers' Magazine*.[1]

With every good wish and my very warmest thanks for two wonderful experiences, and kindest regards,

Yours sincerely,

George Shackle

George Shackle

1 For the published address by G.L.S. Shackle to the Ashburn Group, see G.L.S. Shackle, 'Business and Uncertainty', *The Bankers' Magazine*, vol. 189, no. 1392, March 1960, pp. 209–13.

115

The University of Liverpool
Department of Economics
11 Abercromby Square
Liverpool 7
3rd February 1960

My dear Frowen,

Thank you very much for sending me the proof [of 'Business and Uncertainty']. There are only two trifling corrections. I am returning proof and typescript as required.

With all good wishes and kindest regards,

Yours sincerely,

George Shackle

116

The University of Liverpool
Department of Economics
11 Abercromby Square
Liverpool 7
16th March 1960

My dear Frowen,

I need not tell you with what great distress I read your letter. It is most especially sad that you have given up the Editorship, in which you have so greatly triumphed. The only consolation is that your reputation now stands so high, and everyone who has had any close knowledge of your work is so well aware of the tremendous drive, thoroughness and, above all, imagination that you have put into that Editorship, that I cannot suppose you will have any trouble in getting another post of comparable scope.

Nor need I say how happy I shall be if I can help by way of testimony to your qualifications and achievements.

I do especially hope that it may not be necessary to go so far afield as Washington, or to disturb your life at home in England.

Academic vacancies are already hard to fill, and are going to increase very rapidly in the next decade. I am quite certain you will be able to obtain one if you wish, though the pay may be much less than even your salary with Waterlows which you told me was not good. But the rule which many Universities have, of filling vacancies at the Assistant Lecturer level (Grade III lecturer), is having to be more & more often disregarded, & posts are being filled higher up the scale. Would you like me to consult any friends on this matter? But I have no doubt you have many friends at LSE and elsewhere who can do more than I in finding out about such things.

I shall, need I say, be *most delighted* to write briefly on your achievement in recreating *The Bankers' Magazine.*

I have just received the March issue, which you so kindly sent me in advance. If you could spare me two or three copies I would be most grateful, but please let me pay for them.

I am sure that all will come right: but meanwhile I do know very well indeed how terribly exhausting and anxious a business it is, when one is not settled. But never fear, all will be well.

With kindest regards,

Yours sincerely,

George Shackle

George Shackle

117

The University of Liverpool
Department of Economics
11 Abercromby Square
Liverpool 7
21st March 1960

My dear Frowen,

I enclose my Note as I promised.[1] Your achievement speaks for itself in the pages of the *Magazine*, but perhaps this will put it in focus for less perceptive readers.

With kindest regards,

Yours sincerely,

George Shackle

George Shackle

1 See G.L.S. Shackle, 'Stephen Frowen: Editor of *The Bankers' Magazine* 1955–1960', *The Bankers' Magazine*, vol. CLXXXIX, no. 1393, April 1960, p. 290. See also 'Editors of *The Bankers' Magazine*', 'vol. CLXXXIX, no. 1390, January 1960, pp. 14–16.

118

The Bankers' Magazine
85 & 86 London Wall
London, E.C.2
22nd March 1960

Dear Professor Shackle,

I cannot tell you how touched and moved I was when I read your Note on 'the retiring editor'. Nothing could have made me happier than the knowledge that you approve of the work I have been doing for *The Bankers' Magazine*. I only fear that I do not deserve to be praised so generously.

It was exceedingly kind of you to devote so much of your precious time to this matter and I am unable to find words adequate to express my gratitude. Outside my closest family circle there is nobody to whom I owe as much as I owe to you, and I shall always be deeply grateful for the kind interest you have taken in me over so many years.

I was most happy when I received your encouraging letter on Saturday. It certainly had the effect but I was able to overcome a slight depression caused by the somewhat unsatisfactory nature of my present job.[1] However, things don't look quite as bad as they did when I wrote to you. I had a very amiable talk with Lord Piercy and things might sort themselves out in the end. I also had a charming letter from Philip Andrews who is doing his utmost to help me.

With many thanks, kindest regards and all best wishes,

Yours sincerely,

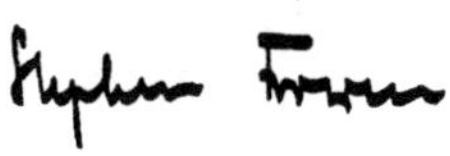

Stephen Frowen

1 This refers to an appointment as Economic Adviser to the Industrial and Commercial Finance Corporation Ltd. (now 3i), London.

119

The University of Liverpool
Department of Economics
11 Abercromby Square
Liverpool 7
25th March 1960

My dear Frowen,

I was tremendously glad to read, in your exceedingly kind letter, that things are now, for the time, settled again. I am so glad, although it seemed impossible that they would be really wrong.

I am delighted to insert Mr. Saunders's name and ought to have thought of it for myself.[1]

I am returning the proof herewith, with no corrections.

With all warmest good wishes, and great thankfulness that things have improved.

Yours sincerely,

George Shackle

1 The name of C.T. Saunders was added to G.L.S. Shackle's note 'Stephen Frowen: Editor of *The Bankers' Magazine*, 1955–1960', listing eminent academics among contributors to *The Bankers' Magazine*.

120

The University of Liverpool
Department of Economics
11 Abercromby Square
Liverpool 7
16th September 1960

My dear Frowen,

I was most delighted some weeks ago to see your article in *The Bankers' Magazine*, and the references to it in *The Times*.[1] I am so pleased to have the off-prints. I do hope that all is happy with you in every respect.

The great occasion of the 20th September approaches. I am in communication with G.H. Lee Ltd., a big Liverpool shop, to send Tanya an Italian 'baby' doll, resembling a real baby. I hope they will manage everything correctly and in good time. It is difficult by phone & letter to get things explained, but I have phoned & written to them. We are rather a long way from Liverpool, at Seagull Cottage, 13 King Street, Aldeburgh Suffolk, until 21 September. We leave here too late for me to go to the shop myself.

A terrific storm here last night. I am a bit sleepless this morning!

With all kindest regards,

Yours sincerely,

George Shackle

George Shackle

1 The article referred to on the evidence submitted to the Radcliffe Committee on medium and long-term finance to small- and medium-sized businesses is 'Medium and Long-Term Finance for Small Businesses' by Stephen Frowen, *The Bankers' Magazine*, vol. CLXL, no. 1398, September 1960, pp. 159–66. It led to extensive critical comments on ICFC's policies in *The Times* and by Lombard in *The Financial Times*.

121

The University of Liverpool
Department of Economics
11 Abercromby Square
Liverpool 7
12th December 1960

My dear Frowen,

I am extremely delighted and relieved to hear the splendid news. I was on the point of writing to you when I had the letter from Christopher Saunders, so I first answered that, and then thought there would very soon be news and that I would wait for it.[1]

Your knowledge of overseas trade, especially on the banking side, will be invaluable to the National Institute. The *Economic Review* carries great weight nowadays, *The Times* evidently relies heavily on it, and it must have an appreciative influence on national policy.

What an interesting conjuncture we are in just now. All the old pre-war rules seem to have gone by the board. Then there are the intriguing rumours about radical tax reforms.

I am exceedingly interested to hear of your plans. Do let me know how these develop, and I need not say, do please call on me for anything that I can do in the way of testimonials, although I am sure that nowadays your reputation carries its own message.

I am so glad, indeed, that the trying time is past for you, and I am perfectly sure great things will open out.

With all the warmest good wishes, and kindest regards,

Yours sincerely,

George Shackle

Some illness in our Department has made me rather extra busy; there is one thing about having to give lectures 'off the cuff': it saves the time of preparation!

1 The reference is to Stephen Frowen's new appointment as Research Officer at the National Institute of Economic and Social Research, London.

122

40 Gurney Drive
Hampstead Garden Suburb
London N.2
19th December 1961

Dear Professor Shackle,

I was very distressed when I discovered today that Tanya never thanked you for the most elegant handkerchiefs you kindly sent her for her birthday. I thought Tanya had written to you when she wrote her other thank-you letters and my wife was convinced that I had written to you myself. Please do forgive us for this negligence which is really inexcusable.

Tanya was simply delighted when she received your exquisite gift. She really appreciates things of practical value and likes *pretty* objects. You must have felt and guessed her mentality and taste when you chose this present.

I hope you are keeping well. I am impatiently looking forward to my visit to Liverpool and to seeing you again.[1]

During the first half of January I am going to Germany to lecture at Cologne University and at the Freie Universität in West Berlin. I really enjoy teaching and hope that eventually I shall succeed in getting a lectureship. I am giving one course at present on Comparative Banking Institutions. My wife is now a lecturer at University College London (German Department).

I cannot tell you how much my son Michael enjoys your book *Mathematics at the Fireside.* He just started at University College School (after having passed the 11+) where he is exceedingly happy. Mathematics is one of his favourite subjects.

With all best wishes and kindest regards,

Yours sincerely,

Stephen Frowen

[1] The invitation to address the Liverpool Economic and Statistical Society had been mentioned earlier in a postcard to George Shackle from Stephen Frowen dated July 1961, which reads as follows:

"Dear Professor Shackle,

Just before I left London for a holiday in Switzerland, I received an invitation from Mr. Robertson to address the Liverpool Economic and Statistical Society at the beginning of next year. I cannot tell you how very much I am looking forward to this event, especially as I hope it will give me an opportunity of meeting you again.

I was most interested to see that your new book *Decision, Order and Time in Human Affairs* was published last month. This substantial volume is beautifully produced and I am impatiently looking forward to reading it. *The Bankers' Magazine* is trying to find a suitable reviewer and I suggested Professor Meredith.

Flims is a delightful holiday resort – very peaceful and ideal for a family holiday.

With all good wishes and kindest regards,

Yours sincerely,

Stephen Frowen"

123

40 Gurney Drive
London, N.2
30th December 1961

Dear Professor Shackle,

I wished you could have seen Tanya's joy when she unpacked your Christmas parcel. It was a tremendous success. She is very proud to have her own clock now, and I discovered that it has been her secret wish for a long time (partly, probably, because her big brother has a clock!).

We asked Tanya on Christmas Day which present she would like to keep if she could only keep one. The answer was: My Godfather's clock, of course.

It was exceedingly kind of you to send her such a precious Christmas gift. I am sure that she will treasure it for the rest of her life.

Next week I am going to Germany to give two lectures at Cologne University and three lectures in West Berlin (at the Free University and the Stock Exchange). Did I mention to you that I am also doing some part-time lecturing in London [at the Polytechnic, Regent Street, London (now the University of Westminster)]? It is a course on Comparative Banking Institutions for third-year Honours students. Some of my students are highly intelligent and very responsive. It is a real pleasure to teach them.

I was very happy to get your interesting Christmas card.

With all best wishes and kindest regards,

Yours sincerely,

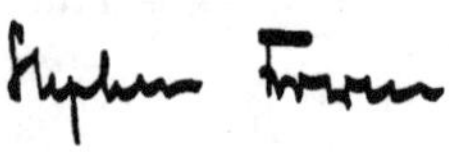

Stephen Frowen

124

The University of Liverpool
Department of Economics
11 Abercromby Square
Liverpool 7
28th January 1962

My dear Frowen,

You will be back now from your German lecture tour and I am all agog to hear from yourself, when you visit us soon, all about this and your other news. I was exceedingly interested to hear that you are lecturing on Comparative Banking Institutions and I wonder whether this course will be published? It is a tremendously intricate, difficult and topically important subject and few people nowadays can be as pre-eminently qualified to write a book on it as you. Does your work at the National Institute give you a chance to do such a thing? I do feel very strongly that your great fund of banking knowledge, gained as Editor as an 'explorer' of other systems in Europe (and beyond?), should be crystallised soon and published for the wide benefit of all the bankers, civil servants, politicians and humble academics who need nowadays to know about it. Of course, Professor Sayers[1] is publishing in this line, but I am sure he would not feel that this field is his closed preserve.

I was delighted, too, to see you writing in *The Observer*.[2] It is all amounting to a very formidable reputation with a momentum of its own. But I am sure you have it all under control, and will follow the path you really wish for, in 'High Financial Journalism' or in an academic career, or *both*.

The colour photograph of Tanya is marvellous. Where was this taken? The Rhine I think? You must forgive my ignorance.

And please forgive, if you can, the time I have let go by before writing. This last vacation was one long rush of distractions, it is rather short for the necessary preparation for a new term, and we are just now in the throes of much re-organisation, with a great increase of students already beginning. Some of them have, and some have not, read economics at G.C.E. Advanced Level, and this is utterly baffling, as we have them in one and the same first year class.

I wonder what are the views at Dean Trench Street about the ICI–Courtaulds business. The Hayek seminar at LSE in my day included both Paul Chambers and Sir Robert Shone.

A terrible clash of dates has just occurred to me: on 23rd Feb. I have to be in London! This is really disastrous. I had been so exceedingly looking forward to seeing and entertaining you. What can we do? We must hope to meet in the South. I really am upset about this. It cannot be helped. Do let me know if your plans or ideas can in any way be aided or promoted by me.

Please give my best love and greetings to Tanya.

With all my warmest and best wishes and kindest regards,

Yours sincerely,

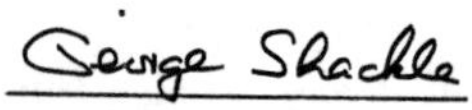

George Shackle

1 Richard Sidney Sayers, Cassel Professor of Economics, London School of Economics, 1947–68.
2 This was an article by Stephen Frowen on 'Booming Berlin Loses Men and Money', *The Observer*, 29 October, 1961.

125
Rosetor Hotel
Torquay
16th April 1962

Dear Professor Shackle,

I was exceedingly happy to receive your long letter at the beginning of February. You can imagine how sorry I was not to see you in Liverpool when I gave my talk to the Liverpool Economic and Statistical Society. However, I do hope that it will be possible to meet in the South sometime soon.

I am greatly enjoying my course on Comparative Banking Institutions. My students are very charming and at least two of them should do very well in their examinations this summer. The idea of publishing a book on this subject had not occurred to me, but the more I think about your suggestion the more I see the advantage of doing so. There is no up-to date textbook on this subject and perhaps I should try to fill this gap.

As the moment I am desperately trying to get a lectureship. I have discussed this at great length with Mr C.T. Saunders[1] and he has encouraged me to apply for vacancies and has promised his support. I like teaching and definitely prefer a combination of teaching and research to a pure research job. Unfortunately there are at present very few vacancies in or near London, and I cannot apply for a lectureship at a provincial university, as I should not like my wife to give up her lectureship at University College London for my sake. Another reason is that we have at last succeeded in getting our son Michael into University College School where he is exceedingly happy and does extremely well. I should therefore not like to transfer him to another school. In recent months London University has not advertised a single vacancy in my field. I did apply for a lectureship at the newly established University of Sussex in Brighton, but so far I only had a formal acknowledgement. I understand that the competition at Brighton is tremendous and I do not really have much hope. Worcester College Oxford advertised a Fellowship, but without an Oxford degree I would certainly not stand a chance there. I also applied for a lectureship at the Polytechnic, Regent Street, where I might stand a chance, as I am already on their part-time staff. My only fear is that it might be difficult to get a University Lectureship for somebody who is a lecturer at a Polytechnic, although my principal task would be to prepare students for the external degree of London University. I should be most grateful to you for your advice in this matter. Would you kindly allow me to give your name as one of my referees when applying for lectureships?

Just now I am enjoying a few days of rest in Torquay with my family. I know Cornwall quite well, but had never been to Devon. I am most impressed by the beauty of this part of England and definitely want to spend more time exploring it. Unfortunately we have to go back to London tomorrow, as we are anxious to spend Easter at home. But I shall certainly come back to Devon as soon as possible.

I have seen your latest publications and can never understand how you manage to do so much research and writing in addition to your extensive teaching. It is indeed a challenge to try and follow your example, but at the same time it is most discouraging as one can never hope even to approach your standards.

With all best wishes and kindest regards,

Yours sincerely,

Stephen Frowen

1 C.T. Saunders, Director of the National Institute of Economic and Social Research, London.

126

The University of Liverpool
Department of Economics
11 Abercromby Square
Liverpool 7
23rd April 1962

My dear Frowen,

What a very special happiness it was for me to have your letter, after the frustrations of not being in Liverpool for your lecture. I am tremendously interested to hear about your Comparative Banking course, and I do urge you to consider early publication. Now is the moment. If Britain joins the European Economic Community, there will begin (I suppose) a long and complex task of aligning institutions and arrangements of all sorts, and banking will plainly be one of the most central. With your extremely distinguished record in the City's high-level semi-academic periodical publications, you will I am sure have no difficulty in finding a publisher. Books are said to be booming and especially those giving instruction in practical matters. On Monday, 30th April, a representative of Longman's is coming to see me. Shall I mention this idea to him?

I have no special knowledge of the firm but a rather vague impression that they do very well for their authors. I am friendly with both Allen & Unwin as with Blackwell, who would both, I am sure, be glad to be given an opportunity to consider your manuscript.

A published book entirely from your own hand would set the seal on your extraordinarily successful career, which would thus be brought to a focus. This would I think be useful in your seeking a lectureship.

I am perfectly sure you are right about the advantage of keeping to one school for Michael. My elder son was moved several times, and although he has now left all that behind (and is nearly 21), I think it was a hardship to him.

I need not say how delighted I should be to reply to any enquiry about you, and that I should try to convey some realisation of your extraordinary achievement.

I feel the greatest hesitation in trying to advise about the kind of post to apply for, but in general I think you should go straight for a post measuring up to your impressive record as Editor of *The Bankers' Magazine*. Do not let them get you on the cheap.

I was most delighted and touched by the message from Tanya. I send her my very best love and good wishes.

With kindest regards,

Yours sincerely,

George Shackle

George Shackle

I found *Economic Issues* in the University Library in Genoa the week before last.

127

The National Institute of Economic & Social Research
2 Dean Trench Street
Smith Square
Westminster S.W.1
26th April 1962

Dear Professor Shackle,

I was exceedingly happy to receive your very kind letter. It is difficult to find words, which could express my gratitude for the great personal interest you have taken in my career. Your encouraging letter has indeed been of tremendous help to me.

I have been shortlisted for the Polytechnic lectureship.[1] The interview has been fixed for 3rd May. But I agree with you that it would be better to go straight for a University Lectureship. The University of Manchester has advertised a Lectureship in Banking and Finance. It seems too good a chance to miss and I shall probably apply. My family would of course stay in London (if I should get the job) and during term time I should try to spend as many weekends as possible with my family in London. It is not an ideal arrangement, of course, but from the strictly professional point of view, it may be a better solution than the acceptance of the Polytechnic Lectureship (if it should be offered to me).

I am now really keen on writing the book on Comparative Banking. The best solution would probably be if I restricted myself to the United Kingdom and the Common Market countries. I should of course be most grateful if you would be so kind as to mention this matter to the representative of Longman's when you see him on Monday. Please accept my sincerest thanks for your generous offer to reply to any enquiries about me in connection with my application. I only hope that this will not take up too much of your precious time.

With warmest wishes and kindest regards,

Yours sincerely,

Stephen Frowen

1 Now the University of Westminster.

128

40 Gurney Drive
Hampstead Garden Suburb
London, N.2
16th May 1962

Dear Professor Shackle,

I thought you might like to know that I was *not* offered a lectureship at the Polytechnic, Regent Street. Mr Pendred, the Head of the School of Commerce, telephoned me after the interview and told me that it was a very close run. Apparently the Principal of the Polytechnic was anxious to save money and they appointed a beginner aged about 25 who was prepared to start at the bottom end of the salary scale. I was not too unhappy as I am of course more anxious to get a University Lectureship.

Meanwhile the University of Birmingham approached me and asked whether I would be interested in a temporary lectureship for one year to replace Dr Harbury who intends to go to the U.S.A. for a year. Provided I cannot get a permanent lectureship in or near London just now, I should of course be very happy to replace Harbury. The courses which he is looking after deal with elementary macroeconomics, including a short advanced course in money and banking; a 14-hour lecture course in social economics; a short course on current economic problems (third-year undergraduate course) and a number of classes and tutorials. I hope to hear from Prof. Hutchison within the next few days.

I have also applied for a lectureship in Monetary Theory and International Trade at Woolwich Polytechnic [now the University of Greenwich], London, S.E.18 to teach degree students. This morning I had a letter informing me that I have been shortlisted. The interview will take place on 23rd May. Although I mentioned the names of three referees when I applied for this job, they nevertheless asked me to forward copies of three testimonials. I should therefore be most grateful if you would be so kind as to let me have a testimonial which I could forward to the Polytechnic. I feel very guilty for taking up so much of your precious time and scarcely dare to trouble you with this request.

With all best wishes and kindest regards,

Yours sincerely,

Stephen Frowen

P.S. The enclosed testimonial from Prof. Rittershausen (Cologne University) may be of interest to you.

129

The University of Liverpool
Department of Economics
11 Abercromby Square
Liverpool 7
18th May 1962

My dear Frowen,

I am so delighted to hear of the invitation to you from Professor Hutchison, to whom I have just written in reply to an enquiry from him. It seems to me that my letter might serve also as a testimonial for your other application, and I enclose a copy of it without the personal address to Professor Hutchison, and with a few names, such as that of the N.I.E.S.R. & the I.M.F., fully spelled out and explained. I do not think Professor Hutchison would mind my letter to him serving as a general testimonial for you. If you took this post, I cannot but feel that it would lead on to a secure academic position for you at one or other British University, with their great expansion or creation of departments of economics.

I have just had a letter from Longman's representative who called on me. He says Longman's are writing to you. I do hope you will be able to spare time to bring your book out.

Do let me know how things go. I rather hope you will take the Birmingham post as I feel it would be more comfortable and more appropriate to your standing than the Polytechnic, though not so convenient; unless of course a London post becomes available.

With all best wishes and warmest hopes that everything will come out for the best, as you deserve, and kindest regards,

Yours sincerely,

George Shackle

George Shackle

130

The National Institute of Economic & Social Research
2 Dean Trench Street
Smith Square
Westminster, S.W.1
22nd May 1962

Dear Professor Shackle,

I was so happy when I received your letter. My indebtedness to you is beyond words and I just don't know how to thank you for your testimonial. I shall have to make the greatest efforts in order not to disappoint those who will appoint me to a teaching job and to justify your very kind remarks which I fear I do not quite deserve. I am also most grateful for your advice. Unfortunately, Birmingham University will not be able to appoint a *full-time* temporary lecturer. I had lunch today with Dr Harbury, the lecturer I was supposed to replace. He told me that Professor Hutchison tried very hard to get permission to appoint a full-time lecturer, but at last Friday's Faculty Board Meeting it was decided (for financial reasons) to replace Harbury by a part-time lecturer and to distribute part of his work among other members of staff. The part-time lectureship now envisaged will probably carry a salary of £400–£600 p.a. I would have to take over most of Harbury's teaching apart from his classes (except one) and tutorials. All these lectures could be given in one day, so that I would only have to go to Birmingham once a week (on Tuesdays or Fridays). With no other University Lectureship in sight, I have agreed to this proposal and hope to hear from Professor Hutchison (who still has to make up his mind whether he wants me or not) within the next few days. From the University of Sussex, Brighton, I had a letter this morning informing me that they do not intend to appoint new lecturers in economics at the moment, but asked me to apply again next year. Apparently one of my present colleagues, Tibor Barna, has just been offered a Chair at the University of Sussex.

I had a very nice letter from Longmans, Green enquiring whether I would be prepared to write a textbook on Comparative Banking Systems. I have accepted and really look forward to this task. There is definitely a gap to be filled. It was exceedingly kind of you to mention my name to Longmans and to encourage me to undertake this task.

I shall of course let you know how things are going. I am quite determined to get an academic post and although the beginning will not be easy as experience has shown, I do hope that I shall succeed. Your practical and moral support has been of tremendous help to me and has given me great encouragement and hope.

With many thanks and warmest wishes,

Yours sincerely,

Stephen Frowen

131

The National Institute of Economic & Social Research
2 Dean Trench Street
Smith Square
Westminster, S.W.1
23rd May 1962

Dear Professor Shackle,

I thought you might like to know that I have just been appointed Lecturer in Monetary Theory and International Trade at Woolwich Polytechnic [now the University of Greenwich]. This is a Grade A Lectureship (salary £1600–1800), and I shall have to teach Degree students only. At present students take the External B.Sc. (Econ) Degree of the University of London – but they will soon be able to take an *Internal* London University Degree. I have also been granted permission to teach part-time at Birmingham University and to continue my annual course at Cologne University. The Principal of the Polytechnic, a very charming man, will probably write to you, as he would prefer a letter from you giving information about me instead of the testimonial originally requested. All he wants, I think, is a confirmation of the contents of your testimonial in the form of a confidential letter addressed to him. You will probably hear from the Principal in a day or two. I am terribly sorry that you will again be troubled in this matter, which has already taken up far too much of your precious time.

My teaching programme will be quite heavy – 20 hours a week at the Polytechnic and 4–5 hours at Birmingham University – and especially the first year might be a bit strenuous. However, I shall struggle through somehow and shall certainly gain enough teaching experience!

With all best wishes and kindest regards and many thanks once again,

Yours sincerely,

Stephen Frowen

P.S. The Principal of the Polytechnic is very keen for me to get a PhD as he would like me to become a Recognised Teacher of London University. I must give some thought to this. Perhaps I could do something in the field of Comparative Banking as a PhD thesis, which could later be published by Longmans?

132

The University of Liverpool
Department of Economics
11 Abercromby Square
Liverpool 7
5th June 1962

My dear Frowen,

So delighted to hear of your splendid (and heroic!) double appointment, also your decision to bring out your book on Comparative Banking. It sounds altogether immensely strenuous but will bring its great rewards. *I have not heard from Woolwich*: ought I to write?

All warmest and best wishes and kindest regards,

Yours sincerely,

George Shackle

133
The Woolwich Polytechnic
London S.E.18
30th September 1962

Dear Professor Shackle,

It was exceedingly kind of you to send Tanya such a lovely birthday gift. She was thrilled to get a railway from you. The competition with her brother is tremendous and anything he has she longs to have herself. You could not have chosen a present which would have given her more joy.

Our term started last Monday, but I only had to give two evening lectures. My day students will start tomorrow. I am really looking forward to my new job. My colleagues are charming and apparently we get some very good students, mainly from overseas. I am making the utmost use of *Economics for Pleasure*, and I am strongly advising all my students to read it with great care.

With warmest wishes,

Yours sincerely,

Stephen Frowen

134
The University of Liverpool
Department of Economics
11 Abercromby Square
Liverpool 7
8th October 1962.

My dear Frowen,

I was delighted to have your letter, and to have some news of your new enterprises. I do very much look forward to hearing more about this as time goes on, and hope to hear that you are not finding the number of hours too great a strain. I was of course extremely happy about your very kind reference to *Economics for Pleasure*. It is just about to appear in a paperback form (the same pages bound up in a soft instead of hard cover). It has also just appeared in Spanish as *Para Comprender la*

Economia, and should, if various publishers keep their promises and make use of the rights they have already paid something for, come out in Swedish, French, Italian and Portuguese.

Tanya's letter is most delightful and I am thrilled to hear of her progress at school: a most beautiful letter. Would you please tell her what very great happiness it gave me.

With kindest regards,

Yours sincerely,

George Shackle

135

40 Gurney Drive
Hampstead Garden Suburb
London N.2
15th December 1962

Dear Professor Shackle,

I should like you to know that I have now received a contract from Longmans, Green & Co. The book they have asked me to write will cover the new subject 'Monetary Institutions', one of the Part II subjects under the revised regulations for the B.Sc. (Econ.) Examination, and will deal with the monetary history of, and current financial institutions in the UK and USA.

Without your encouragement I should scarcely have decided to attempt writing this book, but I am greatly looking forward to this task. It was exceedingly kind of you to suggest this to Longmans, Green & Co., and I am most grateful to you for both your encouragement and your more than generous help.

My first term has been rather hectic, but stimulating and gratifying. I think I like teaching more than anything I have done in the past.. Some of my students are very good indeed and my Part II students (there is only one student doing Money and Banking) ought to get at least an Upper Second. The only distressing aspect of my present job is that many students have obviously come to us because they did not manage to get into a university. They feel deprived (I have little understanding for this snobbishness) and those of our first-year students who do well in their Part I examinations will without doubt try (as they have done in the past) to get into a university for their Part II course. The number of our Part II students is therefore very small. It is possible, of course, that technical colleges will be granted university status and things might change as a result of this. Our teaching load is really too heavy. Twenty hours of teaching at degree level is more than one can manage if one wants to do it at all well, especially during the first year of one's teaching career. In fact, I was rather dissatisfied with some of my lectures, although the students apparently liked them. I think eventually I might try to get a University Lectureship, which would leave me more time for preparing my lecture courses and for writing and research. I am quite looking forward to my lectures at Birmingham University next term (on Money and Banking), which I hope to be able to prepare during the Christmas holidays.

I feel I must apologise for writing so much about my own activities and myself but I thought you might be interested in a short progress report. (I am not sure whether the word 'progress' is justified.)

Tanya's school report is quite satisfactory. Her best subject is Poetry!

I was very pleased to see the paperback edition of *Economics for Pleasure*. It must be a best seller by now. There was quite a display of it recently at the Economists' Bookshop.

With all best wishes and kindest regards,

Yours sincerely,

Stephen Frowen

136

The University of Liverpool
Department of Economics
11 Abercromby Square
Liverpool 7
22nd December 1962.

My dear Frowen

I was more delighted that I can say to have your letter. It is a really inspiring account of your new undertakings and I wish that all the discontented young men, who have everything given them without question, could be made to study your career and see what can be achieved in the face of *real* difficulty.

I am most thrilled about the contract for your book. I do most earnestly hope you will be able to give *this* your best efforts rather than exhaust them wholly in the teaching which, as always happens with a first-rate teacher, drains away a flood of nervous energy in the service of people of whom only a few deserve it. I am frankly horrified at your teaching load. I do hope before long you will transfer to a university. Your teaching experience at Woolwich ought after very few terms to be a sufficient basis for applications for one or other of the many posts that are now coming up. You know how exceedingly happy I should be if I could do anything to forward such an application, though you would nowadays have massive support from many others. I hope Birmingham will be congenial to you, and I feel sure that if they should in future have the necessary vacancy and finance, they would be anxious to have you. There are all the new universities too. Your book, of course, will be a tremendous help.

I was so very pleased to hear of Tanya's excellent progress. I hope she will enjoy *The Wind in the Willows*, which I sent a few days ago, as much as my own children did. I found it an ideal book for reading aloud, but perhaps nowadays children no longer appreciate that.

There will of course be some among your students who, though seeming now rather passive recipients of instruction, are quietly filled with excitement and ambition by your teaching. They will remember it all their lives and always be grateful to you.[1] One has to be careful not to think of the whole body of one's students as a homogeneous mass, they range through a large part of the variety that the human being can achieve. But they are a marvellous subject for study.

How kind of you to refer to *Economics for Pleasure*. The Spanish edition published in Mexico City and Buenos Aires is also paperback, and I have agreements for Swedish, French, Italian and Portuguese editions. I cannot help feeling a sort of shy pleasure, though a slightly ironic one.

With all my warmest good wishes and kindest regards,

Yours sincerely,

George Shackle

George Shackle

1 One of the most outstanding students attending some of Stephen Frowen's lectures at Birmingham University was Stephen Littlechild, who later held Chairs at the Universities of Aston and Birmingham, became a member of the Monopolies and Mergers Commission and ultimately Director-General of Electricity Regulation. G.L.S. Shackle always felt that Stephen Littlechild was among those with the deepest insight into his thoughts and works and would have loved him to write his biography.

137

The University of Liverpool
Department of Economics
11 Abercromby Square
11th January 1963

My dear Frowen,

I do hope I have not caused you anxiety and dismay by not sending before now a copy of my lecture amended in respect of the italic. I wonder if it will be in time if I send it next Thursday 16th January? By then I can have revised it and got it typed.

It was extremely kind of you to think of seeking to get the Woolwich Papers published by Cambridge University Press. They do everything so beautifully, and it would have pleased me very much. I sounded them on the subject. The Assistant Secretary (there are several) who handles my affairs was most kind but after carefully discussing it he left me the impression that they might be reluctant to do it because it would cost a good deal more than they could charge. They are not mercenary (they have been extraordinarily generous to me) but I think the principle is that the subsidies must be used for the benefit of members of the Cambridge University (as you know, I am *not* one). I did not feel that I ought to intervene further in the matter, since I have no authority from you and I had the feeling that my friend at the Press was trying very tactfully to discourage me. It is sad, but in view of the urgency of getting it printed, it does seem as if we should do best to make other arrangements. I am so very sorry.

You are always so immeasurably much too kind in what you say about my writing. *You* are a master of *two* languages (*at least* two, you may have many more at your fingertips!). It would have been of the greatest value to me to know German. But things conspired against me a little. Now I think it is too late. I don't suppose we can get that command of a language which makes its use a pleasure, except in youth. My father [Robert Walker Shackle] took up Spanish when he was past 70, but did not really master it. (As he was an excellent Latinist, he would easily get that sort of reading knowledge, which consists in treating any Romance language as a sort of emulsified Latin.)

I am very much distressed indeed that Tanya's book did not come. I cannot think what muddle can have happened. I ought to have telephoned to Heffers instead of writing, but I gave them a whole week.

I fear it will be a miracle if you can decipher this letter.

With all my very best wishes and kindest regards, and I do hope no delays of mine have caused you trouble.

Yours sincerely,

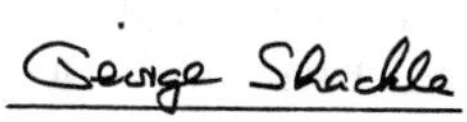

George Shackle

138

40 Gurney Drive
Hampstead Garden Suburb
London, N.2
29th April 1963

Dear Professor Shackle,

I do apologise for troubling you again, but as you will see from the enclosed letter, I may have a chance of getting a lectureship in the Department of Economics at Birmingham University where I have been doing some part-time teaching during the session 1962–63.

I should be most grateful if you would kindly allow me to give your name as one of the three referees required. The second referee will be Mr. C.T. Saunders and the third referee the Head of my Department at Woolwich Polytechnic.

I was late in sending in my application to Birmingham University (closing date 27th April), as I have only just returned from Germany where I had to address a group of industrialists on the problem of Britain's entry into the Common Market. My return to London was delayed by the sudden and completely unexpected death of a cousin with whom I was staying in Frankfurt.[1] It was rather tragic. He was only 40. Three months ago he got his chair of medicine at Frankfurt University and he leaves three children ranging in age from 18 months to 7 years. The cause of his death was an acute form of leukaemia, which apparently could not be diagnosed until a few days before his death.

I hope you are keeping well. I went to the conference of university teachers of economics and hoped to see you there. I was very disappointed when I could not find your name on the list of participants. I assume that you have been far too busy with your research to find the time for attending the conference. Some of the papers and the discussions I found disappointing.

I was very distressed to hear of your illness some time ago. I do hope that you are quite well again.

This morning Tanya had to sit for a three-hour examination at the North London Collegiate. The competition for places is tremendous but we do hope that she will get in. It is an outstanding school and I have the feeling that Tanya would be very happy there.

If I should get the Birmingham job, my family would probably stay in London for the time being. My idea is to take a small flat in Birmingham where I would stay during term time (with occasional weekends spent in London). It would be a bit of an upheaval, but my wife does not feel like giving up her lectureship at University College London and Michael is very happy at University College School in Hampstead where I would like him to stay on. He has done extremely well so far.

I should of course have preferred a lectureship at London University, but my feeling is that I must get more teaching experience before I stand a chance of such an appointment. The LSE seems to be more in favour of appointing Assistant Lecturers, and my chances there are therefore limited at present. I think I would be very happy at Birmingham University. I have certainly enjoyed my teaching there and found the students lively and very responsive.

One of my most precious Christmas gifts was your last letter, which arrived on Christmas Eve. It is difficult to express in words how happy I was to receive it.

With kindest regards and all best wishes,

Yours sincerely,

Stephen Frowen

1 Professor Rolf Frowein

139
40 Gurney Drive
Hampstead Garden Suburb
London, N.2
15th May 1963

Dear Professor Shackle,

To my deepest regret I had to withdraw my Birmingham application. You probably felt how keen I was to get this job and it was not easy to give up the chance of getting the lectureship at Birmingham.

My wife was terribly unhappy about my application and the prospect of having to move to Birmingham. Our discussions went on and on; in the end I was so exhausted emotionally that I did not have the strength to argue any longer. My wife also convinced Mrs. Saunders, a close friend of hers, that my decision was wrong, and Mrs. Saunders in turn made it difficult for her husband (one of my referees) to give me his wholehearted support because by doing so he might indirectly damage our marriage. When things had reached this stage, I withdrew my application.

In a way I can of course understand that from my wife's personal angle, it would have made her unhappy if I had been offered, and then accepted, the Birmingham job, but from the professional point of view it was a unique chance for me. Still, a suitable vacancy might crop up in London in due course. I hear that a vacancy may occur in the Department of Economics at University College London next year. The trouble is that London University does not appoint many lecturers, most of the new appointments being made at the Assistant Lecturer's level. However, I have not given up hope yet.

I was so grateful to you for the kind interest you have shown in my application and for the support you were prepared to provide in my attempt to get the Birmingham lectureship.

Last term Mr. Saunders inaugurated a new public lecture series entitled *Woolwich Economic Lectures*, established at my suggestion at Woolwich Polytechnic. This will be an annual event. If you could possible spare the time to give a lecture during the session 1963–64, I should be exceedingly happy. We should like this lecture to be given sometime in October, but the date could be postponed until later in the year if October would not suit you. I remember a lecture you once gave on 'What makes an economist?' It was a delightful paper and I think our students and staff would greatly benefit from a lecture on this theme. Mr. Saunders's lecture, which was entitled 'Towards Free Trade?' and dealt extensively with the US Trade Expansion Act, will be published in a few weeks' time. I shall arrange for a copy of his lecture to be sent to you.

There is no need to make up your mind immediately, but if you could let me know your decision by the end of June, I should be most grateful. A number of distinguished scientists from universities all over world have so far given guest lectures at Woolwich Polytechnic in the Departments of Mathematics, Physics, Chemistry, Biology and Engineering, but this is quite a new activity in the Department of Economics. We are therefore anxious to make it a great success.

I hope so much that you will be able to accept. The lecture would be preceded by a sherry party and followed by a dinner party given by the principal of our college in his private dining room, but there would be time enough, I hope, to see you privately either before or after the lecture. If you felt able to accept our invitation you would of course receive an official invitation from the Head of the Department of Economics.

With all best wishes and kindest regards,

Yours sincerely,

Stephen Frowen

140

The University of Liverpool
Department of Economics
11 Abercromby Square
19th May 1963

My dear Frowen,

I am most grievously distressed by what you tell me. There is in my thoughts only one comfort: you are a man of immense courage, proved over and over again in a career full of every sort of adversity, discouragement and upset, as well as its marvellous successes; a man whom nothing so far has been able to defeat. Your letter, which brings this sad account, is itself entirely in line with the qualities which have brought you so far. You almost seem able to view this setback with detachment, and most of your letter is devoted to an extremely kind invitation to me, by which I am most deeply touched and very greatly honoured. But things will come right. The academic world is having to recruit itself with people who have nothing to compare with your record; it cannot afford to do without you. Meanwhile I am chiefly concerned about the over-load of work from which we hoped that you would be relieved. I wish we could have a talk to explore what is possible and what is not possible. I have a *viva* at LSE on Wednesday, 5 June. It is fixed for 3 o'clock and should be over by 4.30. I wonder if we could have tea together, anywhere that would suit you, before I catch a train at Euston?

I am afraid I have missed the post (4 p.m. on Sundays). Everything goes with such a rush. If 5th June will not do, I have 3 more vivas later in the summer, (higher degrees at LSE). Also I hope to come to the annual meeting at the Royal Economic Society on 4th July. I would so much love to have a chance of exchanging news.

I did write to Birmingham, there are going to be lots of other opportunities, some of them near enough to London.

All my warmest good wishes,

Yours sincerely,

George Shackle

George Shackle

141

Reform Club,
Pall Mall, S.W.1
23rd May 1963

Dear Professor Shackle,

I was exceedingly happy to receive your very kind and encouraging letter.

I am overjoyed to know that I shall have an opportunity of meeting you at the beginning of next month. It is extremely kind of you to suggest this meeting.

I am quite free on Wednesday, 5th June. May I suggest that I wait for you in the entrance hall of the LSE at 4.30? We can then drive to the Reform Club for tea. Later on I can take you by car to Euston. In case you should be free before 4.30, you could contact me at the Reform Club and I would be at the LSE within minutes.

This morning the Principal of Woolwich Polytechnic, the Head of my Department, our Principal Lecturer and myself interviewed six candidates, who had applied for a lectureship, for $3\frac{1}{2}$ hours. It was quite a new and interesting experience, but I felt terribly sorry for some of the unsuccessful candidates (one of them got a Double First in Cambridge).

I cannot tell you how much I am looking forward to our meeting. With kindest regards and warmest wishes,

Yours sincerely,

Stephen Frowen

142

19th July 1963

Telegram from G.L.S. Shackle to S.F. Frowen

Thrilled and delighted beyond words with incomparable book. Letter follows. Please give Tanya also my love and warmest thanks for her card.

George Shackle

143

The University of Liverpool
Department of Economics
11 Abercromby Square
Liverpool 7
28th July 1963

My dear Frowen,

I have never received any present of such incomparable and inexpressible beauty as the book you sent me. I did not know that such a book existed. I want you to know what intense pleasure it gives me, for its own sake, but much more because of your deep kindness in seeking it out.

The message from Tanya also gave me the greatest happiness.

I expect you will be going on holiday. My wife and I went to Copenhagen for the Econometric Society meeting, just for a week. I do try to keep up with 'the feel' of what is going on, but the pace of things is far too much for any one man to know much about it. I also had a feeling, again, that in some papers an idea that an old-fashioned economist would have had 'in his bones' was being formalised at great and superfluous length.

Hurwicz gave a brilliant and witty lecture. I had never met him. He has a very great reputation, and a few minutes is enough to tell one it is deserved. A quietly powerful personality.

How is your book progressing? I am thrilled by the idea of seeing it. Your knowledge that is going into it is real and practical, and first hand.

My manuscript is behind time. I am doing nothing but struggle with it.

Please forgive this scrappy note. I am trying to catch the post which goes early on Sunday.

How can I possibly thank you in any proper way for the superb and marvellous book?

With all warmest good wishes and kindest regards,

Yours sincerely,

George Shackle

George Shackle

144

Aldeburgh
Suffolk
19th September 1963

My dear Frowen,

I am tremendously excited about the LSE prospect. I should be so extremely happy if you were appointed. At least I tried to make sure, in a long letter, that they know of your achievements and wonderful career, and I well know that Christopher Saunders with his very great influence will have said the same.

Please forgive my delay in answering your letter. I only had it in my hand when I paid a 'flying visit' home to install my younger son at our local Technical College. He wants to become a professional geologist, but there is a long road to travel first.

I had the pleasure of meeting Professor Travaglini when he was in England a good many years ago, and have corresponded with him since. I am delighted to hear of your invitation to lecture in Rome, and proposed exchange visits.

How exciting to have your book in course of writing! It is an all-absorbing goal, causing everything else to seem a little unreal?

I have asked Heffers at Cambridge to send two books to Tanya for to-morrow, but one of them may not come till later because they did not know whether they could get it at once. Phillippa Pearce lived in the same village as I did when I was a child, and the river in her story of 'Minnow on the Say' is plainly derived from the river which flows through Shelford into the Cam. Also, I had a canoe on that stream in the early 1920s! I have never met Phillippa Pearce, but the names of the characters in her story are all plainly suggested by those of real people in the village 40 or 50 years ago.

The other story is a brilliant fantasy which I think Tanya will appreciate.

With all my warmest good wishes, please forgive my bad writing,

Yours sincerely,

George Shackle

George Shackle

145

The University of Liverpool
Department of Economics
11 Abercromby Square
7th October 1963

My dear Frowen,

Well knowing as I do your invincible fibre, your letter fills me more than ever with admiration. The people who put upon you all the strain, tension and exhaustion of an interview, having made up their minds adversely beforehand, I cannot easily forgive, though you seem already to be making allowances for them. All three of us (Christopher Saunders, I am sure, as much as I) necessarily put all our effort and hope into this attempt: that is the only way to succeed: and so our disappointment is out of proportion to the facts. There are *better* (yes, much better) possibilities, and we will get them. Meanwhile, my feelings towards the Institution in question are somewhat contemptuous. (Really, I don't know what is the matter with them. At any rate, they have done themselves a much worse injury than to you).

Let us forget them and come to the practical questions. *Of course* you must not put aside your plan to go right on in the academic line. I am sure you are right in giving your book top priority. I wonder what stage it has reached? But need this prevent you from registering at once for a Ph.D.? The latter would, I think, take whatever time you wished, and if its subject were some aspect of banking, your work on your book would really be work for a Ph.D. as well. I wish I was better informed about the regulations in force at various Universities, the question that bothers me most is whether any, except London, offer *external* Ph.Ds. There is, of course, University College as an alternative to LSE. I wonder if you have considered this? But I think we should *also* explore further afield, which could be done by letter to the Registrars or Heads of Departments.

I do think that great developments will arise from the Robbins Report, and that all existing institutions of high calibre, such as Woolwich Polytechnic, stand a great chance of being turned into Universities. We should soon know. Looked at against the background of the great and ever-increasing possibilities, our disappointment over LSE is really not worth any regrets.

I know very little about Reading. I believe their economics department has been small, and they may need someone to teach a wide range of subjects, which is not a very attractive sort of situation.

I believe you would find Professor G.C. Allen, at University College, a sympathetic person to consult. And that might be a solution to the Ph.D. problem.

It was exceedingly kind of you to write and tell me so fully about your experiences and your plans, which I am intensely interested in. As you know, your hopes are mine

I am perfectly sure all will come right before long.

With all warmest good wishes,

Yours sincerely,

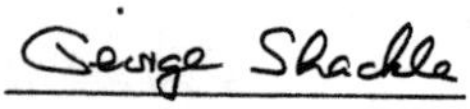

George Shackle

146

University of Liverpool
Department of Economics
11 Abercromby Square
23rd October 1963

My dear Frowen,

I have been re-reading some of your letters, and reflecting what a deep and lasting pleasure our long correspondence has given me. I fear I am getting more and more liable to let time go by before answering. This is partly, just now, because I have had to take up again the duty of giving the first year General Economics course, because of the loss of three principal members of our staff, two to Chairs (Edinburgh and Aberystwyth) and one to the World Bank. I also have now to divide my Second Year class into three groups for seminar purposes. I have never found it possible to use old lecture notes. So everything has to be got ready afresh, at least one must think things out for the purpose of delivery.

I should not feel happy to use an already-written lecture when I come to Woolwich. There are some lectures which have not been published but I want to write something of my very best for the occasion and I fear the dates towards the end of November do not give me time to have it ready four weeks in advance. My delay in starting (I am truly sorry) is the struggle to complete a book which I at last dispatched for the publisher's consideration last Monday. A fearful struggle: in course of writing it changed from one book (the scheme of which the CU Press had already accepted) to a quite different one.

For my Woolwich lecture I would like to write on 'Schemes of thought and the economist'.

This is not very precise but will give me scope to try to make some order out of a number of elusive strands that I want sometime to unravel. If I cannot finish in time for this term (which seems impossible) can it be done next term?

I wonder what the Robbins Report will say to-morrow, especially if it may have some bearing on your own plans.

What a thrill it will be as your book nears completion. Do send me all news.

With kindest regards and warmest good wishes,

Yours sincerely,

George Shackle

George Shackle

My suggestion for the title of my lecture is meant to suggest 'schemes of thought *in general*' not those of economics alone. I want to consider the bearing on economics of those stereotypes of thought that all sciences, and people in their everyday life use, such as 'cause and effect', 'structure', 'evolution' and so on.

147

The University of Liverpool
Department of Economics
11 Abercromby Square
10th November 1963

My dear Frowen,

I have, as so often, to apologise very much for letting the time slip by. It is exceedingly kind of you to be taking so much trouble about the arrangements for my lecture. I am extremely proud of this invitation, and as I am equally anxious to do as creditably as I possibly can, I think it would be best if the date could be arranged for February or March: may I leave it to you?

The title I have in mind is

General Thought-Schemes and the Economist

(I have added the word 'general' to convey the idea that it is the very basic and universal ideas whose part in the economist's thinking I wish to discuss).

I will try to send you the manuscript by the end of the Christmas vacation, if that will be time enough?

I have just had a very kind letter from Mr. Wheble, and am writing to tell him of the ideas that you and I have so far arrived at about the lecture.

I do hope your book is going fast ahead, and that you will soon get more leisure for it. I seldom find any efforts made in the evening yield useful results, but there is an irresistible temptation to try to wring a little more out of the day.

With all warmest good wishes,

Yours sincerely,

George Shackle

148

The University of Liverpool
Department of Economics
11 Abercromby square
Liverpool 7
13th December 1963

My dear Frowen,

In writing the manuscript which I now enclose[1], I had in mind that your students might like a paper which does not stick to well-trodden paths but throws out ideas of my own in an uninhibited way. In delivering it I should urge my audience to regard my remarks as an invitation to close scrutiny and criticism. I hope you will not feel that I have strayed too far from what could be properly regarded as the concerns of the economist. I believe the paper is of about 6,000 words and should take me about fifty minutes to read. I shall be very happy if you feel that this manuscript fulfils in some degree the purpose of the Woolwich Papers.

With kindest regards and warmest good wishes,

Yours sincerely,

George Shackle

I see that I have once more allowed myself to make a grossly excessive use of italic. I must correct this before the MS is printed. But I think you may like to see it now and judge of its suitability for the occasion.

1 This paper entitled 'General Thought-Schemes and the Economist' was published as *Woolwich Economic Paper*, no. 2, in 1964.

149

The University of Liverpool
Department of Economics
11 Abercromby Square
Liverpool 7
29th December 1963

My dear Frowen,

I was most deeply touched by your overwhelmingly kind letter. I only hope my lecture will not seem too remote and abstract; at any rate, in giving it by word of mouth, I can hope to convey to the audience that it merely expresses a struggle and groping exploration.

I am excited by your suggestion that the Woolwich Papers might be published by the Cambridge University Press. You know immeasurably more than I do about the economic aspects of printing and publishing. I hope to go to see some of the staff of the Press early in January, and I would very much like to raise this question. I wonder if you could brief me a little further on how I should put it to them?

I do hope my present for Tanya reached her in good time. It is a story called 'The Roaring 40' (Oxford University Press) but I only saw the review of it a little while before Christmas, had to write to Heffers to send it, and fear the Christmas post may have held things up.

I was tremendously delighted with Tanya's Christmas card, and most tickled by your pencilled remark.

Christmas gets more strenuous every year, and the weight of anxiety, as to whether anyone has been left off the list, more oppressive. Addresses are enough to return one to despair; of course people never put them on Christmas cards, which they send you at the very last moment.

I have made a note that the lecture is to be on 3rd March. I will soon send you a re-typed copy of my paper with greatly reduced use of italic, as I suggested I would like to do.

What wonderful news about your Senior Lectureship, and the further Principal Lectureship in prospect, it is plain that they are on tenterhooks to keep you. I am also delighted that you are fixing up your Ph.D. research at LSE. When this is all settled you will feel much more relaxed.

With kindest regards and warmest good wishes,

Yours sincerely,

George Shackle

George Shackle

150

The University of Liverpool
Department of Economics
11 Abercromby Square
Liverpool 7
18th January 1964

My dear Frowen,

I am exceedingly sorry to hear of your bereavement.[1]

I am most deeply touched by Tanya's beautiful and most charming letter. I would like her to know that its *design* and *symmetry* are not lost upon me. It is most striking and beautiful, a visual composition in the artist's sense. I am, of course, writing to her.

I am now enclosing the new typescript of my paper: unchanged except for the omission of a word or two on the first page, and of almost all the italic. I have, in fact, made a discovery: a method of correcting the excess of underlining that I am so prone to: I have the MS typed with *no* underlining, then put in an italic word or two here and there, disregarding the MS.

I do hope this delay has not upset your programme for the printing.

With all kindest regards,

Yours sincerely,

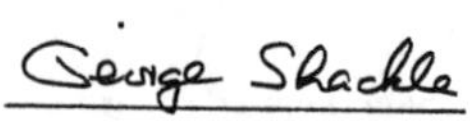

George Shackle

1 The bereavement is the death of Stephen Frowen's father in Germany, Adolf Frowein, on 10 January 1964, member of a well-known West German family of industrialists.

151

The University of Liverpool
Department of Economics
11 Abercromby Square
30th January 1964

My dear Frowen,

I was so very much distressed to hear of your further anxieties. I do hope all is well now.

Writing this paper has given me the opportunity to make some special effort in return for all the kindness that *you* have shown to *me*, over the years (How the time flies!)

My only anxiety is to come up to your expectations and please the members of the Polytechnic who may hear the paper, and to fulfil an occasion which means very much to me.

May I please have 100 copies if this is really not too many to ask for?

The samples are all very attractive but I would like the one you yourself prefer, the gold, Royal 26 LB 100.

It is most kind of you to offer to book my hotel, but I can very easily get it laid on.

With all warmest wishes and how can I thank you enough, for all the trouble you are taking.

Yours sincerely,

George Shackle

152

The University of Liverpool
Department of Economics
11 Abercromby Square
18th February 1964

My dear Frowen,

My Woolwich Paper has been most beautifully printed without a single mistake of any consequence. I have marked just two things: in one place a capital letter O has been printed instead of numeral zero; in another, dashes (thin long lines) have been printed where the intention was two hyphens.

I only received the proof yesterday and have read it attentively as quickly as I could, and now hasten to send it to you according to your instructions.

Perhaps you will be sending me directions as to the time of the lecture (or please forgive me if I have had them, I keep your letters at home).

I do hope all is going well.

With kindest regards and all best wishes,

Yours sincerely,

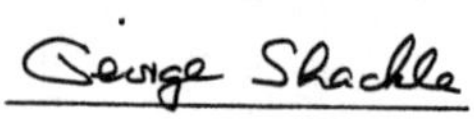

George Shackle

153
Reform Club
Pall Mall. S.W.1.
18th February 1964

Dear Professor Shackle,

I hope you will forgive me for the delay in writing to you. My mother-in-law is still critically ill and the last four weeks have been rather upsetting and hectic. Since the beginning of January everything seems to be going wrong. First my father's death, then my mother-in-law's accident and a number of minor upsets. Still, there is one occasion I am looking forward to with joyful anticipation, similar to the joy I experienced as a child when I was impatiently looking forward to Christmas Eve and yet did not want the great occasion to happen too soon out of fear that it might all be over far too quickly.

I am enclosing a proof of your paper but I hope that you received a proof directly from our printers last week.

I have checked these proofs with great care. There were only two printing errors, I think, which have been corrected. (On page 7 'F=O' should read 'F=O~' and on page 20 third line from bottom the word "itself" is misspelled. If there are any further errors you may discover, or if there are any other amendments you would like to be made, I should be grateful if you would kindly contact our printers Besley & Copp Ltd., Courteney Road, Exeter.

Cambridge University Press have taken up my suggestion and decided to advertise two of your books in our Paper in the form of a one-page advertisement on the inside back cover.

I am also enclosing a sample of our invitation card and poster. Tea will be served at 4.30 and sherry and a small dinner party in the Principal's Dining

Room will follow the lecture. Sir Ralph Hawtrey, Mr. C.T. Saunders and Professor M.J. Bonn will be among the invited guests.

I should like to take you myself to Woolwich by car on 3rd March and perhaps we could meet on Monday night or have lunch together on Tuesday. Alternatively (if this is not convenient) we could discuss any further details on our way to Woolwich.

We are having leaflets printed advertising the *Woolwich Economic Papers*. I wonder whether you would agree to the following brief description of your paper entitled *General Thought-Schemes and the Economist*:

> This paper deals with 'schemes of thought in general', not those of economics alone. The author considers the bearing on economics of those stereotypes of thought that all sciences, and people in their everyday life, use, such as 'cause and effect', 'structure', ' evolution' and so on.

There is no need to return the galley proof to me.

I am so very much looking forward to this event and it is impossible to express in words how much your visit means to me.

With all warmest wishes and kindest regards,

Yours sincerely,

Stephen Frowen

154
The Reform Club
19th February 1964

Dear Professor Shackle,

Many thanks for your letter of 18th February,

It was very kind of you to return the proof so quickly. The two mistakes have been corrected and if everything goes according to plan, you should receive 100 copies of the paper by Monday, 2nd March.

If there is anything you would like me to do in connection with your stay in London, please do not hesitate to let me know. I should only be too happy to be of help to you.

With all best wishes and kindest regards,

Yours sincerely,

Stephen Frowen

P.S. I have just heard from the hospital that my mother-in law's condition is improving. This is one load off my mind!

155

The University of Liverpool
Department of Economics
11 Abercromby Square
11th March 1964

My dear Frowen,

I can now look back on one absolutely perfect and unflawed occasion, when everything conspired to make me happy, and I owe it all to you. Superbly organised with every detail thought of, the whole day not only went from start to finish without the smallest hitch, but it had a warmth and ease that enabled me to do my very best. The audience was supremely kind to me, this I could feel within a few moments of starting to speak: what a tremendous tribute to you! For it is, of course, for your sake that they were ready to accept my effort, and myself. I did not feel a stranger, and I can only hope to have seemed what they expected. I have never before spoken with such a feeling of relaxation and of unity with my audience. Their questions were ideally chosen to enable me to put my feeling about the subject in a clear light, and no speaker can ever have had more help or sympathy from those he addressed.

I was indeed most deeply touched by *everyone's* kindness, very specially indeed by the unmistakeable care and pains that my questioners took to make their questions (so extremely to the point!) sympathetic in tone. In addressing so highly sophisticated an audience, as many of you were, I ought to have felt nervous (there is, of course, an inevitable aftermath of reaction and feeling of being spent, the second day rather than the first after the occasion) but I felt relaxed and happy.

Mr. Heywood asked me to elucidate a question about the arrangements at Liverpool, and I therefore wrote to him the other day. I took the opportunity to thank him for his own kindness to me, and indeed the obviously happy atmosphere at Woolwich is the greatest tribute he could wish for. The Woolwich Polytechnic is a *wonderful* place, I could not be more eager about anything than to hope it will get its so immensely deserved recognition.

How quickly you have established your own remarkable ascendancy. Everything speaks of your success. And of course, I know how to interpret this effect into terms of its source: – relentless concentration and unsparing effort. May I say, you looked so happy, and if anyone has deserved to do so, you have.

I was delighted with the newspaper cuttings, and proudly showed them to my family. I was extremely interested in the report of Sir Edward Boyle's remarks, and this seems much more encouraging than I had supposed.

I shall write to Mr Wheble to thank him also for his very kind welcome and entertainment of me, and it was such a pleasure and great privilege to meet Professor Bonn.

I think I shall write in the first instance to Professor Carter about Professor Rittershausen's book.

I do hope all is well with your family and anxiety relieved.

What a wonderful day: it was all *your* doing, but I feel like one of those Mayors or members of the Royal Family, who open a new bridge with a golden pair of scissors, and walk about proudly as though they had built it with their own hands!

All my warmest and best gratitude, and kindest regards,

Yours sincerely,

George Shackle

George Shackle

156

The Woolwich Polytechnic
London S.E.18
16th April 1964

Dear Professor Shackle,

I hope you will forgive me if I ask you once more for advice. You may have seen the two vacancies advertised by University College London two weeks ago. One of the two Assistant Lectureships *or* Lectureships will be in Monetary Economics. I feel greatly tempted to apply provided I can be reasonably certain that my application will be seriously considered by Professor Allen and his colleagues.

You know how happy I am at Woolwich. The only reason why I should like to apply for one of the UCL jobs is that I would not have to teach 20 hours per week and this would leave me with more time for research. I have just registered for a higher degree at LSE and my supervisor will be Dr. Pressnell (formerly Lecturer in Monetary Economics at UCL). The subject of my thesis is "Central Bank Discount Policy in the UK, USA and Western Germany since 1951".

I would be prepared to accept *some* drop in salary but I would not be too happy if even a Lectureship at UCL would initially be a temporary appointment; but the latter may only be a formality, of course.

I should hesitate to apply at UCL unless I stand a reasonable chance of success. Woolwich Polytechnic and Mr. Wheble have been very kind to me, and I would not like to upset them unnecessarily. Is there any chance of finding out from Professor Allen whether he would be interested in my application? You may remember that in 1954 I applied for an Assistant Lectureship at UCL. I was shortlisted on that occasion and was told later that I *nearly* got the job. Applications for the present job have to be submitted by 27th April.

I hear from the Economists' Bookshop that your paper on *General Thought-Schemes and the Economist* is selling well. If you could let me know the name and address of the University Bookshop in Liverpool, I should like to inquire whether they would be interested stocking our *Woolwich Economic Papers*.

I hope you are keeping well. I cannot tell you how deeply impressed we all are with your stimulating paper. I am so glad that it now exists in print.

With all good wishes and kindest regards,

Yours sincerely,

Stephen Frowen

157

The University of Liverpool
Department of Economics
11 Abercromby Square
18th April 1964

My dear Frowen,

I am most delighted and excited to hear of this possibility at UCL. I opened your letter this morning, an hour ago, and have spent the intervening time writing a long letter to

Professor Allen. I hope he will encourage you to apply. Whether you can feel it worth while to do so will depend, I think, on the wording of his answer to me. I shall try to get some real insight into the situation, but I do most completely agree with your feeling that it would be a great pity to upset Mr Wheble unless this opportunity at UCL is likely to come off. I am delighted to hear of your having registered for Ph.D. This will make a great difference to everything, I believe, although it is a wretched pity that all your achievements and your wonderful career should need to be backed up by a formal qualification.

I will write as soon as ever I hear.

With all warmest good wishes and kindest regards,

Yours sincerely,

George Shackle

George Shackle

158
40 Gurney Drive
London N.2
20th April 1964

Dear Professor Shackle,

I was deeply moved to see from your letter that immediately after receiving my note you wrote to Professor Allen. Although I ought to know by now that there are no limits to your kindness, I never cease to be absolutely overwhelmed by the imaginative and wholehearted way in which you support my plans, by your faith in me and your readiness to help whenever I am in need of whatever it may be. My indebtedness to you grows deeper and deeper and there are no longer any words, which could even in the remotest way express the gratitude, and admiration I feel towards you.

With all my very best wishes and kindest regards,

Yours sincerely,

Stephen Frowen

Stephen Frowen

P.S. I can honestly say that I shall not be too disappointed if Professor Allen should discourage me from applying. As I mentioned to you before and as you realise yourself, my present position, despite all its disadvantages, has considerable attractions in its own right, some of which I appreciate and others I treasure.

159

The University of Liverpool
Department of Economics
11 Abercromby Square
22nd April 1964

My dear Frowen,

I write in haste having just this morning had a reply from Professor G.C. Allen. His letter is extremely kind but leaves me in some doubt as to what our next move should be. He says: 'Our closing date is not until next Monday': but the rest of his letter leaves me in doubt whether he wants you to apply or whether he will himself get in touch with you. However, it does not seem to me that you can do any harm by applying.

Please forgive this note in the greatest haste, typed to save time

With kindest regards and all best wishes,

Yours sincerely,

George Shackle

George Shackle

160

40 Gurney Drive
London N.2
26th April 1964

Dear Professor Shackle,

It was exceedingly kind of you to find the time to let me know Professor Allen's reaction to your letter. I really feel guilty that I troubled you with this matter knowing fully well how busy you must be just now at the beginning of term.

I have decided not to apply. Your letter seems to indicate that Professor Allen has not really given any indication that he would like me to apply. It is of course possible that he will himself get in touch with me if he is short of suitable applications which, I think, is most unlikely. There must be many Lecturers in Monetary Economics all over the country who are anxious to move to London and the competition will probably be fierce enough for UCL to be able to get a much "cheaper" lecturer than myself, although as I indicated to you I would have been prepared to accept *some* drop in salary.

I think your very great kindness in writing to Professor Allen has prevented me from applying for a job I would have stood a very small chance of getting. I would probably only have upset Mr. Wheble, the Head of my present Department, and spoiled my chances at Woolwich.

Yesterday I received a letter from Mr Matthews, the Associate Editor of *The Economic Journal*. He would like to have a review from me of Professor Rittershausen's book for the December issue. This will be my first opportunity of contributing to *The Economic Journal*. It was so kind of you to write to Professor Carter and to mention my name to him as a possible reviewer of this book. I shall try to do my very best to justify your recommendation without which I would not have been asked to review this book.

Professor Rittershausen has just invited me to give two lectures at Cologne University (12th and 13th May) which I understand will be attended by 400 students. I shall also be a guest speaker at a special seminar arranged by the University of Bonn (where I graduated myself) on 11th May. One of my former teachers who is still Head of the Economics Department at Bonn University had invited me to present this paper.

Fortunately some of my lecture courses finished last week (we only had two weeks off over Easter) and I can gradually begin to devote more time to my book and my Ph.D. thesis.

I wonder when your next book will be coming out. I have not seen anything mentioned yet by Cambridge University.

With all warmest wishes and kindest regards, I remain, in deepest gratitude,

Yours sincerely,

Stephen Frowen

161

40 Gurney Drive
London N.2
6th May 1964

Dear Professor Shackle,

You may like to know that I wrote a few words to Professor Allen pointing out that I was not quite sure whether he expected me to apply for one of the vacancies or whether he intended to get in touch with me in case he wanted me to apply. I received the following reply to my letter:

> Dear Mr. Frowen,
>
> Thank you for your letter of 30th April. I think that we had better regard your letter as confirming the view that I had gained from Professor Shackle that you are interested in the Lectureship in Monetary Economics. We are considering the question of the appointment and I shall write to you again if we think it possible to carry the matter any further.

I was very pleased to see from this letter that I am still being considered, although I fully realise that the chance of being offered this post is probably very remote. One of our Assistant Lecturers, a girl aged 23, was interviewed for the Assistant Lectureship in Economics by Professor Allen on Tuesday. I understand from her that Professor Allen intends to make four appointments (two in Monetary Economics) and that more interviews have been arranged for tomorrow (Thursday).

I shall fly to Germany on Sunday and intend to return to London on Thursday, 14th May.

With warmest wishes and kindest regards,

Yours sincerely,

Stephen Frowen

162
40 Gurney Drive
London N.2
14th July 1964

Dear Professor Shackle,

You may like to see the enclosed letters received in response to your paper on *General Thought-Schemes and the Economist*.

I am now concentrating on my book and hope to get as much of the work done as possible during the summer break. At the end of July I am going with my family to the Bürgenstock, a resort in Switzerland above the Vierwaldstätter Lake, for a few weeks' holiday.

I hope you are keeping well. With all best wishes and kindest regards,

Yours sincerely,

Stephen Frowen

163
The University of Liverpool
Department of Economics
11 Abercromby Square
29th July 1964

My dear Frowen,

Your exquisite gift for my birthday is characteristic of everything you do – a precision and imagination in generosity which are incomparable. I shall never forget your rescuing a copy of my book from a poor shop, and taking it to where it might be acquired for use. This exceedingly beautiful book about Albrecht Dürer will give me immense pleasure and I shall be a little less ignorant after reading it.

The Post Office trouble is even yet not quite sorted out, and packets are still arriving 10–12 days late. The news of your progress with your book on Comparative Banking is tremendously cheering – I am so glad that in spite of your fearful teaching load you can still work on it. Perhaps the vacation will see it finished.

I have allowed myself to be saddled with a lecture course on the history of doctrines – but only those of 1926–39, with some attempt to unravel their origins. I have the gravest misgivings whether I should have attempted this.

It was extremely kind of you to send me the paper by Mr O. Prochazka. I mean to write to him when I can send some fresh off-print or other, there should be one available sometime in the autumn.

I do hope your holiday will be all that you deserve – peaceful and restful. It is a district of mountains I think? I am a lowlander – I only admire the mountains from below.

With every good wish, and all that words can say of my gratitude for your beautiful present,

Yours sincerely,

George Shackle

George Shackle

164

40 Gurney Drive
Hampstead Garden Suburb
London, N.2
10th February 1965

Dear Professor Shackle,

The other night Tanya was reading one of the two books you sent her for Christmas and in the course of our conversation about the book I discovered to my horror that she never thanked you for these gifts. She felt rather embarrassed herself when she discovered this. Two days before Christmas we went to Switzerland for a short skiing holiday and it must have been the rush before and after our journey (we returned on 3 January and on 4 January spring term started at Woolwich) which accounts for this unforgivable neglect. I hope you will accept our sincere apologies. Tanya wants to write to you over the weekend because she intends to write a 'proper letter'. She is quite an imaginative child and adores reading. I don't think you could have made her happier with any other present. It was extremely kind of you to send her these gifts which have been chosen with so much care and intuition.

Our Economics Department at Woolwich continues to expand rapidly and next month the Minister of Education will open our new extensions on the occasion of the 75th anniversary celebrations (the Polytechnic was founded in 1890). The next *Woolwich Economic Paper* will be by Sir Ralph Hawtrey on *Incomes Policy*. Mr. L.A. Dicks-Mireaux, a former colleague of mine at the National Institute of Economic and Social Research who is now Acting Head of the National Economic Development Office, has kindly agreed to give the Third Woolwich Economic Lecture. He intends to cover wage and price behaviour in the United Kingdom. However, despite all these activities and expansion I am not too happy about the future of our Degree Course, as we are unlikely to be granted University status. The Government left us in no doubt that there is no intention of creating any more new universities. This means that we shall find it increasingly difficult to get enough students for our Degree Course in the years to come. It is for this reason that I decided to apply for a Lectureship with special reference to Money and Banking advertised by the University of Kent at Canterbury. This is not too far from London so that it would be possible for my son Michael to complete his education at University College School and for my wife to continue with her work at UCL. However, I don't really expect to be shortlisted as there will probably be enough applicants who are prepared to start as Assistant Lecturer (the job was advertised an Assistant Lectureship or Lectureship). I have taken the liberty of giving your name as one of three referees. The closing date was 5 February and it was already after this date when I submitted my application. Please don't hesitate to let me know if you would rather not act as referee. Unfortunately I don't know the Professor of Economics at Kent. Somebody told me that Hagenbuch got the Chair. My other referees are Mr C.T. Saunders (who is now with the Economic Commission for Europe in Geneva) and Mr Wheble (I have asked Kent not to approach the latter before letting me know first as I did not want to upset him unnecessarily by mentioning my application to him without even knowing whether I shall be shortlisted).

You may have seen the enclosed review of *General Thought-Schemes and the Economist* which appeared in the *Asian Economic Review*. This essay of yours is still selling very well and continues to receive much attention.

In haste (I am trying to catch the last collection) and with grateful thanks and all warmest good wishes,

Yours sincerely,

Stephen Frowen

Stephen Frowen

165

The University of Liverpool
Department of Economics
11 Abercromby Square
Liverpool 7
17th February 1965

My dear Frowen,

How kind of you to send me the review of my *Woolwich Economic Paper*. Any reactions to this essay are invaluable to me, since this is how I hope to learn and improve. I have a strong feeling that one should not hesitate to express speculative opinions, for though they are likely to meet with objections and criticism, they may start a line of thought which would lead somebody else to get at a useful truth. It is marvellous that you have secured Sir Ralph Hawtrey to give the next paper. What a wonderful vitality he has.

I am most delighted to hear that Tanya liked the Arthur Ransome books. My own children were always reading and re-reading them (my elder son who is now 23 can easily be found re-reading one of them!) and so I thought she might like to try them. I do not think they 'date' at all, though I never found I could read them aloud very comfortably.

I am very interested indeed to hear that you are applying at Canterbury. I know Hagenbuch, a very nice man. I had not heard that he had been appointed to that chair. Everything I can possibly do, need I say, I will do to the utmost. If we could only go and actually buttonhole these people and tell them face to face! I do hope something comes of it.

There is undoubtedly a great shortage of qualified staff. I have had to take up again the first year lectures, which I gave for ten years and then thought I would give up. I enjoy them but it takes a great deal of time and energy and there is so much I want to do.

I also write in haste, to get this letter posted in good time, because I so often write a letter and then fail to get it posted for days.

With all warmest good wishes and kindest regards,

Yours sincerely,

George Shackle

George Shackle

166

The University of Liverpool
Department of Economics
11 Abercromby Square
Liverpool 7
30th April 1965

My dear Frowen,

It was exceedingly kind of you to think of me when sending out your invitations to the Third Woolwich Economic Lecture and the first Annual Dinner. I should have loved to come, if only my commitments did not keep piling up even while I was wondering whether it would be possible. I am very sorry indeed to have to give the idea up. I have been so much hoping for news of you. Your enterprise in getting five *Woolwich Economic Papers* out already is marvellous and characteristic.

The other day at the Royal Economic Society Council meeting, Professor Austin Robinson spoke with the deepest affection of Professor [Moritz] Bonn.[1] I am so happy to have had the privilege of knowing him, thanks to you.

With kindest regards and warmest good wishes,

Yours sincerely,

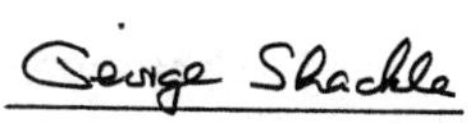

George Shackle

1 Professor M.J. Bonn was the German representative at the Brussels Conference (1920) and Technical Adviser to German Goverment, writer of a foreword to and co-translator (with C. Brinckmann) of the German edition of Keynes's *The Economic Consequences of the Peace* (German title: *Die wirtschaftlichen Folgen des Friedensvertrages*, 1920, reprinted 1920–1 four times).

167

The Woolwich Polytechnic
Wellington Street
London, S.E.18
3rd July 1965

Dear Professor Shackle,

I am extremely sorry for the delay in thanking you for your letters and for your kindness in allowing me to give your name as a referee when I applied for a lectureship at the University of Kent. Naturally, I was a bit disappointed that I was not even shortlisted, especially as the University of Kent had taken the trouble to write to all my referees. But their decision did not really come as a surprise. I suppose most universities prefer to appoint assistant lecturers or lecturers who are prepared to start at the bottom of the salary scale. In the case of more senior appointments, my academic achievements as far as publications are concerned are perhaps insufficient at this stage. Yet in view of my very heavy teaching load it is quite impossible to find the time for serious academic work. But even if I did publish more, it would probably be just as difficult to get a university lectureship with a beginning salary near or above the efficiency bar (and even this would mean some financial sacrifice in my case) for anybody teaching at a Polytechnic.

There is no hope for Woolwich Polytechnic to be granted university status. This was made quite clear by Mr. Crosland, the Minister of Education, when he attended our 75th Anniversary Dinner. In view of these adverse developments it is quite possible (probably likely) that our external B.Sc. (Econ.) Course will have to be discontinued in the course of the next few years. We already have difficulties in getting as many students for the course as we would like to accept – and this at a time when the universities are turning away thousands of would-be students!

I hope you are keeping well. It would be so nice to see you again. Will you be in London for the Annual Meeting of the Royal Economic Society on 8th July? I suppose you will be too busy for even a brief meeting during your short stay in London! If you could spare the time I should be overjoyed if you could join me for lunch, tea or dinner at the Reform Club or any other convenient place.

The Third Woolwich Economic Lecture was quite successful and well attended. I was so sorry that you could not be with us on this occasion.

On 19th July I shall be going to Germany to lecture in Düsseldorf and at the Free University of Berlin. From there I intend to go to Switzerland and Italy for a short holiday. I shall probably not be back in England until the end of August as I hope to do some research for my thesis in Germany before returning to London.

Tanya is making satisfactory progress. She is very keen on acting and painting. One of her paintings for which she got the second prize at a painting exhibition was bought by a collector of childrens' paintings! I have started painting a bit myself in my spare time (encouraged by Christopher Saunders and his wife Cora who are keen amateur painters), and it was when watching me that Tanya became interested in painting herself. Michael is just taking his O-Level exams.

I suppose your latest book must soon be due for publication. Or has it already been published? I have not seen anything in the bookshops yet.

With all warmest good wishes and kindest regards,

Yours ever,

Stephen Frowen

168

Goethehaus Frankfurt am Main
Dichterzimmer
Undated

Dear Professor Shackle,

Many thanks for your letter and for returning the proofs. I was so busy the days before my departure that I did not manage to write the letter I had intended to write. My wife and I are having a lovely time in Germany and professionally the journey has been very successful indeed. The Deutsche Bundesbank and Professor Günter Schmölders of Cologne University have been greatly interested in your article. At present we are spending a few quiet days in Königstein, a peaceful village in the Taunus near Frankfurt.

With all good wishes and kindest regards,

Yours sincerely,

Stephen Frowen

169

The University of Liverpool
Department of Economics
11 Abercromby Square
Liverpool 7
6th July 1965

My dear Frowen,

I have just this moment received and read your letter. I do wish we could meet at the Royal Economic Society meeting, but my wife has persuaded me to go for a week's holiday in Scotland, and I felt that this would give me a fresh start on my commitments for the summer. But when you are back at the end of August we can surely meet, for I hope to be in Cambridge for the British Association meeting. I have also just opened the other letter with the seventh *Woolwich Economic Paper*. What a tremendous impetus you give to everything you take up! This is a marvellous enterprise, and the growing list will in a year or two amount to the contents of a book. I met Professor Sir Ralph Hawtrey at the corner of Houghton Street a month or two back, and he told me about his *Woolwich Economic Paper*. He is amazingly full of vitality and seems to have as keen a mind as ever. If he was not so unassuming and gentle, his reputation would far outshine some of those who make much stir in the world. I am *delighted* to see that you yourself are writing the ninth paper. Also I am delighted to hear that your German lecture will provide material for your thesis.

I was extremely interested to hear that you are an artist. I should love to see your work, I do wish I had known of this earlier. Six years ago my wife and I had a week in County Kerry (Ireland) and I had to go to Ireland as an external examiner. We took oil paints etc. and I tried my hand. My wife complained bitterly that she could not paint anything herself because she had to spend all her time cleaning me up. But I *did* put paint on one piece of canvas! Having absolutely no knowledge, skill or plan, I simply slapped the paint on (mainly with a knife) and let it take its chance. It will be thrilling if Tanya is going to be famous, as she is evidently already becoming! My own daughter is also taking O-levels, but she has no high academic ambitions I think.

My eldest son has taken up colour photography and produces some astonishing results. It seems to have advanced greatly in the last few years.

I am now looking forward to new books by James Meade, Hicks, Ozga and Lamberton: what a lot of reading to do!

I must post this now, in haste, or you will not get it by Wednesday. I am very sorry indeed that I abandoned my plan to come to the meeting.

With kindest regards and all best wishes,

Yours sincerely

George Shackle

George Shackle

170
40 Gurney Drive
Hampstead Garden Suburb
London, N.2
19th January 1966

Dear Professor Shackle,

I cannot tell you how happy I was to receive your letter. I had intended to write to you for such a long time and feel terribly guilty because of my long silence. It was such a relief to see from your letter that you are still interested to have news of me. My personal life went through a lengthy period of considerable stress, mainly due to the fact that my wife went though a period of great emotional instability. There were moments when I was near a breakdown myself. All this greatly interfered with my work at a rather crucial period of my life. To recover from the effect of these difficulties, we took the children on a skiing holiday over Christmas and the New Year. The complete change of surroundings did us all a lot of good, although it was not as much of a success as we had hoped, and in the end my wife had a skiing accident and I got tonsillitis. However, things look much brighter now and I pray that soon all the clouds overshadowing our life will have disappeared.

Christopher Saunders and his wife joined us over Christmas. He is now with the United Nations in Geneva. He asked me to remember him to you.

I was delighted to see from *The Economist* that your latest book has just been published. I am anxiously looking forward to seeing and reading it and shall buy a copy immediately after my return from Berlin where I am giving a talk on the problem of sterling at the Free University. I shall be away from 22nd January until 29th January.

I applied for a lectureship in monetary economics at Southampton University and have taken the liberty of giving your name as a referee, to which I hope you have no objection. I should have asked you beforehand, but it was a last-minute decision and the closing date was on 15th January. The reason why I might stand a slight chance is that I have met Professor D.C. Rowan. He succeeded me as Editor of *The Bankers' Magazine* when my immediate successor Roger Opie gave up the editorial chair. Professor Rowan is in fact still the Editor of the *Magazine*. I would be overjoyed if something materialised, and I should quite like the prospect of living in Southampton.

Michael and Tanya are both delightful and give us tremendous joy. Michael is quite successful at school (he is studying physics, chemistry and pure and applied mathematics) and Tanya is working hard for her 11+ examinations. She was exceedingly happy to receive your Christmas gift, which she is enjoying tremendously – especially during the last few days when she was in bed with influenza.

Please forgive me for mentioning my personal problems. But I wanted you to know and understand why I found it so difficult to write to you for so many months.

With all warmest good wishes and kindest regards,

Yours sincerely,

Stephen Frowen

P.S. The enclosed letter from Professor Sayers may be of interest to you.

171

The University of Liverpool
Department of Economics
Social Sciences Building
Liverpool 7
22nd January 1966

My dear Frowen,

I am so happy to hear that there is a possibility of your being appointed at Southampton. I wrote some weeks ago to Professor Rowan and felt, from his letter of enquiry, that he would be sensitive to the very great claims that I am able to make (and always seek to express with the utmost force) in your regard. I do hope that in this case there will not be the usual unimaginative and earth-bound insistence on purely formal and stereotyped qualifications. You have such a tremendous lot to offer to a Department of Economics. I fear you are too modest in stating your own case.

I am asking the CUP to send you a copy of my book A Scheme of Economic Theory; it will be most kind of you indeed to tell me how it strikes you. So far I have had no reviews except a brief note in *The Economist* and one in a French journal. However, Harrod wrote me an extremely kind letter, and Douglas Hague at Manchester said he was surprised that someone could find something fresh to say about Marshall. I have become much inured to reviews, but they necessarily cause one alarm and despondency.

I am so very much interested to hear of your lectures in Berlin. The problem of sterling is certainly going to be the most crucial and red-hot topic in the next year or two. How we are ever to repay our international borrowings if our costs go on going up is difficult to see. I think the big crunch for sterling is still to come. I see the idea of a floating exchange rate is being advanced again. I think we shall have to come to it, unless we get a real world-monetary system.

How splendid to have got your pupil the Stern Scholarship. I am *most delighted* at what Professor Sayers says, you have deserved it a thousand times over.

With all kindest regards and very best wishes,

Yours sincerely,

George Shackle

172
10 Church Row
Hampstead
London, N.W.3
4th August 1966

Dear Professor Shackle

I scarcely dare to contact you any more after my long silence, and specially as I did not thank you for your last letter I cannot tell you how happy I was to receive a copy of your latest book *A Scheme of Economic Theory*. I wanted to read it before replying to you but the problems I had to cope with in my personal life were such that I was constantly at the point of a breakdown and just don't know how I managed to get through the Spring and Summer Term. I was terribly worried about my students – I tried to do my best, but my teaching was rather erratic. As it turned out, my students did best in their Finals this year (as last year) and the Head of my Department who seemed rather worried about me, seems to be quite pleased with the results.

My wife and I actually separated in May. At first, Tanya and Michael stayed with my wife, but Michael – after a suicide attempt at the beginning of May – decided to live with me. I managed to get a very nice furnished flat in Hampstead, just big enough for the two of us, but I am in the process of buying Christopher Saunders's flat in Hampstead (he now works for ECE in Geneva).

Some weeks ago I was offered an appointment by the University of Surrey (formerly the Battersea College of Technology) in the Department of Linguistics and Regional Studies and the Sub-Department of International Economics. In the former I would have to provide courses on German economic development and in the latter cover international monetary economics. However, the official appointment cannot be made until the beginning of next year. The appointment is for October 1967. I have been asked to give two lecture courses and take one seminar per week during the session 1966–67.

Meanwhile I have been approached by Professor J.R. Sargent of the University of Warwick, Coventry, whose letter I am enclosing. I would definitely prefer a Warwick appointment and very much hope that I shall be successful. Apart from the fact that for professional reasons I prefer Professor Sargent's Department, I am also looking forward to leaving London with all my unhappy experiences. Michael left school at Easter but has now decided to attend an A-Level course in Economics, British Constitution and Economic History, as he would like to read for a degree in economics. He will start in September at the North-Western Polytechnic and could, if necessary, continue his A-Level preparations at a Technical College in Coventry.

I have taken the liberty of giving your name as one of the referees required and would be most grateful if you were prepared to act as my referee.

I should be so happy to see you again. Is there any chance of you coming to London in the foreseeable future?

With all very best wishes and kindest regards,

Yours sincerely,

Stephen Frowen

173

The University of Liverpool
Department of Economics
Liverpool 7
10th August 1966

My dear Frowen,

How *much* I hope that the letter from Professor Sargent means that at last your true value is going to be in some measure recognized. I have told many people in its most decisive terms that in appointing you they would be rewarding themselves a hundred fold. I cannot help being angry with some of those to whom I have tried to convey what is to me so vividly and speakingly plain about your gifts and achievements, and the quality of spirit which has carried you through all.

Please forgive this brief line: I think it best to write quickly, and when we meet we will exchange all news more easily.

With all best and warmest wishes,

Yours sincerely,

George Shackle

174
Reform Club
Pall Mall, S.W.1
11th January 1967

Dear Professor Shackle

Please forgive me for the delay in writing to you. The past year has been rather upsetting and particularly strenuous, but things are moving again in the right direction and I hope that I shall now be able to settle down to some serious writing.

At the moment, life is still rather hectic as, in addition to my full-time job at Woolwich, I am also an Associate Lecturer at the new University of Surrey (the former Battersea College of Advanced Technology) and I hope to take up a full-time appointment there next October. It will be a Lectureship in Economics, with special reference to German Economic Development. The post will also involve some teaching of macro-economic theory and monetary economics in the Sub-Department of International Economics, attached to the Department of Linguistics and Regional Studies. However, my appointment as such will be to the Department of Linguistics and Regional Studies as a specialist on German economic development. The post will probably be advertised before the end of January in accordance with university regulations. In about two years' time the University will move from Battersea to their new, rather attractive campus in Guildford which is in the process of being built. The Head of the Department, Mr. Lord, appears to be keen to have me in his Department, but the final decision will of course be taken by the appointments committee consisting of the Vice-Chancellor and Members of the Senate.

I am glad to say that my son Michael has now got completely over his emotional difficulties. He decided last summer to start a new A-Level course in Economics, British Constitution and Economic History, but did not want to return to his old school. I was lucky to get him a place at the North-Western Polytechnic where he is very happy. The teaching appears to be very good. He intends to read economics. So far he has been offered two conditional places at the University of Essex (minimum two B's or one B and two C's) and at Leeds University (minimum two B's). He has quite a flair for mathematics and may well develop an interest in econometrics, although mathematics is not one of his A-Level subjects.

Michael and I are sharing a new flat at 83 Cholmley Gardens, Fortune Green Road, N.W.6, and Tanya is sharing our previous house with my wife. I see her [Tanya] quite often and she frequently enquires about you. She is now attending South Hampstead High School for Girls and she seems to be really happy there. At present mathematics appears to be her best (and her favourite) subject.

On 22nd January I shall be going to Berlin with Michael where I have promised to give a series of three lectures.

I hope that you are keeping well. I saw your latest book[1] at the Economists' Bookshop the other day and greatly enjoyed reading your article in the December issue of *The Economic Journal*.[2]

With all warmest good wishes and kindest regards,

Yours sincerely,

Stephen Frowen

Stephen Frowen

1 *The Years of High Theory: Invention and Tradition in Economic Thought, 1926–1939.*
2 'Policy, Poetry and Success', *The Economic Journal*, vol. 76, no. 304, December 1966, pp. 755–67.

175
83, Cholmley Gardens
Fortune Green Road
London N.W.6
13 February 1967

Dear Professor Shackle,

The University of Surrey has now advertised the post I have been asked to apply for. It is a Lectureship in Economics with special reference to Monetary Economics and German Economic Affairs. The closing date was last Friday and I just managed to apply in time after my return from my German lecture tour. As the candidate to be appointed should preferably be a native German speaker, my application is – not surprisingly – the only one received by the University. The Heads of both the Department of Linguistics and Regional Studies and the Sub-Department of International Economics seem to be anxious for me to join their Departments. I therefore do not expect any of the difficulties I had to cope with in the case of previous applications at other universities. As you know, I am already an Associate Lecturer in both Departments.

I hope that you will forgive me for having given your name as one of my referees without having asked for your permission. I should be most grateful if you would be so kind as to act as my referee. You have been so exceedingly kind to me in the past and I scarcely dare to ask you for yet another favour. The other three referees are Mr. C.L. Wheble, the Head of my Department at Woolwich Polytechnic, Professor Alan Day (London School of Economics) and Mr. C.T. Saunders.

I cannot tell you how much I am looking forward to my move to the University of Surrey, although personally I have always been happy at Woolwich. What I am looking forward to most is to have more time for research and the preparation of my lectures.

I have not heard from you for some time but I hope that you are well. Michael has been offered a place at Essex and Leeds University and is very much looking forward to his University course. He appears to have a flair for both economics and mathematics.

With all warmest good wishes and kindest regards,

Yours sincerely,

Stephen Frowen

176

The University Club
Pittsburgh Pa. 15213
USA
22nd February 1967

My dear Frowen,

I was *tremendously* pleased to read about your prospects at the University of Surrey. The post sounds ideal for you, it would be the very greatest thrill to hear that you were installed there. I do hope to have this news quite soon. I cannot think how it has happened, but I have come to suppose that I must have failed to answer your letter of 11th January. I had been convinced until yesterday that I had done so, but your letter of 13th February shows that I had not. I do not think this has ever happened before. It must be the state of my mind I was in on account of having just arrived here (for one term, $3\frac{1}{2}$months). I had also had a most frantic term last autumn, making 2 book indexes (one in French), reading the proofs of a book, preparing 2 courses for the University of Pittsburgh, and preparing for publication a book called *On the Nature of Business Success* which is meant to contain 10 papers given in Section F of the British Association last summer at Nottingham. I am exceedingly sorry indeed that I failed to answer your letter, but I was certain I had done so. What splendid news of Michael! I will get this off quickly as there has been such a delay in my writing already.

With all warmest wishes and kindest regards,

Yours sincerely,

George Shackle

George Shackle

177

University of Surrey
Annex, 14 Falcon Road
London S.W.11
9th June 1967

Dear Professor Shackle,

Thank you so very much for your letter. I was exceedingly happy to hear from you. I wanted to write to you for a long time and in the end was not sure whether you would still be in the United States or back in Liverpool. I was anxious for you to know that I did get the job at the University of Surrey. It is a Lectureship, but the appointment was made above the efficiency bar. The title of my appointment is 'Lecturer in Monetary Economics and German Economic Affairs'. I shall be teaching in two departments: the Department of Linguistics and Regional Studies (where I shall lecture on German Economic Affairs) and the Sub-Department of International Economics (where I shall lecture on monetary and international monetary theory at advanced level and on macroeconomic theory at Part II level. I shall also have to supervise postgraduate students in these subjects. There is no undergraduate course in economics but the University intention is to start one in September 1968. It is unlikely that the first Professor of Economics will be appointed until the beginning of next year at the earliest. The Lecturer-in-Charge of the Sub-Department of International Economics is most unlikely to get the chair but hopes to remain in charge of the postgraduate courses in international economics. I don't think that her chances are very good and my personal feeling is that for a variety of reasons it would not be in the interest of both the University and the Lecturer concerned. As in many universities the fights going on below the surface are unbelievable and quite unpleasant. I think I shall always prefer an appointment, which allows me to concentrate on teaching and research. I am completely devoid of any wish for power. To see people devoting all their energy to achieve a position of power is a rather sad spectacle.

Of course I shall be glad to skim through the book by Hans Schneeweis and write a note for *The Economic Journal*'s New Book List. I am quite sure that your German is more than adequate to judge whether the book does justify a review; a note will probably be sufficient. However, I shall let you know if the book should in my view deserve a short review. I shall only be too happy to assist *The Economic Journal* – now and in the future – in any way I possibly can. I am in fact most grateful to you for mentioning my name to Professor Austin Robinson.

I was thrilled to hear that there is a chance of getting another paper from you for the *Woolwich Economic Papers*. Could you possibly let me have your paper "On the Nature of Profit" fairly soon? I should be so happy to publish it before leaving Woolwich on 31st August. I am going to Germany on 24th June to give four lectures at the Universities of Berlin and Bonn and shall be back in England on 5th July for our examiners' meetings. It would be nice if I could send your manuscript to our printers before leaving for Germany. It will not take more than 3 or 4 weeks to get it published from the moment I receive your manuscript.

Meanwhile I have bought a small bungalow 5 miles south of Guildford and hope to move there on 22nd June, but shall not actually live there until my return from Germany on 5th July.

My new address will be Mulberry Croft, Littleford Lane, Shamley Green, Surrey.

It is a charming spot between two villages – Shamley Green and Blackheath – on top of a hill overlooking the rather beautiful Surrey landscape. I am quite excited about the prospect of living in the country after so many years in London. I so much hope that you will soon visit me there on one of your trips to the south. But if you cannot spare the time, there will always be the Reform Club.

It will be a great honour to publish your paper and I shall look forward to receiving your manuscript.

Michael is in the midst of his A-Level examinations in Economics, British Constitution and Economic History. Both Essex and Warwick University have offered him a conditional place (he was keen to go to one of the new universities).

With all warmest good wishes and kindest regards,

Yours sincerely,

Stephen Frowen

Stephen Frowen

178

University of Surrey
Annex, 14 Falcon Road
London S.W.11
2nd November 1967

Dear Professor Shackle,

I hope you will forgive me for the delay in thanking you for your last letter. It took a little while to settle down in my new surroundings and the last few weeks have been rather hectic.

I am so glad to know that your paper "On the Nature of Profit", my last issue of the *Woolwich Economic Papers* (Mr.Wheble has now taken over as Editor), has at last appeared. I asked the Polytechnic to send you 50 complimentary copies, which I hope you have received by now. I could also spare another 50 copies of your previous paper in this series if they are of any use to you. In fact, they are already packed and ready for dispatch. I understand that review copies of your latest paper have only just gone out.

Yesterday I spent a delightful day with Sir Ralph Hawtrey who visited me at my new cottage in Surrey. He spent the war years in the neighbouring village of Wonersh and was, I think, happy to see the district again after 20 years. We walked for miles and I don't think I have ever met anybody of his age with such intellectual power, alertness and physical strength. Actually one of the reasons for writing to you today is in connection with Sir Ralph. He kindly came to our Department last term to read a paper on 'International Liquidity', a copy of which I am enclosing. We should very much like to publish this paper in our series *International Economics*, the first issue of which I am also enclosing. The difficulty is that in each case, the University will only publish papers which (a) have been delivered at the University, and (b) have been externally assessed (quite regardless of how distinguished the author is). I am wondering, therefore, whether you would be prepared to send me a formal, short letter saying that in your view the Hawtrey paper is worth publishing. It is certainly a strange request and I feel really quite guilty for asking you. But the only way to continue our series and to publish the Hawtrey paper is by producing such a letter to our University administration. Please do not hesitate to disregard my request if for any reason you should feel unable to help us in this matter.

Is there any chance of persuading you to read a paper yourself at our post-graduate seminar sometime this term or, maybe, next term? If you should be willing to consider this proposal you will perhaps be so kind as to let me know which date would be convenient from your point of view and the subject you would like to cover. I cannot tell you how happy I should be if you accepted this invitation.

Unfortunately, my son Michael does not appear to be too happy reading economics at Warwick University. He likes mathematics and economics but cannot develop any enthusiasm for politics and economic history, which I am afraid are two compulsory subjects. He is now considering switching to the English Department, but I still hope that he will stick to economics.

You must be hectically busy just now and I feel quite guilty for troubling you with all this.

With all warmest good wishes,

Yours sincerely,

Stephen Frowen

179

Department of Economics
University of Liverpool
27th November 1967

My dear Frowen,

I have read with the utmost intellectual and aesthetic delight the paper by Sir Ralph Hawtrey on *International Liquidity*, which you so kindly sent me. In its perfect simplicity and clarity, its almost a miraculous unravelling of so elusive a skein of inter-penetrating problems, it illustrates the extraordinary and special qualities of mind which have long since given Sir Ralph Hawtrey a unique position amongst the world's great economists. His direct personal experience and memory of monetary history now give him an unapproachable eminence and authority. His is an intellect at whose touch problems seem to be dissolved rather than solved. The mark of the supreme expert is to make everything he does look easy. Sir Ralph's paper may do more than clear our minds of a tangle of difficulties and carry us to an incisive practical recommendation. It may persuade us that the finest vehicle for economic thought, the one which allows all its subtleties and depths to be in some degree taken into account, is still the English language, provided it is handled with such supreme unassuming mastery as Sir Ralph Hawtrey here exemplifies.

It is a very great privilege to have been allowed to read this paper. Its urgent and even desperate topicality has been heightened, its deep wisdom made vividly plain, by the events of the past week. It is, if I may venture to say so, quite imperative that this guidance should be made publicly available in print as soon as ever it can be done.

With very kind regards,

Yours sincerely,

George Shackle

George Shackle

180

40 Gurney Drive
London N.2
17th November 1968

Dear Professor Shackle,

I don't know whether you will ever forgive me for not thanking you for your last letter. My intention to reply by return somehow did not materialise and the more time passed the more difficult it became to write to you. It was so very kind of you to assess Hawtrey's paper for us and thanks to your assessment we obtained permission to publish it. You may have seen the paper in print by now, but just in case this should not be so, I am sending you a copy under separate cover.

I hope that you and your family are keeping well. I have followed your publications with the intense interest they deserve and they have been of tremendous help to me, especially as far as my teaching to postgraduate students is concerned.

My son Michael has just started his second year at Warwick University reading economics. Fortunately he came top in last June's examinations in mathematical analysis and macro-economics so that he has been accepted for Warwick's special course in advanced econometrics. He appears to have a special flair for both economics and mathematics.

Tanya is also doing quite well academically at South Hampstead High School for Girls after a relatively slow start. She is highly intelligent but less intellectual than Michael and terribly keen on sports, which Michael hates. Yet the two, perhaps partly because of their differences, are very close to each other. Tanya still remembers you well and treasures your presents.

The University of Surrey is now in Guildford but my department and a few others will not move there until the completion of the Arts Block next summer. The University still does not have an economics department and the Vice-Chancellor appears to be reluctant to change the present arrangement whereby we have a Sub-Department of International Economics attached to the Department of Linguistics and Regional Studies. There is a newly appointed Professor of Economics, Colin Robinson (an industrial economist), who will be teaching in the Department of Humanities. I understand that he will have nothing to do with our Sub-Department of International Economics and that his main task will be to start combined degree courses in engineering, other science subjects, and economics. Meanwhile my Sub-Department of International Economics offering post-graduate courses in international economics also provides a certain amount of service teaching to undergraduates in the Linguistics and Regional Studies Department. It is, as you can see, a very strange set up and I only hope that something will be done to streamline the economics teaching within the university. However, because of the many vested interests, things do not look too hopeful at present. Nevertheless, I do enjoy my teaching tremendously, especially as I get quite a number of mature students with, in some cases, quite extensive practical experience.

My wife, who asked me to send you her regards, still teaches at University College London and has just completed a rather exciting lecture course on the nature of tragedy. She intends to continue teaching at UCL when my department moves to Guilldford, also to enable Tanya to complete her O and A-Level courses at her Hampstead School where she is very happy. I shall therefore stay at my cottage in Shamley Green on my own during term time with occasional visits to London.

I assume that your visits to London during term time are not very frequent, but if on one of these occasions you could spare the time to join me for lunch or dinner at the Reform Club or visit us in Hampstead, I should be exceedingly happy.

With all warmest good wishes,

Yours sincerely,

Stephen Frowen

181

University of Surrey
14 Falcon Road
London, S.W.11
12th June 1969

Dear Professor Shackle,

I have just returned from a short visit to Germany where I gave a series of lectures at Bonn, Berlin, Hamburg and Würzburg University. I was delighted to see in all the German bookshops I visited copies of the German translation of *Economics for Pleasure* prominently displayed.

On the day of my departure for London, I discovered the enclosed review of your book in the *Frankfurter Allgemeine Zeitung*. Please let me know if you would like me to translate the review for you.

I hope you are keeping well. It is a long time since I last heard from you.

My son Michael is still enjoying his economics course at Warwick University. He specialises in econometrics and computer science. He treasures your book *Mathematics at the Fireside*, which you sent him for his second or third birthday.

With all warmest wishes and kindest regards,

Yours sincerely,

Stephen Frowen

182

The University of Liverpool
Social Studies Building
Bedford Street South
P.O. Box 147
Liverpool L69 3BX
15th June 1969

My dear Frowen,

How exceedingly delighted I am to have your letter. It is most kind of you indeed to tell me about the German edition of *Economics for Pleasure*, and to send me the review from the *Frankfurter Allgemeine Zeitung*. I should like very much indeed, if I may, to accept your offer to translate it, the fact that I must do so is, I fear, disgraceful for me, the only excuse I can make is that at school we were so soaked in the Romance languages that all my early energy was taken up in learning Latin and French. I can of course understand the general gist of it in some passages, but not all. This is the first time any book of mine has been published in a German edition.

Your lectures will have been thrilling for your audiences, since they will no doubt have dealt with the most burning economic questions of the day. It is very fascinating to consider how fashions change in economics. Richard Sayers told me that when monetary theory and policy were out of fashion, his classes dwindled to two or three, but when 'money' became an active theme they filled up enormously. I wonder what you think of the newspaper references nowadays to the 'money supply theory'. I am perfectly astounded nowadays to read articles whose authors seem never to have heard of the Quantity Theory, Irving Fisher, Marshall or the Banking and Currency School controversy. They give the impression of thinking that 'money supply' as an influence on the price level was discovered in the last few weeks.

I am just on the point of retirement from the University. I shall be 66 in July and feel that I am 'expendable' or should I say, a spent force. I will send you my address when it is finalised, but letters to the University will, I think, always be forwarded, as I shall, I believe, still be a member (emeritus).

I am sending (separately) two books which have recently appeared. One is the second edition of my first book, published in 1938 and re-issued after just 30 years by the Clarendon Press, with a new chapter of a slightly autobiographical flavour. The other is the volume of papers given at the British Association Section F in 1966, which I edited.

I should be *extremely* interested to hear about your work, and I do hope to hear from you.

With my very best and warmest wishes,

Yours sincerely,

George Shackle

George Shackle

183
University of Surrey
14 Falcon Road
London, S.W.11
20th June 1969

Dear Professor Shackle,

You cannot imagine how very happy I was to receive your letter. I had almost given up hope of ever hearing from you again. I was overjoyed when I discovered your letter and your parcels among my mail.

It was exceedingly kind of you to send me a copy of the second edition of your first book and a copy of the volume of papers given at the British Association Section F in 1966. I tremendously like the new chapter in *Expectations, Investment and Income*. It will be prescribed reading for all my students – undergraduates as well as postgraduates. The tendency for students to read Samuelson, Lipsey and Ackley as a short cut, but never Keynes's *General Theory* (not to speak of earlier economists), is so strong that one could despair. How many of them are really giving serious thought to their subject? In the case of those who do it is thanks to your writings that they have a chance of acquiring more than just some technical skill.

From the students' point of view it is sad to think that you will no longer be teaching after the summer term. But through your past and future writings they will fortunately still be able to learn from you. You must be very happy that, undistracted by so many other duties, you can now concentrate entirely on your writing.

I am enclosing an English translation of the German review of *Economics for Pleasure*. The bulk of it appears to consist of a brief summary of Chapter 3, Part a, of your book. The translation of your book appears to be quite good but a closer look does reveal a number of, fortunately, minor discrepancies.

Will you be coming to London for the Annual General Meeting of the Royal Economic Society? It would give me the greatest possible happiness if you could spare the time to join me for lunch or dinner at the Reform Club.

By the way, I love the title of your paper 'Policy, Poetry and Success'.[1] It is a beautifully written and a most interesting essay.

With all warmest good wishes

Yours sincerely,

Stephen Frowen

1 The paper appeared in *The Advancement of Science*, vol. 23, no. 111, September 1966, pp. 265–73, and in *The Economic Journal*, vol. 76, no. 304, December 1966, pp. 755–67.

184

The University of Liverpool
Social Studies Building
Bedford Street South
P.O. Box 147
Liverpool L69 3BX
28th June 1969

My dear Frowen,

I was exceedingly happy to have your letter, which is just such as have always given me a feeling of the worthwhileness of things. It would be lovely if we could meet and have a long talk as we used to do. I have had to give up any idea of coming to the General Meeting of the Royal Economic Society this year, as my own affairs have been so distracting. We are giving up our house near Liverpool and going to Aldeburgh in Suffolk, where we have spent our summer holiday for many years past. I have for some years been sending consignments of my personal papers (MSS, collections of letters, my printed books and so on) to the Cambridge University Library. But there still remained a vast mass of records of the process of getting books through the press, and a large collection of off-prints, and so on, and I have been trying to put all this in order so that it could go to the Liverpool University Library. I expect they will discard a lot of it as of no value, but some may serve some purpose. We have also, of course, have had to dispose in various ways of the domestic accumulations of 14 years, and reduce the remainder to what will go into a bungalow. At the same time there have been the summer examinations. My wife and I have just escaped to Scotland for a week, before the final effort of our actual house-move.

It is a strange experience to have, every now and then, a sudden thought that I need not prepare any lectures for next term! However there seems to be some suggestion of giving lectures in Belfast, which would be a way of gradually getting used to a new state of my affairs. I am not sure whether you will have met Professor R.D.C. Black or Professor Norman Cuthbert. I have known them well since the years when I went to Belfast as external examiner, and Black has taken a leading part in the two conferences on the History of Economic Thought which have taken place at Sussex and Nottingham, respectively, in January '68 and '69.

I do hope we may meet very soon, and much more often when I have set up house at Aldeburgh, from which London is quite accessible.

With all warmest and best wishes and kindest regards,

Yours sincerely,

George Shackle

Thank you *ever so much* for the exceeding kindness of translating the review. The review itself gave me very much pleasure, as it was a great thrill, earlier this year, to hear from CUP of the German edition. They have promised me a copy. It is fascinating to study the renderings in German and English which you provide. Translation is a most exacting and difficult art which I believe can throw much light on the ideas themselves.

185

Reform Club
Pall Mall, S.W.1
12th July 1969

Dear Professor Shackle,

I should like to send you my warmest congratulations on your 66th birthday. The small gift I am sending under separate cover is a completely inadequate token of the gratitude and affection I feel for you. My whole life and career in England have in a most decisive way been influenced and determined by you. How can I ever thank you enough for the keen interest you have taken in me and for your wise counsel? My whole thinking in the field of economics changed when I was privileged to attend your lectures at Leeds University. I shall never forget the tremendous impact those lectures had on me. The continuation of our contact and, if I may say, friendship has always been a source of the greatest possible happiness in my life.

I was delighted and exceedingly happy to receive your letter of 28th June. I was so thrilled to hear of your move to Aldeburgh. What an enchanting place it is! On a number of occasions I attended the Aldeburgh Music Festival – and on one occasion with Sir Ralph Hawtrey and his late sister. They both loved Aldeburgh.

I shall be going to Greece at the end of July but hope to be back in London at the beginning of September.

One of my tasks at Surrey University will be to arrange a seminar programme with external speakers. Could you possibly spare the time for taking over one of these papers on a topic of your choice? The subject does not need to, but should preferably have some bearing on international economics. Your talk could be given any time during the session 1969–70, but if you are already overcommitted during this period, we could arrange something for the following session.

My son Michael just had a letter from the Head of his Department at Warwick University saying that it had been decided at the Staff Meeting to commend him for his work in micro- and macro-economics. It was just the encouragement he needed.

With all warmest good wishes and kindest regards,

Yours sincerely,

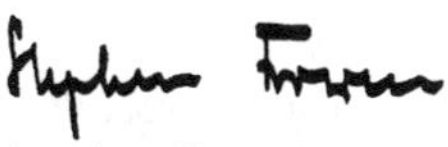

Stephen Frowen

186

Rudloe
Alde House Drive
Aldeburgh
Suffolk
20th July 1969

My dear Frowen,

I am sure you cannot know what our friendship through all these years has meant to me. You have been the most unchanging and perfectly constant, the most unwearied of all, amongst a host of friends with whom I have been blessed. Reading your letters amongst the many hundreds which I have kept from thirty-five and more years of professional activity, during this period of sorting and packing my papers for removal, I have realised more than ever what is meant by elevation of the human personality. Your example has been a shining one to any who has had the good fortune to know it.

The superb gift,[1] which I received a little before your letter, really took my breath away. It is a perfect combination of beauty and use, and I need not tell you that I shall treasure it always for the sake of what it will remind me of, as much as for what it is.

I decided in March or April that I would retire a year early. I was tired in many senses, and I have begun to feel a little out of sympathy with recent trends in our subject. The tendency to trust in supposedly self-contained mathematical models; the belief that mere attention to 'facts' and the application to them of arbitrarily chosen, *ad hoc*, principles for their interpretation, can give us knowledge; the neglect of the history of ideas (so that we have the absurdity of the daily press treating the Quantity Theory as though it was invented in the last month or two), and the belief that 'facts' can exist without pre-conceived classifications or concepts, seem to me likely to lead the subject into disrepute. I am trying to get my feelings and thoughts about all this into a book, but it will be a 'groping' one.

I should be extremely honoured and delighted to be allowed to give one of the lectures in your programme. I am not qualified to try to deal with International Affairs. I wonder if a general survey of the scope of economics and its traditional methods would be in any degree interesting to your students, if you should have some who would not consider such a paper a mere plodding over ground they have already covered?

I have been preparing a new edition of *Decision, Order and Time*, with a fairly long new additional chapter. I think it should be out in the autumn.

How can I thank you, with any words that can possibly convey my feelings, for your marvellous gift and deeply sustaining words?

With kindest regards and warmest gratitude,

Yours sincerely,

George Shackle

George Shackle

1 The gift was an antique silver ruler made in London in 1916. George Shackle's second wife, Catherine Shackle, delighted in using it after her husband's death in 1992. Her nieces and heirs, Hilary Clapham and Frances Ferneyhau, generously returned it to Stephen Frowen as a memento of deep emotional value after her own death in 2003.

187

University of Surrey
14 Falcon Road
London, S.W.1
9th October 1969

Dear Professor Shackle,

It is difficult to put into words the happiness I felt when I received your last letter. Please accept my belated but sincere and warmest thanks for your exceedingly kind remarks.

I was so pleased to hear that you are willing to give one of the lectures in our seminar programme. The subject you suggest 'a general survey of the scope of economics and its traditional methods' would be *most* suitable and welcome. At first I intended to spread the special lectures throughout the session, but as most of our postgraduate students will be unable to submit their seminar paper until the end of November, my colleague, Mrs. Troeller, would prefer the special lectures to take place during the first half of the Michaelmas Term if this can be arranged at this late stage. Our first lecture by Harry Johnson will take place next Monday and Dick Sargent of Warwick University has agreed to come on 21st October. Is there any chance of persuading you to come on either 28th October or 4th November? If you cannot do it at such short notice, a later date would also be possible. Our postgraduate seminar normally takes place on Tuesdays from 2–3.30p.m. but as I have to teach myself from 3.30–5.30p.m. during the first 5 weeks of term, I would try to arrange the seminar for 5.30–7p.m., so that we don't need to separate and can go straight on to dinner.

I cannot tell how very much I am looking forward to seeing you again and to listening to the fascinating paper you have so kindly proposed to present to our seminar.

When do you expect the new edition of *Decision, Order and Time* to appear?

With all warmest good wishes and kindest regards,

Yours sincerely,

Stephen Frowen

188

University of Surrey
14 Falcon Road
London, S.W.11
31st October 1969

Dear Professor Shackle,

I am tremendously looking forward to Tuesday. To my great regret the Seminar had to be arranged for 2–3.30pm as my colleague, Mrs Troeller, has a long standing appointment in Guildford in the late afternoon and she is most anxious to be present when you read your paper. I sincerely hope that this arrangement will not inconvenience you too much.

It would be nice if you could join us for lunch at 12.30 or better 12.40 as I am teaching until 12.30. I should have loved to meet you at the station, but in the circumstances you could perhaps be so kind as to take a taxi to our Department (14 Falcon Road, S.W.11). I shall be quite free after the Seminar and perhaps you could spare the time to join me for dinner at the Reform Club. Afterwards I shall take you to the station in time for your train to Cambridge at 9.30 p.m. I hope these arrangements will meet with your approval.

With all warmest wishes, until Tuesday,

Yours sincerely,

Stephen Frowen

Stephen Frowen

189
Reform Club
Pall Mall, S.W.1
9th November 1969

Dear Professor Shackle,

I should like to thank you again for the quite outstanding paper you read to our postgraduate seminar on Tuesday. It can only be described as a masterly treatment of the subject and it was beautifully presented. In fact some of my students said to me quite spontaneously that it was one of the most memorable occasions of their whole university life. Only a scholar with your philosophical mind, tremendous experience, knowledge, insight and the gift to give expression to all these accomplishments could have written it. The copy of your paper in our possession is now making its round, as more and more students wish to read it.

It is difficult to find words which could express my gratitude for the tremendous trouble you have taken in preparing and delivering your paper. To see you again has given me the greatest possible happiness and the evening at the Reform Club will remain among my dearest memories. I wished we had the opportunity of meeting more often in the future than has been possible in the past.

As arranged, I shall be at the air terminal in Cromwell Road at 6.30p.m. on Wednesday. Please don't worry if you get there later. I shall do some reading while waiting for you.

With all warmest good wishes, until Wednesday,

Yours sincerely,

Stephen Frowen

190

University of Surrey
Guildford
Surrey
19th September 1970

Dear Professor Shackle,

I was delighted to receive your letter on my return from the continent. I stayed longer than I originally intended and was immediately faced with qualifying examinations, resits, etc. when I got back to London.

I was exceedingly happy to hear that you will be able to come to London. I could manage any evening (except 1st, 10th and 13th October).

At daytime, I would be free on Friday, 25th September, Monday, 28th September, Thursday, 1st October and Friday, 9th October. From then on the only weekday I could be in London at daytime would be Friday (but I would be free for dinner any evening as my last lectures in Guildford finish at 5 p.m.).

If you prefer to join me for lunch at the Reform Club, the best time to meet would be 12 or 12.30. Or better still I could collect you by car at your hotel.

If you can manage to join me for dinner, we could perhaps meet at 6 or 6.30 p.m. Perhaps you could be so kind as to let me know which day and time would be most convenient for you. The prospect of having a long talk with you makes me exceedingly happy and I am impatiently looking forward to hearing from you. I hope that your crowded time-table will not prevent a meeting at an early date; kindly let me know if none of the dates suggested are possible for you. I shall then try to cancel some of my existing engagements.

I intend to look out for your new book *Expectation, Enterprise and Profit* at the Economists' Bookshop tomorrow. May I congratulate you most warmly on the addition of yet another title to your truly impressive list of publications? It must be one of the longest in the British Library!

It is most kind of you to make the time for a meeting in London, especially in view of your heavy commitments during the next few months. I was so glad to hear of the Visiting Professorship and the invitation to Cleveland. What an experience it will be for the students privileged to listen to your lectures.

With all warmest good wishes and kindest regards,

Yours sincerely,

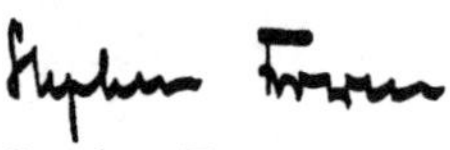

Stephen Frowen

P.S. Loughborough University is obviously not interested in my application. I am not unhappy about it, as I don't really mind staying on at Surrey University. Things here have improved greatly.

191

Rudloe
Alde House Drive
Aldeburgh
Suffolk
22nd September 1970

My dear Frowen,

Your extremely kind letter has just come, by the second post. It would have been lovely to have dinner together, and I am very sorry indeed that things have worked out to prevent it. I can't keep up with the way the time flies. The last fortnight has been busy with other things besides writing. I attended a conference at Sheffield the weekend before last, where Milton Friedman was the star performer. He is a delightful and most unassuming man, I will try to give you some account of what went on when we meet. Then I had to go to London the very next day after getting home, as I have been reading a series of book manuscripts for a publisher. It was an interesting but exhausting day. My time-table has been a little thrown out by having to have an X-ray, for which I have to go to hospital, I think for one night, this week or early next week.

Now I am very anxious in case you have altered your own arrangements in order to be so exceedingly kind to meet me on Wednesday, 30th Sept. I couldn't have hoped for such a splendid and consoling send-off, it will be marvellous. This term I am dabbling in the history of economic thought, not of choice but in order to fill the particular gap for which they have appointed me. But this fits very nicely with what I am trying to write, and the library at Queen's is excellent on the subject, thanks to Bob Black who of course is a very great authority on it. He is completing his book on Jevons.

I am very nervous about my book on the theory of the firm, *Expectation, Enterprise and Profit*, and got Charles Carter to explain on the jacket that it is not an orthodox account of the matter.

I shall look forward extremely to the 30th, and if all goes well I will be on the train arriving at Liverpool Street at 11.40. I do hope that it is not wrecking your time-table, but I shall be happy to have this great pleasure just before I leave for Ireland.

With very kind regards,

Yours sincerely,

George Shackle

George Shackle

192
University of Surrey
Guildford
Surrey
22nd September 1970

Dear Professor Shackle,

I am so very grateful to you for your tremendous kindness in writing immediately and in such detail to Loughborough University despite your many other commitments. I had really given up all hope of being considered for this chair and was most surprised when I heard from Professor Walz (University of Surrey) that he had received a request for a reference from Loughborough.

I apologise for the intrusion this morning, but I was a bit worried as I had not supplied you with the information you requested.

I am greatly looking forward to Wednesday, 30th September. I shall be at Liverpool Street Station at 11.40 a.m. There will just be enough time for lunch at the Reform and I shall then take you to London airport. By coincidence I have to go to the airport anyhow that afternoon, as our new au pair girl will be arriving from Zürich at 4.20 p.m.

With many thanks once again and all best and warmest wishes,

Yours gratefully,

Stephen Frowen

P.S. Loughborough University must be flooded with applications for this chair and my chances can't be very great. However, it is nice to know that at least I am being considered for this position.

193
University of Surrey
Guildford
Surrey
2nd October 1970

Dear Professor Shackle,

Our meeting in London on your way to Belfast has been the source of great happiness to me. It meant so much to me to talk with you and exchange views and hear of the exciting and fascinating book you are in the process of writing. Thank you so much for making it possible to see you in London.

I hope that you had a pleasant flight without further delays and that your Cottage exceeds your expectations.

I am enclosing the script of your Surrey lecture. I have not yet had a chance of showing it to Professor Robinson, the Chairman of our Editorial Board, but I have no doubt that he will be delighted and honoured to see it published in our series *Surrey Papers in Economics* (I have just changed the name of the series from *International Economics* to this broader title). It will take about 4 weeks to get it printed. If you could return it to me by the end of October, it should be published before the end of the year.

When I looked up the address of Queen's University of Belfast in the 1966 edition of the *Commonwealth University Yearbook*, I noticed that D. Swann, now

Professor of Economics at Loughborough University, was at that time a lecturer in the Economics Department at Queen's University Belfast.

With all warmest good wishes,

Yours sincerely,

Stephen Frowen

194

The Queen's University of Belfast
Belfast BT7 1NN
Northern Ireland
15th October 1970

My dear Frowen,

It was most delightful indeed, for me, to experience yet again your great kindness, and to have a talk after almost a year since we last met. I was concerned to hear that you had a meeting which you might have been at. I do hope that your kindness to me did not involve you in inconvenience.

I was most interested to hear about your son, and the golden opinions he won at Warwick, and of course he will go from strength to strength.

I am distressed to think it is already a fortnight since we met, and I am only now writing to thank you; my one excuse is that I have been attending to the manuscript you wish me to read over. It occurred to me that as the xerox will not be very easy for the printer to use, I would look out for the typescript which I have at home, and get the hand-written sections at beginning and end typed and attached to the central part which is typed already. I have accordingly copied out, with some slight revisions, those beginning and end sections and I am sending them off to Cambridge to be typed by the agency I always use. When the typed copies come I will attach them and send the whole typed version to you. There is just one other thing that bothers me: the paper was originally written to be read aloud, and I had in consequence given rein to the impulse to underline many words and phrases which would be emphasized in speaking. These are far too frequent to be italicized in print, and I thought that before I send you the typescript I would write 'rom' in the margin against most of them. I think this will be sufficient without making any mark in the text (bound to look messy)? I hope to send you the typescript well before the end of October.

I do wonder whether there is any news from Loughborough? I am sure your other project, of getting some study leave with a research Fellowship, would be a splendid idea and would result in a mass of writing and make available the immense knowledge you must have of banking affairs on the international scene. There are so many obscurities that no one bothers to disentangle, no one could do it so well as you! And I do look forward exceedingly to hear that the book of your collected papers is in train.

With all very best and warmest wishes,

Yours sincerely, and most gratefully,

George Shackle

195

University of Surrey
Guildford
Surrey
3rd January 1971

Dear Professor Shackle,

I hope you will accept my sincere apologies for the delay in thanking you for your letter of 15th October. I had a rather hectic and difficult term with a number of personal upsets. First my wife had to enter hospital for an operation and soon after her return from hospital, a police officer informed us one night that our son Michael who is reading for a M.Sc. in Economics at Warwick University had been taken to a Coventry hospital for an emergency operation. The surgeon who performed the operation from midnight until 2 a.m. discovered an acute and rather extensive pancreatitis – an apparently rare and often fatal disease. He remained critically ill for some time but in the end got over the critical point and was able to leave hospital just before Christmas. He will have to lead a very careful and protected life during the next few years as there is always the danger of a recurrence of the inflammation. However, for all of us to be well and together again, Christmas was a particularly happy one this year. So often one only fully appreciate one's blessings when one is in danger of being deprived of things or in danger of losing those one loves most.

You must have had a most interesting but probably also an exceedingly busy time at Queen's University of Belfast.

In your letter you mention the manuscript of your paper we are anxious to publish. You must have been far too busy to attend to this matter last term.

However, if you could let me have the typescript as soon as you can manage, I should be most grateful.

I should also like to raise another matter. Professor Colin Robinson and I are in the process of arranging two or three public lectures in economics for the remaining part of this session. We should be delighted and honoured if you accepted our invitation to give one of these lectures at a date and on a subject of your choice. If you decided on 'Expectations in Economics' as your main theme,we should be very happy. But if you preferred another subject,we would be equally happy. Our Spring Term finishes on 26th March and our Summer Term lasts from 26th April until 2nd July, but the second half of the Summer Term is of course taken up mainly by examinations.

I was shortlisted for the chair at Loughborough, but failed to be appointed . The University received 80 applications for this post and I was one of the six candidates invited to attend for interview. The interview was quite tough but went reasonably well.

However, the University was obviously anxious to appoint an expert in the field of politics – in fact I was the only economist shortlisted – as the University already has a Professor of Economics and a Professor of Social Sciences, but no Professor of Politics in the School of Social Sciences. I was a bit disappointed, of course, but genuinely believe, after reflection, that it might be better for me to stay at Surrey for a while without being burdened by administrative duties. What I should like to pursue in the near future, however, is the project of getting some study leave with a research fellowship. I am greatly indebted to you for taking so much trouble over recommending me to Loughborough. My being shortlisted at all was no doubt the result of your strong letter of recommendation,and I should like you to know how very grateful I am to you. Your encouragement throughout my career has been of decisive importance. It would be so nice and would make me exceedingly happy to see you again at Surrey in the foreseeable future. If you wish to discuss the project of your public lecture personally, perhaps lunch or dinner on one of your journeys to Belfast via London may be possibility.

With all warmest good wishes for a very happy New Year to you and your family,

Yours most gratefully,

Stephen Frowen

Stephen Frowen

196

Rudloe
Alde House Drive
Aldeburgh
Suffolk
2nd November 1971

My dear Frowen,

I am most delighted indeed to hear the splendid news of your sabbatical term next summer, and the opportunity for you to write the magnificent book which your deep insight and knowledge will produce. This will be precisely the kind of book which is needed to give back to economics its respectability with the public, lost by its over-ambition to become a mathematised exact science with absurd claims to predictive powers. Your mastery of theory and great knowledge of that particular economy whose monetary experience has been most dramatic in many respects will bring the two sides of the subjects together and make them illuminate each other in a real and cogent analysis.

It would be a very great happiness to me if we could soon meet, as soon as I am far enough through Mr. Lepper's thesis (rather more than one third read so far) to enable me to discuss it. I think I should give myself another fortnight, and I wonder if we could find a date in the week starting 14th November? The Monday would be the 15th, the Wednesday 17th, either would be easy for me, would you let me know if one of them would be perfectly convenient for you?

I am due to attend Professor R.D.C. Black's lecture on Jevons on this Wednesday and have an appointment with a publisher (not on my own account) in the afternoon. I should have liked to suggest this date but I was already committed to these engagements and so it was impossible. I look forward extremely to hear how the Menger conference went. I was to have attended two conferences on Jevons this summer, one at Bellagio and the other at Manchester, but I did not feel equal to going to either of them. I wrote a paper for the Bellagio conference and I believe the proceedings will be published.

The other day I remembered that it was just a year since, with such extreme kindness, you put me on my aircraft for Dublin and gave up your whole afternoon to see me off. It was a great comfort to me. I had a term which was very fruitful in several ways but had to withdraw in the last week of November through not being well. In the spring term this year I went four times for two nights each time, and finished my course for the students.

There is so much to discuss. I shall look forward extremely to our meeting, and I hope I may then have finished reading the thesis and formed an opinion on it.

With kindest regards,

Yours sincerely,

George Shackle

George Shackle

197

University of Surrey
Department of Humanities and Social Sciences
Guildford
Surrey
7th November 1971

Dear Professor Shackle,

I was delighted to receive your exceedingly kind letter and to hear that we shall be able to meet soon. Wednesday, 17th November, would be convenient for Professor Robinson and me. Would it be too early for you to meet at 12.15 a.m. at the Reform Club? Unfortunately, Colin Robinson has to be back in Guildford for a lecture at 3 p.m. I have no teaching commitments myself on Wednesday afternoon.

I am so much looking forward to seeing you again and to be able to resume our discussions.

With all best wishes and kindest regards,

Yours sincerely,

Stephen Frowen

Stephen Frowen

198

Rudloe
Alde House Drive
Aldeburgh
Suffolk
14th November 1971

My dear Frowen,

The arrangement for Wednesday will be splendid, and I look forward so much to our being able to have a talk over all the many things we are interested in, in common. It will be a great happiness for me, also, to meet Professor Robinson.

I hope to have formed some view of Mr. Lepper's thesis, though I am afraid I shall not have quite finished reading it. The middle chapters have been much slower going, and I need increasingly, of course, to think back over what he has said in order to see how his argument stands as a whole, and where it leads. He himself insists that this is an exploratory work, and not the presentation of a finished view. This is of course not only reasonable but inevitable; it would be disturbing if anyone claimed to have dealt finally with the question of Cause. It is no doubt my chief duty to consider the argument from the point of view of an economist. Large allowances must I think be made by all the professionals of exact thinkers, mathematicians, logicians and philosophers, to the economists whose subject-matter appears daily more intractable, and nowadays seems every week to defeat old explanations and make nonsense of forecasts. I think economic theory provides an admirable, necessary and neglected field for the philosopher's astringent critical methods. And these methods do, as they have always done, show a tendency to turn their swords up on themselves.

It is all very fascinating. It is also increasingly topical, and even increasingly urgent, for economists ought to make up their minds what sort of economics they are justified in teaching.

I look forward with the very best happiness to our being able to meet, and continue our discussions which have gone on now so many years, interrupted but unbroken. And I shall be delighted to meet your friend and colleague.

With kindest regards and very best wishes,

Yours sincerely,

George Shackle

George Shackle

199

Rudloe
Alde House Drive
Aldeburgh
Suffolk
27th November 1971

My dear Frowen,

Our gathering at the Reform Club was delightful and relaxed for me. I enjoyed it very deeply and that is my excuse for having, as I realised with a pang of conscience, taken up far too much of your time. Your resources of deeply-examined monetary theory, and your exceedingly impressive knowledge of contemporary and recent affairs always give me a very great stimulus and store of ideas.

I am very sorry to say that I have not an available, and presentable, extra copy of the paper I am to give on Tuesday, as the carbon typescript is in London. I will collect it on Tuesday morning and bring it with me.

I have made fairly copious notes on the thesis, and have made out in writing a list of themes that, if agreed, I should very much like to invite the candidate to discuss, at his own pace and taking his time. The talk on them that we might have would interest me exceedingly and, I hope, may give him a feeling that all his efforts have had at any rate one interested reader with a sympathetic anxiety to hear him discourse on them.

I do look forward to this occasion.

With very kind regards,

Yours sincerely,

George Shackle

George Shackle

200

Rudloe
Alde House Drive
Aldeburgh
Suffolk
4th December 1971

My dear Frowen,

I had a marvellous visit. I enjoyed every moment of it, and I am filled with gratitude to you for proposing it to the authorities and for your superb hospitality and all your exceedingly thoughtful kindness, which is incomparable.

The seminar gave me just that exacting criticism which I wanted, and left only one thing to be desired: you yourself withheld what would have been the most telling comments of all, for you are a 'citizen' of the real financial world.[1] When your book on the recent German financial history is published, it will be plain to everyone (as it has been for a dozen or a score of years to me) that what is awaited next is a definitive general treatise by you on financial policy.

My visit raised my morale tremendously, (it has needed constant rebuke from me recently) and I was very happy indeed to feel that for a short time I had been of some use to somebody.

With all very best wishes and kindest regards,

Yours sincerely,

George Shackle

1 The paper was subsequently discussed intensely between G.L.S. Shackle and Stephen Frowen.

201

University of Surrey
Department of Humanities and Social Sciences
Guildford
Surrey
2nd June 1972

Dear Professor Shackle,

I was so very happy to hear that I have been awarded the Leverhulme Fellowship for a period of six months starting on 1st August. I honestly did not dare to hope that my application might be successful as the number of applications received by the Lerverhulme Trust has been very heavy indeed this year. I know that it is only thanks to your warm and strong recommendation that my application has been considered at all. How can I ever thank you enough for your great kindness? It will make all the difference to my work to be able to spend this time in Germany on my research without being distracted by so many other duties. It is the first time since I took up teaching that I will be in this position.

I already spent seven weeks with the Deutsche Bundesbank in Frankfurt and I have only just returned to London for the summer examinations at Surrey and London University.

At the Bundesbank I met Jerry Jordon of the Federal Reserve Bank of St. Louis who spent four months with the Bundesbank as an adviser. He has already done a lot of ground work for me and we shall probably collaborate to some extent. I also met Karl Brunner at the Bundesbank who kindly invited me to participate in his annual Monetary Seminar at the University of Constance from 28th to 30th June. Alan Meltzer, Harry Johnson and other leading monetary theorists will also be present.

I shall be in London until 23rd June and should be exceedingly happy if we could meet one day during one of your visits to London. The only two days I would not be free because of examiners' meetings would be the 19th and 20th June.

I cannot tell you how very happy I was to see a copy of the volume of essays in your honour at the Economists' Bookshop shortly before my departure for Germany.[1] I immediately added it to my students' reading list for next year as some of the essays are highly relevant to my syllabus. It is a very handsome volume, beautifully produced and I do like the photograph of you. I wish I could obtain a print from the photographer. Unfortunately, his name is not mentioned.

I was pleased to hear that my colleague David Reisman has now completed his Ph.D. thesis. It ought to be quite an interesting study. He always strikes me as one of the few people with an original mind in our Department.

In 1974 I may have the chance of spending six months with the Federal Reserve Bank of St. Louis. I shall have to discuss the details with Dr. Andersen at Constance.

With many, many thanks once again and all warmest good wishes,

Yours sincerely,

Stephen Frowen

1 See Carter, C.F. and Ford, J.L. (eds), *Uncertainty and Expectations in Economics. Essays in Honour of G.L.S. Shackle* (Oxford: Basil Blackwell,1972).

202

Rudloe
Alde House Drive
Aldeburgh
Suffolk
6th June 1972

My dear Frowen,

I am most delighted to have all your splendid news: Everything is evidently going perfectly. Your success is surging forward irresistibly, as it was bound to do. You will have been in the thick of controversy over monetary policy, which *The Times* has been full of, between Herr Schiller and the Bundesbank. You arrived in the nick of time!

I am not sure whether I shall be able to arrange my affairs so as to come to London while you are here, as I am buried under an avalanche of commitments. One of them is Mr. Reisman's massive thesis, which I have promised to read by about 6th July. I have also proofs to correct, and a syllabus to prepare for lectures which I am supposed to give in Wales in the autumn, which I ought to send in before the end of term. I feel I am in a jam, and ought to grind away 16 hours a day for the next month. But I hope to escape for a day, and will write to see if we can manage to meet, I should so like it.

The book of essays they have given me is a dream-like experience, seeming to me quite unreal, and I cannot really bring myself to believe that it is for me at all. I am still engaged in studying the essays and writing to thank, as well as I can, the contributors for their immense kindness.

It is really a great thing that the flood-tide of interest in monetary theory and banking policy is flowing so strongly. In such a vast field, collaboration is evidently a great advantage, but I cannot help hoping you will write your own, solely your own, book.

I do hope we can meet, but things have piled up for me!, and it seems you will only be here for a fortnight?

With kindest regards and all warmest wishes,

Yours sincerely,

George Shackle

George Shackle

203

Mulberry Croft
Littleford Lane
Shamley Green
Guildford
Surrey GU5 0RH
16th March 1973

Dear Professor Shackle,

I feel very guilty for not writing to you earlier. My thoughts have been with you so often, but somehow I never managed to find sufficient peace. I tend to take on too many things and my whole life is becoming more and more of a rush. I have got to make a completely new start, drastically reducing my commitments. This year my colleague, Mrs. Troeller, is spending a year in the States. She decided on this late in August and we were unable to find a replacement at such short notice. As a result, I was landed with 15 contact hours per week, and it was quite impossible to continue with my research on the German economy. However, life will be easier from now on, and I hope to complete my research project in Germany during the summer when I intend to spend another month or two with the Bundesbank. Last year's stay with the Bundesbank was most successful and fascinating. It was most kind of you to recommend me to the Leverhulme Trust for the Research Fellowship. It made all the difference receiving this award. To justify your recommendation, I am trying hard to produce something of sufficient merit.[1]

It is such a long time since our last meeting and I sincerely hope that you are keeping well. If you should have an engagement in London one day, it would make me very happy if you could join me for lunch or dinner at the Reform Club. Apart from seeing you again, I should greatly enjoy to hear more of the work you are engaged in at present. How is the book we discussed at our last meeting progressing?

I hear that Benjamin Britten's new opera *The Death in Venice* will be performed at the Aldeburgh Music Festival. I don't know when it takes place, but if it should be before 3rd July and if I can get tickets, Irina and I should very much like to hear it.

Tanya has just had an acceptance from Bedford College of Physical Education. She intends to specialise in the training of physically handicapped children. She will be taking her A-Level examinations in May and June. Michael is reading for a M.Sc. in Economics at Surrey University this year. He has definitely decided to go into teaching.

I do hope that we shall have an opportunity of meeting soon. It would give me great happiness.

With warmest wishes and kindest regards to you and Mrs. Shackle,

Yours sincerely,

Stephen Frowen

1 The findings of the research undertaken on the demand for and supply of money in the Federal Republic of Germany were published as follows: (1) 'Some investigations of demand and supply functions for money in the Federal Republic of Germany, 1965 to 1974', *Weltwirtschaftliches Archiv*, vol. 112, no. 1, 1976, pp.136–64; and (2) 'The demand for and supply of money in the Federal Republic of Germany 1965–1974', in S.F. Frowen, A.S. Courakis and M.H. Miller (eds) *Monetary Policy and Economic Activity in West Germany* (Surrey University Press in association with International Textbook Company, 1977), pp. 129–42.

204

Rudloe
Alde House Drive
Aldeburgh
Suffolk
21st March 1973

My dear Frowen,

I am extremely delighted to have a letter from you. I have been wondering very much indeed how things were going. Your book will come endowed with every possible advantage: its perfect timing, as a history and unravelment of these years, so dramatic for the whole field of money, banking and currency exchanges; its immense advantage of your experience both in British banking and research and now your 'inside' view of the continental systems; and above all your depth of insight and unerring eye for the crucial questions. I wonder whether you will find space to urge a reconstruction of the *language* of currency exchanges and related questions. Until recently people have talked of 'money *flowing over* the exchanges', as though it was water over a sluice. It seems to me they have only recently recognised explicitly that such transactions can involve vast *creations* of national currencies. There are a number of mysteries which many people would be glad to see cleared up and explained from ground level up, such as the exact nature of Euro-dollars and where the book-keeping takes place which brings them into existence, and so on. At any rate, no-one could be better equipped than you with every gift and circumstance, save only the frightful over-work which seems always to pursue you. I do hope you really mean to escape from this decisive action, and I am quite sure your department must be anxious to free you from this strain, so wasteful of splendid possibilities.

I should be so happy if we could meet for a talk, there is so much news for you to give me of yourself. I am getting towards the end of my commitments, and do not think I shall do any more lecturing. I found it rather a strain last term, when I was going to Cardiff and then to Swansea, at first weekly and later fortnightly. Some day, when you would in any case be in London, if you would just send me a line, I would love to come up for lunch; but I must not take up more than a reasonable amount of your time. I fear that 'pensioners' are inclined to think others have as much time as they have, and when you are so over-pressed it is a scandal that I should keep you talking.

With all warmest and best wishes and kindest regards,

Yours sincerely,

George Shackle

205

University of Surrey
School of Humanities and Social Sciences
Department of Economics
Guildford
Surrey GU2 5XH
7th March 1974

Dear Professor Shackle,

Yesterday I received an inspection copy of *An Economic Querist* – a most instructive and delightful book I would like all my economics students to read. It will certainly be on my reading list for next year.

I am so very sorry about my long silence caused by a number of unfortunate circumstances. However, it would give me tremendous happiness if you could spare the time to join me for lunch at the Reform Club if possible on Thursday, 28th or Friday, 29th March. Another possibility would be Monday, 25th March. If none of these dates should be convenient, I should be grateful if you would kindly let me know the day and time most convenient to you and I shall try to be in London on that day. In the evening I would be free for dinner almost any day (except 19th, 21st and 22nd March). On 2nd April we intend to go to Sicily for a fortnight. If you should be free for lunch on 28th or 29th March, the best time to meet may be at 12.30 a.m. at the Reform. I could also meet you at the station if you will kindly let me know the time of your arrival.

I also hope that it will be possible for you and Mrs. Shackle to attend Tanya's wedding on 20th April in Surrey. She is only $18\frac{1}{2}$ years old and will start a teachers' training course at Goldsmith College in the autumn. Four years ago she met one of my wife's former students [Richard Hosburn] and they have been friends ever since. He graduated last June and now works as a journalist. It is a bit young to get married, of course, but nothing could be done to induce her to wait.

I am so very much looking forward to seeing you again. There is so much I would like to discuss with you. If for some reason it should be difficult for you to come to London, we could perhaps meet for lunch or dinner in Aldeburgh.

With all warmest good wishes and kindest regards to you and Mrs. Shackle,

Yours sincerely,

Stephen Frowen

206

Rudloe
Alde House Drive
Aldeburgh
Suffolk
13th March 1974

My dear Frowen,

It will be most delightful to look forward to meeting again at the Reform Club for lunch on Thursday, 28th March. I have very often wondered how your work was going, and it will be a very great happiness to me to hear about it, and your experiences on your journeys abroad. I should be so glad if you would let me know the address to which I should send my present for Tanya's wedding. I am afraid my wife and I would find it rather more than we could manage to accept your very kind invitation, we are not so mobile as in former years. We shall think of you on this great occasion and wish you, and her, every possible happiness.

I write in great haste to catch the post. I found your letter on returning from a very brief visit to Oxford, which I had found extremely interesting but tiring. Please forgive this very brief note. I only have a few minutes to go about a half-mile!

With kindest regards and very best thanks,

Yours sincerely,

George Shackle

George Shackle

207

University of Surrey
School of Humanities and Social Sciences
Department of Economics
Guildford
Surrey GU2 5XH
23rd March 1974

Dear Professor Shackle,

Just a few words to thank you for your kind letter and to let you know how very much I am looking forward to meeting you at the Reform Club on Thursday, 28th March, at 12.30 p.m.

I was very sorry to hear that you will be unable to attend Tanya's wedding, but I quite understand that a journey from Suffolk to Surrey would have been rather difficult to arrange without a car.

I shall be very happy to see you again on Thursday.

With warmest wishes and kindest regards,

Yours sincerely,

Stephen Frowen

Stephen Frowen

208

Rudloe
Alde House Drive
Aldeburgh
Suffolk
17th April 1974

My dear Frowen,

I think you will be home again now from your holiday, and I do hope it was perfect in every way and will have given you some rest and release.

Yesterday I took to the typing agency an outline of ideas for the possibility which we discussed of a collaborative work on the history of economic thought. What I have written comprises a page or two seeking to show that the study of the history of ideas is essential to the understanding of ideas; a page of brief notes on my suggested scheme for such a work; and the scheme itself, amounting to a table of contents in the form of headings for divisions ('Books' in the sense used to denote their main divisions by Adam Smith, Ricardo, Marshall and Keynes) and under each heading a list of chapters. All this sounds and looks alarmingly ambitious and, I am afraid, pretentious, if regarded as other than a mere illustration of one sort of plan for such book. I do not for a moment mean it to be taken as my considered and serious plan or draft. Indeed, I do not wish to be considered as other than the merest outsider or chance contributor in your gathering of ideas for such a book, if such a proposal is ever formulated. I felt that you wished to know if I had any ideas. I have put down on paper such ideas as I had. I hope the typed copy will be ready in a week or two.

I do hope that everything will be perfect at Tanya's wedding, and that you and she will be exceedingly happy. Yesterday I arranged for my wedding gift, a very modest and humble one, to be dispatched to your house, Mulberry Croft at Shamley Green. I hope this was the right place to have it sent.

With all very best wishes for the great occasion and kindest regards,

Yours sincerely,

George Shackle

George Shackle

I wrote to the Cambridge University Press to ask them to send you a copy of *Epistemics and Economics*, and heard from them in reply that they had sent with it, most disastrously and (need I say) against every intention of mine, an invoice. Please send me the invoice. I phoned them to put this right but did not get from them any clear assurance. I am so very sorry that this blunder of mine should have happened, one cannot think of everything and I *always* have books charged to my own account. But there have been changes in the staff of the Press and reliance on old settled arrangements is not now to be automatically assumed, it was my own fault not theirs.

209
The Reform Club
12th July 1974

Dear Professor Shackle,

I am so very sorry not to have written to you before to thank you for your great kindness in sending me a copy of your book *Keynesian Kaleidics* that I was so anxious to have. It will be of tremendous help in revising my Economic Theory course for M.Sc. students. It is certainly one of the most stimulating and thought-provoking books I have come across in recent years.

Tanya and Rick [Hosburn] were delighted to receive your beautiful and generous wedding present, the only sherry glasses they got. Tanya is terribly afraid that one of these glasses might one day get broken and I promised to ask you where it could be replaced if this should happen.

One of the reasons why I did not write earlier (although this is not an excuse) is that I was rather busy preparing a conference on West German Monetary Developments which took place this week at the University of Surrey. We had about 60 monetary theorists and central bankers from both Britain and Western Germany as delegates. My own paper written jointly with Philip Arestis was on the Demand for Money in Western Germany, covering the period 1965–73. It is an empirical test of a model first developed by Feige and subsequently tested for the UK by Laidler and Parkin. If I may, I should very much like to send you a copy of the revised version as soon as it is ready as I should be very grateful and interested to hear your comments. I have not yet finalised arrangements but I hope that either Cambridge University Press or Macmillan will publish the conference proceedings.[1]

In your last letter you mentioned that you will let me have some suggestions in connection with the study we discussed at our meeting at the Reform Club. I shall be most interested to receive your comments as I am very interested indeed in this project.

On Wednesday I shall be going to Manchester for a conference on inflation arranged by Michael Parkin. Is there any chance of meeting you there? On the following Monday we shall be going to Switzerland until the end of August.

May I conclude by sending you my warmest wishes for a very happy birthday and many happy returns.

It gave me tremendous happiness to see you again at the Reform Club after such a long time. There is so much more I would have liked to talk to you about but the time always seems too short. But perhaps it will be possible for us to meet again in the not too distant future. If the journey to London is too strenuous for you, we could also meet one day for lunch in Aldeburgh which in any case I would like to see again after so many years.

With all warmest good wishes and kindest regards,

Yours sincerely,

Stephen Frowen

1 Surrey University Press in association with International Textbook Company did in fact publish the conference proceedings entitled *Monetary Policy and Economic Activity in West Germany*, edited by S.F. Frowen, A.S. Courakis and M.H. Miller, in 1977.

210

Rudloe
Alde House Drive
Aldeburgh
Suffolk
9th September 1974

My dear Frowen,

This letter is only a desperate apology for my failure to keep up our correspondence. My summer has been distracted in many ways including some spells of troublesome health, and events seem to go by faster and faster. On getting your letter of 12th July saying that you were going to Switzerland immediately, I resolved to write at your return, but that date has gone past by a week or more. You will now be engrossed in preparations for the new term, but sometime perhaps we can meet in London and exchange our news (I fear this a one-sided offer, I have no news to exchange!) I think my health is improving, and so I could fit into any arrangement that you might suggest, but I do hope you will not give up time which I know you cannot spare. I have a permanently guilty conscience on this score.

Please forgive this note, which is nothing but an apology for my failure to write. I hope to amend my performance.

With all very best and warmest wishes,

Tanya wrote me a most charming and delightful letter.

Yours sincerely,

George Shackle

George Shackle

211
Mulberry Croft
Littleford Lane
Shamley Green
Guildford
Surrey GU5 0RH
12th November 1974

Dear Professor Shackle,

Your letter of 9th September was in fact awaiting me at Mulberry Croft on my return from the Oxford Seminar, having been forwarded by the Reform Club. Although, as always, I was exceedingly happy to hear from you, I suddenly realised how inconsiderate and selfish I have been in taking up so much of your precious time with our correspondence – time which I am convinced you desperately need to accomplish more important tasks.

The only reason why I dare to write to you again today is to send you the enclosed copy of Wicksell's *Value, Capital and Rent*, as you mentioned to me that you do not possess a copy yourself. I should be very happy indeed if you would be so kind as to accept this copy with my renewed and sincerest thanks for all your help and support in so many directions over several decades.

Through Blackwell's I discovered that the book is being kept in print by Augustus M. Kelley of New York and I immediately ordered the enclosed copy for you. A letter I received from Charles Furth of Allen & Unwin in this connection may also be of interest to you (copy enclosed).

Another matter I should like to raise concerns one of my Ph.D. students, Mr. Philip Arestis, a Senior Lecturer at Thames Polytechnic. He is writing a thesis on 'Optimal Choice of Monetary Policy Instruments: The UK Case' which he hopes to complete by next July. His first paper on this topic to our Research Seminar will be presented at the beginning of February. I should be exceedingly happy if you could spare the time and would be willing to be his external examiner. Before committing yourself I could of course send you a copy of what he has produced so far. He has been granted a year's leave of absence and is working full time on his thesis.

I was greatly distressed to hear of your spells of troublesome health and hope that by now you have completely recovered.

With all warmest good wishes,

Yours sincerely,

Stephen Frowen.

212

Rudloe
Alde House Drive
Aldeburgh
Suffolk
1st December 1974

My dear Frowen,

It is extremely kind of you to send me Mr Brian Kantor's very striking paper. I think he is the first to contend so explicitly and incisively that attempts by government at discretionary stabilisation measures are disabled by uncertainty. He brings his guns to bear from many quarters with boldness and originality. I have long intensely disliked the phrase 'fine tuning', which seems to me to be a contradiction in terms when applied to the nominally 'free enterprise' sector. But Mr Kantor's argument goes beyond this, and shows that the uncertainty of the timing of the effects of so-called 'stabilisation' measures makes them dangerous and likely to do damage. We used to argue, when James Meade was Director of the Economic Section of the Cabinet Office, that it might be two years or more from the start of *designing* a public works scheme before it had any effect on employment; I should think that was an *under*-estimate.

I should like very much indeed to meet Mr Kantor, and in any case I am writing to him. My affairs are very crowded just now and I am losing the race against my correspondence, but I will try to get to London to have a talk with him.

With all warmest wishes, and very best thanks,

Yours sincerely,

George Shackle

213

Rudloe
Alde House Drive
Aldeburgh
Suffolk
8th March 1976

My dear Frowen,

I was delighted by our few minutes' talk, even if only on the telephone. I am a little worried about Mr Arestis's thesis. Will he be upset at waiting for two months or even more? I will try to read it as soon as I am free from the present pressures, which do not give me time even to meet accepted obligations. It is also an anxiety to have this manuscript in my charge. I hope there are two or three other copies in existence?

Your expeditions to Casablanca and Berlin seem most adventurous. I do hope you are in every way prospering.

With kindest regards,

Yours sincerely,

George Shackle

214

Rudloe
Alde House Drive
Aldeburgh
Suffolk
2nd June 1976

My dear Frowen,

I hav e finished studying Mr Arestis's thesis, and I wonder if you would like to suggest a date for the viva voce. I could reach Guildford by the early afternoon on any day next week or the following, or of course I could meet you and him in London if that suited better. I should like if possible to catch a train home from Liverpool Street at 4.50. If we could meet after lunch that would give ample time either at Guildford or London. We could still have time for a little exchange of news.

With kindest regards,

Yours sincerely,

George Shackle

215

Rudloe
Alde House Drive
Aldeburgh
Suffolk
20th June 1976

My dear Frowen,

Friday's occasion was for me an extreme happiness and delight. The candidate's extraordinary excellence and his irresistible personality and charm, given their best possible setting by your own inexpressible kindness, consideration and insight, made this the most truly and movingly happy *viva* in which I have ever been privileged to take part. I have tried to convey the remarkable quality of our discussion and the thesis which made it possible, in the brief report which I enclose.

With kindest regards,

Yours sincerely,

George Shackle

Mr Philip Arestis seeks to answer the question whether the size of the national income of the United Kingdom, measured by quantities and production at constant prices, can best be influenced by taking as the explicit instrument of policy, on the one hand interest rates, or on the other hand the size of the stock of money. In the form of an equation-system carefully based on theoretical considerations, he constructs a model of the governance of the United Kingdom national real income by the variable through which either form of monetary policy would have to work. The parameters of the equations are determined, and their stability tested, by econometric analysis of the statistical record of recent years. The result is a table of *dynamic multipliers* expressing the effects which a unit change of the Treasury Bill rate would exert on national income in the first, the second, … , the eighth quarter-years up to the eighth quarter-year after the change of interest rate; and similarly the dynamic multipliers for the effect, after the same time-lags, of a unit change in the Bank of England's portfolio of Government debt. His conclusion is somewhat in favour of interest-rates as the more reliably precise means of policy.

Mr. Arestis here shows himself a master of the theoretical field and of the statistical and computational techniques required for its quantitative study. Mr. Arestis is aware of subtle theoretical enigmas which will remain debatable, and in oral discussion he revealed a deep insight into the difficulties and hazards of his intellectually audacious and exceedingly exacting investigation. One cannot revise such a work immediately after completing it. When some time for recuperation has passed, he may feel able to make some concessions, in early chapters, to the ordinary reader's need for guidance, in order that a published version may have a market worthy of its quality.

G.L.S. Shackle

G.L.S. Shackle
20th June 1976

216

University of Surrey
Department of Economics
Guildford
Surrey GU5 0XH
27th December 1976

Dear Professor Shackle,

I was so very happy to receive your letter of 20 December. It is difficult to find words which could adequately express how deeply moved I was when reading your exceedingly kind remarks which I fear I scarcely deserve. Whatever I may have done or achieved is so minute and unimportant in comparison to your own accomplishments that I cannot help feeling terribly humble and inadequate. It is indeed a great honour to be counted among your friends and there is nothing that could give me greater happiness.

I cannot thank you enough for your immediate response to the request from Reading University, knowing how extremely short of time you are. One of my colleagues from the Department of Linguistic and International Studies recently gave a guest lecture at the University of Aston in Birmingham and I understand that this University is also interested in my application, although references have not so far been taken up. From Birmingham University there has been no response until now except a formal acknowledgment of the receipt of my application.

The enclosed offprint[1] may be of interest to you. Philip Arestis and I have extended the analysis to four OECD countries and we hope that this paper will in due course be accepted by the quarterly journal *Public Finance* for publication in 1977 or 1978.[2]

With all warmest good wishes to you and your family for much happiness and the best of health during the coming year,

Yours sincerely,

Stephen Frowen

1 S.F. Frowen, and P., Arestis, 'The Dynamic Impacts of Government Expenditure and the Monetary Base on Aggregate Income: The West German Case, 1965 to 1974', *Kredit und Kapital*, vol. 9, no. 3, 1976, pp. 368–83.
2 The actual publication details of this paper are as follows: P. Arestis, S.F. Frowen, and E., Karakitsos, 'The Dynamic Impacts of Government Expenditure and the Monetary Base on Aggregate Income: The Case of Four OECD Countries, 1965–74', *Public Finance*, vol. 33, nos 1–2, 1978, pp. 1–22.

217

Rudloe
Alde House Drive
Aldeburgh
Suffolk
19th January 1979

My dear Frowen,

The date that I am obliged to put on this letter makes me most grievously conscience-stricken. The past twelve months have been an exhausting, sad and baffling time for me. Susan[1] died on 10th April after a fortnight which caused me heart-breaking grief. She had until then seemed comparatively content and still interested in things. But then she began to give up, wanted to go back to her parental home, (of course, it was given up 30 years ago) and she seemed frightened and despairing. She had a stroke on 1st April and was said to be going to die that night. My daughter and I sat up with her all night. She made a recovery, and one day in the week that followed I actually made her laugh. Saturday, 8th April was a day of dreadful sadness, her last conscious day.

The months that followed were a nightmare. The doctor, whom everyone here rightly regards as a saint from heaven, came to see me many, many times, sometimes in the evening spending as much as an hour with me. He came each week for many weeks, until there befell the most terrible blow, he had a stroke himself. He has made a marvellous recovery, can walk, goes to London by himself, but cannot speak except a little. This was for me a crushing disaster.

In recent months, I have found a source of serenity and hope which has again given my life some sense of purpose. All this turmoil has left me, however, rather drained of strength for the ordinary obligations of life, especially at Christmas. I hope you will forgive my long delay in answering your exceedingly kind letter. I should love to hear about your Professorship at Würzburg University and your lectures. It would be splendid if we could meet some day. I will not ask you to come to Aldeburgh as my home is ill-organised for receiving visitors at present. I am due to be away from home until later in the Spring, but I would like to write to you when I am back, and perhaps we could meet in London. I have been working at one or two things and am much behindhand in replying to correspondents.

With all warmest gratitude for your letter and kindest regards,

Yours sincerely,

George Shackle

George Shackle

1 First wife of G.L.S. Shackle and mother of his four children.

218
Mulberry Croft
Littleford Lane
Shamley Green
Guildford, Surrey
14th June 1979

Dear Professor Shackle,

When I received your last letter I intended to reply immediately, but it was a difficult letter to write during the turmoil of term-time activities. I was so very distressed and sad to hear of the passing away of your wife and in particular of the extreme suffering her extended illness has caused both of you. But I think the fact that you could be close to your wife and spend so much time with her must have been a tremendous help in her agony. One cannot be grateful enough that you have had in fact the physical and emotional strength to cope with this exceedingly difficult situation for so long. I only hope that during the past few months you have had a chance of recovering from this ordeal, the magnitude of which would be impossible for an outsider even to imagine. I do hope that your health is now very much better than when I saw you last.

A few weeks ago, on election night, Christopher Saunders introduced me to Sir Eugene Melville (an old friend of his) at a Reform Club reception. As you know he lives in Aldeburgh not far from you and apparently knows you. I was delighted to hear from him (and I do hope so very much that this information is correct) that you did get married again a short while ago. Not knowing whether this really is true I scarcely dared to congratulate you. It would make me very happy indeed to know that you are not lonely and have in fact found renewed happiness.

If at any time you felt like coming down to Surrey I would like you to know that I would be only too happy for you to stay with us. It would in any case be so nice to see you again and perhaps to have the opportunity of meeting your wife.

We had a rather worrying time over our son Michael who has been suffering from a serious addiction problem and had to spend extensive periods in hospital. I am glad to say that he seems better now – I only hope that it will be a lasting recovery.

Tanya has just gone back to College to complete the course she interrupted when she expected our granddaughter, Carly, who will be 3 tomorrow. She is reading for a B.Ed. Degree. It is so nice to see how very happy she and her family are. She asked me to remember her to you and to send you her warmest greetings.

On the professional front not much has happened to me – apart from a few additional publications (including a book I recently edited on International Banking[1]). I am in touch with the European University Institute in Florence – in fact I did apply there for a 3-year professorial appointment. Unfortunately, my application was received too late, but I believe they are still trying to see whether I can be fitted in somehow to participate in their new research project in the banking field. I have also applied for a recently advertised Readership at the LSE. This would be a more permanent position, of course, and therefore perhaps preferable, but I don't have too much hope. The competition for this post must be tremendous and I don't know whether their need is really for somebody with a principal interest in monetary economics (this Readership was previously held by Dr Ozga).

I have actually taken the liberty of giving your name as one of my three referees (together with Christopher Saunders and Colin Robinson). I apologise for not asking you beforehand, but the application had to be in at rather short notice – I decided at the last minute to apply. However, the LSE may well decide not even to take up references for the reasons mentioned.

I suppose that you are gradually getting back to your writing, having, I hope, recovered somewhat from all you had to go through during the last few years. It would make me so happy to see your next book in print in the not too distant future.

With all warmest good wishes,

Yours sincerely,

Stephen Frowen

1 Guilford Educational Press published this volume entitled *A Framework of International Banking* in 1979.

219

Rudloe
Alde House Drive
Aldeburgh
Suffolk, IP15 5EE
19th June 1979

My dear Frowen,

It was a very great joy to me to see your handwriting on an envelope, and still more, to read your letter. There is such a wealth of news in it that I must arrange my thoughts carefully in the effort to be coherent. I, also, met Sir Eugene Melville a few weeks ago, at a concert given in our church by a most brilliant group of singers from.* Sad to say, I am not musically educated, but the large (and musically highly expert) congregation were tremendously appreciative. It is always a deep pleasure to observe a performance of consummate excellence and seemingly effortless mastery. Sir Eugene Melville gave you news of me, which is true. Last August, I began going once or twice a week to read aloud to a lady who, despite an abounding vitality, does not see quite well enough to find reading a pleasure. She used to give me supper, my visits were soon daily, and I found in her companionship a deep solace. At the end of January we were married. I have been engaged for these succeeding months in meeting a great host of her friends. Aldeburgh and the neighbourhood, across the width of Suffolk, is full of very interesting people, and I have found new vistas opening. My wife is herself musically very accomplished. She sang in the Bach Choir for very many years. During my lonely time last summer, I tried to work, but found it fruitless. I am now very well cared for and have made what I hope will be a fresh start at some writing.

I am so delighted to hear that Tanya is happy and that her family is flourishing, what a wonderful joy it must be for you to watch the new generation developing. It also interests me extremely to hear of Tanya's course for B.Ed. I am sure she has every prospect of brilliant success. It is wonderful, and amazing, to be able to combine family life and scholarly life. For a man it is possible but the demands it must make on a mother seem superhuman.

It is your own achievements and plans which, after all, are for me the central focus in your letter, and I am eager to hear good news of them. I need not assure you of my intense wish for your further success and that I shall of course do everything I can to promote it. I must confess, though, that I have a feeling that my efforts on behalf of candidates for appointment are of little help to them, or even a disadvantage, The trouble seems to be that I am regarded (rightly, of course) as a propounder of heterodox and 'heretical' ideas, which are at odds with the mainstream of our subject. Despite the account I can so enthusiastically give of your unsurpassable dedication as a teacher, your brilliant success as editor of *The Bankers' Magazine*, your regular lecturing engagements in Europe and Africa, and your extremely impressive insight and knowledge of economic, especially monetary affairs, which I realise must have deeply impressed Sir Ralph Hawtrey, it does not seem that I can get people to understand that in you they have a man of vast experience, utter devotion to the profession, and gifted with every qualification. Believe me, I have stated, urged and developed this theme to the utmost. I am almost fearful of being an item on the debit side of your account.

I wonder whether you have seen the obituary written by Bob Black (Professor R.D.G. Black of Queen's University, Belfast) of Sir Ralph Hawtrey. It pays a touching tribute to his extraordinary and beautiful gentleness and warmth, as well, of course, as to his high scholarship and splendid career. I am enclosing it.

I am increasingly out of touch with what goes on in our profession. I have always disliked committee meetings (they seem designed for the delectation of those whose joy is administration), and so I hear no news and have quite dropped out of things.

Do let me know how things go, be assured I am at all times delighted and eager to help in any way, and wishful to the utmost degree for your success.

With kindest regards,

Yours sincerely,

G.L.S. Shackle

G.L.S. Shackle

* I cannot find the programme of these concerts.

220

2 Alde House
Aldeburgh
Suffolk
10th October 1979

My dear Frowen,

Catherine[1] and I are very happy with the change of date for our visit to 30 October, and we look forward to it very much. We both send you our very best wishes.

Yours sincerely,

G.L.S. Shackle

G L S Shackle

1 Catherine is G.L.S. Shackle's second wife.

221

Mulberry Croft
Littleford Lane
Shamley Green
Guildford, Surrey
16th October 1979

Dear Professor Shackle,

Thank you so much for agreeing to the change of date which will be of great help to the other speaker, Professor Pickering. A copy of our full research programme is enclosed, as it may be of interest to you.

I was so very delighted to meet you both [George Shackle and his second wife Catherine] at the money study group conference in Oxford. Nothing could have given me greater happiness than to see you both looking so happy and to be in your company. It is a long time since we had the opportunity of spending time together, and I am really glad to know that we shall soon meet again.

I am enclosing some of the photographs I took in Oxford which I hope you will like. Unfortunately, on the photograph taken by Tony Courakis of both of us, only part of your jacket is visible! We must have another photograph taken when you come to Guildford.

Personally, I had a rather unhappy time recently as my application for promotion to Senior Lecturer was rejected .... This treatment after 12 years at the University (having joined at the top of the lecturer's scale where I have been ever since) I find deplorable.[1] I am trying to get away from Surrey University, of course, but it is not too easy as a result of all the financial cuts universities suffer from. I am just now exploring the possibilities of transferring to another department (Department of Linguistic and International Studies) at this University. Attempts are being made by this Department – where I have many friends – to raise funds in Germany for a Personal Chair or at least a Readership. If this does not materialise, I shall apply for a year's sabbatical leave, which I would try to spend in America.[2]

With all warmest good wishes to both of you and greatly looking forward to 30th October,

Yours sincerely,

Stephen Frowen

P.S. I shall be waiting for you at the *main* exit at Guildford Station at 3p.m. (or 3.30 if you should miss the earlier train).

1 It seems likely though that in the case of this promotion Surrey University preferred a member of staff with special interests in administration and committee work.
2 Stephen Frowen was subsequently promoted to a Senior Lectureship at Surrey University, but left the University in 1987 for a Chair at Frankfurt University to be followed by the Bundesbank Chair at the Free University of Berlin.

222

Mulberry Croft
Littleford Lane
Shamley Green
Guildford
Surrey GU5 0RH
31 October 1979

Dear George and Catherine,

I would like you to know how extremely happy I was that your visit to Guildford did materialise yesterday afternoon. It was lovely to have had a chance of seeing you both again.

The paper George presented was simply splendid. Most economists nowadays seem to be quite incapable of doing what you, George, have done, that is getting down to simple but essential and crucial issues and discussing the basic principles economics is really about. The way you showed the evolution of thought in economics can only be described as masterly. Not for a long time have I enjoyed a lecture as much as yours. I have reason to believe that this was the general feeling among all those present.

You know how much I would like to publish your paper in our series *Surrey Papers in Economics*, perhaps even with some of your answers during the discussion being included. Please let me know if you feel that this can be arranged. I am returning the carbon copy of your paper which you kindly allowed me to photocopy.

I am only sorry that after your long and strenuous journey to Guildford, there was no time left after your lecture to stay for dinner. You must have felt absolutely exhausted and starved by the time you got back to Aldeburgh!

I do hope that it will not be long before we meet again. Meanwhile I would like to thank you both most warmly for the joy you have given to so many.

With all warmest good wishes,

Yours sincerely,

Stephen

Stephen

P.S. We do have quite a generous fund to cover travelling expenses for external speakers. Please do let me know your total expenses.

A copy of the recording of the lecture should be ready by Tuesday, and I shall send it to you immediately. It can be listened to on any cassette player.

223

University of Surrey
Guildford
Surrey, GU2 5XH
26th June 1980

Dear George,

As promised I am sending you a copy of a review by Ian Steedman of your book entitled *Imagination and the Nature of Choice*, which appeared in the March

1980 issue of *The Manchester School*. I do hope that economists will take note of the last paragraph of this review!

The same issue also contained a review by Steedman of Hicks's *Causality in Economics*, which may also be of interest to you (copy enclosed).

I shall always remember, with gratitude, the discussion we had in your study on Sunday morning. Time passed far too quickly, as far as I was concerned. I do hope that we shall soon be able to meet again. The weekend with you and Catherine meant so much to both of us.[1] How shall we ever be able to reciprocate your most generous hospitality?

With all my warmest and best wishes,

Yours ever,

Stephen

Stephen

1 It was a visit by Stephen Frowen and his wife Irina to Catherine and George Shackle.

224

2 Alde House
Aldeburgh
Suffolk
8th July 1980

Dear Stephen,

It was extremely kind of you to send me xerox copies of the two reviews. The two books, Hicks's and mine, were both reviewed by Professor Ian Steedman and by Henri Guitton (the latter in a French journal in one article), and I was given Hicks's book to write a review-article on.

It was such a joy to us to have you and your wife here and our talks were delightful and stimulating.

We both send to you both our very best thoughts and wishes,

Yours sincerely,

George Shackle

George Shackle

225

2 Alde House
Aldeburgh
Suffolk
16th July 1980

Dear Stephen,

Your superb gift heaps coals of fire on my head. This wonderful volume would in any circumstances have been an overwhelming pleasure. It has everything: superlative beauty, utmost authority of editing by one of the greatest experts of any era on the history of economic thought, its intrinsic interest and the story of one of the most brilliant minds of our profession. But there are special factors which raise my enthusiasm to a tremendous glow. I am writing an article to which Jevons's opinions are vital. I was working at Queen's during those very terms when Bob Black was editing the volumes, and watched his super-secretary transcribing the letters from the actual pieces of paper on which Jevons had written with his own hand. (I was the nominal stand-in for Bob Black during his study-leave term, and by his great kindness had the occupancy of his room for the Autumn Term, 1970). My delight in this book is beyond words, thank you a thousand times. But I have also a most oppressive mistake to apologise for: In thanking you for the Reviews of INC [*Imagination and the Nature of Choice*], I referred to xerox copies. I realised later that you had sent me the pages themselves from a copy of *The Manchester School*. It is most generous indeed.

In a frightful haste, I must finish: the post goes, quarter mile off, in 5 minutes.

With every utmost thanks,

Yours sincerely,

George Shackle

George Shackle

226

Christmas Card To George Shackle

9 December 1980

Dear George,

Sorry I could not get vol. II at the Economists' Bookshop. I hope vol. III will also be of interest.

I very much hope to see you both before going to Rutgers University in February. Paul Davidson invited me to be their Visiting Professor.

With all warmest good wishes,

Stephen

227

2 Alde House
Aldeburgh
Suffolk
10th November 1982

Dear Stephen,

The idea you propounded on Thursday evening, of a conference on my efforts to make, as I would say, a theory of business as essentially an imaginative process, is for me gratifying in the extreme. To do its proper job, it should of course include a variety of potential creative critics, if there are people who would think such a task worthwhile. I think, too, that in order to be fertile, the discussion should bear on certain questions where I have most radically discarded the received notions of the purpose, style of thought, and conceptual tools of a theory of business decision. The ideas I should specially like critics to regard as the essence of my scheme are these:

1 The right word is not uncertainty but *unknowledge*. We know a little about the texture of the material, but nothing about how history will cut the garment.

2 Knowledge of the texture can perhaps tell us what can be made to seem possible by specified use of specified resources, on condition of exposing us to what misfortune. The right question for the enterprise-investor to ask is: *At best*, and *at worst*, what *can* the sequel be if I do this, or this?

3 If, in the elemental sense, history is made by human decisions (that is to say, if a decision can be in some respects an uncaused cause) the sequels of specified action will be in principle (and not merely in practice) *unlistable*.

4 If so, the claim of any hypothetical sequel to be taken seriously, its *epistemic standing*, cannot be appropriately expressed as a *share of certainty*, for this share will be affected by the number of rival hypotheses, which number (we are

assuming) can increase without limit. We therefore cannot say that any given list of them is complete, nor that it is completeable. Instead, my scheme requires imagined sequels to be judged possible or not-possible. Then by taking *disbelief* instead of belief, as the expression of epistemic standing, we express perfect (subjective) possibility as *zero disbelief*. This is a non-distributive variable and enables the highest level of epistemic standing to be assigned to each of an unlimited number of hypotheses.

5 *Disbelief* can be given an emotional interpretation (a meaning in terms of feeling, so as to be deemed capable of different intensities) and thus made quantifiable, by identifying it with potential surprise. If we wish, we can then refine in some sense the notion of 'best' and 'worst' imagined sequels amongst those deemed *possible*, by referring instead to the best and worst *not too difficult* to envisage as coming true.

* * *

A remarkable thing that I should tell you of, is that on the last morning of our stay in Brasenose, the same day we came to you, Tony Courakis made a suggestion of trying to have a small conference (of six or seven people only) on my ideas at the end of the Spring Term just before he starts a sabbatical year. Your suggestion and his thus arose simultaneously. I do not know how the two suggestions can be reconciled, and I wonder if you and he would wish to consult.

* * *

Please forgive my sending you this fearful tract. My real wish is to thank you for the hours of delight we spent with you, the visit to the supremely beautiful little church[1], and to the astonishing Watts Gallery in the heart of the woods.

We both send to you our warmest thoughts and wishes,

Yours sincerely,

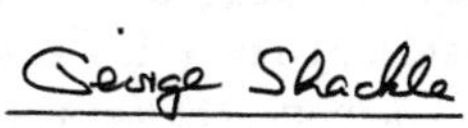

George Shackle

1 This was the Church of St Nicholas in Compton, Surrey, where Stephen Frowen's daughter Tatiana, George Shackle's goddaughter, was married.

228

Mulberry Croft
Littleford Lane
Shamley Green
Guildford
Surrey
5th December 1982

Dear George,

I hope you will forgive me for this note being very brief, but I just want to thank you for your letter of 10th November. I was delighted to receive it and greatly appreciate the immense trouble you have taken in setting out in such detail and so clearly the ideas you specifically like critics to regard as the essence of your scheme. This will be tremendously helpful in planning the programme for the proposed conference next summer.

Immediately after receipt of your letter I contacted Tony Courakis and we shall be meeting in Oxford on Monday, 20th December, for a thorough discussion of the project. I shall immediately report back to you the results of our deliberations. I understand from Tony Courakis that you would rather have younger than established colleagues present at the conference. He would be quite prepared to arrange something jointly on a larger scale at Brasenose to take place either in the spring or in September when he will interrupt his sabbatical for a one-month stay in Oxford. David Reisman is also most anxious to participate actively in whatever we decide. The possibility of *two* conferences, a smaller one at Brasenose and a larger one at Surrey, is not excluded, of course.

I shall answer your letter in greater detail as soon as I get some peace after the end of term. Meanwhile, I should like to say how much I enjoyed the days I was privileged to spend with you and Catherine at Mulberry Croft and how delighted I was to receive Catherine's sweet note which I greatly appreciated. The two enclosed photos are meant as a little souvenir of your stay in Surrey. I do hope that you will both be able to visit us again soon and hopefully at a time when Irina can be present as well. Wilfrid Blunt came for lunch the other day. He greatly enjoyed your visit and very much hopes to see you both again next time you come to Surrey.

With all warmest good wishes to Catherine and you,

Yours ever,

Stephen

Stephen

229

University of Surrey
Guildford
Surrey
7th December 1982

Dear George,

My intention to send you the enclosed book for your birthday unfortunately never materialised. May I therefore present it to you for Christmas with all my warmest thoughts and best wishes.

Yours,

Stephen

Stephen

230

2 Alde House
Aldeburgh
Suffolk
21st December 1982

My dear Stephen,

Your vigour, decisiveness and system in making this plan and setting it in motion leave me with no sufficient expressions of admiration and gratitude. You have thought of everything, and the whole prospect is something I should never have imagined. Since you phoned this morning, I have been trying to think what I can do to be of use. Of course, I must not make suggestions and I am no more than a looker-on. It may be that you would like copies of some recent (relevant) things I have written which are not yet in print, and I will collect and send them. Tell me, please, if there is anything else.

Catherine and I send to you both our utmost thanks and warmest wishes.

Yours sincerely,

George Shackle

George Shackle

231

2 Alde House
Aldeburgh
Suffolk
26th January 1983

Dear Stephen,

Catherine and I are so very often talking about you, and sending you, in thought, our utmost good wishes.

I have just heard from Jim Ford (Professor J.L. Ford, who has moved from his former Chair at Sheffield to Birmingham) that he has almost completed the revision of a book-manuscript which is to be published this summer by Martin Robertson (Oxford) with the title: *Expectations, Uncertainty and Investment. An Inquiry into G.L.S. Shackle's Theory with special reference to Portfolio Choice.* I wondered if you or Tony Courakis would be willing to invite him to one or other of your planned conferences? He was a member of my classes at Liverpool, and was the originator of the idea of giving me a Festshrift in 1972. I expect you may know him or know of his earlier book on interest-rates.

I have been working as hard as I can on two papers for the Keynes centenary, but I fear they are too heretical to earn me any credit.

Catherine and I remember our visit to Shamley Green and to Hampstead with a deep and poignant feeling of the serenity which you, in an extraordinary degree, spread over your surroundings.

We send to both of you our warmest affection and our utmost wishes for your happiness.

Yours sincerely,

George Shackle

232
2 Alde House
Aldeburgh
Suffolk
25th March 1983

Dear Stephen,

I have been trying for a long time to find words to express all that I feel of gratitude and happiness for what you are doing for me. I cannot find words to do it. Perhaps you will understand.

Instead of a letter, I am sending now the book we spoke of and two off-prints. When you and Irina come, we will all have unlimited talk, and open our hearts.

Till then, every best and warmest thought,

Yours sincerely,

George Shackle

George Shackle

233
Mulberry Croft
Littleford Lane
Shamley Green
Guildford
Surrey
20th April 1983

My dear George,

Before we meet I must thank you in writing for the most precious gift of the British Association volume *Beyond Positive Economics?* and the off-prints of your two papers on Cantillon and 'Means and Meaning in Economic Theory'. Your dedication deeply touched me and words fail me to express my deep gratitude. I have gained so much from reading your papers and I am greatly looking forward to discussing them with you. They have also been tremendously helpful in my understanding of your basic ideas, especially as expressed in your contribution to the British Association volume.[1] I also learned a considerable amount from the other two papers. What an outstanding and original thinker Cantillon was only became fully clear to me after reading your paper.

Irina and I are so very much looking forward to our weekend with you both. We shall arrive after tea in the late afternoon on Friday, 22nd April.

With all very warmest good wishes to you both,

Yours sincerely,

Stephen

P.S. The enclosed reply from Jim Ford may be of interest to you. I am so glad to have the confirmation of his participation in our conference.

I would have written earlier but we have only just returned from a delightful trip to Vienna.

1 This paper by G.L.S. Shackle, entitled 'The Bounds of Unknowledge', examines the potential of concepts of possibility. It appeared in Jack Wiseman (ed.), *Beyond Positive Economics?* Proceedings of Section F (Economics) of the British Association for the Advancement of Science, York 1981 (London: Macmillan, 1983).

234

2 Alde House
Aldeburgh
Suffolk
26th April 1983

Dear Stephen,

It was a truly thrilling time for us, electric and sizzling with ideas, brimming over with intellectual excitement, a draught of wine. We hope it was also refreshing for you and Irina, her letter this morning gave us great joy.

I now enclose a copy of the paper I wrote for Tony Courakis, which he decided to send to the *South African Journal of Economics*. This is the paper I hope either to read, or to use as the basis of a talk, at the Middlesex Polytechnic on May 18th.

I have wondered if there might be any possibility of Ludwig Lachmann's coming to the conference in September. He has been since 1935, when he and I were working under

Hayek at LSE, one of my greatest sources of encouragement. He is a brilliant and most erudite scholar, and profoundly subjectivist in conviction.

He is a very few years younger than I. It would be a deep gratification to me if he were able to come, but unless he means to be in Europe for some other reason, it seems hardly practicable. I thought I would just put up the idea to you (address on the next page).

I am *exceedingly* concerned about the exertions and work and expense of time the organising of this occasion is causing you.

Catherine and I send to you and Irene our warmest and best thoughts and wishes.

Yours sincerely,

George Shackle

George Shackle

address for Lachmann:
Professor Ludwig M. Lachmann
40 Kerry Road
Parkview
Johannesburg 2193
South Africa

235

2 Alde House
Aldeburgh
Suffolk
8th May 1983

Dear Stephen,

All the trouble you are taking is beyond anything I can say in gratitude. Of course everything concerning the September meeting is in your hands and Tony Courakis's. There is just one thing that it may be permissible for me to suggest. It seems evident from many of the letters you have received that there will not be many papers in finished form. I think therefore that the idea of publication should be abandoned. There would be great difficulty, long delay and doubtful success in endeavouring to produce a book. I should greatly prefer the conference to be simply a gathering for oral discussion. It would be highly valuable for me to hear views freely expressed and they would be far more uninhibited by word of mouth than on paper.

Catherine joins me in sending every best thought and kindest regards to you both.

Yours sincerely,

George Shackle

George Shackle

236

Mulberry Croft
Littleford Lane
Shamley Green
Guildford
Surrey
10th May 1983

Dear George,

I was thrilled and so very happy to receive your letter of 26th April and the copy of your paper on 'Levels of Simplicity in Keynes's Theory of Money and Employment' which only you could have written. It gave me a completely new insight into Keynes and his ideas – it was such an eye-opener. I do hope that we shall have a chance of discussing some of the points you raise in this paper.

Meanwhile, I have received the enclosed replies in connection with our September conference. Geoff Harcourt, too, is *very* anxious to attend. The only paper he could present would be on Keynes and his contemporaries, but the paper has already been placed for publication. I had a long session with Macmillan last Friday – they are quite anxious to publish the September conference proceedings. They also pressed me to write a book for them on international banking and gave an undertaking that the Saunders Festschrift will be published by the end of August.[1] What a struggle it was to get his book out! But I think the end-result is quite satisfactory.

We are so very much looking forward to seeing you on Tuesday.

With all my warmest good wishes and affectionate thoughts to both of you,

Yours,

Stephen

Stephen

1 See Stephen F. Frowen (ed.), *Controlling Industrial Economies. Essays in Honour of Christopher Thomas Saunders* (London: Macmillan, in association with the Vienna Institute for Comparative Economic Studies, 1983).

237

Mulberry Croft
Littleford Lane
Shamley Green
Guildford
Surrey
12th May 1983

My dear Catherine,

I was so pleased to receive the note you so kindly enclosed in George's letter and to know that you derived some joy from listening to the Britten record.

The weekend with you revived us physically and mentally to an extent I should have thought impossible in so short a period of time. We arrived at Alde House feeling rather exhausted and left your sanctuary full of energy and new ideas, which we are anxious to pursue. It was a magic weekend with not even the unexpressed wishes and desires remaining unfulfilled.

The photographs came out rather well, I think. I don't have them handy just now, but I shall give them to you on Tuesday.

We are so very much looking forward to your visit. I shall be waiting for you with joyful anticipation at Liverpool Street Station on Tuesday at 17.45.

With much love,

Stephen

Stephen

238

2 Alde House
Aldeburgh
Suffolk
25th May 1983

Dear Stephen,

First, to tell you as far as words can how immensely grateful I am to you and Irina for making my engagement at the Middlesex Polytechnic a joyous and exhilarating occasion with your wonderful companionship and your inexpressible kindness in transporting us everywhere. Thanks to this, I reached the Polytechnic with no anxiety or bother, and felt fresh, instead of weary with travelling.

I ought to have kept a note of the addresses you wished for. I have found those I think you wanted, with one or two others that I thought worth mentioning. The names that I feel most relevant are Kirzner, Rizzo and Frank Stephen. I have not been in touch with Boussard for many years, and the address I have of him (on his envelope) may be out-of-date. I do not know what the last line of it means.

Please forgive this untidy letter.

Catherine joins me in warmest and best thoughts and wishes and gratitude.

Yours ever,

George Shackle

George Shackle

239

Mulberry Croft
Littleford Lane
Shamley Green
Guildford, Surrey
31st May 1983

Dear George,

I am writing just a brief note to say that the preparations for our September conference are making satisfactory progress as you can see from the enclosed copies of letters I received from Jack Wiseman, whom I have now asked to introduce the discussion on some relevant topic, and G.C. Harcourt. I have also asked for a notice to be included in the next Newsletter of the Royal Economic Society.

I managed to get in touch with Tony Courakis and we are going to meet in Oxford next Tuesday to discuss further details. Instead of subjectivism in economics related to your theory, he appears to have a preference for 'Keynesian Economics and the Economics of George Shackle' as a title for the conference which would of course be much broader than what I had in mind.

I wish you both a really happy and restful time in Fiesole with lots of sunshine.

With all my best and warmest good wishes,

Yours,

Stephen

240
14th July 1983

TO GEORGE
BEST WISHES
AND MANY HAPPY RETURNS
OF YOUR BIRTHDAY

on this very special occasion.[1] We so much hope that the next decades will be as happy as the one you have just completed.

With all warmest good wishes for much happiness and health during the coming years and in deepest gratitude for your unending kindness,

Yours,

Stephen and Irina

1 The occasion was George Shackle's 80th birthday.

241

Mulberry Croft
Littleford Lane
Shamley Green
Guildford
Surrey
8th November 1983

My dear George,

Please forgive me for my long silence. In various ways life has been particularly hectic in recent months and time passed far too quickly.

I still regret tremendously that our Oxford conference did not materialise in the memorable year of your 80th birthday. As far as next year is concerned I have now devised the following plan to which I hope you will give your assent. The History of Economic Thought Study Group meeting will take place at Surrey University from 4th September 1984 until Friday (lunchtime), 6th September. It occurred to me that it might not be a bad idea if instead of Oxford we would hold the conference on your main theories at Surrey immediately following the History of Economic Thought meeting, that is from Friday (lunchtime), 6th September until Saturday evening, 7th September 1984. On Friday morning, Dieter Helm and David Reisman would already present papers on your work to the History of Economic Thought Conference so that for the 'Shackle Conference' there would be time for 6 papers, 2 on Friday afternoon, 2 on Saturday morning and 2 on Saturday afternoon. On Friday evening there would be a Conference Dinner in your honour.

I do hope that arrangements on these lines will meet with your approval and that the dates mentioned will be convenient to you. We would of course be delighted if you would be prepared to say a few words either during the final session on Saturday or maybe at the Conference Dinner. However, we would be quite happy for you just to attend the conference without giving any formal speeches, if you prefer. I have made a provisional booking for 40 participants for the 6th and 7th September 1984. Jack Wiseman and Stephen Littlechild will present a joint paper on 'Crusoe's Kingdom: Cost, Choice and Political Economy', and Jim Ford has also promised to give a talk. I was greatly interested to see the latter's recent book on your work published, but have not yet had a chance of reading it.[1] But I did read your delightful autobiographical article in one of the recent issues of the Banca Nazionale del Lavoro's *Quarterly Review*.[2]

With all my best and warmest good wishes,

Yours ever,

Stephen

1 This refers to J.L. Ford, *Choice, Expectation and Uncertainty: An Appraisal of G.L.S. Shackle's Theory* (Oxford: Martin Robertson, 1983).
2 See 'A Student's Pilgrimage', Banca Nazionale del Lavoro *Quarterly Review*, vol. 145, June 1983, pp. 107–16, reprinted in S.F. Frowen (ed.), *Business, Time and Thought. Selected Papers of G.L.S. Shackle*, pp. 230–9.

242

2 Alde House
Aldeburgh
Suffolk
17th November 1983

My dear Stephen,

I am intensely moved by all your kindness. Your imaginative thought and endless exertion in arranging a conference on my ideas is marvellous and generous beyond any words of mine. I shall be exceedingly happy to do whatever is required of me. I feel that I ought not to make any suggestions for the enterprise, which I must leave to those whose kindness has proposed and agreed to it. How can I thank you enough? Catherine will tell you all about our adventures and explain the pressures which seem to have built up for me.

With all best and warmest thoughts,

Yours sincerely,

George Shackle

243

Mulberry Croft,
Littleford Lane
Shamley Green,
Guildford
Surrey GU5 0RH
3rd December 1983

My dear George,

Thank you so very much for your letter of 17th November and for your kind remarks, which far exceed anything I deserve. I feel greatly relieved to know that the dates suggested for next year's conference in your honour are convenient to you and that you are in general agreement with my suggestions. Meanwhile Surrey University has confirmed the dates and all reservations have been made. I shall of course let you know the exact details of the conference programme in due course.

Last Monday we had a small presentation party for Christopher Saunders at the Reform Club when he was presented with the volume of essays in his honour (details of which I am enclosing) entitled *Controlling Industrial Economies.*[1] The whole project took nearly five years to accomplish but it was a task I gladly undertook, although I am obviously happy that it is now off my mind. I think it is quite an interesting volume and Macmillan seems to be happy with the final outcome. Mr. T.M. Farmiloe, the Editorial Director of Macmillan you know, kindly made it possible, despite his many other commitments, to attend the presentation party at the Reform and told me how much he likes your contributions to two volumes published by Macmillan during the last 2 years.[2] He regards them as the most outstanding papers in these volumes and told me how much he would like to publish a volume of your papers, which have appeared in various journals and collected works over the last few years. He really would appreciate it if you contacted him in this connection in the near future. I had to promise him to write to you about it, especially when he heard that I had already made suggestions to you on these lines. I think he may also be interested in publishing a new edition of *Mathematics at the Fireside.* If I can be of any help to you whatever in connection with the work involved in these tasks you know, I hope, that you only need to let me know.

I do hope that the pressures which have built up for you are gradually diminishing, and that you will be able to celebrate a happy and peaceful Christmas. Aldeburgh must be especially enchanting during the present sunny and crisp winter season.

With all my warmest and best wishes to you and Catherine,

Yours sincerely,

Stephen

P.S. I was very happy to receive Catherine's letter and shall be writing to her separately.

1 See Frowen, S.F. (ed.), *Controlling Industrial Economies. Essays in Honour of Christopher Thomas Saunders* (London: Macmillan, in association with the Vienna Institute for Comparative Economic Studies, 1983). G.L.S. Shackle wrote a review article of the book, published in *Kyklos*, vol. 38, no. 1, 1985, pp. 120–2, reprinted in Frowen, S.F. (ed.), *Business, Time and Thought. Selected Papers of G.L.S. Shackle*, pp. 200–3, and a review, which appeared in *Economic Modelling*, vol. 1, no. 4, October 1984, p. 440.
2 The two papers concerned are (1) 'F.A. Hayek, 1899–', in D.P. O'Brien and John R. Presley (eds), *Pioneers of Modern Economics in Britain* (1981) (pp. 234–61), and (2) 'The Bounds of Unknowledge', in Jack Wiseman (ed.), *Beyond Positive Economics?* (1983) (pp. 28–37) – both reprinted in S.F. Frowen (ed.), *Business, Time and Thought. Selected Papers of G.L.S. Shackle*, pp. 165–191 and 60–69 respectively.

244

2 Alde House
Aldeburgh
Suffolk
7th December 1983

My dear Stephen,

Your letter is an elixir of life. It compels me to try to emulate your inexhaustible zest and power of work. I realise that your plan for the conference is surging ahead. I shall get immense instruction and illumination from it, and if the proceedings are recorded, be able to absorb the critical suggestion in an efficient and relaxed study of them.

The prolonged effort which made possible the presentation to Christopher Saunders is one more example of your generosity.

I am of course exceedingly interested in your talk with Mr Farmiloe. His kind remarks about my chapters in two of his recent economics books give me a deep pleasure. Things have strangely converged and co-incided in these last weeks in the matter of collecting my articles of the last few years. Catherine and I met Mr Farmiloe at breakfast after the Keynes seminar at Canterbury on 11th November. He is extremely engaging. Catherine is urging me to consider putting together some of the pieces I have written since retirement, and I think there would be a dozen or so without overlap or repetition. I am not sure how soon such a collection could be published, since many of the articles are very recent and editors of books and journals might not give permission. But when I have had a chance to go into the possibilities I will write to Mr Farmiloe.

A year or two ago Colin Day of CUP said he would like to see a copy of *Mathematics at the Fireside* and I lent him one, but he concluded 'the world has changed too much' in the intervening years.

Our trip to Dijon from 23rd to 28th Nov. was tremendously interesting. I had to take part in what with us would have been a simple viva-voce examination for a doctorate, but which in the French system is an archaic ceremony of 'soutenance' of the thesis by the candidate. This was a thesis at a most formidable level, at the Institut de Mathematiques Economiques of Dijon University. The young lady showed an astonishing combination of modesty, aplomb and intellectual brilliance.

I am submerged in manuscripts, but Catherine is incomparably splendid in support and encouragement.

We both send you and Irina every best possible wish and kindest thoughts.

Yours sincerely,

George Shackle

245
The Reform Club
2nd January 1984

My dear Catherine and George,

What a lovely surprise to receive your most generous and beautiful Christmas gift. How could you possibly have guessed that we anxiously desired to have a copy of the exquisitely produced catalogue of this Great Japanese Exhibition, which was sold out at the time we saw the exhibition? Nothing could have given us more joy. The parcel from the Aldeburgh bookshop arrived just in time for Christmas. Many thanks from both of us for this simply splendid present.

I am so glad you liked Wilfrid Blunt's book.[1] I, too, found it compulsive reading and felt quite sad when I got to the last pages. However, Wilfrid promised to let me read the manuscript of the second and final volume of his autobiography as soon as it is completed. He does not wish it to be published during his lifetime as too many people he refers to and close relatives are still alive.[2] He is the last person, who would wish to give offence to anybody, yet he quite rightly wants to be frank. The enclosed review of his book may be of interest to you.

We had quite a difficult time before Christmas. Michael had an extremely serious relapse and almost died. He had reached a point of such despair that he did not wish to live any longer and refused all medical help. All we could do was to sit at his bedside and watch him getting weaker and weaker. At the last minute (like a miracle it seemed to us) his attitude changed and he agreed to be taken to our house in Gurney Drive so that with the help of our doctor and Dr. Max Glatt, one of the world's leading psychiatrists specialising in alcoholism who happens to live near us, we managed to get him back on his feet. After many years of inactivity he will now go back to his old job with a computing company — hopefully next week.

Did I mention to you before that my chow-chow Leonard died in a tragic car accident in September? A young RAF sergeant speeding late at night caused the accident. I was quite heartbroken, as you can imagine. He had been my constant companion for over 13 years and it still seems strange not to have him around me any longer.

I hope 1984 will be another really happy year for you both full of exciting and fulfilling tasks and events. How nice it would be to see you again early in the New Year. Please let us know next time you will be in London.

We went to see the magnificent Venice exhibition last week and took the opportunity of becoming Friends of the Royal Academy — partly to meet you both at Private Views!

Last but not least let me thank you most warmly for your lovely Christmas cards. The one with the photograph of George — indeed a picture of contentment — is standing on my desk, while the Russian one sent with the book was immediately 'confiscated' by Irina.

With all our warmest good wishes and lots of love,

Stephen

Stephen

1 This was the first volume of Wilfrid Blunt's autobiography *Married to a Single Life*, published in 1983.
2 The second volume of Wilfrid Blunt's autobiography did in the end appear during his lifetime in 1986 under the title *Slow on the Feather. Further Autobiography 1938–1959*, also published by Michael Russell (Publishing) Ltd., Wilton, Salisbury, Wiltshire.

246

2 Alde House
Aldeburgh
Suffolk
13th February 1984

Dear Stephen,

Your expression of delight in the catalogue of the Japanese Exhibition was a very great kindness to me. Catherine and I saw it the moment we entered the bookshop, and we felt that this was a piece of inspired good luck. I deeply wished that it might please you, and it is the utmost happiness to me to know that it did.

I hope that nowadays a lighter load of teaching gives you the feeling that time spent resting and listening to music is a vital ingredient in intellectual production, and that you can enjoy such highly productive relaxation without feeling the need to be 'visibly' doing something. It is not an easy thing to convince oneself of. I am thankful to say that we are not planning to go anywhere, except to see some of our relations the other side of the county. Later plans are comfortably vague.

One thing I have on my mind is to complete the adaptation of a lecture which you published in *Woolwich Economic Papers*, and which Philip Arestis very kindly (but not at my suggestion) wishes to re-print in *Thames Papers*. I have written a new introductory section, which I sent him last year, but commitments are pressing on me and I now again owe him more and more apologies.

Catherine and I send to you and Irina our very best and warmest thoughts and wishes.

Yours sincerely,

George Shackle

George Shackle

247

Mulberry Croft
Littleford Lane
Shamley Green
Guildford
Surrey
12th March 1984

My dear George,

I was so very happy to receive Catherine's letter and your letter the other day. I was getting rather worried not having heard from you for so long. It was a real relief to hear that you are both well and as active as ever.

I immediately told Philip Arestis that you are in the process of revising your *Woolwich Economic Paper*, which made him very happy indeed. I suppose you will mention that it was first published in my series *Woolwich Economic Papers*.[1]

You will be pleased to hear that the preparation for the conference planned for so long is now going ahead at full speed. I am enclosing a copy of the preliminary programme. I am still waiting for Paul Davidson's topic. To Mark Perlman I suggested giving a shortish talk at the Conference Dinner on Friday evening, 7th September, rather than a formal evening lecture. This would leave more time for an informal gathering after the Conference Dinner.

As soon as I have a chance I should appreciate the opportunity of discussing with you the topic of my own contribution. I still have to clarify my thoughts on this subject (Interest Rates and the Theory of Business). There would still be time, of course, to change the title if this seemed advisable. I am anxious to concentrate on your major contributions to the theory of business, yet I must try to avoid any possible overlap with the other papers.[2]

Irina and I will be going to Germany and Switzerland on 23rd March and we shall be back immediately after Easter. It would be nice, of course, if there were an opportunity of seeing you either in London or in Aldeburgh sometime in May. As members of the Friends of the Royal Academy (we joined a short while ago) we shall be going to the Private View on 17th May. Perhaps we could join up on this occasion. We should be only too happy if you could then stay with us overnight.

During the conference period in September you will, I hope, both be staying with us at Mulberry Croft. I am most impatiently looking forward to this exciting event.

With all my warmest good wishes to both of you, in haste,

Yours ever,

Stephen

Stephen

1 G.L.S. Shackle's two *Woolwich Economic Papers* — 'General thought-schemes and the economist' (no. 2, March 1963) and 'On the nature of profit' (no. 13, July 1967) — subsequently appeared as reprints in the Thames Polytechnic series. 'On the nature of profit' was also reprinted in S.F. Frowen (ed.), *Business, Time and Thought. Selected Papers of G.L.S. Shackle,* pp. 104—23.
2 Stephen Frowen's contribution to the conference in honour of G.L.S. Shackle was a paper on 'Interest Rates and Investment Decisions'. See Stephen F. Frowen (ed.), *Unknowledge and Choice in Economics,* pp. 156—67.

248

2 Alde House
Aldeburgh
Suffolk
16th March 1984

My dear Stephen,

To have brought the conference preparations to such a pitch of completeness, in face of endless difficulties and frustrations, is heroic in the strict meaning of the word, and shows the work of a man of iron as well as of most perfect grace, that I have known you to be since Leeds thirty years ago.

The programme is triumphant in its variety and the promised presence of loyal and splendid friends. Mark Perlman is a man of immense moral weight and worth, a deeply learned scholar in a field far removed from economics, that of religious tradition. Like you, he is a rock-like figure unmoved by vicissitudes. I am most deeply touched that Paul Davidson is coming, I have long admired his bold resourceful work, but I only met him for the first time at Cambridge last July. I am most delighted and excited at the prospect of hearing from Stephen Littlechild and Jack Wiseman about their long-maturing text-book. Your own chosen subject is of course the absolutely right one. There can be to-day very few people who can speak with your authority on international banking.

Catherine and I look forward with delight to meeting you and Irina in May at about the time of the Summer Exhibition private view. Catherine wonders if we might even ask to stay two nights with you on that occasion? It would enable us to consult about

September, to hear of your visit to Germany and Switzerland, and perhaps to hear about Rainer Maria Rilke.

We both send to both of you utmost good wishes and kindest regards.

Yours ever,

George Shackle

George Shackle

249
University of Surrey
Guildford
Surrey
27th April 1984

My dear George,

We only returned from our Continental trip late last night but I did rush to the University this morning to attend to any mail.

In connection with our September conference, the enclosed letters may be of interest to you. I am so very happy to know that Mark Perlman, Ludwig Lachmann and Paul Davidson will all be contributing papers. I am not sure yet how to respond to Kregel whose work was highly praised to me by Paul Davidson in his last letter. What would you suggest?

Irina and I are enormously looking forward to seeing you and Catherine next month and for you to stay with us for two nights. Please let me know the time of your arrival at Liverpool Street Station so that I can meet your train.

With all warmest good wishes to both of you,

Yours ever,

Stephen

Stephen

250

2 Alde House
Aldeburgh
Suffolk
28th April 1984

My dear Stephen,

Your energy is limitless. It is exceedingly good of you to take up the threads the moment you are home. I am so happy that Lachmann will send even a brief paper. Mark Perlman's presence will be a joy to me. It is extremely interesting to hear of Paul Davidson having 'several papers nearing completion'. I wonder if this is a book? We should not wish to encroach on such a book, but it occurs to me that if he were to give a paper on 7th–8th September which is a key chapter in his book, it would be possible for it to appear there *and* in the proceedings of your conference, by agreement between the publishers?

I am delighted by Kregel's letter. It would be splendid if we could fit him in?

Catherine and I are joyfully looking forward to seeing you and Irina on Thursday 17th May, and to hearing about the book on Rilke. We are most eager indeed to hear about your lecture tour. Your zest and stamina are beyond my understanding, such a circuit would kill me.

We both send to you both all the best wishes that can be thought of.

Yours sincerely,

George Shackle

251

Mulberry Croft
Littleford Lane
Shamley Green
Guildford
Surrey, GU5 0RH
23rd May 1984

My dear George,

It was tremendously joyful and stimulating talking to you during your stay in London and you left me full of new ideas and a far deeper insight and understanding of some of the problems I have been tackling recently. I really do look forward to the continuation of our talks next time we meet in Aldeburgh. While talking to you I never noticed how quickly time was passing. Time just seemed to fly.

As promised I am sending you a revised and expanded list of your papers published since 1969. There are only a few items left on this list where more precise information may be desirable. Could you also let me know if there are any papers on this list which you may not like to be included in the volume of your collected essays. In which order would you place the papers?

With all warmest good wishes,

Yours,

Stephen

252

2 Alde House
Aldeburgh
Suffolk
4th June 1984

My dear Stephen,

I am sorry it has taken me so long to prepare the list, which I enclose, of articles of mine that seem to me the possible contents of a book. The sequence in which I have listed them is carefully considered. It begins with a piece which I wrote at Ceriani's repeated request for the Banca Nazionale del Lavoro. This is a sort of brief statement of faith. The next is a 'public lecture' given at York in March 1980 at Jack Wiseman's suggestion, made possible by a touching kindness on the part of Berrick Saul the Vice-Chancellor who was formerly my colleague at Liverpool. He took the chair at this lecture, himself. Then there is a lecture which *you* published for me in *Woolwich Economic Papers* (The Finlay Lecture at University College Dublin). Next the annual lecture (1982) of the Scottish Economic Society, which ends with a highly provocative section called 'The Unquiet Market'. These four make up a first section on my own ideas.

A sharp break is provided by a piece written for the Bellagio conference (early 1970s) on the Marginal Revolution.

After this, in historic sequence, there is Cantillon, Keynes (3 pieces), Hicks (2 pieces) and a survey of 1926–1939.

* * *

In this project (yours and Catherine's) there seem to me to be many doubts and questions:

1. The book would be very short, say 160 pages.
2. Permissions will be required from all editors or publishers, though some copyrights are mine.
3. I would write a preface, to make my peace with a few to whom I may have appeared rebarbative. But this might seem to make matters worse.

I have assembled (after despairing searches) a complete set of off-prints, or in two cases, typescripts for pieces not yet known to be in print. I think there is no possibility of publication by September. It will take weeks to get replies from editors and publishers. Some may refuse, or require delay. Please forgive these hesitations.

Catherine and I are looking forward most warmly to seeing you and Irina at the end of the month.

With kindest regards,

Yours sincerely,

George Shackle

George Shackle

253
Mulberry Croft
Littleford Lane
Shamley Green
Guildford, Surrey
20th June 1984

My dear George,

Thank you so very much for your letter of 4th June and the enclosed list of articles to be included in your volume of collected essays. I am in touch with Macmillan and hope to see Mr. Farmiloe before we meet at Alde House. I am sorry to have put you to so much trouble, but I do think that the papers you have selected will make a most fascinating volume. I am really happy to know that this exciting project can now go ahead.

Today I discovered the enclosed review by John Hey just published in the June issue of the *Scottish Journal of Political Economy*. I have not had a chance yet of reading it, but I do like the title 'Unshackling Economics'!

You may have received a copy of *Controlling Industrial Economies*, the volume of essays in honour of Christopher Saunders I recently edited. In this connection I wonder whether I may express a great wish. Would you be prepared to review the book for a new journal entitled *Economic Modelling*, edited (and founded) by Homa Motamen of Imperial College (a former colleague of mine at Surrey University) who also contributed a chapter to the book. If you could write a short review by the end of July, it would be included in the October issue of *Economic Modelling* (no. 3).

I scarcely dared to ask you to do this, knowing of your eyesight problem and knowing how overworked you are already. If you could do it by glancing through the book, perhaps looking more closely at just one or two papers (without of course reading the whole book) I should be really happy. Two or three hand-written pages would be quite sufficient which I could type myself and send to Homa Motamen to save you as much time and trouble as possible. But please do not hesitate to say no if you feel that you would rather not do it. I will understand.

Unfortunately, Paul Davidson's son has decided to get married at the beginning of September so that he had to cancel his European trip. This late cancellation of a major speaker causes certain problems, of course, but I shall try to get Geoffrey Harcourt or M. Beaugrand as a replacement. In case of need David Reisman would also be willing to fill the gap. By chance I had today a letter from Joseph Labia of the University of Johannesburg (who is unknown to me) offering to give a paper. Do you know him or of his work by any chance?

There is so much to talk about and I am impatiently looking forward to seeing you both again next week.

With my very best and warmest wishes to Catherine and yourself and with kindest regards,

Yours sincerely,

Stephen

Stephen

254

5th July 1984

My dear Catherine and George

How can we ever thank you adequately for your unbelievingly generous hospitality. No wish of ours remained unfulfilled however strenuous for you. We arrived in a state of utter exhaustion and left revitalised and full of high spirits on Friday morning. And we do like your house rule of going to bed early although we did not always succeed, but even then I was still early by our London standards. But I am sure that you must have felt extremely tired after our departure. I am so glad to know that in September we should have a chance of spoiling you, although we can never hope to reach your peaks of perfect hospitality.

Incidentally, the journey to Guildford from Aldeburgh took only just over 3 hours so that I could not have been more punctual for our examiners' meeting.

At the University, I immediately photocopied George's last paper for his collection (from *Modern Economic Thought*) and sent the complete set of papers to Macmillan. I spoke to Mr. Farmiloe today and a positive and formal reply should reach me early next week. I shall then immediately contact you.

With much love and all warmest good wishes from both of us,

Yours,

Stephen

255

University of Surrey
Guidford
Surrey
12th July 1984

My dear George,

I was delighted to receive the enclosed reply from Mr Farmiloe this morning (the letter is dated 6th July but was not in fact posted until 11th July!). He certainly seems keen for both volumes to be published by Macmillan. I shall let you know as soon as I hear from Mr. Farmiloe again in this matter.

Geoff Harcourt has kindly suggested one of his younger colleagues to take Paul Davidson's place at our September conference. His name is Omar Hamouda. I understand he has written a book on Hicks and is thoroughly familiar with your work. I am waiting to receive the title of his paper for inclusion in our conference programme.

With all best wishes and kindest regards to you and Catherine, in haste,

Yours sincerely,

Stephen

Stephen

256

University of Surrey
Guildford
Surrey
25th July 1984

My dear George,

I wonder whether I may possibly trouble you in connection with the enclosed draft questionnaire I am intending to send to a number of selected companies. It is in connection with the paper I am working on for the September conference. Do you think some of the questions should be amended or further questions added? The ultimate aim is to test some of your theories of the effect of interest rate changes on investment.

I have not heard from you for some time and assume that you must still be in Spain.

Warmest wishes to you and Catherine,

Yours,

Stephen

Stephen

257

2 Alde House
Aldeburgh
Suffolk
30th July 1984

My dear Stephen,

It has been a joy to me to write this review. Thank you most warmly for giving me this splendid book, and thank you more than I can say for what you wrote in it.

Catherine and I send to both of you our warmest and best thoughts.

Yours sincerely,

George Shackle

George Shackle

258

Hotel Bewallerhof
Bewaller
Eggen – Ega
Italy
8th August 1984

My dear George,

How shall I ever be able to thank you adequately for your absolutely splendid review of *Controlling Industrial Economies*[1], which only you could have written? It is itself full of the most interesting and inspiring thoughts and ideas and I do hope that your comments, concentrating on the essence of the problems involved, will be a guide to others in any further research. I am sure that the editor of *Kyklos* will be delighted to get your article for publication in his journal, which I think is an ideal outlet for your paper. *Kyklos* is truly international (with a circulation of 3500) and a journal read by many prospective readers of *Controlling Industrial Economies*. I have asked the Editor to send the galley proofs direct to you. If accepted, there is a chance that the article will still appear this year (no. 4).[2]

Your kindness in writing a short review for *Economic Modelling* as well surpasses anything I dared to hope. I am impatiently looking forward to reading it (my secretary has promised to send me a copy immediately).[3]

In the Dolomites I am gradually recovering from all the strain I was subjected to before leaving London. On my International Banking Summer Course I had forty participants (for a fortnight!), double the usual number, and being burdened with the sole responsibility as Academic Director, it really was a strain greater than I anticipated.

Please do let me know in due course when you will be arriving at Liverpool Street Station early September so that I can meet your train and drive you to Guildford. Would it be all right if I would take you back to London on Sunday, 9th September? Unfortunately, I have to fly to Belgium later on Sunday for a talk I have to give at Namur University on Monday afternoon. You are of course more than welcome to stay on at Mulberry Croft if you wished – I shall be back from Namur late on Wednesday, 12th September.

In deepest gratitude and with warmest wishes from both of us to you and Catherine,

Yours sincerely,

Stephen

1 Stephen F. Frowen (ed.), *Controlling Industrial Economies. Essays in Honour of Christopher Thomas Saunders* (London: Macmillan, in association with the Vienna Institute for Comparative Economic Studies, 1983).
2 The review article by G.L.S. Shackle appeared in *Kyklos*, vol. 38, no. 1, 1985, pp. 120–2.
3 This review appeared in *Economic Modelling*, vol. 1, no. 4, October 1984, p. 440.

259
Bolzano, 20th August 1984

My dear George,

I was overjoyed to receive a copy of your excellent review of *Controlling Industrial Economies* for *Economic Modelling* from my secretary this morning. I am convinced that the Editor, Homa Motamen, and the contributors to the volume will be equally delighted. I have no doubt that your comments will raise considerable interest in Christopher's Festschrift. He will certainly wish to thank you himself for all you have done.

We shall be leaving Italy on 23rd August to spend a few days in Germany and will be back in London on 30th August.

I am tremendously looking forward to our reunion at the beginning of September.

With all our best wishes to you and Catherine,

Yours sincerely,

Stephen

Stephen

260

2 Alde House
Aldeburgh
Suffolk
6th October 1984

My dear Stephen,

Catherine's letter to you, I am sure, will have brought to you the glow of admiration and gratitude for you that fills our thoughts of your wonderful organising vision, energy, charismatic persuasiveness which made the G.S. Conference so encompassing a success. Though I did nothing but sit and listen, I found myself fine-drawn and emotionally *épuisé* at the end of it.

Such an experience must deeply affect one. It seems to turn a page, and close a chapter. If it gave to you even a small part of the feeling of triumph you deserved, I think you must have been pleased. Catherine is never tired of uttering your praises. I hope that publication of the proceedings will not be too tiresome and time-consuming.

I know that you had no pause for breath after so generously delivering us to the train, before setting off on another conference trip. I hope this also was in every way gratifying.

We are to be in Spain, if all goes well, from 13th to 27th October. Catherine is full of zest; if I come through without dismay it will be thanks to her.

With every grateful thought and kindest regards,

Yours sincerely,

George Shackle

George Shackle

261
University of Surrey
Guildford
Surrey
29th October 1984

Dear George,

I have just received the enclosed proof of the review of *Controlling Industrial Economies* you have so kindly written for *Economic Modelling*. I have already returned one of the corrected proofs to the printer in Guildford so that you only need to return your enclosed copy to the printer if you should discover any further errors or wish to make any amendments.

Mark Perlman has been exceedingly kind in sending me a set of superb photographs (particularly of you) taken at the conference. You will probably have received the same, but if this should not be so, please let me know. I shall then pass some of my prints on to you and Catherine.

Every journey is a strain and I guess that you both feel rather tired after your lecture tour to Spain. However, I hope that it was an exhilarating and joyful experience. You will probably be extremely busy now trying to catch up with your correspondence!

With my warmest regards to you and Catherine,

Yours sincerely,

Stephen

262
University of Surrey
Guildford
Surrey
19th November 1984

My dear George,

I am enclosing the revised copy of your delightful, informative and much appreciated Conference Speech. Please feel entirely free to make any further amendments you think appropriate. The text is on our word processor and it takes my secretary just a few minutes to amend the text according to your instructions.

I was so very happy to talk to you the other day and to receive your letters to which I shall reply properly tomorrow.

There is some slight improvement in the condition of my son-in-law and we are now much more hopeful.

With warmest wishes – in haste –

Yours sincerely,

Stephen

263

2 Alde House
Aldeburgh
Suffolk
23rd December 1984

My dear Stephen,

I am later than I should have been in writing to you, but I hope this has not upset your plans. It is only in these last few days that I have felt that I have got on terms with my commitments and can hope to work efficiently on them.

The matter most on my conscience is my bibliography. I worked out the two sections of it, which seem to matter most, afresh about a year ago, and had them typed out in proper form. Until a few years ago I had my papers all orderly arranged and listed, but in the last five years things have accelerated so, for me, that now my papers have got out of hand and I have searched in vain for the new bibliography. I have the materials for it but I shall have to get a typescript made.

Amongst the endless things you have done for me with such immense generosity of time and effort, the new typed copy of my speech at the conference especially touches me. The speech was a pure improvisation, and had its omissions and an all too freehand flow, but there are only one or two things I want to amend, very slightly. The omissions are what matter, and in the typescript which I now return I have marked the place for a fresh passage which I attach.

The manuscript which you have just sent me by Domingo Castelo Joaquin gratifies me extremely, since it shows that here is one economist-philosopher who has been interested in my work and has become thoroughly acquainted with it. I shall write to thank him and to send him a book, but I do not think his article fits in with the conference collection. It would be more suitably published as a journal article, perhaps in *Econometrica*, but I will consult Paul Davidson, to whom I will also write, since he has been so kind as to send this article, in the midst of his sad pre-occupations.

The article by Dr. Domingo Castelo Joaquin will need considerable editing in the matter of its notation, not from any fault of his, but because he has had to use the letter 'a' as an algebraic or logical symbol without being able to distinguish it as such. I am sure no such editing or copy-preparing can be suitably done by us. My feeling is that you might perhaps explain to the author, or Paul Davidson, that the editorial process has proceeded too far for radical changes of content. I shall do all I can to ensure that Dr Joaquin does not feel that his interest is not appreciated. It is greatly appreciated by me, and I hope his work will secure publication in some journal.

I do hope your anxieties are lessening. Catherine and I constantly talk of you and your family. (You may wonder why I write the 'wrong way of the paper'. It is because I write resting the block on my knee).

With every best thought and wish,

Yours sincerely,

George Shackle

264

2 Alde House
Aldeburgh
Suffolk
29th December 1984

My dear Stephen,

The letter to which I attach this note was written before our yesterday's telephone conversation. When I have the copy of your letter to Dr Domingo Castelo Joaquin, I shall write to him on similar lines to yours. I enclose one copy of his article and the letters addressed to you by him and by Paul Davidson.

I will send my bibliography, as complete as I can make, together with the slightly amended transcript of my conference speech, to reach your Hampstead address by 14th January.

Catherine and I send to you and Irina every heartfelt best wish for a happy lecture tour in Germany and the dissolving of anxieties.

Yours sincerely,

George Shackle

265

2 Alde House
Aldeburgh
Suffolk
14th January 1985

My dear Stephen,

Except for the last-but-one paragraph, I have made only trifling changes in this text of my speech. I would like that paragraph to be replaced entirely by the passage I have written on a piece of paper attached to the page. The last paragraph of all would stand unchanged.

The bibliography has greatly troubled me. An intensive and repeated search has failed to find the carbon typescript of what I sent to Frank Stephen of Strathclyde University, which is a complete and re-organised list of *books* and of *chapters contributed to books* up to the time of our conference. The rest of my bibliography consists of reviews and short notes, of which I have complete lists properly typed. I think I must ask Frank Stephen if he would make a xerox copy of what I sent him. That would enable me to send you a complete and tidy list of everything published up to date.

We are more or less snowed up here. I do hope your lecture tour was happy and in every way satisfying, and that all is well. Catherine will, I think, try to phone you tonight.

With very best thoughts and warmest wishes,

Yours sincerely,

George Shackle

Excuse these scrappy lists of paper, I am incarcerated with a cold.

266
2 Alde House
Aldeburgh
Suffolk
4th March 1985

My dear Stephen,

We have been anxiously hoping for news of you and have tried many times by telephone to get in touch. Meanwhile Catherine has been giving me miraculous help in completing my bibliography to the utmost degree we can encompass. I cannot be quite certain that nothing has eluded me, but I am sure nothing of substance has escaped. There are several things awaiting publication: the lectures I gave respectively at Paris II, 1983, and at Madrid 1984; a foreword to a thesis to be published at Dijon in the first half of this year; an introductory chapter to one part of a volume being produced at Bordeaux; and a chapter for a Festschrift. These of course cannot yet be included in 'published work'?

The typing of the bibliography was finished on Saturday, and xerox copies were made this morning. I will send a copy to you as soon as I know where it should go.

I was delighted to have the chapters from Paul Davidson and Jim Ford. No comments of course are required from me, but I shall read them with utmost interest.

We both send to all of you our warmest and best thoughts and wishes.

Yours sincerely,

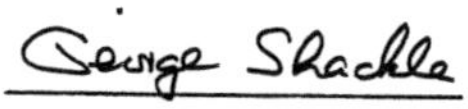

George Shackle

267
2 Alde House
Aldeburgh
Suffolk
22nd March 1985

My dear Stephen,

Your telephone call immensely relieved our minds, while leaving us with a wondering impression of the relentless difficulties you are coping with. To remain, as you do, unmoved in face of them is beyond admiration.

Catherine and I have had a week or more of the most violent influenza I ever knew, causing one's sleep to be subject to disturbance of a kind I never experienced before. We are both better, but I fear that Catherine is exhausted.

Excuse my erratic writing, it is not due to this illness but to some decline of my eyesight. It slows me up, but leaves me untroubled. The doctor is highly encouraging, though rules out an actual improvement.

The bibliography was completed many weeks ago, but I did not feel it should be sent without your instruction of address. There are just two things I would mention about it. Two of the books: *Uncertainty in Economics* (1955) and *The Nature of Economic Thought* (1966) consist of 'selected articles' which are also listed under 'articles'. I think I ought to have indicated this.

Secondly, I have just received the Italian language edition of *Years of High Theory*, called *Gli anni dell'alta teoria* (Roma: Istituto della Enciclopedia Italiana, 1984) pp. ix + 418.

I do not know whether you would wish this to be added to the typescript. There are of course other things not yet in print, so the bibliography cannot be definitive.

Catherine and I send to both of you our utmost good wishes and warmest thoughts, and our love.

Yours ever,

George Shackle

George Shackle

268

3rd April 1985

My dear Catherine and George,

I so often think of you both and hope that by now you are well on the way to a complete recovery from your nasty attack of influenza. I can imagine how much it must have weakened you and disrupted your life. How despite of it all, George managed to compile his complex bibliography seems a miracle to me. It is beautifully done – just perfect, as everything George does.

I treasure the reproductions of the drawings of you both, which Catherine so kindly sent us.[1] Nothing could have made us more happy. Our house in

London is nearing completion and we are looking forward to putting them up in a place of honour. Shall be writing in greater detail soon.

With all good wishes for Easter and much love from both of us,

Affectionately yours,

Stephen

Stephen

1 After the death of Catherine Shackle, the originals of the two drawings of George Shackle and of Catherine Shackle by Oliver Thomas were generously given to Stephen Frowen by Catherine's two nieces, Frances Ferneyhau and Hilary Law.

269

2 Alde House
Aldeburgh
Suffolk
7th July 1985

My dear Stephen,

All the thought and work you gave to the enterprise of editing a collection of my recent essays, in the midst of intense pre-occupations, was a kindness beyond words. After thorough consideration, I have left out three of the essays in your main list, and replaced them with three from your supplementary list.

It was a happiness and privilege for me to write the foreword of your translation of Wicksell's *Value, Capital and Rent*, but I am afraid of seeming to claim to be a Wicksell scholar, which I am not. I would therefore feel happier to leave this one out.

My contribution to the *Annals of the American Academy of Political and Social Science* is too similar, I think, to for example 'The Bounds of Unknowledge' and the same applies to 'Imagination, Unknowledge and Choice'.

Thus I would omit number 1, 4, and 7 in your main list.

I would replace these from your additional list with 'News from Sweden' (a tribute to Brinley Thomas), my chapter on Hayek in D.P. O'Brien's book, and 'The Bounds of Unknowledge' in Jack Wiseman's book of the proceedings of Section F of the British Association in 1981.

There is, of course, a more-than-astronomical number of sequences in which the 18 essays could be arranged. I suggest that after 'The Origination of Choice', which is meant to be a readable condensed account of my oft-repeated theme, the second item should be a sample of my kind of writing at its wildest (Section 3, 'The Unquiet Market'). The third is a long lecture (given in Madrid 1984) on Keynes, which may be expected even by those with sated palates for that subject. That lecture sprang originally from a suggestion of Lucas Beltràn, for whose Festschrift I wrote the piece on Cantillon which I would make number 4. My number 5 'The Bounds of Unknowledge' is I think the best statement of my decision-theory that I have done.

My general principle throughout the list has been to make successive essays as *different* from each other as possible. To group the essays by similarity of subject would invite anyone who picked up the book to omit whole groups.

May I now consult you about the agreement with Macmillan? It calls for 'three copies of the typescript'. Many of the essays are already in print. I have collected in a large box two copies of every off-print and everything which is at present only in typescript. Some items are chapters in bound books. Here I have put in only one. I will try to do whatever you feel to be necessary. Until I have consulted you on this, I thought it best to wait before signing the agreement.

I have sent off three letters asking for permission to reprint essays, and I will write in hand-writing to, e.g. Jack Wiseman.

Catherine and I are most anxious indeed to have your news.

With every best thought and warmest gratitude,

Yours sincerely,

George Shackle

George Shackle

Enclosed: A list still to be typed of the essays proposed to be included, in the sequence I suggest. They are numbered with your numbers as well as the straight forward numbering.

270

2 Alde House
Aldeburgh
Suffolk
15th July 1985

My dear Stephen,

Your letter gives me the utmost joy, your card for my birthday delights us both. We are most deeply thankful that you and Irina are safely back and had good news on getting to London. Your letter came this morning, and I have dwelt on it all day. However, the solution I wish to offer you to the question of the title of the collection of essays came into my head without long search. I think it in fact much better than the one Mr. Farmiloe rejects. My feeling is that, since *you* approve the present sequence of titles, and there is I think some principle running through it, it would be a pity to disturb it. If we keep it, a title for the collection as a whole should be invented on its own, not borrowing that of any essay.

My suggestion is:

Time and Thought
An Economic Skein

I think the brevity of the main title, and its reference to the core-ideas of these essays, and the 'economy' in two senses, of the subtitle, may please Mr. Farmiloe. I do hope so, for I feel that if this suggestion does not hit the target, I cannot offer anything.

I will send in a day or two typescripts of the 4 papers that are still not in your file.

[Letter continued on 6th July]

Yesterday Catherine and I studied your letter very carefully. It answers every question. I will keep my set of copies of the papers in readiness, in case any query arises.

We send to you both our warmest thoughts and wishes. I will get Catherine to add a word or two to this letter.

As ever,

George Shackle

George Shackle

We are so glad to know you are home again and found Michael better. I hope *Time and Thought* passes muster! And I always love George's use of the word 'skein'; to me it means a hank of wool or silk.

With love,

C.

C.

271

2 Alde House
Aldeburgh
Suffolk
30th July 1985

My dear Stephen,

I now send one typed copy of each of the four papers still required:

The Origination of Choice
Treatise, Theory and Time
Keynes the Meeting Point of History and Thought
News from Sweden

Except for 'News from Sweden', all are xerox copies made from original typescripts carefully checked when first typed.

'News from Sweden' was typed this morning by a professional typing agency, from xerox copies of the pages of the book where it appeared. We will get on with applying for permissions to reprint, without delay.

I also have copies which I will send to you later of the eight letters, asking for permission to reprint, which I wrote yesterday: The two others, to the editor of the *Scottish Journal* and to the editor of the *South African Journal*, will be quite straightforward since those articles were published about two years ago. That will leave only the one to Professor Rafael Rubio de Urquía concerning '*Treatise, Theory* and Time' and I will not delay long in writing it.

I am so sorry that there was confusion at this end about your telephoning, and that you were put to such trouble, but I gained extra time and was better able to cope.

Every best thought and warmest wish from us both,

Yours ever,

George Shackle

272

2 Alde House
Aldeburgh
Suffolk
2nd August 1985

My dear Stephen,

Our phone conversation just now was most perfectly satisfying and carried us a great stride forward. Your thoroughness and capacity to think of everything (an imaginative gift, in essence) are giving this enterprise its whole chance of success.

I am enclosing the 3-page brief note I wrote last night. I think it expresses my thoughts as I wanted to put them to you, starting off with the suggestion that I hope will *please* Mr. Farmiloe:

Business, Time and Thought

Mr. Farmiloe dislikes *Time and Thought* because it suggests philosophy. But these essays *are* concerned with philosophy. It is the philosophical aspect of economics that I have always been mainly interested in. My books are concerned with philosophical problems: with 'epistemics', especially with the inescapable need to decide in face of *unknowledge*. Economics is as wholly entangled with time as history itself is (see Alfred Marshall, soon to have his *Principles* celebrated (1990)).

These essays are not about cut-and-dried simplified 'models' but about the mutual forming of thought and event, linked by the middle term of action, enterprise. This has always been my slant on economics, and it is known to be. The title *Means and Meaning in Economic Theory* was given to *one* essay. For the collection as a whole it would be gimmicky and journalistic, also *narrow*. I do not understand why Mr. Farmiloe is so set on it.

I have a title which would bring the philosophical problems right into the market place: *Business, Time and Thought.*

'Business' describes our field better than economics, a word fudged up from two Greek ones. You yourself, Stephen, have spoken of the 'theory of business'. That suggests a rather detailed technical concern. I do not claim to discuss as wide and complex a field as 'that', only the business of business-decisions.

Mr. Farmiloe should not think of these essays as conventional economics. That description would elicit a roll of Homeric laughter.

G.L.S. Shackle

G.L.S. Shackle

273
2 Alde House
Aldeburgh
Suffolk
9th August 1985

My dear Stephen,

When I had put down the phone and sat thinking for a very few minutes, I had the strongest feeling that I would like again to try to carry Mr. Farmiloe with us. Since you consented to my making an approach myself, I have written a letter to Mr. Farmiloe which I have left open for you to decide whether to give it to him or not.

The word 'decide' or 'decision' belongs of course in the context of this title, but there is quite a danger of its becoming hackneyed. I feel now that the *best* would be if we can convince Mr. Farmiloe to accept *Business, Time and Thought* as right on the target.

If we cannot persuade him at present, let us wait until your return. I am so set on this title that I would rather make all efforts for it than think about others.

(I am writing this way of the paper because I can see better where I am.)

It was exceedingly kind of you to 'phone. We look forward to having you here in October for a rest and relaxed happy conversation.

With all my gratitude,

Yours as ever,

George Shackle

George Shackle

274
2 Alde House
Aldeburgh
Suffolk
9th August 1985

Dear Mr. Farmiloe,

I feel a very real hesitation in seeking to enter my own plea in the matter of the choice of title for the book of my recent essays. This book is *entirely* Stephen's enterprise and only exists through his initiative. You yourself have been at much expense of time in the matter, and we are grateful.

My excuse for intruding is that the title *Business, Time and Thought* attracts me so powerfully. I do feel that in this short phrase it expresses *exactly* what this diverse but highly consistent body of pieces has as its theme from end to end. Business is imagination and nerve, it is able to yield brilliant successes because it can also yield failures and misfortune. The essence of all this is that the business man embarks his hopes on time-to-come. No one can surpass yourself in real and exigent direct knowledge of business, and I feel that the words 'business' and 'time' are almost extensions of each other's meaning. The business of the business man is thought. Please forgive this endeavour to show reason for my faith in my suggested title.

With kindest regards,

Yours sincerely,

G.L.S. Shackle

G.L.S. Shackle

275
2 Alde House
Aldeburgh
Suffolk
20th January 1986

My dear Stephen,

I marvel unceasingly at your power of work and endless zest and drive in the enterprise of the two books that you are editing and getting into print with Macmillan.

I was delighted to have our telephone talk this morning regardless of the actual matter in hand, but I now enclose the letter from JAI Press which I took for a refusal of permission to re-print my chapter on Harrod. I did not answer the letter. If Mr. Farmiloe can get their consent, there is one sentence in my piece which has plainly gone wrong. I will correct it and sent a note to you.

Catherine and I are looking forward with the greatest happiness to see you both on 5th February.

With every best thought,

Yours sincerely,

George Shackle

George Shackle

276
The Reform Club
2nd February 1986

My dear George,

Words fail me to express fully how deeply moved I was when Philip Arestis showed me the Foreword you have written for the volume he has embarked on. It is a splendid and most interesting piece on the indeed mysterious and elusive nature of money. I only feel that I scarcely deserve your exceedingly kind remarks about myself. How will I ever be able to thank you adequately for responding immediately and in such generous manner to Philip's request? He was as thrilled as I was when he received your letter and immediately telephoned me. He will no doubt be writing to you.

Many thanks, too, for your last letter. I at once forwarded a copy of the American publisher's reply in connection with the Harrod paper to Mr. Farmiloe. I am now awaiting his answer.

Irina and I are tremendously looking forward to seeing you on Thursday at 4.30pm. It will be so nice to have enough time for talking. I only hope that we shall not cause you both too much trouble and work.

In deepest gratitude,

Yours ever,

Stephen

277
2 Alde House
Aldeburgh
Suffolk
17th February 1986

My dear Stephen,

We were overjoyed to have your letters. Your brief stay with us was a moment of brilliant happiness and warmth. We had the feeling that Irina and yourself were sitting with us round a bright hearth of ideas. There is perhaps a sort of New Renaissance in the air to-day, despite the world's disturbances, that makes scholarship a dance of the spirit. I wrote a new paragraph for the Foreword of Philip's planned Festschrift for you, to replace the one which was at fault. I enclose a copy of it. Your systematic energy got us through a remarkable amount of business, with decisions which I hope were pleasing to you. My feeling is to leave the collected essays in their present sequence, with the addition of the review article on Professor Reekie's book, if I get the consent of the Newsletter editor to reprint it, (though I have actually marked it to retain copyright). I will, as soon as I can, send a correction of a sentence in the Harrod essay which has gone wrong.

We send to you both our very best and warmest wishes.

Yours sincerely,

George Shackle

George Shackle

278

2 Alde House
Aldeburgh
Suffolk
4th March 1986

My dear Stephen,

I have this morning read with critical attention the later pages of my essay on 'Harrod as Economist' and have found the sentence which I thought had something wrong with it. Only one word is wrong: what should be 'and' has been typed, and no doubt printed, 'as'. The passage occurs in the middle of the last full page of the typescript (the printed volume is with you) and reads thus in its correct form:

'He sees those orders justified by the matching of the extra demand and [*] the extra equipment in which they have resulted' [* and, not as].

With love from both of us, as ever,

George Shackle

George Shackle

279

The Reform Club
Pall Mall
London SW1
7th March 1986

My dear George,

Please forgive me for the delay in thanking you for your letters. Life at the university has been particularly hectic in recent weeks.

I was deeply touched about the endless trouble you have taken over the Foreword for Philip's planned Festschrift. It is beautifully phrased and quite poetic – Irina, too, was most impressed. Only you, with your unique gift for perfect prose, could have written it.

Many thanks, too, for the amendment of the chapter on Harrod.

As far as the Harrod chapter is concerned, I sent a reminder to Mr. Farmiloe, as he had kindly promised to contact the JAI Press. I enclose a copy of his reply which also refers to the placing of footnotes. It seems to me that if the notes can't be footnotes it may be best for them to appear all grouped together at the end of the book. Placing them at the end of the chapter concerned would, on the other hand, have the advantage that if somebody photocopies one of the chapters only, he would also have the relevant footnotes at the end of it. Perhaps on balance it may be better to have the notes at the end of each chapter. What is your own feeling on this issue?

I suppose you are still waiting for the details of the Lachmann and Madrid volumes.

I am happy that the volume of your essays is now making rapid progress. I am anxiously looking forward to seeing it in print.

I was surprised to see that Frank Stephen has published the essays on your work as a separate volume – I thought he was planning a special issue of his Journal. I must order a copy of the book.

I was so very happy to receive Catherine's lovely letter which I shall treasure. I shall reply to it next week. Meanwhile Irina and I are sending you both our warmest wishes and kindest thoughts, with much love.

Yours, as ever,

Stephen

280

2 Alde House
Aldeburgh
Suffolk
12th March 1986

My dear Stephen,

Your letter gave us the greatest joy. Catherine has read it to me twice since we opened it this afternoon on getting home from our expedition. At Oxford Catherine read aloud my *extremely* condensed epitome of what has ensued from *Expectation in Economics* since 1949 in England, France and G.H. von Wright's Düsseldorf conference in 1978. She gave it every chance of being understood by a most beautiful delivery. The audience was minute, but included a very purposeful D.Phil. candidate nearly at the end of his thesis, and Tony Courakis himself with whom I had extremely interesting discussions both theoretical and practical.

On the question of the placing of the footnotes, I should of course follow your view, were we alone concerned. But Mr. Farmiloe has made one important concession to our views on the matter of the title, and I do not wish to trade on his good will. Sometimes the collected footnotes at the end of a book can serve as a useful commentary and 'refresher', when read consecutively, and are certainly easier to find while reading the text, if they cannot be at the foot of the pages. If he wishes them gathered at the end, I think we should accept this. You have done a most wonderful job in getting this collection organised and accepted for printing, I can never find words for my gratitude.

I am sorry for the delay in sending the particulars of the Lachmann Festschrift and the Madrid paper. I will write to Professor Rubio de Urquía to ask if he can yet give them for the volume of proceedings at Madrid. I have not yet received either.

I am surprised and delighted to hear in your letter that Frank Stephen is publishing the articles in his special issue of the *Journal of Economic Studies* as a book. I had not heard of it.

Catherine will write to you and tell you of all our adventures in Oxford and of her visit to Roger de Grey's exhibition of his recent paintings. Your letter gave both of us such deep pleasure. We send to both of you every best and warmest wish.

Yours ever,

George Shackle

George Shackle

281

2 Alde House
Aldeburgh
Suffolk
14th May 1986

My dear Stephen,

I was extremely happy that you and Catherine had a long comprehensive telephone call, of which I was able to listen to at one end. We have been sadly distracted by the entirely sudden death of Catherine's sister Jocelyn, and on Friday we are receiving Jane Lidderdale, a great friend who lives alone in London and has been seriously ill, to convalesce with us for twelve days.

I enclose a copy, described as a first draft, of Kregel's paper given at the conference. I have two copies of the 'first draft' but nothing else.

I have received a copy of the Festschrift which Israel Kirzner edited for Ludwig Lachmann's eightieth birthday. It is a handsome book with a prestigious and geographically widespread list of 24 contributors, but I think some of them must have delayed the process of publication, since the index lacks a few page references and one chapter heading has a word left out. This is a pity, for Israel Kirzner is the most thorough far-seeing and devoted editor. However, I am sure Lachmann will have been delighted. The copy I have was sent me by New York University Press, but I saw the book listed also in Macmillan's catalogue in the spring.

Catherine and I were very greatly distressed to hear of your and Irina's illness. We look forward to seeing you both in July.

With every best thought,

Yours ever,

George Shackle

282

2 Alde House
Aldeburgh
Suffolk
21st May 1986

My dear Stephen,

I am deeply moved by your exceedingly kind letter. It immensely revives my spirits in a rather bleak time. Catherine's sister was a pivot on whom so much revolved. The home at Lavenham seemed the family centre. For my part, I am very well again, except for the need to re-organise for work with difficult reading. The nature of the trouble is illustrated by the fact that if I lose the place in a laborious process, I cannot find it again. But it is a thing that can be organised away.

I am sorry to be still unable to send you details of the Spanish language version of '*Treatise, Theory* and *Time*'. Do you think the Spanish title of the volume, if I can get it would suffice? It is unlikely that readers of *Business, Time and Thought* would make use of page numbers?

Catherine has decided that I should not make the trip to London on Wednesday 28th May. I have been delighted with the hope of having lunch with you at the Reform Club but I must look forward to July, when we hope to have you here for many days while Irina is away from you.

The task of organising my papers looms ahead. Catherine has done a great deal, but we have decisions to make about methods of arrangement. At one time I had everything most *tidily* put away, but it was not arranged so that anything could easily be found. I had two large sheets of cardboard, on which a complex and cryptic index was displayed, but now we are going to have a regular filing and proper system.

Catherine is writing to you at the moment. We are both pinning all hopes on July, when we hope you will be able to rest and relax down here and that we can have marvellous discussions.

With every warmest wish, and every most grateful thought,

Yours as ever,

George Shackle

George Shackle

283

The Reform Club
Pall Mall
London SW1
16th June 1986

My dear George,

I had a most exciting time reading the entire typescript of *Business, Time and Thought*. It is sparkling with the most original, exhilarating and stimulating ideas and thoughts. I felt as elated as you as you did when attending the LSE in the 1930s! It is a splendid book and will be compulsory reading for all my future students.

I handed two copies of the edited version to Mr. Farmiloe last Friday and sent one copy to you for your information. The only pieces to follow will be the Preface attempting a true appreciation of Catherine's essential and unique part in the creation of this volume and my Introduction. Both I hope to discuss with you when we meet in July. Incidentally, the Preface to your Finlay Lecture (p. 119 of the typescript) will of course be retained (it was crossed out by mistake).

Meanwhile, Tanya had another little girl (no. 3) called Cassie.[1] Both are doing very well. We are all extremely thrilled. The sad event is that I had to take her husband Richard to the Royal Free Hospital last night with severe pain in his chest. He is now in the intensive care unit of the coronary department suffering from an inflammation of the linings of his heart. He can scarcely breathe or move. The doctors are still carrying out tests to establish whether it is caused by a virus or bacteria. This latest illness comes so soon after the virus infection of his brain. We are quite worried, of course, also about Tanya having to cope on her own with the three children.

Tomorrow I am supposed to fly to Switzerland to give some lectures at St. Gallen University, next week we have all our examiners' meetings and the week after I shall be lecturing in Berlin. I still hope to be able to fulfil all these obligations and, if everything goes well, to see you in July.

You have both been through so much suffering yourself recently that you will understand how we feel.

With warmest thoughts to you and Catherine,

Yours ever,

Stephen

1 Stephen Frowen's granddaughter Cassie Hosburn's first publication at the age of 17 appeared in the *Bulletin of the British Neuroscience Association*, Autumn/Winter 2003. In her final year at Lancing College, she was offered a place at St. Catherine's College, Oxford, and at four other leading British universities.

284

2 Alde House
Aldeburgh
Suffolk
18th June 1986

My dear Stephen,

Your letter moves me beyond words. It is an exertion of the spirit to give another person happiness, made despite worrying pre-occupations, which is truly heroic. Your letter gives me intense pleasure. The book owes its existence to you. Catherine's ecstatic delight, when I showed her the dedication, would have rewarded you very deeply.

We are wondering whether permission to reprint the Harrod piece has been given by JAI Press. If not, I wonder if the offer of a token payment, which I would be very glad to make, might satisfy them?

You refer to the Preface and Introduction! Your Preface will speak for us both in making clear, in some degree, the overwhelming good fortune I have had in Catherine's encouragement and all kinds of practical assistance. (Not least, as noted by Geoff Harcourt, her cooking).

The Preface and Introduction will be your crowning gift to the book.

We look forward with the greatest joy to seeing you here in July. I am amazed at your limitless energy in visits to lecture on the Continent.

The picture of your new grand-daughter gave Catherine tremendous pleasure. I think we told you that I also have a new grand-daughter, born on 15th January this year.

With every utmost grateful thought,

Yours ever,

George Shackle

George Shackle

285

Alde House
Aldeburgh
Suffolk
23rd July 1986

Dearest Stephen,

You were indeed a good brother to me while you were here. I was so afraid George's malaise was, or was going to be, a stroke, and your support was truly 'eine feste Burg'(? or is it 'berg'?). The doctor's report when it came was an immense relief, as I know it was to you too. But I was sorry you had to arrive at a moment when George wasn't well because we both wanted you to have a good rest in absolute tranquillity, and I am afraid we couldn't quite give you that.

George is definitely better, though he still has moments when he is not quite so good, and we are leading a very quiet life as ordered by the doctor. We have begun to read Lachmann's new book which has *just* arrived from Blackwell's, and in his better moments G. is doing some writing which in my view is as lovely as anything he has ever done.

We did love your letter; you always say such heart-warming things. And thank you too for *Slow on the Feather*[1] which continues to enthral, and the lovely bottle of wine.

I *did* enjoy our visit to Snape, I hope to see Mrs. H. again one day.

We are enormously gratified by your getting the German chairs.

With much love from your much older sister (though I don't feel like it!)

Catherine.
C. [Catherine]

1 Wilfrid Blunt, *Slow on the Feather: Further Autobiography 1938–1959* (Wilton, Salisbury: Michael Russell, 1986).

286

University of Surrey
Department of Economics
Guildford
Surrey GU2 5XH
4th August 1986

My dear George,

I am so very happy that you are now feeling better and even had the strength to take up writing again – and with such vigour, working on two papers simultaneously.

I am enclosing the invoice of the JAI Press together with two accompanying letters. It is most generous of you to settle it. All you need to do is to leave the invoice and your instructions with your bank.

In haste but with all my warmest good wishes to both of you,

Yours,

Stephen

Stephen

287

2 Alde House
Aldeburgh
Suffolk
6th August 1986

My dear Stephen,

We are delighted to have your letter, and exceedingly happy that your patient efforts have solved the difficulty over the Harrod paper. Yesterday I arranged with the bank to send $150 with the invoice to the JAI Press. It is a deep satisfaction to me that my tribute to Harrod can go in and that the volume can be complete just in the way we planned.

I am enclosing a copy of the paper I finished at the week-end. It is not meant for publication, was written for something to do, and is just free ranging reflections.

We do hope you will have a real rest in Italy.

Catherine joins me in all best and warmest wishes,

Yours ever,

George Shackle

George Shackle

For this piece on 'Method in Economic Theory' I have borrowed a phrase of my own from the Foreword that I wrote to Philip Arestis's Festschrift for you, but few people will ever see this enclosed piece.

288

Hotel Bewallerhof
Eggen – Ega
Italy
26th August 1986

Dearest Catherine and George,

Irina and I are spending a most restful holiday among close friends on our beloved Bewallerhof – a most peaceful place amidst the most magnificent mountain scenery. The mood of the mountains seems to change from day to day and each walk is full of surprises. Such a pity you can't be with us. We shall be back in London on 6th September. Hope you are both well.

With much love,

Stephen

Warmest wishes and affectionate thoughts from me as well,

Irina

289

Bewallerhof
27th August 1986

My dear George,

I am *most* grateful to you for sending me a copy of your latest paper 'Method in Economic Theory'. It is one of the clearest statement I have ever read on this issue and I have no doubt that it should be published to make it known to a wider public. Would you like it to be included in the forthcoming volume of your essays?

One small point which occurred to me is that output and employment may no longer be as closely interrelated as previously because of the increasing importance of technology. Technological progress and the need for labour in the productive process seem to be inversely related.

The passages on money are so subtle and penetrating and belong to the best I have read on this subject. In a few sentences you express what in the case of many authors requires a book! Also the limitations of economic theory emerge only too clearly from your paper. What a blessing for economic literature that you have regained your strength and are writing again!

One of our old friends who joined us in the Dolomites at the Bewallerhof is Erich Heller who teaches at the Northwestern University in Chicago. He has written perhaps the finest and most penetrating book on Thomas Mann *The Ironic German*. His most recent book on *The Age of Prose* I would also recommend to you and Catherine. To everybody's delight he has given several readings during our stay here.

I do hope that you are still feeling much better and that your health will progressively improve.

With affectionate thoughts and all warmest good wishes,

Yours ever,

Stephen

Stephen

290

2 Alde House
Aldeburgh
Suffolk IP15 5EE
3 September 1986

My dear Stephen,

The kindness of your letter moves me beyond words. It is a deep happiness to me that you found 'Method in Economic Theory' worthwhile. I will amend the passage which suggests that an increase of output implies in these days an increase in employment. Fifty years ago Keynes could resort to his characteristic use of employment as a proxy for output, and this was the more legitimate in the context of his short-term outlook. But now I think we have to envisage a production economy almost wholly self-operated and an employment economy where everyone is an artist-craftsman making beautiful objects by hand, for a society educated to desire and demand them. I suggested this to Charles Carter a few years ago, but it plainly poses immense practical organizational problems. The essential is that there would be *two* economies. The link between them is the complex matter.

I have had it in mind to keep 'Method in Economic Theory' as a reserve against future occasions, since the practical difficulty of writing makes it a slow business. I think perhaps it would be upsetting to your plans and Mr. Farmiloe to include it in *Business, Time and Thought.*

I am thoroughly absorbed in working on my piece for Philip Arestis's Festschrift for you. It seeks to give the word Policy a systematically expectational basis and meaning.

Catherine and I were thankful and delighted to feel that you and Irina were having a really restful and relaxed holiday in a place you love.

With all warmest and best thoughts,

Yours sincerely,

George Shackle

291

2 Alde House
Aldeburgh
Suffolk
26th September 1986

My dear Stephen,

Let me say yet again how deeply appreciative we both are of your superlative organising of the preparation of *Business, Time and Thought.* Catherine has listed the questions in Macmillan's form which we think we have to answer-:

2a. List of Books. Reverse the order of *Imagination and the Nature of Choice* and *Epistemics and Economics.*

3. THE TEXT. Accents. The Cantillon paper (chapter 4) deliberately preserves his inconsistent accentuation.

3. Last Point. We suppose that Oliver Thomas's drawing of GLSS is being used as frontispiece.

PROMOTION. 4. Add Heffers, Cambridge.

MEDIA. 2. Name the *TLS* instead of *The Economic Journal.*

THE BOOK. 4. Second half of comment to read: Chapter 3 '*Treatise, Theory* and Time' has been published in Spanish in a translation by Professor Lucas Beltrán and Chapter 14 'Keynes the Meeting-Point of History and Thought' in French in a translation by Professor Frédéric Poulon; the first publication of the original English versions will be in *Business, Time and Thought.*

1. THE JACKET/COVER DESIGN. GLSS thinks the dust cover should simply present the title of the book and the names of the Editor and the Author in large, highly visible lettering without decorative detail.

We hope these suggestions will be easily understood.

With kindest regards from us both,

George Shackle

George Shackle

We do hope there is good news at home.

292

Alde House
Aldeburgh
Suffolk
21st January 1987

My dear Stephen,

Here, at last, is my cheque for the photographs; I am deeply grateful to you on two counts – first for having taken such beauties, and then for having let me have extra copies. One day I shall ask you for more of the full-face one of us, both laughing, because I think it is the best of all and I sent all copies away at Christmas. One & all were received with acclaim.

We have been wondering if you both got home safely on the 16th, or if you were snow bound in Germany. I shall ring up to find out. We have had venomous weather here with vicious winds blowing straight from Siberia, and of such strength to be frightening at times. Aldeburgh was cut off from the outside world for some days, with milk and bread running short in the town. We were all right with a good stock of everything we need, and *all* the heating on *all* the time *everywhere*. George hasn't been well, and I kept him in bed some of the time, and in our bedroom (a cosy, friendly room) for most of the time. I have been anxious about him on occasions, and sometimes I look at him with the knowledge that I must steel myself to the pain of living without him. This fairly takes me by the throat, and at the same time I pray that I may outlive him, that the pain be mine and not his. I do believe in a God of goodness and a continuing life; I must believe; but sometimes I have to struggle to believe. For you, a man of faith, I hope it comes more easily.

Wilfrid Blunt's death has set us thinking and talking of you such a lot. For him, I am glad it has come quickly, more quickly than the doctor forecast. For you, I grieve in the loss of a friend, and perhaps even more in the loss of a man to whom *you* were such a wonderfully good friend. We need people to love, to be good to, to help. Don't you agree? I was glad the obituary stressed the loving way in which Wilfrid wrote of Anthony in *Slow on the Feather*. To me that was the best part of the whole book, a sign of a generous heart.

We were dreadfully distressed to hear of Michael's relapse and of your great anxiety, and we hope very much that the hospital kept him for a good long time and that matters have eased now. And did you have a satisfactory and enjoyable time in Germany? And not too exhausting? And did you get a lovely welcome home from the children? I am sure you did!

Much love to Irina, and to yourself, from us both,

Catherine.

Catherine

293

2 Alde House
Aldeburgh
Suffolk
18th February 1987

My dear Stephen,

Your letter moves me far beyond anything I can express. It will be treasured as long as I live, and if all goes well preserved far beyond that with a collection of letters only a handful of which can come near it in value for me.

Business, Time and Thought would of course never have come into being but for your extreme generosity and prodigality of time, effort and care. Nothing, I feel certain, could have given Catherine such pleasure as the dedication of this book to her. You have brought this enterprise to within sight of its goal despite distracting pre-occupations and difficulties that would have daunted and worn out any ordinary man.

I am delighted to have a book published by the great house of Macmillan which for a century or more has been the most honourable embodiment of economists' work.

Catherine and I both feel that the question of the jacket is a vital one for the success of the book in the measure that your superlative editing deserves. We feel that the jacket design should immediately convey the serious purpose of the book and the intense efforts of both you and me that it represents. The jacket that Macmillans have proposed seems to us very far from achieving this. We feel that the design was in a lighthearted mood in letting the three little emblems intrude themselves. Do you not think that your name and mine should be printed so as to be legible at a distance of several feet; for example, through a bookshop plate glass window. We like the plainness of the rest of the design but we would prefer a lively colour rather than black.

Catherine has spent the morning designing an arrangement which we think suggests what we have in mind. She will I think explain more fully her ideas in her own letter to you.

With all warmest feelings,

Yours ever,

George Shackle

George L.S.S.

294

2 Alde House
Aldeburgh
Suffolk
4th March 1987

My dear Stephen,

This morning brought us the inexpressible excitement of the proofs. Catherine is ecstatic, and I am more deeply moved than I can put into words. The intensity and all-encompassing skill of the work you have given to this book, the glowing warmth of your friendship, have given us a tremendous lift of the spirit. Catherine will put all this into living speach on the phone far better than I can write it. She read long passages to me this morning, and we have, in fact, one or two suggestions to venture on. Catherine has been given a supreme happiness by the dedication to herself, but should it not read:

We, the editor and the author, dedicate this work to Catherine Shackle.

In 'A Student's Pilgrimage', p. 230, third paragraph, the wording should be: 'As a child I had at first only one playmate ...' (We both think that the original order of words has a natural rhythm that should be preserved.)

My wording, a few lines lower, is 'I told the manager of the bank of my ambition ...' Here, too, I would like this wording to be retained. Catherine thinks she will not have time to read aloud the whole proof in time to be of service to you and we would therefore be doubly and trebly grateful if your editorial eye could guard the printed text from departing from what I wrote.

We are both delighted with the reproduction of Oliver Thomas' drawing. My remark to Catherine was: 'It gives my face that faint, elusive hint of self-mockery, of ironic detachment that, I think, every product of the fallible human mind should bear.'

Our utmost gratitude and warmest affection go to you

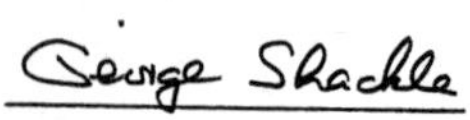

George Shackle

295

2 Alde House
Aldeburgh
Suffolk
19th March 1987

My dear Stephen,

It occurred to us that we might just possibly be of some service to you in what must be an exacting and exhausting task. We found that by listening to Catherine's reading aloud I could tell, as it were by ear, whether there was any departure from the original texts. We found a number of things needing adjustment and we are sending you Catherine's notes of them. She has also marked the proof itself – Shall we send this?

On page 210 there is a sentence in which I am very anxious to insert 5 words so that it would read: '... and these will not be shaped until that time, as Lachmann has vividly insisted.' (Third paragraph down).

On page 211, first paragraph, 10 line down, there appears to be a line missing.

We have checked Chapters 1–10, inclusive, and Chapters 14,15 and half 18.

We both send love and are anxiously awaiting news of Irina.

Yours ever,

George Shackle

296

2 Alde House
Aldeburgh
Suffolk
26th March 1987

My dear Stephen,

Thank you very much for pointing out the confusions that have occurred in the printing of the algebraic expressions on pages 116 and 117. In the Thames paper two different ways of writing the expression were used (Thames pages 19,20).

We can either write:-

$$v = \sum_{i=1}^{L} \frac{Q_i}{(1+r)^i}$$

or

$$v = \sum_{i=1}^{L} Q_i(1+r)^{-i}$$

In the Thames paper they have used the first expression but each time have printed it incorrectly (pages 19 & 20). On page 116 of the proof they have used the first version but have printed it incorrectly; on page 117 of the proof in trying to save vertical space they have mixed up the two versions, but the space could be saved by using the second version.

On page 118 of the proof in expressing the elasticity of profit they should have printed:-

$(\Delta G/G)/(\Delta R/R)$

and

$(\Delta J/G)/(\Delta R/R)$

I fear that some of these errors may have appeared in my manuscript of the Thames paper though I do take great care.

I am exceedingly sorry, my dear Stephen, for the trouble and delay that you have suffered over these mistakes. I must have failed to correct some of them in the Thames paper that I sent you.

We greatly hope that today's news from the hospital is good. Catherine joins me in sending you our best love.

As ever,

George Shackle

297

Alde House
Aldburgh
Suffolk
7th April 1987

My dear Stephen,

We were mistaken in thinking that there is anything wrong with the sentence on page 211, first paragraph which reads: 'But this business must be carried through with urgency and decisively consummated in action at some external deadline or some sense of excellence.' This is as I meant it to read and should stand.

Yours as ever,

George Shackle

Just an added word to say we are both so thankful Irina is making a steady recovery. We realise that you are tremendously tied up, and we don't want you to try to make a dart down here if it is difficult to find the time.

Much love,

C.

298

Alde House
Aldburgh
Suffolk
16th August 1987

My dear Stephen,

My gratitude and admiration for what you have done for me in seeking an appointment for me with a neurologist are beyond words. You have cut through the endless complications and difficulties of getting advice from your cousin, Professor Reinhold Frowein [neuro-surgeon], and making contact with Professor Symon with infinite patience, resources and generosity of spirit. I am much deeply moved by your extraordinary patience.

Catherine writes this:-

'I want to remind you of that chap on the road to Jericho who fell among thieves, and lo and behold who should come along but the kindest of kind Samaritans who saw what was wrong and rang up his cousin in Cologne to get the name of the specialist, and took endless trouble, and spent much time which he could ill afford being a very busy man, to make an appointment. The Jericho-traveller, and his wife, could hardly believe they had such a kind friend. Talk about loving your neighbour as yourself, that Samaritan is an example to the whole world, and I say that on the best authority.'

You suggested very kindly that you would bring my bibliography up to date. The four papers I have recently written are:

1 A review article of *Richard Cantillon: Entrepreneur and Economist* by Antoin Murphy, Jarenden Press (the review will be published this autumn).
2 An article 'Decision' published in the *Journal of Economic Studies*, vol. 3, no. 5, 1986.
This issue of the journal was headed: Essays on Reappraisal, ed. Frank M. Stephen.
3 'What did the *General Theory* do?'
A paper to be read at the Mannheim Conference (not yet published).

4 A paper called 'Possibility: Interpretation, inverse measure, marginal comparison (not yet published).

With warmest love and every good wish from us both,

Catherine and George

Catherine and George

299

The Reform Club
Pall Mall
London SW1
20 August 1987

My dear George,

I was deeply moved to receive your letter of 16th August and particularly happy to see that despite your reduced eyesight you are still able to write to me by hand. Your words are far too kind. The little I was able to do for you is scarcely worth mentioning. I so much wished I could do more. I am longing to see you quite well again. You have still so very much to give. It must have been a tremendously stimulating experience for everybody present at this week's conference to listen to your paper (which I am sure could not have been better presented than Catherine did) and to have the privilege of meeting you in person. I do hope that the paper will in due course be published. If you could let me have a copy I should be ever so grateful.

I am enclosing the letter I received this morning from Professor Symon (which his secretary had already read out to me). I have also sent a copy of it to your G.P., Dr. Ian Tait. The enclosed details relating to Dr. Kocen may also be of interest to you and Catherine. I was interested to see that he was trained at Leeds. He certainly seems extremely well qualified. I do hope that the medication he will prescribe will make you feel your usual self again. I am sure that you could not be in better hands. I shall be waiting impatiently for your news. I am only sorry that I shall not be in London to meet your train at Liverpool Street Station and to take you to Queen's Square for your appointment on Tuesday, 25th August, at 2.30 p.m. at 23 Queen's Square, London, W.C. !.

With all my very best and warmest wishes, and love,

Yours ever,

Stephen

Stephen

P.S. I am most grateful for the details of your latest publications, prepared with such care, which will enable me to bring your bibliography for the conference volume right up to date.

300

Alde House
Aldburgh
Suffolk
25th November 1987

Dear Stephen,

I believe you told me some time ago that you had proposed to Mr. Farmiloe of Macmillan the setting up of an annual prize under my name. I am, of course, most deeply gratified by this idea.

I am writing to consult you now because I have just heard that Professor John Pheby of Birmingham Polytechnic has arranged with the publisher, Edward Arnold, to give a biennial prize to have my name attached to it. I ought not, of course, to have any involvement in these matters, but it occurs to me that I am perhaps the only person who is aware of *both* these arrangements. It seems plain that the sponsors of the two proposals ought each to be informed of the other, since some co-ordination would be in order. Please forgive my troubling you. I hope the strange conjuncture can be sorted out.

Catherine and I send you our very best wishes.

Yours as ever,

George Shackle

301

Free University of Berlin
Stiftungsprofessur Deutsche Bundesbank
Internationale Währungs – und Geldpolitik
D-1000 Berlin 33
15th January 1988

My dear Catherine and George,

For a long time I intended to write to you in some detail but never found the peace to do so. Life is still rather hectic. We are getting to the tail end of the

Wintersemester, although a lot of time is now taken up with the preparation for the Sommersemster which will start on 4th April.

We shall be in London from 12th February for one month and shall then have a two-week holiday in Ascona.

Belatedly I should like to send you our warmest wishes for 1988 in the hope that the coming months will bring you the best of health and much happiness.

I am afraid that Michael suffered serious neurological damage as a result of his last relapse. Periodically his right hand shakes quite violently – it may be an illness known as focal Jacksonian epilepsy. During our stay in London over Christmas Professor Lindsay Symon treated him for a few days at the National Hospital in Queen Square. They did a brain scan and various other tests. It is a terrible worry.

However, we do enjoy our stay in Berlin. The tasks before me are challenging and exciting and I am greatly looking forward to the months ahead.

My conference on 'Monetary Theory and Monetary Policy – New Tracts for the 1990s' is now taking shape and will take place at the Guest House of the Land Central Bank [Landeszentralbank] in Berlin from 31.8-2.9.1988, beautifully situated right on the shores of the Wannsee.[1] I so much hope that you will both be able to come. A paper would be more than welcome or a contribution as a discussant. But you could also just attend. I should so much love to introduce you to Berlin – officially the European Cultural City for 1988.

I am so very happy to know, George, that you are again able to work. I do hope that there will be enough books which merit being reviewed by you. What a chance for young and not-so-young economists to be able to benefit from your criticism and encouragement.

I should like to write more but time is pressing and I am anxious to get at least this short greeting off to you today.

With all my love to both of you,

Yours affectionately,

Stephen

1 For the conference proceedings, see S.F. Frowen (ed.), *Monetary Theory and Monetary Policy: New Tracks for the 1990s* (London: Macmillan; New York: St. Martin's Press, 1993).

302

Free University of Berlin
Stiftungsprofessur Deutsche Bundesbank
Internationale Währungs- und Geldpolitik
D-1000 Berlin 33
17th May 1988

My dear George,

I do apologise for my long silence. For so long I intended to congratulate you on the great and so well deserved honour bestowed upon you by the University of Strathclyde. I am very happy to know that Catherine was able to represent you at the ceremony. What a splendid ambassador she must have been. I am longing to hear all the details of this great and memorable occasion.

Life has been even more hectic than usual here in Berlin with a stream of visitors from London and New York in addition to my increasing university and other duties. But I do enjoy it all enormously. On 19th May we shall fly to Helsinki for a conference, returning to Berlin on 22nd May (the day of my 65th birthday) and shall then fly to London on 25th May where we shall be (at 40 Gurney Drive, London N2 0DE) until 30th May.

We had so much hoped to see you both at the Reform Club on Friday, 27th May, for my birthday dinner but quite understand that it would be difficult for you to subject yourself to the strain involved. It is needless to say that the gap created by your absence will be felt intensely. But I know that you will be with us in spirit. We still hope that Catherine may be able to come on her own – following the Strathclyde example. We are expecting about 50 guests from the UK, Germany and the US. I am beginning to feel quite nervous about the event.

I am so anxiously awaiting receipt of a copy of 'our' book. It surely cannot be long now even for a publisher as meticulous as Macmillan. Mr. Farmiloe will of course be at my birthday dinner on 27th May, I am glad to say.

Today I received a copy of the enclosed book jacket design for the conference volume *Unknowledge and Choice in Economics*. I think it looks rather attractive. There are, I am afraid, a few queries still to be answered relating to your bibliography. The four titles in question are listed separately (see enclosed sheet). Perhaps you can let me have the information required in due course. I have to return the copy-edited typescript to the Macmillan copy-editor by 30th May. The best may be for you to reply to my London address where I shall be from 25th to 30th May.

I am so much longing to see you both again. Meanwhile I hope that you are well and that your health continues to improve. The summer ahead of you in your lovely garden should greatly contribute to restore your strength.

I am still busy with the preparation of my August/September conference in Berlin. The enclosed conference programme may be of interest to you. How nice it would be if you could both be with us on this occasion. I should have loved to introduce you to the attractions of Berlin.

I shall of course telephone you when I am in London next week.

With much love to you and Catherine and all my warmest good wishes,

Yours affectionately,

Stephen

303

Alde House
Aldeburgh
Suffolk IP15 5EE
24th May 1988

My dear Stephen,

We were delighted to have your letter of May 17th.

In answer to the queries on the Bibliography:

I. I am afraid I do not know the name of the Editor of Lucas Beltrán's Festschrift nor have I ever received a copy.
II. Title of book: *La herencia de Keynes*. Madrid: Publisher – Alianza Universidad © Alianza Editorial. Date: 1988. Chapter title: El Treatise. La Teoria General y el Tiempo (*Treatise, Theory & Time*), pp. 211–234.
III. Nature, Notion et Notation de l'Incertitude: This paper was written in English, read at a Conference at Paris II University whose proceedings so far as I know were never published.
IV. *Reason in Human Affairs*. This was a slight and disappointing book in view of its pretentious title and I think it best to delete the reference to it. I have no knowledge of the publication of any review.

Thank you very much indeed for the list of lectures for the First Monetary Conference at the end of August. I wish we could be there, but I find travel a great strain and difficulty and have had to resign myself to not attending conferences at distant places.

We are extremely happy to think of the very great personal success you are having in Berlin. It is evident that you will be a memorable figure in academic and business circles there

With all warmest good wishes and kindest regards,

George Shackle

And love,

C.

304

POSTCARD FROM BERLIN – SCHLOSS CHARLOTTENBURG

4 September 1988

To: George and Catherine Shackle

Dear Friends,

Stephen [Frowen] has just organized the most wonderful conference on the future of monetary policy and we all think of you. – Michael Ambrosi, Victoria Chick, Elias Karakitsos, Mike Artis, Stephen [Frowen] with much love. Best regards – Paul Davidson.

305

2 Alde House
Aldeburgh
Suffolk
14th March 1989

My dear Stephen,

No words of mine can tell you how deeply I was moved, delighted, and overwhelmed by what you told me on the telephone last night. I cannot hope to deserve such commendation, but if I can ever seem distantly to aspire to it, I shall not have altogether failed to see what life might be at its rarest moments of inspiration. Your friendship is, if any can be, the source of such inspiration: A gift beyond compare that you give me.

The writer's art is a mysterious one. All of us build with the same bricks, the words of our vocabulary universally shared. Yet these words have in them the seeds of beauty that germinate by their mere arrangement. Rhythm of words is not, I think, a mere matter of sensuous delight. The meaning of a passage is built up by the carrying over of meaning from its early to its later phases by rhythm, the surge and resource of phrase and sentence. I am not a classical scholar and cannot compare English and Greek in the matter of aural enchantment. But I do think the saying is true that form and content are one.

The feeling that I have tried here to express will be the same whether or not your letter is published.

Yours sincerely,

George Shackle

G.L.S. Shackle

306
The Reform Club
Pall Mall
London SW1
10th August 1989

My dearest Catherine and George,

How can I ever thank you adequately for a most wonderful and relaxing weekend? I tremendously enjoyed every second of this exhilarating stay with you both and the many fascinating discussions we had. The memorable hours with you have done me a lot of good. I only hope that I did not leave you behind feeling totally exhausted!

I hope you will forgive me for being so late with my expression of thanks, but I literally did not have a minute to myself since I left you on that lovely sunny afternoon. Glyndebourne I reached just in time for the beginning of the long interval, i.e. *after* the second Act, as Irina's car broke down two miles before I got to the Dartford Tunnel. There was a very strong smell of petrol and the AA man said that I was lucky the car did not blow up with me inside it. It was also fortunate that it did not happen inside the tunnel itself. However, I did enjoy the third and final Act and bought myself a video of Britten's *Midsummer Night's Dream* to watch the first two Acts at home!

The second week of my course went well but was totally exhausting (the heatwave did not help, of course!). I then rushed back to Sylt to fetch Irina and during the three days I stayed there, the most terrible storm did not stop for a minute. I was glad when we got to Kiel where I saw my old friend, Hubertus Mueller-Groeling, the editor of the *Weltwirtschaftliches Archiv*. He was delighted when I told him that George is well and would probably be prepared to review one or two books for the *W.A.* He immediately picked two books on Keynesian Economics, one by Alan Meltzer, we both thought might appeal to George. He wanted to write to you (I gave him your address), George, immediately before going on holiday. I hope his letter has arrived by now.

John Pheby and Vicky Chick very kindly pressed me to come to the Malvern Conference. It's a bad timing for me because of Irina's birthday to which we have invited a number of guests. However, I have decided to be present just for the day on Wednesday, 16th August. It will be so lovely to see you both again. It also sounds an interesting conference programme. I shall come by car and leave soon after the conference dinner.

With all my love and warmest wishes to both of you, and many, many thanks once again,

Yours,

Stephen

Stephen

307

The Reform Club
Pall Mall
London SW1
14th August 1989

My dearest Catherine,

I forgot to attach the enclosed card of *the* Buddenbrook-Haus to my last letter. We inspected it carefully during our two-day visit to Lübeck just before returning to London. What a fascinating city! Like the Venetian Palazzos the Buddenbrook-Haus is considerably larger than one would expect from the outside as it extends far into the back garden. It belonged to the Mann family but Thomas Mann's grandparents were the last to occupy this splendid patrician building. I hope you are enjoying the novel!

I had lunch with Tim Farmiloe the other day (what an absolutely delightful person he is). It seems that of *Business, Time and Thought,* they have so far sold 135 copies in the UK and 724 copies overseas, the latter including 525 copies taken up in the US by the New York University Press. For the Festschrift *Contemporary Issues in Money and Banking,* UK sales amount to 165 copies and overseas sales to 326 copies (there was no American edition, as in the case of George's book [*Business, Time and Thought*]). Both volumes are of course rather expensive (£ 35 each) and there have not been many reviews so far. I am trying to arrange for more journals to be supplied with review copies.

So much looking forward to seeing you both on Wednesday.

With much love to both of you,

Yours affectionately,

Stephen

308

Alde House
Aldeburgh
Suffolk
23rd August 1989

My dear Stephen,

The debt of gratitude I owe you for what you have done in bringing into being with consummate editorial skill, with inexhaustible brilliance of ideas and perfect judgement in their exploitation, and with a thoroughness beyond praise and almost unexampled is measureless and beyond words.

In *Business, Time and Thought* Macmillan have produced something truly beautiful in appearance and workmanship. What a pity they did not have faith enough to send it out widely for reviews. At any rate, you have two admirers of your work whose admiration of it could not be surpassed.

May I turn to the questions I mooted at the end of our conversation this afternoon. We need a successor to Knight's great classic *Risk, Uncertainty and Profit*. Perhaps if we were to wait until John Pheby's next conference, a session might be devoted by a few chosen spirits to getting out the reasons for such an enterprise and trying to make a plan for finding the right author. If you yourself were willing to engage in this demanding and very difficult task that would be a great service to the profession.

With every warmest and heartfelt wish,

Yours,

George Shackle

George Shackle

309

40 Gurney Drive
London, N2 0DE
5th September 1989

My dear George,

I thought you might like to know that I went to Cambridge last week to see Mr Owen, the Head of the Manuscript Department at Cambridge University Library. He was delighted to receive the originals of the letters you so kindly wrote to me from 1953 onwards right up to 1989. I have of course kept a copy of the entire correspondence. I shall see him again in October as I still have some of your manuscripts which he is also keen to have. I am too afraid nowadays to keep originals at home as it would be such a tragedy if they were not preserved.

This morning I received two books for review from the *Weltwirtschaftliches Archiv* (Journal of the Institut für Weltwirtschaft, Kiel) and I trust that yours (among them a volume by Alan Meltzer) arrived as well.

From Henry Boettinger I received a most charming letter of which I am enclosing a copy. I am so happy to have copies of all your letters to him for the proposed volume of your correspondence which Jim Ford and I are planning to edit. Mr. Owen, too, was most enthusiastic about this project and promised every possible support.

At the Malvern Conference I casually mentioned my interest in the history of monetary thought to Edward Elgar and in response received the enclosed letter. It is a task I should really like to concentrate on over the next year or two.

I have now promised to let him have a brief synopsis and chapter outline by the end of October. I should of course greatly appreciate the opportunity of discussing my outline of the book with you before submitting it to the publisher.

Irina and I will fly to Germany on 22nd September for three days to attend a concert and reception at the Burg Hohenzollern in the South of Germany. Prince Louis Ferdinand (grandson of the last German emperor Kaiser Wilhelm II), the present Head of the House of Hohenzollern, had kindly invited us to the occasion. He like his ancestor Frederick the Great and other members of his family is a highly talented composer, and some of his new works will be performed for the first time.

On 27th September we will be flying to Lund to attend the annual meeting of the Rilke Society at which Irina will read a paper on Rilke and Kierkegaard, a rather demanding subject. The trip to Sweden will be followed by a brief journey to Siena from 6th to 9th October to attend the wedding of the daughter of a close friend of mine from student days, Norbert Kloten, who also contributed to *Contemporary Issues in Money and Banking*. This I hope will be our last journey this year!

If it suited you and Catherine and if you are not too busy, I could perhaps come to Aldeburgh just for the day after 15th October to discuss the proposed volume of your correspondence, collect your microfilms and any copies of letters you have written in recent years, and perhaps discuss my own project. The greatest joy of course would be to see you both again.

With all warmest good wishes to you and Catherine, and much love to both of you,

Yours as ever,

Stephen

310

40 Gurney Drive
London N2 0DE
6th September 1989

Dearest Catherine,

What a tremendous joy it was to see you and George again at the splendid Malvern Conference. It was such a pleasant and friendly gathering.

As I mentioned to George in yesterday's letter, we shall be back in London from our various trips abroad by the middle of October and I should very much like to see you one day during the second half of October or at the beginning of November if that suited you better. I would make an early start and just come for the day as Irina hates being alone in the house over night. The best may be for me to telephone you when we are back from Siena on 10th October.

I was delighted to receive Henry Boettinger's charming letter and copies of George's illuminating letters to him in which he discusses much of his work and ideas. The correspondence starts in July 1967 and continues until March 1984. In his last letter to Henry Boettinger (dated 4 March 1984) George writes "Catherine says, it would be a pity now to 'dull the edge' by trying to write more".[1] Although one has obviously to be aware of this danger, I am personally extremely happy to see George still producing papers and reviews because whatever he writes is always interesting, illuminating and profoundly thought-provoking. He continues to be full of original ideas, more so than most younger members of the profession. I have suggested to Henry Boettinger to let Cambridge University Library have the originals of George's letters to him and I am glad to say that he has kindly agreed to do so immediately. He has apparently not yet received the copy of *Business, Time and Thought* you so generously offered to present to him. I could send him one of my own copies if you should no longer have a spare copy. He is of course most anxious to read it.

You and George may like to have the enclosed copy of George's bibliography as it will appear in the conference volume [*Unknowledge and Choice in Economics*] – with the [book] reviews still to be written being included!

* * *

I had to interrupt writing this letter as lunch had to be prepared. While doing so the postman arrived with the second delivery, among which was George's most touching letter. Nothing could have moved me more than his most kind and generous words. I shall reply to him tonight.

I hope you and George are well and that you have recovered from the enjoyable but no doubt strenuous journey to Malvern.

Irina joins me in sending you our love and warmest wishes.

Yours affectionately,

Stephen

1 There is an entry on the margin of this letter by Catherine Shackle stating: 'This is a mistake. I always encouraged George to write! CSS.'

311

40 Gurney Drive
London N2 0DE
7th September 1989

My dear George,

I was moved beyond words and close to tears when I read your exceedingly kind letter and your most generous remarks. I can only say that to be entrusted with the exciting task of editing your collection of essays *Business, Time and Thought* is the greatest honour anybody could have bestowed upon me. I shall never forget the happiness I felt when for the first time I held a copy of this handsome volume in my hands. I am now so much looking forward to the imminent appearance of the Guildford conference proceedings *Unknowledge and Choice in Economics*. The preparation of both volumes has given me joy and satisfaction beyond any imagination. I am disappointed, of course, that Macmillan have made so little effort to promote *Business, Time and Thought*. I have now discovered that the only journals supplied with a review copy were the *Economic Journal, World Economy*, the *TLS, THES* and the *FT*. New York University Press who published the American edition appears to have been much more active. I have now prepared a list of 30 journals complete with the names of the Book Review Editors and exact addresses for Macmillan with an urgent request to supply a review copy. I feel that I am really doing the job their publicity department ought to be responsible for. I only hope that we shall now get the reviews the book so amply deserves.

Your suggestion for John Pheby to have a session next year devoted to setting out the reasons for the need of a successor to Knight's *Risk, Uncertainty and Profit* is excellent and I shall immediately write to John Pheby. However, this session must be closely related – as it will be by necessity – to your own work and I am sure that this plan and suggestion will be most enthusiastically received.

I was deeply touched by your suggestion that I might engage in this certainly most demanding and extremely difficult task, and greatly moved by the confidence you showed in me. You know how very much these problems are at the heart of my thinking and I should certainly like to play an active part at the Malvern discussions next year and see what will emerge from the deliberations. I am tremendously and impatiently looking forward to this exciting event.

You mentioned in the course of our telephone conversation that you do not know the book by D.M. Lamberton on *The Theory of Profit*, published in 1963. Perhaps the enclosed copy of the chapter especially devoted to your work may be of interest to you. I could send you the book if you would like to see it.

I also enclose the obituary of Richard Kahn which Geoff Harcourt wrote for *The Independent*. It may have escaped your notice. I was deeply impressed by this extremely fine piece of writing – a moving tribute to Richard Kahn.

With all my very warmest and most affectionate wishes and greetings,

Yours,

Stephen

312
40 Gurney Drive
London N2 0DE
12th September 1989

Dearest Catherine,

What a treat and joy it was to receive your long and much treasured letter this morning. It was so lovely to hear from you and to have your news.

I am sorry I forgot to enclose Edward Elgar's letter. I am doing so now together with a copy of a letter I received from him this morning.

I am of course also very keen on the idea George put to me in his last letter regarding Frank Knight's book. Meanwhile I have taken up this matter with John Pheby. As you know he is anxious to devote half of next year's Malvern Conference to George's work and would like me to present one of the papers. As part of this session, he would be quite happy to see half a day reserved for setting out the reasons for the need of a successor to Knight's classic work on *Risk, Uncertainty and Profit*. Such a discussion would by necessity again be closely linked to George's own work.

As far as my quotation from George's last letter to Henry Boettinger is concerned, you may like to see the enclosed copy of the letter referred to. I am of course the first person to know the extent to which you have always encouraged George to continue writing – right up to the present day and the assistance you have given him in every respect to make it possible for him to do so. After all *Business, Time and Thought* would never exist without you. It is your book as much as George's. However, you may have felt quite rightly that the time had come for George to relax, enjoy life and devote time to subjects other than economics, such as music, for example.

I was so glad to hear that George did write to Henry Boettinger and sent him a copy of *Business, Time and Thought*. I can imagine the tremendous joy he will derive from both. Lachmann, too, must have been thrilled to hear from George.

As far as my visit in October is concerned, Thursday, 26th October, may be preferable, as we only get back from Italy on the 10th October, and immediately have visitors from Berlin until 14th and then from Switzerland until 17th. We are then expected in Windermere for two or three days. However, if the 26th October should not suit you, I could try and rearrange all this to see you on 19th October.

I am glad to know that the Kiel books have arrived. Will you not forget to send me a copy of George's reviews? I am anxious to see his comments and hear his views on these two volumes.

With much love and all warmest good wishes to both of you,

Yours affectionately,

Stephen

Stephen

313

Alde House
Aldeburgh
Suffolk
17th September 1989

My dear Stephen,

Your project of a History of Monetary Thought is exciting to the last degree. Here theory and history can come together in perfect mutual support. It will engage your splendid powers to the full, for an indefinite stretch of years. Will you seek some single seminal idea which has run through the minds of all writers on the subject of money, or will you start with the questions that monetary theory ought to answer? I hope your publisher will not press you for a fixed date for completion. Keynes's *Treatise* is sixty years old. His own later ideas did much to add new greatness.

I am most deeply touched indeed by your extraordinary generous kindness in proposing to arrange for a collection of my letters to be made and published. I began some years ago to have xerox copies made of my outgoing letters and perhaps these may be of service. My handwriting did not become as atrociously bad as it now is until a number of years ago. Mr. Owen's interest is this plan is of course a very deep pleasure to me, and this has suggested to me a search among my papers for manuscript material that might interest him. With Catherine's help and Mrs. Dyter's, I hope still to be of some use in these projects.

Catherine joins me of course in sending you our warmest and best wishes.

Yours,

George Shackle

314

Alde House
Aldeburgh
Suffolk
25th October 1989

Dearest Stephen,

We have just seen the [death] notice in *The Times* and our hearts go out to you in a yearning of love and a longing of sympathy.[1]

This is the end of a long tragedy for you and Irina, and please God may it be *the end* of it for surely we can say of Michael this is the beginning of a new life, fresh and clean, and the boy he once was he is now again. This is a fresh start. Bonhoeffer comes into my mind. When he was called out by the guards from the rest of the group of prisoners he said to the Englishman beside him: 'This is the end for me; and the beginning of something splendid.'

We can't be with you next Tuesday but we shall follow you in our thoughts. And we shan't of course expect to see you here until later on.

I want to write to Irina separately.

With much love as always,

Catherine

1 This refers to the death of Stephen Frowen's only son Michael who died as a result of a tragic accident on 19 October, 1989. George Shackle's letter to Stephen Frowen, dated 29 October 1989, reads as follows:

My dear Stephen,

Catherine and I think of you in these days, and especially we think what joy you have in Tanya and her three daughters [Carly, Josie and Cassie Hosburn]. News of them will always be of the greatest interest to us.[1] My grandchildren also are all girls, varying in age from tot to grown-up.

We send you our warmest love and wishes.

As ever,

George Shackle

1 George would have been delighted had he lived long enough to hear of Carly's two children, Josie's studies at the Royal Holloway College, University of London, after obtaining four Grades A in her A-level examinations, and Cassie's success at Lancing College.

315

University College London
Department of Economics
Gower Street
London WC1E 6BT
5th December 1989

My dear Catherine and George,

Irina and I are deeply grateful to you for your kind and helpful letters and for contributing to the 'Michael Frowen Memorial Fund'. The Royal Free Hospital School of Medicine will use the income from the contributions to award a biennial or maybe annual prize for outstanding medical research in those fields where Michael was most in need of expert medical help which the Royal Free Hospital has provided to him over so many years.

The realisation of his death is still so difficult for us to accept and often we hope that it was nothing but a bad dream. I feel quite paralysed and unable to concentrate. For a time I had a high temperature without any other symptoms, just a feeling of total exhaustion. I don't think any pain can be greater than the pain one feels sitting at the death-bed of one's own child and then to take him to his grave. Michael's closest friend during the last phase of his short life was the priest of the Anglican Parish Church in Hampstead.[1] His support throughout this tragic period I just cannot praise enough. On the day of the accident we spent the afternoon with Michael and his young wife (he was married only three weeks before the accident). He seemed reasonably well, although he was going through another bad period intending to enter a private dedoxicating clinic in London the following day. In the evening he choked on a piece of steak during dinner. By the time the ambulance car reached the Royal Free Hospital his heart had stopped beating for up to 20 minutes. The doctors managed to resuscitate him, but the brain damage was such that he peacefully died four days later on 19 October. We stayed with him day and night and most of the time the priest, David Michaels, was at our side. We had a small family service on the eve of the funeral when Michael's body was taken to the Church where he rested overnight. I was amazed how crowded the church was for the Funeral Eucharist the following day, 31 October. He was then laid to rest at the Highgate Cemetery. So many letters we received express the thought that he is now enjoying peace and eternal life. My hope and belief is that this is true but the thought occurs why even strong believers do not want to die. Surely if life after death is the really desirable one, our only wish should be to die! If only I could find an answer to this question.

After the inquest on 27th November we went to Germany for a fortnight to get away from our immediate problems, but we shall be back in London on 14th December in time for Christmas with Tanya and her family. Our three granddaughters, too, are such a joy and have been a great support during these trying weeks.

This is one of the first letters I am able to write since Michael's death. I hope it does not sound too confused. I am longing to see you both again early in the New Year. Hopefully *Unknowledge and Choice in Economics* will be published by then! I so much hope that you are both keeping well. I was so glad to hear from Vicky Chick that she found you both looking extremely well and fit at the Keynes Conference.

With all my warmest good wishes,

Yours ever,

Stephen

1 This was the Hampstead Parish Church of St. John and the priest, still a close friend of ours, was the Rev. David Michaels, now the Vicar at Wolvercote Church, Oxford.

316

University College London
Department of Economics
Gower Street
London WC1 6BT
28th December 1989

My dear George,

I am gradually recovering from the shock and utter despair I felt after the death of my son Michael last October. I have got to make a new start. I am sure it will help if I now take up my work again. During the weeks following the tragic events I was quite unable to concentrate and did not feel well at all. However, I hope our life will follow a more positive course from now on. I firmly believe in eternal life and a reunion with Michael after my death, whatever form this reunion may take.

I am still planning to visit you and Catherine one day, but it may be best to leave my visit until the early spring or the first half of March. In February I hope to give some talks at the Universities of Berlin, Münster and Frankfurt.

I was delighted to see a short but very positive review of *Business, Time and Thought* in the December issue of *The Economic Journal* (p. 1232) – copy enclosed. It is disappointing, of course, that the Journal did not publish a full-length review of the volume, but perhaps this is their policy in the case of collections of previously published essays.

You will probably be pleased to hear that I have been able to arrange for the 'George Shackle Foundation' to operate under the auspices of University College London and for this purpose all income from capital (to be held by Barclays Bank, Kingsway Branch, London) will be transferred regularly to a special UCL account. As UCL has charitable status, this arrangement also avoids having to set up an independent charity with all the work this would involve. The prize-awarding 'George Shackle Foundation' will also be officially listed in all relevant UCL publications which again seems to me a great advantage. Both the *EJ Newsletter* (September issue) and the *Review of Political Economy* published a note inviting essays to be submitted to the Foundation by June 1990 for then first award to be made. One essay (more the length of a monograph) has already been submitted by a young American economist!

When sorting out some papers the other day, I at last traced another batch of your (mainly early) letters to me dating back to the 1950s and early 1960s, which I shall take to Cambridge University Library next week. I shall take this opportunity to discuss with Mr. Owen the publication of your correspondence, a project we discussed at the Malvern Conference.

I had so much hoped that *Unknowledge and Choice in Economics* would be published by the end of 1989, as promised by Mr. Farmiloe. I shall talk to him about it next week.

I have not heard from you for some time but very much hope that Catherine and you are in the best of health and that Christmas with no doubt many visitors was not too strenuous for you. Irina joins me in sending you both our very warmest wishes. I feel closer to you than ever before.

Yours affectionately,

Stephen

Stephen

317

Alde House
Aldeburgh
Suffolk
7th January 1990

Dearest Stephen,

Your heartbreaking letter about Michael's death, written when you were in Germany, has lain close to my hand for a long time. I couldn't answer it until I had a time of concentrated quietness to think about it, and the hurly burly of Christmas, its preparation and aftermath, and since then the very welcome visit of a cousin didn't provide it.

I can't think of anything more heartrendering than to have to watch your child die. In the war I came to realise that we can bear, and have to bear, almost anything for our generation and almost nothing for the generation younger than our own. I sympathise quite desperately with you and Irina over this.

I have been thinking about your problem of why we should dread dying. This isn't a problem to me. I am not afraid of *being* dead (nor are you I am sure) but I have certain qualms about the act of dying and the sickness or accident leading to it. This doesn't mean to say I am not in great need of a period of life, call it purgatory or what you will, in which to learn the many things I still need to learn and to divest myself of what is bad in my make-up. I am not afraid of this and am in fact keen to get on with it. But fear of death is still there and this is surely an age-old instinct of our physical-animal-nature. When I was a child I was afraid of the dark. I didn't believe in bears under the bed but night was a time of terror to me and I used to lie in bed frozen in stillness. This was an instinct of the fawn in the grass. And so it must be with the fear of death. Watch your birds in the garden; always on the look out; afraid of danger, of being attacked, of dying. We are here as the survival of the fittest, of the most wary, the most afraid. But then on top of that – and thank God for it – we have our God-given spiritual nature to curb fear and to give hope. To me one of the most moving moments in the whole gospel story is when Christ says: "I go to my Father and to your Father." If that is so then all manner of things must be well and we can treat our fears for what they are worth and laugh at them.

Oh I do hope that doesn't read like preaching. I am the last person to be qualified or to wish to do that. But if there is a thought here which helps you in the smallest way I want to share it with you.

One happy thing which comes from your letter is the knowledge of what the Hampstead parish priest meant to Michael and to you.

George is all right but tires very easily and his memory has deteriorated. He is still working. If you feel like coming to Aldeburgh, COME. It would make us so happy to have you.

Much love as always,

Catherine.

Catherine

318

2 Alde House
Aldeburgh
Suffolk IP15 5EE
[Letter undated – a reply to Stephen Frowen's letter of 28 December 1989]

My dear Stephen,

It is a great privilege to receive your deeply moving letter of 28 December. Catherine has read it to me several times, and it fills me with sympathy, admiration and love.

Your generosity in editing *Business, Time and Thought* was a kindness beyond words.

I have been working for some weeks on an essay asked for by Philip Arestis as an entry in his proposed volume. It has been very difficult to write, for technical reasons. It has to deal with two entirely separate themes, an account of how I got 'hooked' on economics, and yet one more [intolerable? redundant? enraging?] statement of my ideas about decision under uncertainty and time. Regarding uncertainty, I have tried to disguise the all-too-familiar theory in a new approach, starting with a definition of uncertainty. I have now to consider how I can squeeze the argument of *Time in Economics* into the second half of the essay.

Really, I feel that I said all that was worth saying, on both matters, in 'A Student's Pilgrimage'.

Catherine is pleased with her new Metro, and it seems more efficient. The back seat is not as comfortable as in the old car. This does not prevent me from enjoying my favourite pastime of eavesdropping, when Catherine has a visitor sitting beside her as she drives.

Listening to such conversations, I have gained a quite new realisation of the complexities of life! When we are children at school, we do not appreciate the wonderful simplicity of life. All you have to do is to elicit a sufficient number of favourable marks (in writing, in your school report) from your teachers, and then you can switch your thoughts on to other things, such as motor cycles and aeroplanes.

Sixty years ago, I used to convey my mother about in a Bath chair. This is an immensely better thing than a wheel chair. Its wider body allows the passenger to recline in comfort. Its big wheels ride easily up a kerb. And it steers like a dream as we push it.

Catherine and I send you our very best love and wishes.

George Shackle

319

Department of Economics
University College London
Gower Street
London, WC1
10th January 1990

Dear Catherine and George,

It is with the greatest possible pleasure and joy that I am today able to present you, also in the name of Macmillan and in particular of Mr Farmiloe, with the enclosed copy of *Unknowledge and Choice in Economics*, the first copy to arrive by air from Hong Kong. I was thrilled and overjoyed to find this elegant volume waiting for me together with Catherine's much treasured letter, when I got back to London from a short stay at Mulberry Croft.

It would make me so happy to know that the book has met with your approval and given you at least some of the joy I experienced myself when producing it – at times, I am afraid, not under the easiest of circumstances: therefore the delay for which Macmillan and I share the responsibility; but the advantage is a really up-to-date list of George's publications at the end of the volume.

I shall write separately to you, Catherine, in response to your deeply moving letter which I found so very helpful and comforting just now when Michael's 40th birthday is approaching (17th January). We shall have a memorial service for him at 6.30pm at St. John's Parish Church in Hampstead.

With much love to both of you,

Yours,

Stephen

320

Alde House
Aldeburgh
Suffolk
13th January 1990

Dearest Stephen,

The opening of your package with *The Book* has brought such a surge of happiness into this house as never was. It is splendid in all ways: easy in the hand, a clear type, a delicious dark blue shiny dust cover, and above all the contents. I straight away read aloud to George your preface and Geoff Harcourt's introduction and when we had finished them I said to G, 'Now we can say: "Lord, now lettest Thou Thy servant depart in peace."' The tears came into his eyes and through a small crack in his armour-plate of modesty he said 'Yes'. Geoff Harcourt not only understands George's work but he sees the inner man, and his article is all the heart could desire in exposition, accuracy, humour and loveliness of writing. And as for you, you can't really know what you have done for both of us in this book and in

Business, Time and Thought. I hadn't known I was to be included in this new dedication and I am proud. And the things you have said about me enable me to discard elements in earlier life which I don't like, and to know myself as George's loving wife; and that is all I need to know. You can't imagine what happiness that is.

Another source of joy to us is the knowledge that the book has brought happiness to you at a moment when you so badly needed it. The book is worthy of you and of the great effort you put into its publication and into mounting of the conference. Bless you for it.

A much loved friend of mine, and latterly of us both, has just died. Eve Balfour, founder of the Soil Association and of early experiments in organic farming. Do keep an eye open for her obituary notices. Niece of one prime minister (A.J. Balfour), great granddaughter of another (Lord Salisbury), kin to half the nobility of the realm and the notable intellectuals of the latter half of the nineteenth century, she was utterly sincere, of the earth earthy, and totally without pretensions. She was a friend of Dr. Schumacher ('small is beautiful') and read the lesson from Corinthians at his requiem mass in Westminster Cathedral (though herself not a Catholic). She told me she felt the Spirit had entered into her at the reading, and after the service Cardinal Hume came to her and thanked her for the way she had done it. She had a stroke and was in the Aldeburgh Cottage Hospital for some weeks when I saw her pretty well daily. I loved her.

Early March would be the perfect time for you to visit us. Would Irina come too, and then you could stay for a night or two?

Much love as always,

Catherine.

Catherine

321

2 Alde House
Alde House Drive
Aldeburgh
Suffolk
18th January 1990

My dear Stephen,

The debt of gratitude I owe you for bringing into being, as editor, organiser and moving spirit, the two collections of essays on my ideas, first the selection of some papers of my own writing called *Business, Time and Thought*, and then the set of papers given at the Guildford Conference on my work, the conference organised by you, can only be expressed by saying it is inexpressible and overwhelming. The book *Unknowledge and Choice in Economics*, containing the Guildford papers, contains passages by yourself which have moved me as few things have ever done. Of the papers themselves I have so far only had Geoff Harcourt's chapter read to me.

[Letter incomplete.]

322

Alde House
Aldeburgh
Suffolk
2nd April 1990

Dear Stephen,

Catherine has now finished reading to me *Unknowledge and Choice in Economics*. It is as though I were to practice at the Bar, and had listened to the evidence and the speaker of the Counsel of the defence in this case, and now the jury must retire and decide their verdict. I am old enough to think there is a possibility that in 10 or 20 years, some of my ideas will seem to have validity. If any notice is ever taken of them, this will be very largely due to your superlative editing of the two books. I have always thought that Robertson's title: *Banking Policy and the Price Level* was in itself almost a summary of this century's contribution to price-level theory.

Writers sometimes single out what they call 'neglected economists'. I think there are neglected economic ideas, and that in rescuing the word *profit* from this category, you are doing a great service to economic theory. But this will be an enterprise of hazard and tough going, with, I think, very great rewards for audacity and vision. Whereas such words as employment, income and interest are impregnably respectable, *profit* causes the less hardy souls to consider moving over to the opposite pavement, in order to avoid dangerous associations. I think you will rescue *profit* from this slur.

I join with Catherine in thanking you from our hearts for your generosity in spending a whole day to come and refresh our spirits.

All warmest and best wishes and utmost gratitude,

Yours,

George Shackle

323

Alde House
Aldeburgh
Suffolk
2nd April 1990

Dearest Stephen,

It was true delight to see you here and to listen to George talking to you with such animation and interest. It did him a world of good, and you supply the one thing which Aldeburgh lacks: a colleague from the world of economics. It was a most generous act to spare a whole day for us when your time is always in demand, and is something greatly appreciated by us.

I am looking out of the drawing room window at the cherry trees and the Crown Imperials all of which are at the peak of perfection. I do hope this lovely spring will be an element in helping you to recover from the trauma of Michael's death.

With much love as always, and to Irina,

Catherine.

Catherine

324

POSTCARD FROM POTSDAM – SCHLOSS SANSSOUCI
14th May 1990

Dear Catherine and George,

Our brief stay in Berlin is passing far too quickly – a most exciting period this great city is now going through. But there is also some sadness among our friends in East Berlin and considerable fear of the unavoidable difficulties to come. Greatly looking forward to talk to you soon. It was such a joy to see Michael Ambrosi again with whom I am just enjoying a few minutes of relaxation and discussion.

Love and warmest wishes,

Stephen

Stephen

Dear Friends,

Sitting together with Stephen we think and talk much of you and of George's relentless intellectual vigour. The sight of Sanssouci in Potsdam, which was in the 'East' although it is *west* of West Berlin, may be a 'motto' for you, too.

Warmest wishes,
Michael [Ambrosi]

325

POSTCARD FROM KESWICK, LAKE DISTRICT
30th May 1990

Dear Catherine and George,

What a delight the Lake District is. We are greatly enjoying our togetherness with Hal and B Hillmann, whom George knows so well from his Leeds days, in Windermere. Yesterday we went to Coniston Lake to visit Brantwood – John Ruskin's residence from 1872–1900. Since my Leeds days in the early 1950s, I have not been to the Lake District and what an overwhelming experience it is to see it again. Delighted to get your card from Malvern.

Love,

Stephen

Kind regards from Hal Hillmann.

Affectionate greetings from this lovely part of the world from
Irina

326

BIRTHDAY CARD TO GEORGE SHACKLE FOR HIS 87TH BIRTHDAY
14th July 1990

To George

Happy Birthday

And many happy returns. 87 and almost time to start with the preparations for the grand occasion of your 90th birthday! All our warmest wishes are with you for a healthy, happy and in every way fulfilling year to come.

With much love and deep affection,

Yours,

Stephen and Irina

327

Quellenhof Kur-und Golfhotel
Bad Ragaz
Switzerland
11th September 1990

My dear Catherine and George,

We arrived last night at the Quellenhof, having left London on 6th September, and shall be staying here until 25th September, mainly for Irina to receive treatment which hopefully will help her over the winter months without too much arthritis pain. The rest here will no doubt be beneficial to me as well, as I felt totally exhausted by the time we left London. Apart from work, the burden of a stream of visitors, with Irina being fairly incapacitated did not exactly help. I almost felt like running a hotel with some visitors leaving in the morning and the next guests having to be picked up at the airport in the afternoon! We have to be more careful next year. In addition I had to empty Michael's flat – a difficult and painful task – to get it ready for letting to an American teacher from the American School in Hampstead. But I am glad that it is all done now. A Requiem Eucharist will be held for Michael on the occasion of the first anniversary of his death at St. John-at-Hampstead Church on 20th October at 6 p.m.

Irina saw Professor Bird again at the Moorfields Eye Hospital in London. The second eye is now beginning to be affected by the same illness [macular degeneration], and reading – still possible but increasingly difficult – will probably become impossible. It is an age problem and there is no treatment. Nature will have to take its course. You and George know it only too well. Irina will have to see an expert recommended by Professor Bird for some magnifying devices which may help temporarily.

It was so lovely to have seen you both again at Great Malvern. I sent a reproduction of Queen Victoria's stained glass window, with her grandson – later the Emperor Wilhelm II – standing behind her, to Prince Louis Ferdinand [grandson of Wilhelm II]. He was thrilled to get it and writes:

> 'My grandfather was the favourite grandson of my great great grandmother [Queen Victoria]. As a present she gave him Kilimanjaro for his East African Colony and no doubt had a decisive influence in the return of the Isle of Heligoland to the German Reich. On 10 August we celebrated the hundredth anniversary of this memorable day on the Isle of Heligoland.'[1]

I was so happy to see both of you in such splendid form at the Malvern Conference. I do hope that this important event in honour of George gave him some happiness.

Just before leaving London I discovered the enclosed excellent review of *Business, Time and Thought* by K.W. Rothschild (Vienna) at the LSE Library in the German *Journal of Economics*. It is gratifying to see that at last notice is being taken of this splendid volume and I hope the review will give some joy and well deserved satisfaction to George.

From Bad Ragaz we shall proceed to the Rilke Conference in Leipzig and Weimar on 25th September, from there to Berlin and Würzburg for the meeting of the German Economic Society from 3rd to 5th October at which I have to chair a morning session. We shall be back in London on 10th October.

I do hope that you are both well and able to continue enjoying your magnificent garden during the rest of this unique summer.

Irina joins me in sending you both our warmest wishes. With much love and affection,

Yours,

Stephen

1 Letter from HIH Prince Louis Ferdinand of Prussia to Stephen Frowen, dated 28 August 1990. The original German text of this passage reads: 'Mein Grossvater war der Lieblingsenkel meiner Ur-Urgrossmutter [Königin Viktoria]. Sie schenkte ihm den Kilimandscharo for seine Kolonie Ostafrika und sicherlich hatte sie auch einen entscheidenden Einfluss auf die Rückgabe der Insel Helgoland an das Deutsche Reich. Am 10. August haben wir die hundertjährige Wiederkehr dieses denkwürdigen Tages auf der Insel Helgoland gefeiert.'

328

Alde House
Aldeburgh
Suffolk
17th September 1990

Dear Stephen,

My first word, in response to your most moving and extraordinarily interesting letter must be to hope that you have had some rest and quiet to regain peace of mind and physical strength. Your stamina and energy are astonishing and fill me with admiration. I hope, too, that the long review of *Business, Time and Thought* will have pleased you as much as it did me. Catherine will read it to me again, and of course we shall carefully file it.

Your knowledge of languages must by now be such that you can compare several of them as means of thought and expression in economics. I believe the question has never been settled whether Cantillon wrote his *Essai sur la nature du ammeice* originally in French or English.

It begins to seem that the appearance of *The Economic Journal* for September has been affected by some special circumstance. I suppose it will be celebrating the centenary year of Marshall's *Principles*, and this could well account for delay.

It was most kind of you to come to the Malvern Conference. I did not realise at the time what this involved for you. Catherine is writing to you and will enclose her note with mine.

We both send you our most intense wishes for your and your wife's continuing happiness.

George Shackle

329

Alde House
Aldeburgh
Suffolk
17th September 1990

Dearest Stephen,

Your lovely letter has given us so much pleasure, *AND* a feeling of dismay (though not of surprise) that the activities and sorrows of the past year have left you so utterly tired and exhausted. Try to let up a bit from now on, it is only to please those who love you.

It was good indeed to read K.W. Rothschild's review of *Business, Time and Thought* and it left both of us purring not only for George's sake but for yours too as its faithful editor.

I was tremendously amused by Prince Louis Ferdinand's reaction to the stained glass picture of Queen Victoria (barely recognisable) at her diamond Jubilee with Edward P. of W. and Kaiser Wilhelm II. It evidently gave him much pleasure to receive the card. Fancy it being 100 years since Heligoland was transferred back to Germany; now it is surely an island of birds rather than big guns. Did I tell you that my sister Jocelyn and her husband got to know Prince L.F. and his wife when he, Pat [Brigadier Patrick Clapham], was Commander at Oldenburg soon after the war? A rather formal acquaintance perhaps since British troops were occupying Germany at the time.

George has had one or two rather disturbing attacks, the most distressing aspect of them being his intense conviction that he was about to die at any moment. The doctors tell me this is a typical symptom of this kind of trouble, that the attack is a passing one and leaves no damage to the brain. So I am reassured, in part at least. He is better now and seems to be responding to the treatment which is the mild one of a small daily dose of aspirin. I am telling you, but not others, about this.

We both sympathise from the heart with Irina over her eye trouble and can do so with full knowledge of what it means. As for the arthritis, we hope very much that the present treatment will ease matters. We shall be thinking of you very dearly at 6p.m. on October 20th. There is no better way of strengthening your links with Michael.

With much love,

Catherine.

Catherine

330

2 Alde House
Aldeburgh
Suffolk
11th December 1990

My dear Stephen,

Catherine and I believe you will find this book consisting of letters addressed by an American ambassador to Britain to Lady Lyttelton as entertaining and engaging as we have done.[1] It is evident from their quality and insight that James Russell Lowell was a man of understanding and humanity, indeed the kind of friend one would be deeply pleased with and one who would give life an extra spice and stimulus. Alethea Hayter was asked by Lady Lyttelton's granddaughters, Lavinia Mynors and Elizabeth Home of the Hirsel who were great friends of hers, to edit the letters. Alethea is a much loved friend of ours in whom you would delight.[2]

Best love from us both,

George Shackle.

1 The book edited by Alethea Hayter is entitled *Portrait of a Friendship, Drawn from New Letters of James Russell Lowell to Sybella Lady Lyttelton, 1881–1891* (Salisbury: Michael Russell, 1990).
2 Stephen Frowen was subsequently introduced to Alethea Hayter by Catherine and George Shackle and a bond of friendship was soon established.

331

Alde House
Aldeburgh
Suffolk
7th January 1991

Dearest Stephen,

We were so happy to know you were safely through your operation and that all was going well and that you had had good care from surgeons and nurses.

We were delighted too to know how much you had enjoyed *Portrait of a Friendship*. You must certainly meet Alethea one day; you would enjoy each other. The provenance of the book will interest you I think. Lady Lyttelton's youngest daughter Hester married a Dr. Alington who became headmaster of Eton and then Dean of Durham. Two of their daughters, Elizabeth who married Lord Home and Lavinia who married Roger Mynors, are, or were for Elizabeth, great friends of Alethea's (I think she and Lavinia were at LMH together); they came into possession of the Lowell letters and asked Alethea to edit them. The Mynors connection may interest you: identical twin brothers Roger and Humphrey; they both became Sir-ed, Humphrey as Governor, or perhaps Deputy Governor of the Bank of England and Roger as a distinguished classical don at Oxford. They lived, plus families, in a small Castle in Herefordshire called Treago where Alethea often stayed. The brothers are unhappily both dead.

By the way, I copied out the part of your letter which refered to the book and sent it to Alethea because I knew how much it would please her. I hope you don't mind? You will be amused to know I supplied one incident to the book. I was browsing in Ethel Smyth's *Impressions that Remained*, an old favourite, and came on her rain-soaked visit to Lady

L. in Hereford when Lowell was there – and didn't like him! So I let Alethea have it and she was grateful and incorporated it.

All's well here and we keep going very quietly. Don't try to answer this letter; you'll be off in a few days and we hope you will have a lovely *restful* time in California with lots of sun and warmth to do you both good.

With much love,

Catherine

Catherine

332

40 Gurney Drive
London N2 0DE
25th January 1991

My dear George,

I was so very sad to hear of the death of Jack Wiseman at such an early age and with so much still to be accomplished. His book on *A New Political Economy* still in preparation would I am sure have been a main contribution. The enclosed obituary by Arthur Seldon may have escaped your notice as you and Catherine are taking *The Times*.

I also enclose a very nice and penetrating review of *Business, Time and Thought* by Jan Kregel which has just appeared in the Dutch jounal *De Economist*. I hope you will be as pleased with it as I was when I discovered it by chance at the LSE Library.

We decided in the end not to go to California in view of the terrible war situation [the Gulf War] and I am now so glad we took this decision. This leaves us free to visit you in Aldeburgh earlier than I visualized, provided an earlier date would suit you. I shall telephone you and Catherine in a few days' time to fix a date for our visit. But our visit may not suit you at all at this time of the year. In this case, we could perhaps postpone it until the spring. In any case, I do hope that you and Catherine are both keeping well.

Irina joins me in sending you and Catherine our warmest wishes.

Yours affectionately,

Stephen

Stephen

333
2 Alde House
Aldeburgh
Suffolk
6th February 1991

Dear Stephen,

With your most kind consent I am enclosing to you copies of the three articles I have recently written.[1] One of them, called 'Word-Efficiency and the Economist' bears on a theme that I believe to be given less attention than it deserves, namely, the successful transmission of thought depends on extremes in the use of words. Words are as important to the economist as they are to the poet, or musical notation to the musical composer. It is *not* true, as is sometimes asserted, that one cannot *think* without words. The carpenter building a fence does not instruct himself in words at each step; the mathematician takes what are very short cuts compared with the verbal statements of the textbooks. But words are the vessels of meaning for the purpose of communication. I shall value any comments you may have on any of these papers as a symbol of friendship at its highest level.

With all warmest and best wishes,

George Shackle

[1] The three Shackle articles were the subject of intense discussions during Stephen Frowen's subsequent visit to Aldeburgh.

334
Alde House
Aldeburgh
10th March 1991

Dearest Stephen,

Here is a copy of George's latest paper 'The economist's thread of thought' which you said you would like to see. He is leaving it to you and John Pheby to decide whether, and in what way, you would like to use it together with the other three papers which the two of you already have.

We are sad not to see you here today, but truly a visit would be better a little later on when the bulbs are in bloom and the Crown Imperials out. At the moment everything is very green and full of promise, but there is little colour in the garden, the crocuses, which were brilliant being over. And of course Irina's sad state of health make a visit out of the question at the moment. We hope so very much that the dermatologist will be able to cure this horrid skin trouble. She has enough to contend with without that.

George shows signs of his increasing age but he is not unwell. We think the day is not far off when he won't be able to manage the stairs and we have a plan ready to put into operation to bring down our beds to the drawing room. I lived happily in a bed-sit when I first started work in London and see no reason why I shouldn't do so again! Nor do we think the friends we are fond of will object. You are forewarned!

I have just sold a couple of pictures at Sotheby's. Not a good time to do it but I got a gross £1600 which covered what they cost me, and I now have my drawings back on the wall where I like them. So I am happy about it.

When you see Vicky Chick will you give her our love? We still hope that one day you will bring her down here to see us. Meanwhile we both send lots of love to you and Irina and warmest wishes for her return to better health. Kindly look after yourself too.

Catherine.

Catherine

335

St. George's House
Windsor Castle
Windsor
23rd April 1991

Dearest Catherine,

I do feel so terribly guilty for the unforgivable delay in thanking you for your lovely letter and for sending me a copy of George's latest and splendid paper. I shall treasure both.

The reason for this impressive notepaper is that Irina and I have just spent three memorable days at St. George's House attending a conference on 'Economic Activity and Personal Responsibility'. Among the participants were leading theologians, economists and managers of large industrial concerns. My own paper was on 'Pressures in Macro and Micro-economics'. The discussions went very well and it was a tremendously interesting exchange of views. One evening we had a most delightful harpsichord concert given by a Professor of the Royal College of Music in the old Library where Shakespeare appeared in the *Merry Wives of Windsor*, especially commissioned by Elizabeth I. Afterwards there was a private conducted tour of St. George's Chapel by the Master of St. George's House. The whole evening was a sheer delight.

I am now writing from Ascona where we have been spending the past week with an old friend, the widow of Karl Kerényi; the latter was a brilliant Hungarian classicist and mythologist who left Hungary in 1943 and settled in Switzerland. Another reason for our stay in the Ticino was the 90th birthday celebrations of our friend Anita Forrer (whose correspondence with Rilke was published a few years ago), given by her nephew, who is the President of the Swiss Parliament, at the Hotel La Palma in Locarno where Anita has her apartment. At 90 she is in the best of health and devotedly looks after her 92 year old friend Mimi, the widow of Don Salvador de Madariaga, the Spanish scholar and writer who for several decades taught at Oxford after leaving Spain under General Franco. She unfortunately suffers most terribly from cancer but is still engaged from her bedside in editing and translating some of her husband's works. It is touching. The serenity with which she witnesses the end approaching and her eyes emanating strength and tremendous warmth and taking in the beauty of her surroundings in full measure is something I shall never forget. Every minute we were able to spend with her seemed a gift from heaven.

Irina is not too well, I am afraid, and tomorrow we are going to a special eye clinic near St. Gallen to see whether her by now very limited reading ability can be prevented from further deterioration. But this is a problem nobody could be more familiar with than you and George. Irina's arthritis will be helped, we hope, by our 2 1/2 weeks of treatment in Bad Ragaz from 24.4.–11.5. (Hotel Quellenhof). In addition to all this she suffers from a serious skin disease, a pre-cancerous state which is being treated and has to be closely watched. But she continuous writing and is trying to keep as active as her health permits.

I have myself been held back rather badly by lots of domestic duties Irina can no longer cope with. I am therefore greatly enjoying our journey which gives me the chance of getting some rest and getting on with some of my neglected tasks – one more pressing than the other.

From Ragaz we shall proceed to Berlin for the viva of one of my Ph.D. students and a few other duties and I shall then accompany Irina to Weimar for the Annual Meeting of the Goethe Society from 22.5.–25.5. Because of her eyesight problem, Irina feels too unsure of herself to travel on her own. We shall therefore not be back in London until the end of May but then hope to see you as soon as possible in Aldeburgh, a visit I have been looking forward to for so long.

I feel quite guilty now for concentrating so much on our own activities instead of enquiring how you are yourself. Your garden must now be getting into its second splendour after the spring flowers, or is the unusually cold weather holding things back? To see that George has regained his strength and vigour, as shown by a flow of further papers full of sparkle and brilliant ideas, expressed with such simplicity, was for me the source of great happiness.

Take care of yourself, Catherine. With your tremendous inner strength, always looking after others, you remind me so much of Anita Forrer. You are so young in every respect that nobody would have a chance of even remotely guessing your age!

If you have a minute to spare some time, it would make me very happy to hear from you while we are on the Continent. I shall write to George separately as soon as I get to Bad Ragaz.

With much love to both of you and all warmest good wishes, always,

Yours,

Stephen

Stephen

336

2 Alde House
Aldeburgh
Suffolk IP15 5EE
30 April 1991

Dearest Stephen,

Your lovely, lovely letter of April 23 has been an absolute delight to us, specially in relation to what you say about George's latest papers and the heartwarming and quite undeserved things you say about me! . . .

We were duly impressed by the St. George's House letter heading and (much better) by your description of the delightful and highly interesting time you had there. I am so glad that Irina was well enough to go too and to enjoy it all with you. But I am not happy to hear the account of her general health and nor can I feel hopeful that the St. Gallen eye clinic will have been able to hold out much hope about her sight, at least as far as reading is concerned. The skin trouble seems a quite gratuitous extra affliction, and a menacing one too for which I feel dreadfully sorry for her – and for you as you must be anxious about it.

(Your letter came at a moment when I heard that a cousin of mine, Roger Norrington, is in trouble with skin cancer. Have you come across him as a conductor? I feel it is very hard on a relatively young man to be removed, if only temporarily, from his profession just when he is making a name for himself.)

What you had to tell us about your friend, the widow of [Don] Salvador de Madariaga [Emilia née Szekely-Rauman (Mimi)], was so beautifully and tellingly expressed that it is as though the beam of courage and serenity from her eyes has made contact with us here. A wonderful woman.

Our garden has been more colourful this spring than I ever remember it. It has been a wonderful flowering year for all bulbs, and the blossom on our two cherry trees has been magical. And now we have rain storms and high winds and everything is torn in shreds and laid flat! But the recollection in tranquillity of its loveliness is still a delight.

My sister's [Jocelyn Clapham's] house in Lavenham is being sold; a sad time & I shall be glad for my nieces when it's all over. Strutt & Parker have produced a brochure with a very lovely photograph of the house on the front. You must see it one day.

And now dear boy remember this: we *love* to see you here and no matter how long the gap we take up exactly where we left off. But we don't want you ever to feel obliged to make the effort to come when it's not easy. We know how busy you are and how valuable is the work you are doing; and we know too that your domestic chores are time-consuming (as are mine). So only come when the coming is easy and then it will be a joy.

George is keeping pretty well on the whole. Ten days ago I did something I haven't done before and doubt it I shall do again. I left him in charge for the day of our kind librarian friend, was driven to London in our car by our tame taxi man, Mr. [S.] Squirrell, and went to a lunch party given in her flat by Alethea Hayter to celebrate the 80th birthday of a dear friend, Kate Warriner. Alethea, Kate and I always sat together in the 1st Altos of the Bach Choir over a period of nearly 20 years. There were a lot of interesting people there, and did I enjoy it! I got back in time for supper.

With love as always,

Catherine.

Catherine

337

Alde House
Aldeburgh
Suffolk
1st May 1991

Dear Stephen,

Your letter to Catherine gave very special pleasure. Your ease of movement about the world brings home to me the very limited extent of my own travels. You must have a working knowledge of many languages, and a far more than merely working one of some. My school, the Perse at Cambridge, gave greater attention to language than anything else, but most of all to classical Latin and Greek. They say that culture is what is left when you have forgotten everything you ever tried to learn. I am rapidly approaching the stage of 'culture'. I think one of the great advances in the technique of living will consist in the devising of a new typography that can be read by a machine: of course read aloud. Do you think such a thing is possible? One can surely conceive of a musical symbolism which could speak directly on an instrument without human intervention. At that rate, human beings will soon become superfluous, or reduced to a merely amateur role. After all, I suppose men could not have gone to the moon without the aid of the electronic computer.

Catherine and her friend, Mrs. Vivien Dyter, are engrossed in research into Catherine's family ancestry, and I hear references to Charles II far more than to, e.g. Mr. Major. Catherine has written you a proper letter which will give you our news, such as it is.

In your visits to various countries, do you get the impression that the new musical work is being conceived and composed by a new generation of composers? I wish I had some feeling of musical response and understanding, but, alas! it's not so. A whole world is denied me, but I think there must be many men in a similar case.

We send you every heartfelt wish for your health.

Yours as ever and sincerely,

George Shackle

338

BIRTHDAY CARD TO GEORGE SHACKLE FOR HIS 88TH BIRTHDAY ON 14th JULY 1991
18th August 1991

My dear George,

With all my heart I wish you a year full of joy, happiness and good and improved health – and many more happy years in good health to follow. My warmest thoughts will always be with you in deepest gratitude for 40 years of unfailing friendship, which so much enriched my life. I only wished that sometimes I could do something for you. If at any time there is any need I hope that you know that I would only be too happy to do everything in my power to help in any way I can.

Please forgive the lateness of my birthday greetings. With me taking Irina to the German Island of Sylt (nr. the Danish border), my Cambridge and Oxford conferences, fetching Irina again in Sylt plus an attack of shingles (!), life has sometimes been difficult to cope with. However, we can now look forward to a quiet and restful week in the Engadin and I am even more looking forward to my visit to you after my return to London on 28th August.

Irina joins me in sending you and Catherine our warmest and very best wishes,

Yours,

Stephen

Stephen

339

40 Gurney Drive
London N2 0DE
24th September 1991

My dear George,

I am so very happy to know that you are now progressing steadily at Ipswich Hospital. The wonderful and substantial letters you are again able to write are sufficient proof that you are well on the way to a speedy recovery. I was delighted and grateful to be allowed to read your splendid letters to Jack Gilbert, Alethea Hayter and your niece Hilary [Clapham]. A copy of your letter to Hilary arrived this morning and I read it out to Irina over breakfast. She was as captivated by your thoughts on poets and poetry as I was. You are so right about the closeness between poetry, music and mathematics. A poet – because of his thought – can express in one line what, writing prose, might require a whole page or more. But as I know from some of our successful and much published poet-friends, it requires great effort, as of course any serious writing does. Rainer Maria Rilke, one of the 20th century's greatest poets, needed absolute solitude for his writing, which he found at the Italian Castle of Duino, where he wrote his famous *Duineser Elegien (Duino Elegies)*, and later at the Castle of Muzot in the French part of Switzerland. What he had in common with you, apart from his brilliance as a writer, is that he wrote beautiful letters which really form part of his literary creation. Most were written quite obviously with publication in mind, and fortunately many were in fact published in due course. This is why I am so anxious to get on with the preparation for the publication of your own correspondence which contains so much untapped material complementary to your published works.

The idea you expressed of a conference in Aldeburgh in the Spring on 'Economics as an Art of Thought' is quite splendid, and those I have mentioned it to are all most enthusiastic and wish to participate. Whenever you feel strong enough to let me have further thoughts on this, I should be most grateful to hear from you, in particular as to the specific topics you would like to be discussed. We can also discuss this further next time I visit you in Suffolk.

Irina and I will be off to Paris tomorrow where she will take a study group to discuss Rilke's poems inspired by Paris as part of the annual conference of the Rilke Society. I hope her eyes will stand up to all this! We shall be back on Monday, 1st October.

Please take care and continue your speedy recovery. We all need you so much.

With much love and all warmest good wishes to you and Catherine from Irina and myself,

Yours ever,

Stephen

Stephen

340

Von Hügel Institute
at St. Edmund's College
Cambridge CB3 0BN
5th October 1991

Dearest Catherine,

I greatly enjoyed talking to you this morning. I was delighted and happy to hear your encouraging news.

Of course, we must go very carefully through the piece I sent you.[1] Fortunately, there is enough time. I regarded it more as a first draft, although I did have to submit it to *The Independent* as they were anxious to have it on their file. However, I did reserve the right to make further amendments. Your cooperation in every way would be more than welcome.

You may have seen the enclosed review by Jim Ford of *Business, Time and Thought*, which appeared in the last issue of the *Review of Political Economy*. I derived great happiness from it, mainly for George's sake. It was of course nice to see the editor getting some praise, too!

The other day I had a reply from Stephan Boehm and a copy of the circular he sent to prospective contributors to the Festschrift on the occasion of George's 90th birthday. Vicky Chick and others have already accepted the invitation. I further enclose a copy of the entry on George in the volume on dissenting economists edited by Philip Arestis. I understand from Edward Elgar that the book is about to appear and he has promised to send one of the first copies he receives to George. This article (the entry on George) sums up George and his work extremely well and should receive considerable attention.

I am so glad that George received my letter and was able to enjoy it, and that my letter to you also arrived safely. I posted both in a hurry prior to my departure for Paris.

With much love, as always, and all warmest and dearest wishes to George,

Yours affectionately,

Stephen

Stephen

P.S. There are a few words in George's letter of 1 May, I still find difficult to decipher. I have typed out the text as far as I could read it, and you would make me very happy if you would be so kind as to fill in the gaps – whenever you can spare a minute or two. Many thanks for your kind help.

1 The piece referred to was a first draft of an obituary of G.L.S. Shackle for *The Independent*. The obituary appeared in *The Independent* on 4 March 1992, the day after the death of G.L.S. Shackle.

341

2 Alde House
Aldeburgh
Suffolk
6th October 1991

Dearest Stephen,

Here is a copy of George's letter to Professor Lucas Beltrán in Madrid which he dictated to me with scarcely a hesitation.

I have just been reading again for the nth time your paper on George and I do want you to know how touched to the heart I am by it. You have presented in lovely words the spirit of the man, his goodness, gentleness and modesty, as well as the achievement of the economist and writer. I am eternally grateful to you for it. And thank you too for the letter you sent with the revised copy: very warming and sustaining to my heart.

I am sorry I was so disorientated on the 'phone when you rang up. Forgive me.

The doctors are starting George's rehabilitation treatment this coming week and we are beginning to look forward to his coming home.

Much love,

Catherine.

Catherine

342

University College London
Department of Economics
Gower Street
London WC1E 6BT
9th October 1991

Dearest Catherine,

How very kind of you to send me a copy of George's letter to Professor Beltrán. It surely is a further and most encouraging sign of George's recovery. Only he could phrase his thoughts in such beautiful prose – a truly poetic style.

I forgot to enclose the copy of George's entry in Philip Arestis's volume on 'dissenting economists'[1] in my last letter. I am attaching it now for you to keep in you files. Please do keep in close touch.

With love,

Yours affectionately,

Stephen

1 The volume concerned is: Philip Arestis and Malcolm Sawyer (eds), *A Biographical Dictionary of Dissenting Economists* (Aldershot: Edward Elgar, 1992. For the entry on G.L.S. Shackle, see pp. 505–10.

343

2 Alde House
Aldeburgh
Suffolk
17th October 1991

Dearest Stephen,

Here are two more items for you: a short statement on 'Form' (I am encouraging George to dictate to me such thoughts so that we may keep them on record) and a letter to Rafael Rubio in Madrid. Rafael sent a delightful letter asking for news of George and I sent G's reply with a covering note. If you want to link up with such letters I can always let you have copies.

Jim Ford's review of *Business, Time and Thought* brought a wonderful sense of satisfaction and a lump to the throat. I don't think we had seen it before – I couldn't have forgotten it.

I have been a tardy correspondent lately. Please forgive me. Most of my day is spent in the hospital or travelling to and fro.

Have a lovely time in Italy.

George is improving – dressed and sitting up in a chair. More himself.

Much love as always,

Catherine

344

The Reform Club
Pall Mall
London SW1
28th November 1991

My dear George,

It was a wonderful occasion seeing you again happily settled at home and even being able to see me to the door when I left. You know how much I treasure every conversation I am privileged to have with you, and yesterday was no exception. It is so wonderful to experience your creative mind working incessantly and to be allowed to participate. One must be grateful that the economics profession has at last moved away from the overemphasis on econometrics and empirical testing, and is beginning to realise the desperate need for new ideas which reflect and can deal with the drastically changed economic environment. We now have an internationalised, global economy to an extent we have never experienced before. And this trend towards internationalisation will no doubt continue. This situation will certainly require some rethinking as far as economic theory is concerned. I wonder how you yourself feel about these developments, which at present are particularly pronounced in the financial sector, but are gradually affecting other sectors of the economy as well.

I have traced the Hey review of Jim Ford's selection of your essays and include a photocopy.[1] I am delighted with it, and feel he is right in his observation that there is a risk of misrepresentation, as your careful writing in book form is excluded from a collection meant to be representative of your entire work.

Please continue to get better from day to day.

With all my warmest good wishes,

Yours,

Stephen

1 This was a Book Note by John D. Hey of J.L.Ford (ed.), *Time, Expectations and Uncertainty in Economics: Selected Essays of G.L.S. Shackle* (Aldershot: Edward Elgar, 1990), *The Economic Journal*, vol. 101, no. 408, September 1991, p. 1337.

345

Alde House
Aldeburgh
Suffolk
3rd December 91

My dear Stephen,

Your exceedingly kind letter gave me immense encouragement. I hope to go on working at our subject for some time yet although I am 88 years old. I feel that if I stop working I shall stop living. One must of course beware of merely repeating oneself but if I fall into this trap you and others will make me aware of it. I try to get hold of the most interesting sounding books so far as their titles are a guide and am always glad to hear of books likely to interest me. I recently had one sent to me called *Capital in Economic Theory*. It was sent me by its author Syed Ahmad and will take a big effort of study and more than one reading to get the full worth of it. I am as you know greatly handicapped by the loss of my reading eyesight but Catherine and some friends are extremely kind in reading aloud to me, though it cannot be said that hearing a book read aloud is at all the same thing as reading it to oneself. These are the inescapable penalties of old age.

I am most grateful to you indeed for sending me a copy of John Hey's review of *Time, Expectations and Uncertainty in Economics*. I am delighted with the praise John Hey bestows on Jim Ford for his editorship.

With all very warmest good wishes and I am most grateful to you for taking the trouble to come so far to see us.

Yours ever,

George Shackle.

346

2 Alde House
Aldeburgh
Suffolk
13th January 1992

Dearest Stephen,

What a *horrifying* story, and I am only thankful to know you are both alive.[1] After you had telephoned me I immediately rang Vicky Chick and she was just as shocked as was I.

I wonder so much how Irina is faring, and I mean to ring up to find out how you both are. I have refrained from telling George because, if he understood it, I think he would be dreadfully distressed. He varies from day to day, sometimes barely waking up and then on another day: 'We must start taking Spanish lessons *at once*; and please explain everything to me about the European Community.' (I came away mentally exhausted!)

Dear boy, I am thinking about you both so much and sending up a constant prayer for you.

With much love as always,

Catherine.

Catherine

1 Stephen and Irina Frowen narrowly missed death when caught in a fire at the house of Stephen's brother and sister-in-law, Kurt and Erika Frowein, in Germany and spent many weeks in hospital with severe burns.

347

2 Alde House
Aldeburgh
Suffolk
23rd February 1992

Dearest Stephen,

I was terribly distressed to learn that Irina's injuries are still so far from recovery and that while she is going daily to the Sanatorium for dressings you are having to do everything for her in the way of feeding, clothing, washing, etc. This is a heavy strain on you and it made me wish the doctors were still keeping her in hospital. Your voice on the telephone sounded as though you yourself were still not fully recovered, so I feel anxious about you dear boy.

Our news here is that George is maintaining his improvement from that bad moment when we all thought he was dying. He varies very much from day to day; sometimes it is distressing to see him unhappy, in discomfort, and sometimes in pain. At other times he is quiet and himself and I can read to him. One lovely sunny day the nurses were able to lift him into the car and I took him for a drive. It seemed like a miracle. But since then he has not been quite so good. A few days ago he said to me, 'Have they finished building the Suez Canal yet?'. 'Oh yes', I said, 'it has been in action for quite a time. It's a good short cut.'

When I got home it suddenly occurred to me that he may have meant the Channel Tunnel, so next day I asked him – and he had!

Vicky and I keep in touch and I can't tell you how much her concern – her *loving* concern – for George moves me. This illness of his has shown very clearly how much his friends and colleagues love him for his sweetness, his goodness and his modesty.

The BBC are broadcasting a reading of [Thomas Mann's] *Buddenbrooks* on Radio 4 on Saturday evenings and of course I am listening. Isn't that splendid?

George has been moved to a new room in the nursing home. It is sunny and spacious with French windows looking across grass to a wood: a big improvement. I keep a bank of flowers and plants going and do my 'gardening' daily. I have hung one or too small pictures there to make it a bit like home.

With much love,

Catherine.

Catherine

348

2 Alde House
Aldeburgh
Suffolk IP15 5EE
12 July 1992

Dearest Stephen,

Thank you so much for sending me the bunch of interesting papers, all of which I have read with close attention.

Your obituary of Georg Seidel [*The Independent*, 3.7.1992] portrays a character of quite wonderful honesty, and I grieve for you in the loss of such a friend. You are a man of many friends (Alethea Hayter is such another) and as the generations thin, inevitably the losses strike home. It is the price we pay for friendship. By the way, if all goes well you will meet Alethea here as she means to come to the memorial service [for George Shackle].

The list of Festschrift subscribers is really lovely – so many honoured and familiar names. It will be a book to treasure.[1] I wish he could have seen it but at the same time I don't wish him back. I am just so thankful that the last rough bit of the road is behind him.

I do hope your conference[2] went well and didn't tire you too much. I have been reading the pamphlet on the Von Hügel Institute with great interest and want to know more. I also want to subscribe and when next we talk will ask you about the best means . . .

The sorting of George's papers goes ahead but is taking us longer than we thought at first. We now hope to have reached a stage by the end of August when we can ask Dr. Zutshi, Keeper of the archives at Cambridge, to come and have a look and decide what he wants (or what we want him to have). Is he the man you met and liked? Then there is Liverpool University who rightly want something, and finally Quaritch for the remainder.

A rambling letter, but a lot of love,

Catherine

1 The Festschrift in memory of G.L.S. Shackle was published in 2000 entitled *Economics as an Art of Thought* (edited by Peter E. Earl and Stephen F. Frowen).
2 The conference concerned was a Von Hügel Institute conference at St. Edmund's College, University of Cambridge, entiled 'Financial Decision-Making and Moral Responsibility'. The conference proceedings under this title were published in 1995 by Macmillan, edited by Stephen F. Frowen and Francis P. McHugh.

349

2 Alde House
Aldeburgh
Suffolk IP15 5EE
9 September 1992

Dearest Stephen,

Here at last is George's letter to you of 1 May '91 with my reading of it. There is only one word I can't get right at the beginning. Perhaps you can make a good guess.

Your address [at the G.L.S. Shackle Memorial Service on 16.9.1992] has things in it of the utmost beauty: the eternal bond between George and us, and through him between us all. That is a saying of deep truth and I treasure it. You can't think how sweet to me are the quotations from his letters, and the Rilke quotation at the end proclaims in the beautiful language of a poet my profoundest hope and belief. I thank you for something very precious.

Will you clear with John Pheby that it is in order for me to read Mark Perlman's paper at the dinner? I don't want to put a foot wrong.

You & Vicky are a wonderful support to me and I send you love for yourself and admiration for your serenity over the car.

Catherine

350

2 Alde House
Aldeburgh
Suffolk IP15 5EE
20 May 1993

Dearest Stephen,

Here is my personal offering for your 70th birthday. It is something infinitely precious to me as I think it will be to you: the first edition of George's first book, *Expectations, Investment and Income*. I love to think of him holding it in his hands, thrilling with happiness and delight to have it in print. He was so filled with joy that he had to express it in movement, so he jumped on a bus (he was in Oxford) and went to Banbury just for the ride! He used to tell me that the dust cover was such a lovely colour and he bitterly regretted not having kept a copy. But after he died we found two copies carefully wrapped in tissue paper – one for you and one for me.

And now dear boy have a very happy birthday. I am sad not to be with you to join in the celebrations, but you understand my position…

I am so happy that you are pleased with the Dictionary and George's table.[1] I shall love to see them in your study and being used by you. George would love it too.

With best love as always,

Catherine.

Catherine

1 The dictionary consisting of many volumes, in two beautiful antique book cases, all inherited by George Shackle from his father, Robert Walker Shackle (1851-1934), *is The Oxford English Dictionary – A New English Dictionary on Historical Principles*, edited by Sir James A.H. Murray. The antique folding table is the one at which George Shackle did all his writings – by hand!

351

2 Alde House
Aldeburgh
Suffolk IP15 5EE
15th January 2002

Dearest Stephen,

Your article on George for the *New Dictionary of National Biography* is a work of erudition and of love. You make your points with a beautiful simplicity and clarity, and your comments on our marriage are heart-moving as is your mention of George's 'extraordinary and beautiful gentleness' – oh, how true.

I have only one small correction to make:- Page 2, paragraph 4, Strathclyde is spelt with a 'y', not an 'i', in '-clyde'. Their degree was an honorary D.Litt (I have the certificate in front of me as I write and it says 'Doctor of Letters'). This gave George special pleasure because it laid emphasis on the beauty of his prose.

I love to know that this account of George's career goes on permanent record and I do hope the Editor will be able to publish it in full.

I have been trying to get you on the telephone but have failed to make connection. I hope all is well with you both.

With love as always,

Catherine.

Catherine.

352
Alderburgh
9 October 2002

Dearest Stephen,

Here is Alethea book[1] and I think you will find much to interest you in it. The book has given me a feeling of intimacy with the Wordsworth family and though I skipped some of the nautical detail I have to respect Alethea's command of it.

I regard your devoted care of Irina as something very beautiful, and I know the joy which comes from giving comfort to someone one loves dearly. I still get a surge of happiness when I remember how you wrote that I was the source of serenity and hope which returned to George after his despair following Susan's death. So keep it up dear boy, and God bless you.

With much sisterly love as always,

Catherine.

Catherine

1 Alethea Hayter, *The Wreck of the ABERGAVENNY: One of Britain's Greatest Maritime Disasters and its Links to Literary Genius* (London: Macmillan, 2002).

353

2 Alde House
Aldeburgh
Suffolk
20th January 2003

Dearest Stephen,

I have been totally immersed in your wonderful article on George for the *NDNB* [*New Dictionary of National Biography*] and love to think it will be read by future students of his work. I am deeply touched by the way you speak of our marriage; it brings me much happiness.

Here are the points I want to make:- Page 2, para. 3: '...daughter of Reginald [corrected spelling. Omit "gardener"] and the late Mita Morgan Weld-Smith of Seend Manor, Wiltshire.'

Page 2, para. 3: '1953, The [Shackle] family lived at ... Easingwold ... On GLSS's appointment to Liverpool University they moved to 15, Devonshire Road, West Kirby, Wirral, Cheshire, and on his retirement in 1969 to ... Aldeburgh...'

After the family moved to the West Country they lived for a time in North Wales but I have failed to find the address. Does it matter?

I do hope I have made my points clear.

With much love as always,

Catherine.

Catherine.

354

2 Alde House
Aldeburgh
Suffolk
26th April 2003

Dearest Stephen,

I have studied the final draft of your Introduction [to *Economists in Discussion*, pp. xi–xviii of this volume], as well as the earlier papers, and I give my warm agreement to its publication. I have flagged two tiny amendments.

You give a beautifully clear picture of George's views on certain aspects of his work, of his shyness, his gentleness, his kindness to those in need of it, and you illustrate your account with your personal experience. This means that anyone reading your Introduction will receive knowledge of the Man behind the Economist, and this is something I most warmly welcome.

Thank you for the invitation to your [80th] birthday celebration. I shall be with you in spirit on May 22nd, but, as I know you understand, the problems of old age make it impossible for me to be there physically.

With much love dear Other Brother,

Catherine.

Catherine.

This is the last letter Stephen Frowen received from Catherine Shackle. Three weeks later, on 16 May 2003, she suffered a severe stroke from which she was not going to recover. Catherine Shackle died peacefully at her beloved home, Alde House, in Aldeburgh, Suffolk, on 14 June 2003.

Appendix 1
The Big Flake

2, Alde House
Aldeburgh
Suffolk IP15 5EE
11th May 2001

Dearest Stephen,

I have been going through my personal papers to decide what should be lodged with the Cambridge University Library after my death. I can't tell you what happiness it gave me to read George's "Big Flake" again. "Flake" to him meant a flake from the sculptor's chisel, and all the notes and letters exchanged between us became flakes. His handwriting was shaky and very hard to read but I found I had copied it all out and xeroxed it. So, dear brother, I want you to have a copy in the hope that it will give you something of the joy I experienced when I read it.

With love as always,

Catherine.

Catherine

* * *

The Big Flake by G.L.S. Shackle

Something for the mind to do that gives it the pleasure of continual gentle surprises, of endlessly wondering "what comes next?", of entering a fresh "imagined landscape with figures", and of transmitting these pleasures as they arise to a warmly attentive other: this is Reading Aloud. This was the ideal prescription for a lonely soul; this was the gift that Catherine gave me in her letter of the 13th August, 1978. There she asked if I would like to come and read aloud to her sometimes. My loneliness vanished in a twinkling. I prided myself at that time on being able to read aloud with clarity (and such grace as the subject matter might allow) anything, as the bankers say, 'sight unseen'. I went to her that afternoon and read at a sitting 50 pages of *Mansfield Park*. Jane Austen became our all-satisfying diet. In the course of some seven years, until my reading eyesight gave up, I read to Cathy each of the novels, except *Northanger Abbey*, six times. Early in that time we read Sir John Eccles' *The*

Human Mystery, a great neurologist's account of the human brain. I was already acquainted with his book [jointly with Karl Popper] *The Self and its Brain*. These brilliantly suggestive titles seized my imagination and we desisted only when *The Human Mystery* became too technical for oral transmission to be possible.

Joy of joys it was to me thus to profit from Catherine's generously exaggerated need for a reader. We noted strange effects. On one occasion I read an entire paragraph with, as Catherine assures me, perfect efficiency and ease of presentation, without, at the end, having the least notion of what I had read. My mind had been busy with some problem that an earlier sentence had suggested. This double activity of the brain, one part scarcely conscious but highly competent and efficient, must be significant to the scientists. Reading aloud is in any case a double activity. The reader must utter the phrase or group of words he has just read while taking in the text. It seems thus to share something with the playing of a musical instrument, where the brain interprets musical notation into patterns of movement of his hands and fingers. The satisfaction it gives to the reader is surely complex. He can watch himself performing with high skill and imparting something to the meaning of the text. But it is only the listener who can perceive the full measure of the enhancement and deepening. It is only since my own eyesight gave up for reading aloud that I have enjoyed the marvellous interpretive richness and consummate skill of Catherine's reading to me. I cannot now read even to myself. At a recent conference, Catherine read a paper of mine aloud. It was a skein of subtle ideas in economics but at the end some listeners were convinced that Catherine is fully conversant with economic argument at this level. And indeed, Catherine's swiftness and precision of thought in seizing the essence of a complex and subtle argument makes her a critic of the utmost value. In practical matters as in theoretical ones she goes instantly to the core of the matter, and she sees it whole.

At first the reading sessions were on days agreed beforehand. But soon it was, "What's wrong with tomorrow?" Tomorrow was all right and so was every tomorrow afterwards. One evening when we had finished the reading Cathy said, "If I was to knock together some supper, just hot soup and such, would you stay and share it with me?" Thus the settled pattern of our days began. I went each evening to read Jane Austen to Cathy, and after the reading she gave me delicious hot soup then and there, and lovely baked custard to take back to my bungalow Rudloe, and eat with my go-to-bed cup of tea. And thus began for me in that late summer a time of serenity, purpose and delight. In November Cathy went away to stay for a fortnight with friends in the New Forest. When the day came for her return I meant to go in the early afternoon to see if she had come, but excitement and impatience made me muddle my domestic chores, and I did not go till 6 o'clock. I pressed the front-door bell, and in a moment our settled way was restored.

Any book which seeks to present a coherent body of ideas about some aspect of the nature and process of the world needs an index. This serves the reader who wishes to refer to some passage which he is reminded of by what he is currently reading on a later page. It thus serves in a special degree the reviewer who must try to grasp and appraise the book's theme as an organic whole. Without an index (and an ample one), a book cannot *converse* with its reader, it can only lecture him. In the autumn of 1978 I was making an index for my book *Imagination and the Nature of Choice*; eventually the publisher of the book, EUP [Edinburgh University Press], rejected my index in favour of one made by a professional indexer, who simply provided a sort of analytical table of contents. I think the author should have been allowed to complete his book in its natural way with his own index. Nonetheless I had this purposeful and scholarly task at the time when Catherine was folding me in a glow of warmth and happiness, a companionship which gave work a special sanction. This was perhaps one illustration of that 'observership' which philosophers say is indispensable even to the very reality of the things that occupy the individual mind. But it was the source of psychic inspiration and of fuel for my thought-engine.

In the time after Cathy's return from the New Forest, the pattern of my day was to work at Rudloe until after tea-time, then to go to Cathy and read, and then to share our simple supper, and then to bask in the glow of Cathy's extraordinary personality. In her were combined a mother's enfolding care and warmth, the keenest mind and most perfect critical judgement a writer could possibly be blessed with, and a capacity for practical decision and action that still after observing it for many years astounds me. I needed Cathy now with a force that centred my whole life on the evening of our day. One evening I expressed this need: "I don't care what happens during the day, if I can come to you in the evening." I had come to her, wholly and utterly.

Nature conspired with us to make our wedding something of exceeding visual beauty. We came to Aldringham Church just before 8 o'clock in the morning of the 30th January 1979. The whole scene in that early twilight was snow-covered, reflecting the lights from the church windows in a fairy-like landscape. Only five people were present: the Vicar, two witnesses and ourselves. This was the true sanctity of marriage. Our wedding service proceeded straight to the Communion Service. Then George and Angela Gibb, our witnesses, took us back to Catherine's home and we had breakfast by ourselves in quietude. George Gibb drove us then to the station, and at last we were man and wife alone together.

At Paddington on our way to Oxford we had some tea, as it were a first picnic. Next day we were bound for Marlborough, beloved of us both. We had to go first to Reading and change there for a train for Pewsey. But at Reading we were greeted by a blackboard announcing that our train had been cancelled; on enquiry, an official told us a train due in ten minutes was to make a special stop at Pewsey. We waited. At the right moment a fine train glided smoothly in, and we got into it. After a while Catherine, looking out at the Thames alongside the line, said, "I think we are going back to Oxford." The ticket inspector came along. "Where is this train going?" "To South Wales. Where do you want to go?" "To Marlborough." "You'll be all right. We stop at Swindon." At Swindon we got a taxi which took us over beautiful snow-clad Hackpen (Soracte?) to look down on the top of the tower of St. Mary's Church, and to the Ailesbury Arms, our haven for our honeymoon.

The whole land was clad in snow and stayed so for the whole fortnight. But to us it seemed high summer.

Looking out over the Kennet valley from our window in the Ailesbury Arms, we saw beyond it Granham Hill still with its belt of trees looking exactly as in my childhood. Yet in more than sixty years the trees themselves could not be the same. We went by bus to Salisbury and sat for a long spell of perfect quiet and solitude in the Cathedral. My uncle, my father's brother, had been an architect living in Marlborough. Had I as a small schoolboy (not at the College) understood better how much he could have told me about the styles of architecture in churches and the technical language of the architect, I could have profited greatly. Salisbury Cathedral drew us again before we left Marlborough. One day we went to Bath. We should have done well to go by taxi to Swindon and then by train, but we went by bus, having to change at Calne both going out and returning, and could find nowhere there to give us a cup of tea. We went one day to Avebury, and in a bitter wind walked round the great earthen ramparts. The winter scene remained, but it did nothing to oppress our spirits or spoil our warmth of happiness.

At Saxmundham, when we came home from Marlborough, a driving snowstorm was reducing visibility to a few yards and adding to the thick drifts blocking the usual road to Aldeburgh which was impassable. No taxi had been willing to take us home from Ipswich, but at Saxmundham a friend, Tom Colchester, got off the train with us and said he had a car waiting there. If he could start it, he would try to get us home via Leiston. He thought he could get a car through most hazards as he had long experience of driving through mud in Kenya. He was as good as his word, and dropped us at our front door. I wrote him a letter saying that few men would have had the courage and fewer still the skill for such a feat.

Appendix 2
Reflections on George Shackle: Three Excerpts from the Shackle Collection*

Stephen C. Littlechild

I am honoured to be invited to say a few words on this pleasant occasion – though it seemed a little daunting to find something that would be of interest both to George Shackle's family and local friends, and to the professional economists here.

At the invitation of Catherine Shackle and Stephen Frowen a year or two ago, my contribution to *Economics as an Art of Thought* was to survey the papers of George Shackle now bequeathed to the University Library at Cambridge.[1] Reading the invariably delightful and perceptive letters that George wrote was a most enjoyable and informative exercise. I propose to read from three of the items that it was not possible to incorporate in the volume itself. These date from the years 1980 and 1981, after his meeting and marrying Catherine in 1979, which revived his spirits after the sadness of losing his first wife Susan in 1978.

As I prepared these remarks, I saw the *The Times* obituary of John Watkins, former Professor of Philosophy at the London School of Economics. Shackle regarded him highly as a philosopher and friend, and the Shackle collection contains several interchanges between them. Two sentences in the obituary struck me particularly.

One is the comment that Watkins "became captivated by critical rationalism – the idea that knowledge grows through a combination of bold, creative guesses, which go wildly beyond the available evidence, and rigorous criticism." This aptly sums up George's own work: throughout his life he subjected the ideas of others to rigorous but generally sympathetic and

* Remarks at the launching by the Aldeburgh Bookshop of *Economics as an Art of Thought: Essays in Memory of G. L. S. Shackle* (Peter E. Earl and Stephen F. Frowen (Eds.). London and New York: Routledge, 2000). Launch held at the Wentworth Hotel, Aldeburgh, Suffolk, 23 February 2001, at the kind invitation of Catherine Shackle. These remarks were finally written up on 7 February 2002.
Kind permission for reprinting this paper from the *Review of Austrian Economics*, vol. 16, no. 1, 2003, pp. 113–17, granted by the Editor, Professor Peter Boettke, and Kluwer Academic Publishers, is gratefully acknowledged.

always courteous scrutiny. But he, more than almost any other economist, was characterised – and attracted – by the bold, creative guess. I want to return later to the second extract from this obituary.

Rational Expectations

The first excerpt from George's papers is his response to Sir Bryan Hopkin, a long-standing friend who was then Professor of Economics at the University of Cardiff.[2] George comments "The term when I was coming to Cardiff every so often seems like yesterday: a vivid unforgettable pleasure." Sir Bryan had evidently invited him to contribute to a symposium on rational expectations. This was not one of George's favourite concepts. But characteristically, he declines with originality and charm.

> 20 August 1980
>
> 'Rational expectations' remains for me a sort of monster living in a cave. I have never ventured into the cave to see what he is like, but I am always uneasily aware that he may come out and eat me. If you will allow me to stir the cauldron of mixed metaphors with a real flourish, I shall suggest that 'rational expectations' is neo-classical theory clutching at the last straw.
>
> Observable circumstances offer us suggestions as to what may be the sequel of this act or that one. How can we know what *invisible* circumstances may take effect in time-to-come, of which no hint can now be gained? I take it that 'rational expectations' assumes that we can work out what *will* happen as a consequence of this or that course of action. I should rather say that at most we can hope to set bounds to what *can* happen, at best and at worst, within a stated length of time from 'the present', and can invent an endless diversity of possibilities lying between them.
>
> I fear that for your purpose I am a broken reed.[3]

Beyond Economic Policy

The exchange is between George and Sir Charles Carter, another long-time friend and correspondent.[4] Sir Charles thanks him for the copy of a book "fully up to your high standard of originality and clarity" and says "I hope you are keeping well, because I need your help again!"

> 26 March 1980
>
> At the Policy Studies Institute, where I am now working, we do a lot of things to find out what policy issues are most on the minds of decision-

makers in Government and elsewhere, so that we can make our research programme as relevant as we can. Naturally enough, 'policies to check the relative economic decline of the UK' are more often mentioned than anything else: and we have become aware that the economics profession is not regarded as saying anything very helpful about the issues. The NIESR takes a fairly old-fashioned Keynesian line, but has little idea of how it might now work; the monerarists tend to be impossibly simple-minded or remote; the new Cambridge school of protectionists is not entirely convincing. Behind this confusion lies the fact that there is no clear analysis of how the economic system *is* now functioning: the various models do not keep close enough to the actual reactions of human beings (including their structure of expectations).

We have it in mind, therefore, to attempt a review of the functioning of the British economy which will reassess what factors *are* now important, and how they interact. This sounds impossibly ambitious, requiring a new Keynes: and so it is, but (in the absence of great men) little ones must do the best they can. I have a shadowy list in my mind of the sorts of issues which should be given prominence, and I hope I may be allowed to submit some thoughts to you for your criticism. But, before I do so, would you feel able to suggest a list of your own? How does the Slump of 1981 differ in its nature, and therefore in its required remedies, from the Slump of 1931? What are to be regarded as the key factors in relative economic decline?

I hope I can provoke you![5]

George is pleased to receive this approach. "A letter from you always gives my spirits a sudden surge of exhilaration. When I think of the many letters from you (carefully treasured) that have thus encouraged me during thirty years, I see and feel what an immense debt of gratitude I owe you." He was indeed also provoked. It was hardly likely that Sir Charles would get (or expect) a conventional response to his question.

10 April 1980

I think your questions go far beyond economic policy in the narrow sense. Perhaps there are two approaches. We could ask what tendencies chiefly threaten our broadly peaceful, humane and tolerable life as a nation. Or we could ask what we should like our national life to become in the next two decades. You ask me to list what I think are the chief issues. I would say:

(1) Food: the need for self-sufficiency.
(2) Occupation: something interesting to do for everyone.
(3) Education: conservation and the arts (music, painting, theatre etc.).

(4) Excellence: a universal dedication to beauty and efficiency in products and performances.
(5) Clarity of tone in our lives: a muting of the blatancy of advertising; a pursuit of ends rather than distractions.

I think these ideas have some underlying coherence and unity.

Richness of experience, variety of possessions and satisfaction in living could be preserved and intensified by a less extravagant and more attentive way of life. If we did not have the feeling that things could be used casually, burnt up and thrown away; if pleasure was taken in having hand-made things, fewer but more individual things; our import bill might be reduced and our extent of satisfying employment increased. If manual skills come back into esteem and use, people would see point and advantage in being trained, in continuing their education, in becoming artist-craftsmen. At a more exacting level, more of them could become medical men and women, musicians, writers, painters of pictures. Education itself would provide employment.

To pay for tropical foods, minerals that we do not have in Britain, and many indispensable imports, a large flow of exports, in value terms, would still be needed. In the end, we shall only be able to sell to other nations things which are better (more efficient, more trustworthy, more beautiful) than other nations can produce. High craftsmanship, high design, high fashion even; and scientific ingenuity and technological virtuosity, rather than mass production, could be our best resource in exports. But also, there is tourism, and for this there must be conservation of historic things and retention of art treasures. For this too, education of everyone who has charge of such things is needed, far beyond the directors of art galleries and museums who of course are keenly striving for this already.

Perhaps such ideas sound like isolationism. But perhaps the one sound motive for protectionism may be the need to avoid paying other countries for things that do us no good.[6]

Perhaps there is more than a hint here of a sympathy for the approach of William Morris[7] a century earlier? It is no coincidence, I'm sure, that George's grandfather on his father's side was curator of paintings at the Fitzwilliam Museum in Cambridge, and his uncle (his father's only brother) was an architect and painter.[8]

An Examination of a Scheme of Life

The final quotation is from a short reflection that George had evidently made, some two years after his marriage to Catherine. He poses and answers seven questions to himself.

Questions for GLSS

1. In order to exist at all, a man needs to have food prepared for him, rest made possible for him, clothes washed and mended for him. Who does these things for you?

My wife.

2. What is her motive?

She finds in selfless exertion a source of pleasure only available to those who have been touched by some special finger, who contain a spiritual fire invisible, a power to see beyond the everyday horizon. These gifts are, of course, only poured out for me as one chance pilgrim whom she has encountered, one among many whose life she has made valuable to them, possible, bearable for them.

3. Does man live by bread alone?

No. The life of thought, of imagination, of the making and seeking of beauty, are as needful, as essential, to some (and to me) as the air they breathe.

4. Beauty, you say. What is beauty?

Beauty is the dream glimpsed in the form and colour of things, the laser-beam whose concentrated energy dazzles the spirit and ignites the tinder-box of thought. Beauty is the needle-magnetic showing a human being the course to lay, the way to the heart of things.

5. Can you not write without a reader?

I have for many years had to write with only the rare accident of some way-farer collecting a page of mine from the gale of life and scanning it.

6. And what now?

Catherine reads and understands, and tells me of her response.

7. Can this be worth her while?

I do not know.[9]

Only Catherine knows the answer to this last question. But I think we can guess. What a hauntingly beautiful examination George has provided.

The World of George Shackle

I mentioned another sentence that struck me from the obituary of John Watkins. This was an extract from what is described as "Watkins's parting gift, the forthcoming *Human Freedom after Darwin*." This deals with the human capacity for freedom of thought and action that was so important to George. The obituary says "Near the end he deftly draws philosophical lessons from a saying which is rather beautiful, but now sadly apposite: 'When a man dies a world goes out of existence.' "

When George Shackle died, a world went out of existence. However, we can still seek to recreate that world by reading George's work and letters. We are grateful to Catherine for preserving those papers for us, and enabling us to enjoy his memory today.

Notes

1 'Disreputable adventures: The Shackle papers at Cambridge' is Chapter 14 in the book. Kathleen Cann, librarian at the University, has added a useful 'Catalogue of the Shackle papers' at Chapter 15. The Shackle papers are at Add. MS 7699 in the library, and the correspondence is in Section 9 thereof. I am most grateful to Ms Cann for providing copies, references and proofreading of the letters cited here.

2 Sir Bryan was Professor of Economics at UC Cardiff 1972–1982 on leave of absence as Head of Government Economic Service and Chief Economic Adviser. HM Treasury 1974–1977.

3 Add. MS 7669/9/12, letter of 20 August 1980.

4 J.L. Ford says that 'Charles Carter (1950) was one of the very first economists to voice his reservations over Shackle's theory . . . However, he . . . believed in the underlying principles of Shackle's approach, and he endeavoured to modify, in fact, extend, that approach . . . 'Ford also refers to Carter as 'the main champion of [Shackle's] cause.' *G. L. S. Shackle: The Dissenting Economist's Economist*. Aldershot: Edward Elgar, 1994, at p. 76 fn. 3 and p. 97. Sir Charles was later Vice-Chancellor of the University of Lancaster 1963–1979. Editor, *Policy Studies* 1980–1988, and President 1989–1991 then Joint President 1991–1997 of the Policy Studies Institute.

5 Add. MS 7669/9/8/105, letter of 26 March 1980.

6 Add. MS 7669/9/12, letter of 10 April 1980

7 '"A man should put his heart into his work and that work should be the kind he can care about." This was the creed of the English poet and artist William Morris (1834–1896), a practical dreamer of extraordinary energy and versatility who had a strong influence upon the literary, artistic and social life of his time. . . . [His] chief aim in life was to beautify things in common use. . . . In his later years he came more and more to realize that the social world was "out of joint," and did what he could to "set it right" and make the world more beautiful for all,' *The New Book of Knowledge*, London: The Waverley Book Company Ltd., p. 2232.

8 Source Catherine Shackle, see 'Disreputable adventures' fn. 28.

9 Add. MS 7669/9/12, memorandum by GLSS dated 3 May 1981.

Appendix 3
Obituary of G.L.S. Shackle*

THE twentieth century has produced, especially in the Anglo-Saxon world, many outstanding economists. George Shackle was one of the greatest of these.

Economic decisions and choice were at the heart of this original thinker's writings, which stretch over a period of nearly 60 years. He constructed an economic theory which was totally opposed to much of contemporary thinking and which, if accepted, would require a complete reconstruction of mainstream economics. Despite his beautiful and lucid prose, it was often difficult for laymen to follow his abstract and philosophical thoughts. Yet he did produce some popular books, such as *Economics for Pleasure* (1959), an introductory textbook deprived of any equations or diagrams, which was translated into no fewer than seven languages (including Czech), and *Mathematics at the Fireside* (1952), a delightful introduction to mathematics written originally for his own children.

The core of Shackle's contribution to economics was in the field of decision-making under conditions of uncertainty, precisely the situation faced by every businessman or woman. He regarded each managerial decision as a unique event and not one of a series of such events and therefore not analysable by classical probability theory. In this connection, Shackle went deeply into concepts such as time, choice and imagination. The titles of some of his books indicate his concern with these factors: *Expectation in Economics* (1949); *Time in Economics: decision, order and time in human affairs* (1951); *Expectation, Enterprise and Profit* (1970); *Imagination and the Nature of Choice* (1979).

As a subjectivist economist, he regarded choice as evidence of man's originative power. This non-determinist view rests on the supposition that the human mind is capable of absolute origination, something not wholly implicit in experience and thus precluding any sure prediction. He believed in the occurrence of uncaused causes, continued creation by human action rather than once-for-all predetermined creation. Apart from these philosophical thoughts, Shackle made numerous contributions to economic theory and the study of economic thought and wrote some penetrating biographical sketches of fellow economists such as Richard Cantillon, Sir Roy Harrod and F.A. von Hayek.

Shackle took up his economic studies fairly late in life. He was born in 1903 as the only child of elderly parents in Cambridge, where his father at one time coached John Maynard Keynes for the scholarship examination for Eton. As family finances were insufficient to take up the place offered him at St Catharine's College, he worked for 14 years, first in a bank, then for a year in a tobacco company and subsequently for nine years as a master in a preparatory school. He did not receive his external London University BA (in Latin, French and Economics) until 1931. This was followed by a London University Ph D in 1937 and soon after, an Oxford D Phil.

Shackle's career as an economist started at the Oxford University Institute of Statistics (1937–39). He then joined St Andrews University for a brief period before becoming a member of the Statistical Branch of Winston Churchill's Admiralty and later Cabinet Office for the entire war period. After a further five years as a member of the Economic Section of the Cabinet Secretariat, he returned to academic life in 1950 as a Reader in

Economic Theory at Leeds University. After only one year he was offered the Brunner Chair of Economic Science at Liverpool University, which he held until his retirement in 1969. As a Fellow of the British Academy he gave the Keynes Lecture in 1976.

The first of Shackle's nearly 200 papers and review articles (some of which appeared in four collected volumes) was published in October 1933 in the inaugural issue of the *Review of Economic Studies*. It was followed in 1938 by the first of 13 books – his London Ph D dissertation *Expectations, Investment and Income*. In this book, Shackle began to develop a theory of man's response to the dilemma of decision in the presence of uncertainty with his concept of the "potential surprise function", which deals with manifold possibilities to which unique probabilities cannot be assigned and which therefore are difficult to rank. Later, potential surprise is combined with elements in the imagined situation which have special power to focus the decision-maker's attention – in particular, prospects of exceptional gain and loss – to enable a decision to be reached.

His concerns extended far beyond the precise moment of decision to the broad sweep of economic theory and its history. *The Years of High Theory: invention and tradition in economic thought, 1926–1939* (1967) is perhaps his most famous book. In its survey from his own distinctive point of view he shows clearly he believed economic thinking had gone wrong. Apart from his brilliance as a writer who firmly believed and practised that form and content are one, Shackle showed equal brilliance as a teacher. His clarity of exposition, the ability to present the most complex thoughts in simple terms understood by all who made the effort to follow his line of thought, and his devotion to students could never be surpassed.

His flow of publications almost came to a halt in the late 1970s when his first wife, Susan, whom he had nursed with devotion for many years, died in 1978. In the following year, he had the great fortune to marry again. It was thanks to the devotion of his second wife, Catherine, and the tremendous interest she took in his work that he felt capable of making a new start. The result was a flow of outstanding journal articles written between the age of 78 and 84, which in 1988 were published in book form under the title *Business, Time and Thought*.

Despite his achievements, Shackle was a man of genuine modesty, always accessible to young colleagues for advice and constructive criticism. But he could also be stubborn when it came to his own work. He would give the most careful thought to the title of a book and once his mind was made up, no publisher could possibly make him change his mind. In fact, he left one of his publishers of long standing over such an issue.

George Shackle was in every respect a good man who brought out the goodness in others. He never spoke ill of anybody, nor would he tolerate such behaviour in others. He was a great and gentle man whose ideas will live on through his writings, and which will continue to inspire economists for generations to come.

Stephen F. Frowen

George Lennox Sharman Shackle, economist, born 14 July 1903, Reader in Economic Theory Leeds University 1950–51, Brunner Professor of Economic Science Liverpool University 1951–69 (Emeritus), married 1939 Susan Rowe (died 1978; two sons, one daughter, and one daughter deceased). 1979 Catherine Squarey Gibb (née Weldsmith), died Aldeburgh 3 March 1992.

* *The Independent*, 4 March 1992, p. 13. Permission to reprint the Obituary is gratefully acknowledged.

Appendix 4
In Memoriam: G.L.S. Shackle, FBA, 1903 to 1992

Address Given at the Service of Thanksgiving for the Life and Work of G.L.S. Shackle at the Parish Church of St Peter and St Paul, Aldeburgh, Suffolk, on Wednesday, 16 September 1992[1]

Stephen F. Frowen

George Shackle, whose life and work we celebrate today, is one of the select few who have achieved greatness in economic theory and the history of economic thought in the twentieth century. Yet, despite his outstanding and manifold achievements as a scholar, covering economics, philosophy and mathematics, and as a writer of considerable distinction, he was a man of genuine modesty and extraordinary and beautiful gentleness. The warmth and love he extended to those he felt close to, and to those who shared his high scholarship, will be with us for the rest of our lives and beyond. It has created an eternal bond between George and us, and, through George, between us.

I shall never forget my first encounter with George ... in 1950 when we both had just arrived at Leeds University – George as Reader in Economics straight from the Economic Section of the UK Cabinet Secretariat, and I as a postgraduate student from defeated Germany. His kindness to students, whom he treated with the utmost courtesy, the time he devoted to us, and the incredible care with which he prepared each of his lectures were experiences none of us will ever forget. I was always aware of the presence of his caring and guiding hand, and I strongly feel that it is still with me today.

When preparing this Address I reread some of the precious letters I was privileged to receive from George, all written in his clear and beautiful handwriting. The most moving one, dated 19 January 1979, was written nine months after the death of his first wife, Susan. In this letter he writes:

> The past twelve months have been an exhausting, sad and baffling time for me. Susan died on 10 April after a fortnight which caused me heart-breaking grief. Saturday, 8 April was a day of dreadful sadness, her last conscious day ... All this turmoil has left me rather drained of strength for the ordinary obligations of life.[2]

But in the same letter I discovered a ray of hope, because George continues:

> In recent months, I have found a source of serenity and hope which has again given my life some sense of purpose.

The exact nature of the 'source and hope' I learned from a letter five months later (19 June, 1979). It reads:

> Last August, I began going once or twice a week to read aloud to a lady who, despite an abounding vitality, does not see quite well enough to find reading a pleasure. She used to give me supper, my visits were soon daily, and I found in her companionship a deep solace. At the end of January we were married.

He then adds:

> During my lonely time last summer, I tried to work, but found it fruitless. I am now very well cared for and have made what I hope will be a fresh start at some writing.

How grateful we in the profession should be to this lady, our beloved Catherine! Thanks to her care, George returned to a creative life and was able to write again. Thus in late life he produced some of his most outstanding essays. These were published in 1988 as a collection, *Business, Time and Thought*: it was dedicated, of course, to Catherine.[3]

Originality is a rare gift and there is no doubt that George's outstanding feature as a scholar is the originality of his mind. Hugh Townshend, reviewing George's first book, *Expectations, Investment, and Income* (1938, second edition 1968) in *The Economic Journal*, judges 'that its most original parts are also the best parts'.[4]

Many years later H.D. Dickinson, reviewing *A Scheme of Economic Theory* (1965), refers to George as being among 'some of the boldest and most original minds active to-day in economic thought'.[5] Sir Roy Harrod refers to George's further work, *The Years of High Theory: Invention and Tradition in Economic Thought, 1926-1939* (1967), as a 'book ... of great originality' and as a 'path-breaking work on the theory of uncertainty', while stressing his gift to 'probe deeply into the essential nature of an economic theory and its relation to the facts of life'.[6]

The concept of 'uncertainty' is of course closely linked with George's name and work. In later years, however, he preferred the word 'unknowledge'. In a letter dated 10 November 1982, he set out for me the ideas he would specially like critics to regard as the essence of his scheme of economic theory and stated:

> The right word is not uncertainty but *unknowledge*. We know a little about the texture of the material, but nothing about how history will cut the garment.[7]

How does anyone act in the face of such unknowledge, knowing only that his own actions are crucial decisions, uncaused causes, which themselves will help to shape the future? George's answer was that choice involved imagining a range of sequels and ranking them by their capacity to surprise. Perfect (subjective) possibility is then expressed as zero disbelief. Then the decision-maker concentrates his attention, amongst the outcomes he deems possible, on the best and worst outcomes.

These ideas were central to George's work, yet his great love for learning and his concern to pass his enthusiasm on to others went further as is revealed in

Mathematics at the Fireside, which was originally written for his children and subsequently published by Cambridge University Press (1952; French edition 1967), and in *Economics for Pleasure* (1959). What a pity that out of the latter's seven foreign language translations, only the one in Czech actually uses the carefully chosen word 'pleasure' in its title!

George's unique gift for words and expression has been aptly described by Sir Charles Carter in his review of George's book *Uncertainty in Economics and other Reflections* (1955) when stating that, '... in expounding his own ideas, he [G.L.S. Shackle] has the invaluable service of a command of the English language such as few economists since Marshall have possessed.'[8]

George was never in the mainstream of economic thinking and never regarded himself as such. He wholeheartedly approved of his inclusion in *A Biographical Dictionary of Dissenting Economists*.[9] In fact, in the final paragraph of his delightful autobiographical essay 'A Student's Pilgrimage' he points to two kinds of economics, one aiming at precision, rigour, tidiness and the formulation of principles which will be permanently valid: an economic science. The other he described as rhetorical, employing reason and appealing to logic. George describes the rhetorician and, eloquently, himself as a user of language at its full compass, where words are fingers touching the keyboard of a hearer's mind'.[10]

Writing was George's life. Just three months before his death, I received a letter from him dated 3 December, 1991, in which he says:

> I hope to go on working at our subject from some time yet although I am 88 years old. One must of course beware of merely repeating oneself but if I fall into this trap you and others will make me aware of it.

These words are ample proof of the long, rich and blessed life we are here to give thanks for – a life from which we have all benefited and will continue to benefit so much. George is not gone. In spirit he is, I am sure, with us today, giving us strength to go on following our own chosen path. This is a thought perhaps best described by Rainer Maria Rilke who as a poet achieved the greatness George achieved in economics:

> When something is taken from us that was deeply and wonderfully ours, to much of our own selves we bid farewell. Yet God wills we should find ourselves again, enriched by all that was lost, enhanced by each infinite pain.[11]

Notes

1 This Address was first published in the G.L.S. Shackle Memorial Issue, *Review of Political Economy*, vol. 5, no. 2, 1993, pp. 263–66. Permission to reprint the Address is gratefully acknowledged. The same issue contains further tributes by The Rev. Dick Hare, Brinley Thomas, Mark Perlman and G.C. Harcourt.

2 The correspondence of G.L.S. Shackle, including his letters to Stephen Frowen quoted from in this Address, can be found in the Manuscript Department of Cambridge University Library.

3 See S.F. Frowen (ed.), *Business, Time and Thought – Selected Papers of G.L.S. Shackle* (London: Macmillan; New York: New York University Press, 1988).
4 See Hugh Townshend, *The Economic Journal*, vol. 48, 1938, p. 521.
5 See H.D. Dickinson, *The Economic Journal*, vol. 77, 1967, p. 107.
6 See R.F. Harrod, *The Economic Journal*, vol. 78, 1968, pp. 660-6.
7 The remaining paragraphs outlining the essence of G.L.S. Shackle's scheme of economic theory can be found in letter no. 227, dated 10 November 1982, on pages 209–10 of this volume.
8 See C.F. Carter, The *Economic Journal*, vol. 66, 1956, p. 701.
9 See P. Arestis and M. Sawyer (eds.), *A Biographical Dictionary of Dissenting Economists* (Aldershot: Edward Elgar, 1992), pp. 505–10.
10 See G.L.S. Shackle, 'A Student's Pilgrimage', *Banca Nazionale del Lavoro Quarterly Review*, vol. 145, 1983, page 116. reprinted in S.F. Frowen (ed.), *Business, Time and Thought. Selected Papers of G.L.S.* Shackle (London: Macmillan; New York. New York University Press, 1988, page 239.
11 See Rainer Maria Rilke, Letter to Princess Cathia von Schönaich-Carolath, Paris, 17 Rue Campagne-Première, 7 May 1908, in Rainer Maria Rilke, *Gesammelte Briefe in 6 Bänden* (Collected Letters in 6 Volumes), vol. 3 (Leipzig: Insel Verlag, 1939). The original German text, the source of which has been kindly provided by Hella Sieber-Rilke (Rilke-Archiv, Gernsbach, Germany), reads as follows:

> *...: denn wenn etwas uns fortgenommen wird, womit wir tief und wunderbar zusammenhängen, so ist viel von uns selber mit fortgenommen. Gott aber will, dass wir uns wiederfinden, reicher um alles Verlorene und vermehrt um jeden unendlichen Schmerz.* (English translation by John Harrison).

Appendix 5
Missing Letters Bequeathed by Catherine Shackle to Cambridge University Library[1]

Mulberry Croft
Littleford Lane
Shamley Green
Guildford
Surrey GU5 0RH
19 March 1984

My dear George,

In my last letter I forgot to mention that I had a reply from Mr. Farmiloe of Macmillan ending as follows:

'Would you recommend me to re-issue *Mathematics at the Fireside*? If so, I will consider that as well.'

I would personally greatly welcome a new edition of this splendid and delightful book. I wonder how you feel about it yourself.

In a further letter – just received – Mr. Farmiloe says that he is 'keenly interested' to consider publishing three further titles I had suggested: a textbook on the main aspects of international banking, a biography of Ralph Hawtrey and the volume of our forthcoming September conference. – I wished the day had more than twenty-four hours!

With my warmest and best wishes,

Yours,

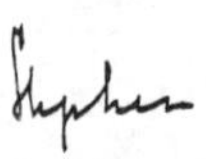

Stephen

[1] These letters were discovered in February 2004, when it was too late for their inclusion in chronological order in the main 'Letters' section of this volume, as the book was then about to go into print. The name and subject indices, too, could not be amended at this stage to include references to Appendix 5.

Alde House
Aldeburgh
Suffolk IP15 5EE
17th September 1984

My dear Stephen,

You have given us a wonderful happiness and satisfaction in all that you accomplished in organising the Conference, and in your sweet cherishing of us at Mulberry Croft. You can imagine what joy it is to me to see George honoured by members of his profession . . .

Catherine.

Catherine
[Letter incomplete]

Mulberry Croft
Littleford Lane
Shamley Green
Guildford
Surrey GU5 0RH
6 October 1984

My dear George,

I am happy to be able to report good news. I had a long meeting with Mr. Farmiloe yesterday (Friday) afternoon and managed to persuade him to publish your collection of essays at the same time the conference volume will be appearing towards the end of next year. Mr. Farmiloe himself was never in any doubt, of course, that your collection of essays should be published but he hesitated because of a negative response from St. Martin's Press, Macmillan's subsidiary company in New York. They apparently never like to reprint published material (although two of your papers selected for inclusion are in fact unpublished), and they also expressed the opinion that the proposed volume of essays would be too slim. However, Mr. Farmiloe is in touch with other American publishers and without so far having reached any definite agreement, he has given me his firm undertaking to go ahead with the publication of your essay collection.[1] This implies that he would like you to write a substantial introduction if possible by the end of November, but the end of December would also be acceptable in case you cannot meet the November deadline. If you had any additional papers you could include, he would be very happy. (What about your forthcoming article in *Kyklos*?[2]) Furthermore, he requested you to obtain permission from the journal editors and publishers concerned for reprinting your papers in the collection.

With regard to the book title, Mr. Farmiloe has a *strong* preference for *Means and Meaning in Economic Theory and Other Essays*, but perhaps you have better suggestions. The title you suggested *A Student's Pilgrimage* he was not too happy with. The enclosed Macmillan Information and Publicity Form should be submitted to Macmillan together with your Introduction to the book. The final point concerns the Index. Would you like this to be prepared by Mrs. Bamber who did the index for *Controlling Industrial Economies* and will also be preparing one for the proceedings of our forthcoming conference in your honour? You may of course prefer to do this yourself. I am afraid Macmillan would not pay for the preparation of the index, but Mrs. Bamber's charges are quite reasonable (Christopher Saunders recommended her to me.)

I have promised to submit the typescript of the conference proceedings by the end of December. Would it be at all possible to let me have your bibliography by then? I would of course get it typed by my secretary if this should be of any help to you, but in this case I would really need it by the *middle* of December. I would also like to have a portrait photograph of you for the conference volume. Would we have to arrange for one to be taken or would you prefer to have the drawing of you by Oliver Thomas reproduced in the book? Mr. Farmiloe was quite enthusiastic about the title I suggested for the conference volume, which is *Unknowledge and Choice in Economics*.

I think I have covered the main points. It only remains for me to wish you both a happy stay in Spain. I can well imagine how much your lectures and seminars will be appreciated by your Spanish colleagues and students.

I was delighted to receive Catherine's sweet letter – it made me very happy. It was such a joy to have you both staying with me at Mulberry Croft. Unfortunately, the time together passed far too quickly.

My conference in Namur was quite interesting and we had a good discussion after my talk. This was followed by three happy days with Michael in Amsterdam.

With all my best and warmest wishes to you and Catherine,

Yours ever,

Stephen

---

[1] The American edition was published by New York University Press.

[2] This paper by G.L.S. Shackle, entitled 'Controlling Industrial Economies', originally appeared in *Kyklos*, vol. 38, no. 1, 1985, pp. 120–2, and was reproduced as Chapter 16 in *Business, Time and Thought*, pp. 200–3.

Mulberry Croft
Littleford Lane
Shamley Green
Guildford
Surrey GU5 0RH
25 October 1984

My dear George,

I was deeply touched to receive your letter of 6th October. I derived the greatest possible happiness from your extremely kind remarks. I hope you know how much joy it gave me to arrange the conference in your honour. Most of all I felt it important to get *your* message across and I sincerely hope that the conference volume will be a further step in this direction. I trust that the book will give some impression of the extent to which many of the more important writings in economics are today deeply influenced by your own ideas and truly original contributions.

Meanwhile, my secretary has been kind enough to type out your delightful and absolutely charming impromptu Conference Dinner Speech which I was fortunately able to record on my little tape recorder. I am enclosing a copy for your perusal and should be, grateful if you would kindly let me know if you wish to amend the text in any way or add to it. It will be included in the conference proceedings . . .

I hope that you and Catherine had an enjoyable and memorable time in Spain.

With all my best and warmest wishes to both of you,

Yours ever,

Stephen

5th June 1985

My dear George,

I am really happy that I have now received the firm contracts from Macmillan for the two books. As far as the volume of your essays is concerned, I have drafted the enclosed list of papers placed in chronological order. Please let me know if there are any papers you wish to be deleted or added. On a separate sheet I have listed some of the papers – mentioned in your bibliography but not part of our original list – for possible inclusion in the volume. You may wish to consider adding some of these to our list.

In which order would you like the essays to appear in the book? I would suggest starting with 'The Origination of Choice' (no. 16 on my list). 'Means and Meaning in Economic Theory', 'Imagination, Unknowledge and Choice' and 'A Student's Pilgrimage' should probably also appear in the first section of the book.

I am planning to write an Introduction of about 3000 words. Would you regard this as the right length?

I am so glad to have your agreement for the establishment of a charitable trust which I propose to be called 'The George Shackle Trust'. The objective would be to award annual prizes for the best essays to be presented in the field of entrepreneurship, choice and the difficulties of prediction in economics. However, the exact terms of reference would have to be worked out very carefully. My instructions to Macmillan will be that all royalties arising from the two books (including any advance payments) should be paid straight into the proposed fund. This would mean that by the time I hand over the final typescripts to Macmillan, the Fund would already have £800 at its disposal, as I shall receive an advance payment of £400 for each book on completion of the typescript. If agreement can be reached, I would like to be joined as a Trustee by Mark Perlman, Brian Loasby, Stephen Littlechild and David Reisman. But perhaps you would like to see others included among the Trustees.

I have written to the University of Kent and let them know that you and Catherine and I would like to attend the next Keynes Conference in Canterbury.

I was so sorry to be unable to get a copy of the second volume of *Contemporary Economists in Perspective* for you. Incidentally, could you possibly let me have a photocopy of your chapter entitled 'Shackle on Harrod'? It may be advisable perhaps to use the printed version rather than the typescript in my possession.

With warmest thoughts and all good wishes,

Yours,

Stephen

Stephen

2 Alde House
Aldeburgh
Suffolk IP15 5EE
12 June 1985

My dear Stephen,

Your two letters give us intense happiness. Each separately gives a surge of warmth and excitement. The wonderful enterprise you have conceived and carried already so far into realisation, of bringing the two books into being and deciding on a further purpose of their publication, is beyond any words that I can find. I am trying to play my part, with Catherine's help in reading to me some of the papers in your list which I felt I should consider specially, as to their inclusion and the sequential arrangement of the whole list.

I am exceedingly delighted by your intention to write the Introduction.

Notes on your proposed list of essays and suggested omissions:

[My] Foreword to Wicksell [*Value, Capital and Rent*]: I feel that this implies a claim on my part to be a Wicksell scholar, which I am not.

I should wish to write a Preface to the collection [of my essays], a main purpose of which would be to delineate the editor in his glowing and radiant personality, and to expound his superlative gifts and unsurpassable care as a translator and his drive and reach of mind as an organiser. This would take the place of the foreword to his translation of *Über Wert, Kapital und Rente*.

Suggested additions:

'News from Sweden': Yes
The essay on Hayek in *Pioneers*: Yes

The other suggested additions I think would be an overlap.

All warmest and best wishes,

George Shackle

George Shackle

The Reform Club
London SW1
18 June 1985

My dear George,

I am enclosing the Agreement I received from Macmillan relating to the volume of your essays which Mr. Farmiloe would like to be signed by both of us. I am so very happy to know that this project can now go ahead at full speed. Perhaps you will be so kind as to return the signed Agreement to Mr. Farmiloe together with the enclosed covering note.

As soon as I get back from Germany, I will have the letters typed to the editors of the journals concerned asking for permission to reproduce your paper in our volume. Meanwhile, could you possibly let me have a copy of your contribution to the Lachmann Festschrift and your Madrid paper?

We again had a most worrying time with Michael. He is so desperate that he again tried to cut his wrists and under an emergency order we managed to get him admitted to the Royal Free Hospital just for the weekend. We hope and pray that he can be admitted later today for a long stay. With all these uncertainties our journey to Germany is still in doubt but we have not given up hope yet that we may be able to leave on Thursday.

With warmest wishes to you and Catherine,

Yours,

Stephen

Mulberry Croft
Littleford Lane
Shamley Green
Guildford
Surrey GU5 0RH
19 June 1985

My dear George,

I managed to make a start by typing at least a few letters of request to some of the editors and publishers concerned. There should be no problem in obtaining their permission for reprinting your papers.

This morning I received the latest issue of *Kyklos* containing your generous review of *Controlling Industrial Economies*. I was delighted. It really was most kind of you to take on this task despite your many other duties. I cannot thank you enough and I have no doubt that Christopher Saunders will be equally grateful to you.

As your paper in *Kyklos* appeared as a book review rather than as a review article, as one would have expected, I am wondering whether it should not now be published as one of the chapters in your essay collection. How would you feel yourself about my suggestion?

I am glad to say that Michael is now safe having been admitted at the Royal Free Hospital. This means that we will be able to meet our commitments and leave for Germany tomorrow morning. We will be back on 6th July.

All my warmest good wishes to both of you,

Yours ever,

Stephen

P.S. I have just received Catherine's lovely letter. Nothing could have made me happier. Thousand thanks. I shall reply to her from Germany.

Mulberry Croft
Littleford Lane
Shamley Green
Guildford
Surrey GU5 0RH
13 July 1985

My dear George,

I was extremely happy to receive your letter of 7th July and your suggestions. I do hope that I am not taking up too much of your time and strength with this project.

I think the order in which you have now arranged the papers to be included in the collection of your recent essays is perfect. I had already given some thought to this crucial problem, of course, but the idea now proposed by you to make successive essays as different from each other as possible had not occurred to me. It quite obviously is the ideal solution.

Of the eighteen papers now to be included, the following four are missing in my file:

1. 'The Origination of Choice' (Lachmann Festschrift)
2. '*Treatise, Theory* and Time' (Madrid volume)
3. 'Keynes the Meeting-point of History and Thought'
4. 'News from Sweden'

Just one copy of each of these papers will suffice as I can easily have further copies done in my office. Of the remaining fourteen papers I already have three copies of each paper.

I shall get the remaining letters asking for permission to reprint typed next week and shall send them to you for your signature.

One small (or rather important) problem emerged. I had a letter from Mr. Farmiloe saying that he does not favour the book title suggested, i.e. *The Origination of Choice*. Instead he prefers *Means and Meaning in Economic Theory* or some other title we may wish to suggest. I should very much like to have *your* views on this matter. Any change of title would also affect the sequence in which the essays are to be arranged, as it may be advisable to place as number one the essay which provides the book title unless a title is chosen which is not also the title of one of the essays.

My German lecture tour went quite well considering that because of Michael I had virtually no time to prepare my talks as carefully as I would have liked. In the case of one of my talks I had to lecture in German from my English script. It was quite a challenge.

Michael is still in hospital but he is feeling much better, I am glad to say. The great worry is what will happen when he leaves hospital.

I hope, George, that you have received my little birthday greeting in time. I hope that you will be able to take things a bit easier from now on and find more time for leisure. If anybody deserves it, it is you. When I see the most impressive list of papers you have published just during the last few years, the majority of us have reason to feel ashamed of our poor and inadequate efforts. Your greatness, which does not require any proof, is nevertheless reflected in the increasing attention your ideas and thoughts are now receiving.

I am longing to see you both again soon.

With all my warmest and best wishes to you and Catherine,

Yours sincerely,

Stephen

The Reform Club
London SW1
23 July 1985

My dear George,

I was so very happy to receive your letter of 15th July and Catherine's personal greetings.

The title you now suggest for the collection of your essays *Time and Thought: An Economic Skein* is ingenious and nothing more suitable could possibly replace it. I immediately wrote to Mr. Farmiloe *strongly* recommending him to accept your proposal. I am anxiously waiting to hear from him.

Do I still have to write to some editors asking for permission to reprint your paper? I will gladly type these letters for you to save you as much time as possible. I assume that you have now forwarded the signed contract to Mr. Farmiloe.

I often think of you both and I am longing to see you again soon. Michael is now out of hospital and will take up his computing job again next Monday. To my surprise and joy, the company directors are most anxious to get Michael back. When not drinking, he is of course the most reliable, considerate and charming colleague they could hope for.

With much love to you and Catherine (I shall write to her soon),

Yours ever,

Stephen

Königstein/Taunus
20 August 1985

My dear George,

Many thanks indeed for your letter and contents which did reach me before my departure. Your letter to Mr. Farmiloe could not have been clearer in stating your position and I should be *most* surprised if your convincing arguments should fail to persuade him. In fact, I do hope that by the time you receive my letter you will have had an affirmative answer from Macmillan agreeing to your suggested title. I shall start preparing the material for Mr. Farmiloe during my stay on the Continent.

Meanwhile we all enjoyed a splendid 70th birthday celebration of Irina at the former Palais Rothschild in Königstein [now the Hotel Sonnenhof]. It was a perfect setting and it was nice for the whole family to be together. We are now greatly looking forward to our holiday in San Angelo d'Ischia in September. My contact address (in case of need) until the end of September will be: c/o. Professor Rolf Frowein, Hohemarkstrasse 24, D-6240 Königstein/Taunus.

I hope you are both feeling well. Irina and I are so very much looking forward to seeing you again in October.

With all warmest good wishes and much love from both of us to you and Catherine,

Yours ever,

Stephen

P.S. I was delighted to receive an invitation to the Keynes Conference in November. This means that I can meet your train at Liverpool Street Station and take you by car to and from Canterbury.

The Reform Club
London SW1
19 July 1986

My dearest Catherine,

My stay with you and George was for me the source of the greatest possible happiness. Once again you have spoiled me beyond words. I feel completely rested and full of renewed energy. There were so many new impressions I was able to absorb and, as always, my discussions with George provided me with a multitude of new ideas, fresh insights and endless inspiration. It is a pleasure and privilege to be in the presence of both of you.

What did sadden me more than I can say was to see George not feeling his usual self; but I felt greatly reassured after our telephone conversation. The doctor's report could not have been satisfactory and I am extremely happy that there is no cause whatsoever for any alarm. However, George will obviously have to take things a bit easier and not burden himself with unnecessary tasks. He needs to relax a bit after his long and uniquely busy and productive life. I shall never forget how kind and attentive he has been to me during my stay with you despite feeling so ill. I shall write to him personally next week.

Once again many, many thanks, Catherine, for all you have done for me.

With love to both of you and all warmest good wishes,

Yours,

Stephen

University of Surrey
Guildford
Surrey GU2 5XH
16 February 1987

My dear George,

Nothing could have touched me more than the efforts you have made to write a paper for the volume which I understand Philip Arestis is preparing for me and despite not feeling too well getting it to him on time. To me your paper will form *the* essential part of the book. Without it the volume, however much appreciated, would have been without a soul. Philip was overjoyed when he received your letter and immediately let me know. I am dying to read your paper but I shall have to be patient and wait until the book is published. I wonder what the title might be![1] The happiness you have bestowed upon me cannot be surpassed and I shall be eternally grateful to you not only for this latest and ultimate sign of friendship but also for the tremendous happiness you have given me through our friendship over so many decades. And it is through Catherine, I fell, that our relationship reached a crowning height. From the moment I met her, I was charmed by her deep and genuine warmth and I felt exceedingly happy that she had entered your life.

This morning I received the enclosed design for the book jacket of our forthcoming volume from Macmillan, which I rather like. As the matter appears to be urgent, you will perhaps let me have your reaction as soon as possible so that I can inform Mr. Farmiloe. I am very pleased that the volume is now making such rapid progress.

I shall be at the University tomorrow (Tuesday) and for the rest of the week in London. On Thursday afternoon and evening I have to give some special lectures at St. John's Seminary in Wonersh on the 20th Anniversary of the Encyclical Letter of Pope Paul VI *Populorum Progressio* which deals specifically with Third World economic and social problems.

I shall write to Catherine separately. With all my warmest and best wishes to both of you and affectionate greetings,

Yours ever,

Stephen

[1] George Shackle's paper, the very last essay he published, is entitled 'Elasticities of Surprise in the Concept of Policy'. It appeared in *Contemporary Issues in Money and Banking: Essays in Honour of Stephen Frowen*, edited by Philip Arestis (London: Macmillan, 1988), pp. 1–6. While working on this paper George Shackle wrote to Stephen Frowen on 3 September 1986: 'I am thoroughly absorbed in working on my piece for Philip Arestis's Festschrift for you. It seeks to give the word Policy a systematically expectational basis and meaning.'

40 Gurney Drive
London N2 0DE
3 April 1987

My dear George,

I am so very happy to know that you are feeling better. However, your sleeplessness must at times be a great disturbance.

I am glad to say that Irina is now making steady progress, although her full recovery will obviously be a slow process. But we must be grateful and are exceedingly happy that everything has been going well so far.

I am enclosing photocopies of some of the passages of the volume of your essays *Business, Time and Thought* where I either have a query or would like your confirmation that the amendments made are correct.

I am now busy correcting the last third of the page proofs. Unfortunately, the last-minute preparations for next week's conference at Surrey have taken up more of my limited time than I expected. However, everything seems to be going well now. Among the delegates there will be a large contingent from the Bank of England, the Treasury, the clearing banks and other City institutions.

I can't wait to see our book in print. Nothing has ever excited me as much as this joint task.

With all my love to you and Catherine,

Yours,

Stephen

2 Alde House
Aldeburgh
Suffolk IP15 5EE
8 April 1987

My dear Stephen,

Many thanks for your letter of April 3rd. George asks me to answer it. His letter of yesterday (posted this morning) will tell you that there is no line missing from the first paragraph on page 211, and it should stand as it is. This is all my fault – I couldn't make sense of it at first reading – and I apologise.

As for the comma to be deleted, it is twelve lines up from the bottom after 'find'. I can't think why I didn't say so originally. As for the algebraic statements, I have read your amendments to George who says they are correct; have also checked them against our written versions and find they agree.

I am afraid that in my first attempt at proof reading I have given you some unnecessary work for which I am sorry. Sorry too for the bad writing of this letter, but I am in bed with a cold.

Yes, this book is one of the most exciting things that ever happened as far as I am concerned.

Our local Music Club (with me in it) has just sung the Messiah, and truly it went well with a life and zest worthy of Huddersfield – and all in the Aldeburgh Jubilee Hall.

We both send love,

Catherine

Johann Wolfgang Goethe-Universität
Frankfurt am Main
26 April 1987

My dearest Catherine and George,

It was so nice to hear your voice again this morning. I derived the greatest happiness from the positive report George had from his doctor. There really seems to be nothing to worry about. I am sure that the warmer weather and the whole summer ahead of us will do the rest and restore George to his usual self – not that you did sound otherwise this morning, George. I so much enjoyed talking to you.

I am enclosing some copies of the Advance Notice Macmillan prepared about 'our' book. It sounds as impressive as it should! Please let me know if you would like to have further copies. I am also enclosing some press comments on Roger and Flavia de Grey's recent exhibition which may be of interest to you . . .

I am most distressed that I have still not been able to return the proofs to Macmillan. However, with Irina and Michael safely settled in their respective clinics in the Taunus and Frankfurt respectively next week, and with the Frankfurt term now well on its way, I should be able to make considerable progress during the coming week.

I am so very much looking forward to August when hopefully we can all be together in Aldeburgh again in a completely relaxed mood with all tasks being accomplished.

With much love, as ever, from both of us,

Yours affectionately,

Stephen

Alde House
Aldeburgh
Suffolk IP 15 5EE
3rd March 1988

Dearest Stephen,

Proofs of the book: I am returning the first page of the Acknowledgements with the correction of the date of the Madrid book (No. 3) from 1987 to 1988. George is happy that the equation on p. 116 is correct, and we agree with your corrections on pp. 116 and 118.

Introduction: I have made various pencil scribbles in the text which I think explain themselves. The doubtful items are: – P.1, lines 17–18, we don't quite understand. P.3, line 2, 'wildest'?? P.3, lines 5–6, slightly mystifying. P. 4, line 9, as G. explained, he would rather have 'scholarly environment'.

I do admire your typing, and I wish I was more familiar with proof correction marks.

The Preface: This rests very comfortably on my heart and I say to myself that if only part of what you say is true, it justifies my having lived. Thank you, dear boy.

I return the typescripts of the Preface and Introduction.

At John Pheby's conference at Malvern last August we met a Professor Michael Ambrosi of the Freie Universität, Berlin. He was a nice chap, quiet and friendly. He knew of the creation of your chair but didn't at that point know who was to fill it. If you should run into him in Berlin, do salute him from us.

Your invitation to attend your conference in Berlin at the end of the summer warmed the heart, but I have to say that I don't think George will be able to do any more travelling abroad, and perhaps no more in this country either. He isn't as strong as he was; I have noticed a change in him during the past few months.

We long to see you but long even more not to be a nuisance or to put extra pressure on you! So we will wait for a visit until the next vacation when, DV [thank goodness], the snow will have gone and the sun will shine. Meanwhile much love as ever,

Catherine.

Catherine

2 Alde House
Aldeburgh
Suffolk IP15 5EE
2 November 1994

Dearest Stephen,

Vivian [Dyter] and I have been sorting some of the last of George's papers and when I came on this exchange with Karl Popper I thought it so interesting and so important that I must send you copies straight away.[1] The originals must go of course to the Cambridge University Library to join the collection already there.

Don't bother to acknowledge this by letter. I know how busy you are with little spare time for writing. Just give me a ring sometime; it is always good to hear your voice.

With much love as always,

Catherine.

Catherine

---

[1] The fascinating exchange of letters between George Shackle and Sir Karl Popper, and the latter's 'highly critical' (Popper's words) report on Shackle's article 'Time and Thought', having had to read, and to re-read, the paper five times, makes most rewarding reading and can be consulted among the Shackle Papers at Cambridge University Library. In response to Popper's sharp criticism, Shackle wrote on 27th May 1958: 'I am quite shamed by your very great generosity of time and trouble over my paper. I have gained more insight and illumination from your comments than I might have got from years of solitary pondering or reading . . . Your "Comments" will provide me with a guide to further thought for many months.' Shackle's paper 'Time and Thought' was published in the *British Journal for the Philosophy of Science*, vol. 9, no. 36, 1959, pp. 285–98.
The exchange of letters between George Shackle and Sir Karl Popper, and the latter's report on Shackle's article 'Time and Thought', make interesting reading and can be consulted in the Shackle archive at Cambridge University Library. In response toPopper's ruthless language, Shackle's response of 27th May 1958 was supremely and characteristically subtle, putting Popper in his place by his own unparalleled courtesy thanking Popper for his great generosity of time and trouble over his paper. 'I have gained more insight and illumination from your comments', writes Shackle, 'than I might have got from years of solitary pondering or reading . . . Your "Comments" will provide me with a guide to further thought for many months.' Shackle's paper 'Time and Thought' was published in the *British Journal for the Philosophy of Science*, vol. 9. no. 36, 1959, pp. 285–98.

40 Gurney Drive
London N2 0DE
9 October 2001

Dearest Catherine,

I greatly enjoyed talking to you this morning and I was glad to hear that you are virtually back to normal. It is simply wonderful and most encouraging how well you were able to cope with this attack.

I am enclosing a copy of my Festschrift *50 Years of the German mark* – the proceedings of a Symposium the Institute for German Studies at Birmingham University organised to mark my 75th birthday in May 1998.[1] It just shows how long it can take to produce a book!

The chapter you might most enjoy reading is the one by Norbert Kloten (pp. xxiv–xxxi) in which quite naturally George features as well (p. xxvi). But the Laudatio by the former Bundesbank President, Hans Tietmeyer, and the chapters by Charles Goodhart and Sir Samuel Brittan might also find your interest. I was glad to see Vicky's [Victoria Chick's] prepublication praise on the back on the book jacket. It would give me great pleasure if you enjoyed reading these pieces.

With all my warmest good wishes and much love, dearest Catherine,

Your 'Other-Brother'

Stephen

Stephen

1 Jens Hölscher (ed.), *50 Years of the German Mark: Essays in Honour of Stephen F. Frowen* (London and New York: Palgrave Macmillan, in association with Anglo-German Foundation of the Study of Industrial Society, 2001).

2 Alde House
Alde House Drive
Aldeburgh
25 October 2001

Dearest Stephen,

50 Years of the German Mark

I have been doing some serious reading of the book, guided by your letter enclosed within it. To start with I simply love the photograph; it is 'the gentle and quiet scholar' to the life; there are the symbols of the German Order of Merit and the Papal Knighthood and I was present on the memorable occasions when you received each one.

I like Tietmeyer's Laudatio and his article, especially his bit about East Germany and the DM as the symbol of prosperity and freedom. 'If the DM doesn't come to us we will go to the DM.'

Goodhart hits the nail on the head when he speaks of a better mutual understanding between the two countries, and this applies not only to monetary policy but to the wide relationship; your work for that most worthy object was in part what brought you the [German] Grand Cross of the Order of Merit.

I am stunned by the volume of the bibliography. How on earth did you manage to write all these books, articles, review, etc. and at the same time honour your home responsibilities? It is a great achievement.

As my Other-Brother I want to give you my thoughts sparked by the book, but they are of small value because they are largely based on ignorance. I shall go on reading and rejoice in the honour bestowed on you. And as always I send you much love.

C.

C.

Name Index

Indexing system

Roman numerals	*page* number.
Arabic numerals	*letter* number.
100	letter No 100 (irrespective of whether Letter 100 covers more than one page number)
100s	*starts* on the second page of letter No 100
100t	*starts* on third page of letter No 100 A321–A326
Appendix	*page* numbers.
n	endnotc
bold	extended discussion

Ackley, Gardner 183
Ahmed, Syed 345
Alington, Cyril 331
Allen, G.C. 41, 43–43s, 45, 48, 51s, 52–53, 80, 145, 156–156s, 157s, 158, 158s(n), 159, 160–160s, 161–161s
Ambrosi, Michael 304, 324–324s
Amundsen, Arne 37s, 58, 79
Andersen, L.C. 201s
Andrews, Philip 114, 118
Arestis, Philip ix, xviii(n11); 209, 211–211s, 213–15, 215s, 216, 216s(n1,n2), 246–247, 276–277s, 279, 290s, 318, 340s, 341, 342s; A343(n9)
Arnold, Edward 300
Artis, Michael 304
Austen, Jane 2–2s; A328

Bagehot, Walter 56(n1)
Balfour, Arthur James, 1st Earl of 320s
Balfour, Eve 320s
Barna, Tibor 130
Baykov, Alexander M. 31
Beaugrand, Phillipe 253s
Beckerath, Erwin von 41, 44
Beltrán, Lucas 269s, 291s, 303, 341–2
Bird, Alan 327
Black, R.D.C. 184, 184s, 191s, 196, 219s, 225
Blunt, Sir Anthony 292s
Blunt, Wilfrid 228, 245s, 245t(n1,n2), 285, 285(n1), 292s
Boehm, Stefan 340s
Böhm-Bawerk, Eugen von 38
Boettinger, Henry 283, 309, 310s, 312–312s
Boettke, Peter A332(n)
Bonhoeffer, Dietrich 314
Bonn, M.J. 153s, 155s, 166, 166(n1)
Boussard, Jean Marc 238
Bowman, Mary Jean 103
Boyle, Sir Edward 155s
Brinckmann, C. 166
Britten, Benjamin 203, 237, 306s
Brunner, Karl 201s
Burchardt, F.A. 40, 42

Cann, Kathleen ix, xvii(n2); A337(n1)
Cantillon, Richard 233–233s, 252s, 269s, 291, 298, 328; A338
Carter, C.F. 63(n1), 155s, 160s, 191, 201s(n1), 290s; A333–A334, A337(n4), A342, A343(n8)
Ceriani, Luigi 252
Chambers, Sir Paul 124
Charles II 337
Chick, Victoria ix; 304, 306s, 315, 334s, 340s, 346, 347s, 349
Chipman, John S. 75
Churchill, Sir Winston A338
Clapham, Hilary 186s(n1), 268s(n1), 339
Clapham, Jocelyn 281–2, 282s, 329s, 336s
Clapham, Brigadier Patrick 329s
Clark, Colin 94

Clayton, George 94
Colchester, Tom A331
Courakis, A.S. 203s(n), 209(n1), 221, 227s, 228, 231, 234–5, 239s, 280
Crick, W.F. 44(n1)
Crosland, Anthony 167s
Cuthbert, Norman 184

Davidson, Paul 226s, 247–50, 253s, 255s, 263s, 264, 266, 304
Day, A.C.L. 175s
Day, Colin 244s
Dickinson, H.D. A341, A343(n5)
Dicks-Mireaux, L.A. 164s
Dürer, Albrecht 163
Dyter, Vivian 313s, 336s, 337

Earl, P.E. ix, xvii(n2); 348(n1)
Eccles, Sir John A328–329
Edey, Malcolm 82
Edward, Prince of Wales 329s
Elgar, Edward 283, 309–309s, 312, 340s
Elizabeth I, Queen 335s

Farmiloe, T.M. ix, xv; 243–4, 244–244s, 253–5, 255s, 270s, 272–4, 274s, 275–6, 279–80, 283s, 290s, 300, 302, 307s, 316s, 319
Feige, Edgar L. 209
Ferneyhau, Frances 186s(n1), 268s(n1)
Fisher, Irving 182s
Ford, P. 40
Ford, J.L. 201s(n1), 231, 233(n), 234s, 241, 241s(n1), 266, 309, 339, 340s, 343–344, 344(n1), 345; A337(n4)
Forrer, Anita 335s, 335t
Fossati, Eraldo 60s
Frederick II (Frederick the Great, King of Prussia) 309s
Friedman, Milton 191
Frowein, Adolf 150(n1)
Frowein, Kurt 346(n1)
Frowein, Erika 346(n1)
Frowein, Reinhold 298, 298s
Frowein, Rolf 138s(n1)
Frowen, Irina xii; 14s, 14s(n3), 92, 92s(n1), 125s, 138s, 139–139s, 164s, 172, 180s, 195, 223s, 232–233s, 234, 238, 250, 306, 309s, 327, 329s, 334, 335s, 338s, 339s, 346, 346(n1), 347, 352
Frowen, Michael, Bernard, James xii; 10, 13, 13(n1), 14, 31s, 85, 90, 92, 104, 113s, 114, 122s, 125s, 126, 133, 138s, 164s, 167s, 170s, 172, 174, 174s, 175s, 176s, 177s, 178s, 180–1, 185, 194, 195, 203, 218s, 245s, 270s(n), 292s, 301s, 314, 314(n1), 315, 315s, 316, 317–317s, 323–324, 327, 329s
Frowen, Tatiana Mary Anne (Tanya) (later Mrs. Hosburn) xiii; 86, 90–1, 92, 100–2, 104–6, 110–2, 114, 120–120s, 122–4, 133–8, 142–3, 144, 149, 150, 164, 165, 167s, 169s, 170s, 172, 174, 180, 203, 205–6, 207, 208–9, 210s, 218, 219, 227(n1), 283s, 315
Furth, Charles 211

Gadamer. Hans-Georg xii, xvii(n3)
Gårdlund, Torsten 106(n1)
Gibb, Angela A330
Gibb, George A330
Gilbert, John C. 339
Glatt, Max 245s
Goodwin, R.M. 75
Grey, Sir Roger de 280
Guitton, Henri 224

Hagenbuch, Prof. 164s, 165
Hague, Douglas 171
Hamouda, Omar 255s
Harbury, C.D. 128, 130
Harcourt, Geoffrey C. 236, 239s, 253s, 255s, 284, 311s, 320–321s; A342(n1)
Hare, Dick A342(n1)
Harrison, John A343(n11)
Harrod, Sir Roy 2, 2(n2), 62, 78, 78(n3,n4), 79–80, 97, 171, 275–8, 278s, 279, 284, 287; A322, A325, A326n
Hawtrey, Sir Ralph 68, 68(n2), 71(n2), 78, 78(n3,n4), 79–80, 153, 164–164s, 165s, 169–169s, 178–178s, 179–179s, 180, 185, 219s
Hayek, Friedrich A. von 32, 49, 114, 124, 234s, 269; A338
Hayter, Alethea 330s, 330s(n1,n2), 331, 336–336s, 339, 348, 352, 352(n1)
Heap, Sir Brian ix
Heller, Erich 289s
Helm, Dieter 241
Hey, John 253s, 344, 344(n1), 345

Heywood, Harold 155
Hicks, Sir John 3, 169s, 223s, 224, 252, 255s
Hillmann, B. 325
Hillmann, H.C. xviii(n5); 77, 77s(n1), 90, 90(n1), 96, 325
Holgate, H.C.F. xiv
Hölscher, Jens xviii(n7)
Home of the Hirsel, Elizabeth Lady 330s
Hopkin, Sir Bryan A333, A337(n2)
Hopson, Sir Oscar 85s
Horton, Anthony ix
Hosburn, Carly 218, 314s(n1)
Hosburn, Cassie 283s, 283s(n1), 284, 314s(n1)
Hosburn, Josie 314(n1)
Hosburn, Richard 205s, 209, 262, 283s
Hosburn, Tanya *see* Frowen, Tatiana Mary Anne
Hume, Cardinal 320s
Hurwicz, Leonid 143
Hutchison, Terence W. 62, 128–130, 130s
Hutton, Graham 103
Hyde, F.E. 107s(n1)

James II 85s
Jevons, William 191s, 196, 225
Joaquin, Domingo Castelo 263s, 264
Johnson, Harry G. 187s, 201s
Jöhr, W.G. 31, 88
Jordan, Jerry 201s

Kahn, Lord 311s
Kantor, Brian 212
Karakitsos, Elias 216s(n2), 304
Kerényi, Karl 335s
Keynes, Lord 2s, 2s(n2), 32–33, 49, 183, 208, 231, 236, 252, 269s, 290–290s, 313; A338
Kira, Princess of Prussia, Grand Duchess of Russia, 329s
Kirzner, I.M. 238, 281
Klein, Lawrence R. 81s, 82s, 104, 104s(n2)
Kloten, Norbert 309s
Knight, Frank Hyneman 308s, 311–312s
Kocen, Dr. 299
Kregel, J. A. 249–50, 281, 332
Kubinski, Z.M. 13

Labia, Joseph 253s
Lachmann, Ludwig 234–234s, 249–50, 279–281, 285, 312s
Laidler, D.E.W. 209
Lamberton, D.M. 169s, 311s
Langdale, James 39–40, 41s, 42s, 60
Law, Hilary (nee Clapham) *see* Clapham, Hilary
Leonard (Chow-Chow) 245s
Leontief, Wassily 32
Lepper, Dr. 196, 198
Lidderdale, Jane 281
Lindahl, Eric Robert 79
Lipsey, Richard 183
Littlechild, Stephen xvii(n2); 136s(n1), 241, 248; **A332–A337**
Lord, R. 174
Louis Ferdinand, Prince of Prussia 309s, 327s, 329s
Lowell, James Russell 330–331s
Lyttelton, Hon. Hester 331
Lyttelton, Sybella Lady 330–331s

Machlup, Fritz 32
McHugh, F.P. ix, xvi; 348s
Macmillan 293, 311
Madariaga, Don Salvador de 335s, 336s
Madariaga, Emilia (Mimi) 335s, 336s
Major, John 337
Mann, Thomas 289s, 307s, 347
Marshall, Alfred 171, 182s, 208, 272, 328
Martin, K. 68, 68(n1), 71(n)
Matthews, R.C.O. 160s
Meade, J.E. 169s, 212
Meltzer, Alan H. 201s, 306s, 309
Melville, Sir Eugene 218–219
Menger, Carl 196s
Meredith, G.P. 63(n1), 103, 122s(n)
Meru, Crispino F. 78–9, 82
Michaels, Rev. David 315, 315s(n1), 317s
Miller, M.H. 209(n1), 203s(n)
Minskers, Harriet 153, 154s(n)
Minskers, Irina *see* Frowen, Irina
Minskers, Sam 14
Morgan, D.J. 78, 78s(n2)
Morgan Weld-Smith, Gilbert xiii
Morgan Weld-Smith, Mita 353
Morgan Weld-Smith, Reginald 353
Motamen, Homa 253s, 259

Mueller-Groeling, Hubertus 306s
Murphy, Antoin 298
Murray, Sir James A.H. 350(n1)
Mynors, Sir Humphrey 331
Mynors, Lady (Lavinia) 330s
Mynors, Sir Roger 331

Newlyn, W.T. 80
Norrington, Roger 336s
Norton, John 13
Nove, Alexander 80

O'Brien, D.P. 243s(n2), 269
Opie, Roger 170s
Owen, A.E.B. ix, xi, xvii(n1); 309, 316s, 313, 313s
Ozga, S.A. 169s, 218s

Paish, Frank W. 46, 62, 92
Palgrave, Sir Inglis 56(n1)
Parkin, Michael 209
Pearce, Phillippa 144
Pendred, Mr. 128
Perlman, Mark 247–50, 261, 349; A342(n1)
Pheby, John 300, 306s, 308s, 311–312, 334, 349
Phelps Brown, E.H. xvii; 46–48, 51s, 52s, 53
Phillips, A.W.H. 45–46, 52
Pickering, Prof. 221
Piercy, Lord 110s, 118
Piris, Joe ix
Please, S. 77, 77s(n2)
Popper, Sir Karl A329
Poulon, Frédéric 291s
Povey, Keith ix
Presley, John R. 243s(n2)
Pressnell, L.S. 156s
Prochazka, O. 163s

Ransome, Arthur 165
Reeckie, W. Duncan 277s
Reisman, David 201s, 202, 228, 241, 253s
Ricardo, David 208
Rilke, Rainer Maria xii, xvii(n3); 208, 248s, 250, 309s, 327s, 335s, 339–339s 349; A342, A343(n11)
Rittershausen, Heinrich 128s, 155s, 160s
Rizzo, Mario J. 238
Robbins, Lord 78s(n1), 79, 79s(n1), 80–81, 89
Robertson, Sir Dennis 90, 322
Robertson, Martin 122s(n), 231
Robinson, Sir Austin (E.A.G.) 166, 177s
Robinson, Colin 180s, 193, 195s, 197–8, 218s, 221s
Rothschild, K.W. 327s, 329s
Rowan, D.C. 170s, 171

Salisbury, Lord 320s
Samulson, Paul Anthony 183s
Sargent, J.R. 172–73, 187s
Saul, Berrick 252
Saunders, Cora 139, 167s, 170s
Saunders, C.T. 92, 119, 119(n1), 121, 125, 125s(n1), 138–9, 139s, 144–145, 153s, 164s, 167s, 170s, 172, 175s, 218–218s, 236–236s, 236(n1), 243–244, 253s, 259
Sawyer, Malcolm 342s(n1); A343(n9)
Sayers, R.S. 40, 64, 124, 124(n1), 170(n), 171, 182s
Scammell, W.M. 105s, 105s(n1)
Schiller, Karl 202
Schlesinger, Helmut xviii(n11)
Schmölders, Günter 168
Schneeweis, Hans 177s
Schneider, Erich 32
Schönaich-Carolath, Princess Cathia von A343(n11)
Schumacher, E.F. 320s
Schwartz, George 56, 56(n2)
Seidel, Georg (pseudonym Ferber, Georg) 348
Seldon, Arthur 332
Shackle, Caroline 85, 111, 169s, 217
Shackle, Catherine iv, xiii–xvii; 186s(n), 219–220, 221s, 223s, 228, 231, 237, 244s, 246, 248–250, 252s, 260, 266–267, 268s(n1), 279–282s, 283s, 284–285, 293s, 294–294s, 295, 298–9, 302, 310s, 310s(n1), 314, 318–318s, 319s, 320–320s, 331–331s, 335t, 336–336s, 351, 354(n); A328–A331, A332, A335–A337, A337(n8), A339, A341
Shackle, children of G.L.S. Shackle 13, 91, 111, 136, 165s

Shackle. Richard 111, 144
Shackle, Robert 91, 111, 126, 165, 169s
Shackle, Robert Walker 137, 350(n1); A338
Shackle, Susan xiii, xiv; 13–14, 17, 20, 51s, 96, 100, 169–169s, 205s, 206, 217–218, 352; A332, A339, A340
Shakespeare, William 335s
Shone, Sir Robert 110s, 111, 114, 124
Sieber-Rilke, Hella A343(n11)
Singer, Sir Hans 31, 88
Smith, Adam 208
Smyth, Ethel 331–331s
Squirrell, S. 336s
Steedman, Ian 223–223s, 224
Stephen, Frank 238, 265, 279, 280, 298
Swann, D. 193–193s
Symon, Lindsay 298–299, 301s

Tait, Ian 299
Thomas, Brinley 269; A342(n1)
Thomas, Oliver 268s(n1), 291s, 294s
Tinbergen, Jan 16
Townshend, Hugh A341, A343(n4)
Travaglini, Volrico 8, 144
Troeller, Ruth 187s, 188, 203
Tupper, H.G. 59
Tustin, Arnold 75

Urquía, Rafael Rubio de 271, 280, 343
Usher, Anne ix

Victoria, Queen 327s, 329s

Wadsworth, J.E. 40–42s, 44, 44(n1), 46, 114
Waller, Geoffrey ix
Walz, Heinz 192
Warriner, Kate 336s
Watkins, Amanda ix
Watkins, John A332, A337
Wheble, C.L. 147, 155s, 156s, 157s, 160s, 164s, 175s, 178
Wicksell, Knut xiv, xviii(n4); 9, 9(n1), 11, 14s, 16–9, 21–21s, 22–27s, 28–30s, 31–33, 37s, 38–38s, 49, 54, 54(n1), 55, 58–9, 64–65, 75s, 76s, 77, 77s(n1), 79–81, 88–9, 106, 106s(n1), 107, 211, 269
Wilhelm II (German emperor) 309s, 327, 329s
William III 85s
Williams, David 76, 80s, 82, 84
Willoughby, L.A. 41
Wilson, J.S.G. 80
Wiseman, J. 233s(n1), 239s, 241, 243s(n2), 248, 252, 269, 332
Wordsworth, William 352
Wright, G.H. von 280

York, Duke of (later James II) 85s

Zutschi, Patrick ix, 348s

Subject Index

Indexing system

Roman numerals	*page* number.
Arabic numerals	*letter* number.
100	letter No 100 (irrespective of whether Letter 100 covers more than one page number)
100s	*starts* on the second page of letter No 100
100t	*starts* on third page of letter No 100
A328–A343	Appendix *page* numbers.
n	endnote
bold	extended discussion

Aberystwyth 146
Accepting Houses (City of London) 14(n2)
accident 153, 170s, 314n, 315s, 317
Accountant (journal) 107, 108
acknowledgements ix-x; A332n, A339n, A342(n1)
Advancement of Science (September 1966) 183n
Adventskalender (Advent calendar) 14
advertising 153; A335
Africa 219s
Age of Prose (Heller) 289s
Aldeburgh 184, 185, 203, 205s, 209s, 217s, 219, 222s, 243, 245, 247, 251s, 254, 292s, 309s, 317s, 323, 332, 335s, 339s, 353; A331
Aldeburgh: Alde House xiii; 237, 253, 354n
Aldeburgh: Rudloe (Shackle bungalow) xiii; 184, 191, 196; A329
Aldeburgh: Seagull Cottage 120s
Aldeburgh: Wentworth Hotel A332n
Aldeburgh Bookshop A332n
Aldringham Church A330
Alice in Wonderland (Carroll, 1865) 110
Allen & Unwin 26, 27s, 30–1, 33–7, 51–2, 54, 58, 61, 75s, 126, 211
anger 173
Annals of American Academy of Political and Social Science 269
architects/architecture A331, A335
art/artists 13, 96, 104, 163, 169s, 334s; A337(n7)
cloisonné enamel 55
drawings 268, 268n, 291s, 294s
painting 167s, 280; A334
Roger de Grey Exhibition 280
sculpture A328
stained glass 327s, 329s
treasures A335
Ascona 301s, 335s
Ashburn Group **110s–114**, 114n
Asian Economic Review 164s
Assisi 104
assistant lecturers 116s, 138s, 139s, 156, 161, 164s, 167s
Association of University Teachers of Economics 40
Aston University 136n, 216
Augustus M. Kelley (publisher) 211
Austrian School (economists) 49
Avebury A331

Bad Ragaz 327s, 335t
Banca Nazionale del Lavoro 241, 241(n2), 252
Bank of England 215, 331
bank managers 100s
Bank Rate 68, 68(n3)
'Bank Rate and Modernisation of Industry' (Shackle, 6.1954) **68–74**
bankers 61s, 94, 95, 124; A328
Bankers' Magazine, The xiv; 67, 104s, 122n, 170s, 219s
general:
Frowein as Assistant Editor (1954–6) xiv; 56, 60, 61s, 75, 81

Frowen as Editor (1956–60) xiv; 88, 91, 93, 101, 111, 113s, 114, 124, 126
Frowen's resignation 116
history (1844–) 56(n1–2)
illness of Editor (November 1954) 80
reprint of articles (ed. Frowen and Hillmann, 1957) xiv; **90–5**, **97–101**, 108s
Shackle's contributions 61s, 62s, **68–74**, 78–80, 89, **106–8**, **113s–115**, **117–19**
specific issues:
May 1954 63n, 65, 68, 68(n1)
June 1954 **68–74**
July 1954 68(n2)
September 1954 77, 77(n1)
October 1954 77
November 1954 77(n2), 78(n2–3)
December 1954 78, 78(n1, n4), 79, 79n, 80
January 1955 80s
April 1955 85s, 85n
October 1958 104s
November 1958 104s
December 1958 104s, 104(n2), 107n
January 1959 105, 105n
January 1960 117n
March 1960 113n, 116s
April 1960 117n
September 1960 120, 120n
banking 42s, 45, 47, 121, 126, 128, 135, 145, 164s, 182s, 204; A338
German 68
international 194s, 218s, 248
lack of cooperation with economists 61s
policy 202
theory 75
Banking in British Colonial Africa (Newlyn) 80
Banking Policy and Price Level (Robertson) 322
Banking World 56(n1)
Barclays Bank 316
Bath A331
Battersea 174
Battersea College of Technology (later University of Surrey) 172
beauty A336, A337(n7)
Bedford College of Physical Education 203
Belfast: Queen's University 184, 191s, 193, 194, 195, 219s, 225
Bellagio 196, 252
Berlin 174s, 213, 283s, 301–3s, 312s, 327s, 335s
Berlin: Free University (*Freie Universität*) 122s, 123, 167s, 170s, 171, 177s, 181, 301, 316
Frowen awarded Bundesbank Chair 221(n2)
Berlin: Landeszentralbank (Land Central Bank) 301s
Berlin: Schloss Sanssouci (Potsdam) 324
Berlin: Stock Exchange 123
Bewallerhof 288
Beyond Positive Economics? (ed. Wiseman, 1983) 233, 233n, 243(n2) 269
'Big flake' (Shackle) x; **A328–A331**
Biographical Dictionary of Dissenting Economists (eds. Arestis and Sawyer, 1992) 340s, 342s, 342n; A342
Birmingham Polytechnic 300
Birmingham University 31, 216, 231
Department of Economics: vacant full-time lectureship (1963) 138–9, 140
Frowen part-time lectureship (1962–) 128, 129, 130, 131, 135s, 136, 138
outstanding students 136s, 136n
birth anniversaries
Forrer, Anita, 90th (1991) 335s
Frowen, 65th (1988) xvi
Frowen, 70th (1993) 350
Frowen, 80th (2003) 354s
Shackle, 51st (1954) 76s
Shackle, 54th (1957) 100
Shackle, 60th (1963) 143
Shackle, 61st (1964) 163
Shackle, 80th (1983) 240–1
Shackle, 87th (1990) 326
Shackle, 88th (1991) 338
Warriner, Kate, 80th (1991) 336s
see also gifts
Black Forest 6s
Blackheath 177s
Blackwell 42, 126, 211, 285
Bolzano 259

Bonn University xii; 3, 41, 160s, 177s, 181
book titles xv; 90, 92, 94–5, 270s, **272–4**, 280
'Booming Berlin Loses Men and Money' (Frowen, 1961) 124, 124(n2)
'Bounds of Unknowledge' (Shackle, 1981/1983) 233n, 243, 243n, 244, 269
brain/mind A329, A330
Brantwood (Ruskin's residence) 325
Bristol 96
British Academy A339
British Association 169, 176, 182s, 183, 233, 233n, 269
British Broadcasting Corporation (BBC) 347s
British Library 190s
Brussels Conference (1920) 166n
Buenos Aires 136s
Buddenbrooks (Mann) 347s
Bulletin of British Neuroscience Association 283n
Bundesbank, Deutsche 168
  Frowen awarded Bundesbank Chair 221(n2) 201s, 202, 203, 221(n2)
Bürgenstock 162
Business Economists Group 109
Business finance (Russian book, 1954) 80
business journalism 75
business theory xv; 227, 272
Business, Time and Thought: Selected Papers of G.L.S. Shackle (ed. Frowen, 1988) xiv, xv-xvi, xviii(n8–9); 241(n2), 243(n1–2), 247(n1), 254, 277, 290s, 302, 310s, 312, 318, 320–1; A339, A341
  choice of title xv; 270s, **272–4s**, 280
  'compulsory reading' 283s
  dedication to Catherine Shackle xv-xvi; 293s, 294s
  dust-jacket 291s, 293s
  footnotes 279–80
  introduction by Frowen 283s, 284
  permissions to reprint 252s, 271, 275, 279, 284
  preface 252s, 283s, 284
  proofs 294–7
  reviews 307s, 308s, 311, 316, 327s, 328, 329s, 332, 340s, 343
  sales 307s
  see also Shackle bibliography
'Business and Uncertainty' (Shackle, 1960) **113–15**

Cabinet Office: Economic Section 212
California 331s, 332
Calne A331
Cam River 144
Cambridge 169, 188s, 194, 248; A328, A338
Cambridge: fitzwilliam Museum A335
Cambridge: Perse School 337
Cambridge: St. Edmund's College ix; 348(n2)
Cambridge: Von Hügel Institute ix; 348, 348(n2)
'Cambridge school of protectionists' A334
Cambridge University 13, 137, 141, 160s
Cambridge University Library ix, xvii(n1); 18n
  Shackle Papers xvii(n2); 184, 282s, 309, 310s, 316, 348s; **A332–7**, A342(n2)
Cambridge University Press xv; 3, **4–6**, 137, 146, 149, 153, 171, 184s, 208, 209, 244s
Canada 80
Capital in Economic Theory (Syed Ahmed) 345
capital theory 32
Cardiff 204s
Cardiff University A333, A337(n2)
cars 318s
Casablanca 213
'Catalogue of the Shackle Papers' (Cann) ix, xvii(n2); A337(n1)
'Central Bank Discount Policy in the UK, USA and Western Germany since 1951' (Frowen, doctoral thesis) 156s, 160s
central bankers 209
Central Statistical Office 92
certainty 227
Chartered Banker 56(n1)
cheap money (Hawtrey) 79
Chicago: Northwestern University 289s
children 13, 31, 33, 91, 106, 110–11, 136s, 165, 203, 292s, 318s; A338

childhood A331
Choice, Expectation, and Uncertainty: An Appraisal of G.L.S. Shackle's Theory (Ford, 1983) 241, 241(n1)
original title 231
Christmas 14, 55, 82, 105–6, 138s, 153, 164, 170s, 195, 226, 229, 243, 245, 292, 317
see also gifts
Christofero Colombo (Italian vessel) 109
City editors 85s
City of London 14(n2), 73
Clarendon Press 182s
classifications or concepts, pre-conceived xvi; 186s
Cleveland 190s
Cologne 122s
Cologne University 123, 128s, 131, 160s, 168
Commonwealth University Yearbook 193
Comparative Banking Institutions
book contract signed 135, 136s
Frowen's course (1961–) 122s, 123, 124, 125, 126
'no up-to-date textbook' (1962), 125
projected book by Frowen 124–7, 130–2, 143–6s, 162–3
Compton (Surrey): Church of St. Nicholas 227s, 227n
computers/computing 181, 245s, 337
conferences
Bellagio 252
British Association (York, 1981) 233n
Düsseldorf (1978) 280
'Economic Activity and Personal Responsibility' (Windsor, 1991) 335
'Financial Decision-Making and Moral Responsibility' (Cambridge, 1992) 348, 348(n2)
Helsinki (1988) 302
Malvern (1989) 306s, 309, 310, 316s
Malvern (1990) 311, 312, 325, 327s, 328
Manchester (1974) 209
Mannheim 298s
miscellaneous 96, 109, 184, 196, 299, 303s, 308s, 315s, 338s, 339s; A329
'Monetary Theory and Monetary Policy–New Tasks for the 1990s' (Berlin, 1988) 301s, 303s, 304
Oxford (1979) 221
Oxford (fails to materialise, 1983) 241
Pittsburgh 103
Rilke Society 327s, 339s
Shackle Conference (Surrey University, 1984) xv; 227s, 228, 230, 232–6, 239, 241–4, 247–50, 253s, 255s, 256, 258s, 260–5, 320s, 321; *see also Unknowledge and Choice in Economics*
Sheffield (1970) 191
university teachers of economics 138
'West German Monetary Developments' (Surrey University, 1974) 209
Coniston Lake 325
conservation A335
Contemporary Issues in Money and Banking. Essays in Honour of Stephen Frowen (ed. Arestis, 1988) ix, xvi, xviii(n11); 290s, 309s
Foreword by Schlesinger (second edition, 1993) xviii(n11)
Foreword by Shackle (first edition, 1988) xvi; 276–7, 279
reviews 307s
Controlling Industrial Economies. Essays in Honour of Christopher Thomas Saunders (ed. Frowen, 1983) 236, 236n, 243
review-article by Shackle 243(n1), 257, 258, 258(n2)
review by Shackle 243(n1), 253s, 258, 258(n3), 259, 261
'Convertibility Problems' (Harrod) 97s
convertibility problems (Harrod-Hawtrey debate, 1954) 78, 78(n3–4), 79
see also sterling
Copenhagen 143
Cornwall 125s
correspondence
literary (Rilke) 339s
Shackle (general): A332, A337
proposed volume 309s, 313, 316
Shackle-Frowen xi, xvi–xvii; 309, 316, 354; A340, A342(n2)
County Kerry 169s
Courtaulds 124

courtship A328–A330
Coventry 172
critical rationalism A332
'Crusoe's Kingdom: Cost, Choice and Political Economy' (planned paper by Wiseman and Littlechild) 241
currency exchanges 204

Dartford Tunnel 306
death, fear of 317
deaths
  Balfour, Eve (1990) 320s
  Blunt, Wilfrid 292s
  Clapham, Jocelyn; sister to Catherine Shackle (1986) 281–2
  Frowein, Adolf (1964) 150, 150n, 153
  Frowein, Rolf (1963) 138, 138n
  Frowen, Michael (1989) **314–17**, 323, 327
  Hawtrey, Sir Ralph 219s
  Holgate, Dr H.C.F. xiv
  Kahn, R. (1989) 311s
  'Leonard' (chow-chow, 1983) 245s
  Seidel, Georg (1992) 348
  Shackle, Catherine (2003) ix; 186n, 268n, 354n
  Shackle, G.L.S. (1992) xiv, xvii; 340, 340n, 341; A337, **A338–A343**
  Shackle, Susan (1978) xiii; 217–18, 352; A332, A340
  Watkins, John A332, A337
  Wiseman, Jack 332
debates
  Harrod-Hawtrey (1954–5) 78, 78(n3–4), 79, 80s
  Hawtrey-Martin (1954) 68, 68(n1), 71n
  Hayek-Keynes (1933) 49
'Decision' (Shackle, 1986) 298
Decision, Order and Time in Human Affairs (Shackle, 1961) 122n
  'new edition' 186, 187s
decision-making/decision-theory xv, xviii(n9); 227, 269s, 272, 273; A333–4, A338, A341
'Demand for and supply of money in Federal Republic of Germany, 1965–1974' (Frowen, 1977) 203n
Deutsche Bundesbank *see* Bundesbank
Devon 125s
Dictionary of Political Economy (Palgrave) 56(n1)
Dijon 266
Dijon University 244s
disbelief 227s; A341
'Disreputable Adventures: Shackle Papers at Cambridge' (Littlechild) xvii(n2); A337(n1)
doctoral studies
  Arestis 211, **213–15**
  Frowen 131s, 145, 149, 156s, 157, 160s, 200
  un-named students 244s, 280, 335s
  Reisman 201s
  Shackle 32; A338–A339
Dollar (Harrod): review by Frowein 62
Dolomites 258s, 289s
driving A331
Dublin 196
Dublin: University College (finlay Lecture by Shackle) 252, 283s
Duineser Elegies (Rilke) 338s
Durham Cathedral 331
Düsseldorf 167s
'Dynamic Impacts of Government Expenditure and Monetary Base on Aggregate Income, 1965 to 1974':
  'Case of Four OECD Countries' (Frowen and Arestis, 1978) 216(n2)
  'West German Case' (Frowen and Arestis, 1976) 216(n1)

Easingwold 38s, 39, 353
East African Colony (German) 327s
East Berlin 324
eavesdropping ('favourite Shackle pastime') 318s
Econometric Society 75s, 143
Econometrica 263s
econometrics 174, 180, 181, 215, 344
Econometrics (Tinbergen) 16
economic
  environment 344
  history 178s, 313
  problems (current) 128
  science A339, A342
  slumps (1931, 1981) A334
Economic Commentaries (Robertson) 90
Economic Commission for Europe (Geneva) 164s, 170s, 172

Economic Consequences of Peace (Keynes):
German translation 166n
Economic Issues: A financial and Economic Debate in the Critical Years, 1954–7 (eds. Frowen and Hillmann, 1957) **90–5, 97–101**
discussion about title 90, 92, 94, 95
Foreword by Shackle 90, 90n, 93–5, 97, 97n, 99
proofs 93, 94, 97–8
reviews 100s
Economic Journal 32, 160s, 174s, 174(n2), 177s, 183n, 291s, 311, 328, 344n
E.J. Newsletter 316
Economic Modelling 243(n1), 253s, 258, 258(n3)
economic policy, beyond **A333–5**, A337(n4–8)
Economic Querist (Shackle, 1974) 205
Economic Review 121
economic theory/thought xvi, xviii(n9); 39, 75, 104s, 146, 179, 184s, 191s, 196, 198, 208–9, 215, 225, 227, 313, 322, 344; A323, A341, A343(n7)
changes of fashion 32, 182s
limitations 289s
Economica (1933) 49
economics 14, 161, 172, 174, 175, 178s, 180, 181, 248, 312, 318, 323; A323
'absurd claims' to predictive power xvi; 196
'brought into disrepute' xvi; 186s, 196
conventional 272
expectational 63, 103, 110s, 195s
philosophical aspect 198, 263s, 272; A340
power of English language xi-xii; 179
pre-war rule 'gone by the board' (1960) 121
recent trends (Shackle out of sympathy with) xvi; 186, 219s
scope 186s
Shackle's slant 272
social 128
traditional methods 186s
'word fudged up from two Greek ones' 272
Economics as Art of Thought (ed. Earl and Frowen, 2000) ix, xvii(n2); 348, 348(n1); A332, A332n
Economics for Pleasure (Shackle, 1959) 110s, 111, 133–4; A338, A342
German review 181–4s
paperback reprint 134, 135s, 136s
translations 134, 136s, 181–4s
economics profession 219s, 308s, 310, 344; A334
Economist 56(n1), 103, 110s, 170s, 171
review of *Value, Capital and Rent* 78
De Economist (Dutch journal) 332
Economist in Twentieth Century (Robbins): Shackle review (1954) **78–80**, 89
'Economist's Thread of Thought' (Shackle) 334–5
economists xvi; 19, 49, 64, 148, 183, 222s, 335, 341; A333
American 103
dissenting 340s; A337(n4), A338
industrial 110s, 180s
influence of language 49
lack of cooperation with business/banking worlds 61s
'neglected' 322
Economists in Discussion (Shackle and Frowen) 354
Economists' Bookshop 135s, 156s, 190, 226
Edinburgh University 146
Edinburgh University Press xv; A330
editors 75
'Editors of *Bankers' Magazine*' 117n
education A334, A335
Edward Arnold (publisher) 300
'Elasticities of Surprise in Concept of Policy' (Shackle, 1988) xvi
elasticity of profit 296s
empirical testing 344
employment 212, 289s, 290, 322; A335
Engadin 338s
enterprise-investor 227
epistemic standing 227
epistemics 272
Epistemics and Economics. A Critique of Economic Doctrines (Shackle, 1972) (xvi), xviii(n12); 208, 291
'groping' book xvi, xvii(n12); 186s

equation-system 215
Essex University 174, 175s, 177s
Eton 331; A338
Euro-dollars 204
Europe 124, 219s, 234s, 284, 335t
European Community 345
European Economic Community 126, 127, 138
European University Institute (florence) 218s
'examination of a scheme of life' **A335–6**, A337(n9)
examiners' meetings 177s, 283s
excellence A335
exchange rate (floating) 171
Expectation in Economics (Shackle, 1949) 1n, 2; 280
  list of alterations 5
  projected Italian translation 8
  projected second edition 5, 8
  projected translation by Frowein **3–8** (postponed, 31s)
Expectation, Enterprise and Profit (Shackle, 1970) 191s; A338
  'new book' 190
Expectations, Investment and Income (Shackle, 1938) 182s, 183s; A339
  gift (1993) of first edition from Catherine Shackle to Frowen 350
  second edition (1969) 182s, 183s
experience A328, A335
exports A335
external examining 184, 196, 198, 202, 211, **213–15**

'F.A. Hayek, 1899–' (Shackle, 1981) 243, 243(n2), 269; A338
'facts' xvi; 186s
faith 292s, 316, 317s
  religious tradition 248
family matters xiii–xiv; 13, 14, 31, 33, 46, 67, 74–6, 85, 93, 100, 103, 105, 113s, 114, 118, 127, 155s, 169s, 170, 172, 174, 175s, 180, 194, 195, **217–19**, 292s, **314–15**, 329s, 334s, 337, 346–7
  education/school stage 91, 126
  'Frowein'/'Frowen' 88n, 150n
  grand-children 283s, 283n, 284, 314n
Federal Reserve Bank of St. Louis 201s
Festschriften 266
  for Beltrán 269s, 303
  for Frowen (1988) ix, xvi, xviii(n11); **276–7**, 279, 290s, 307s, 309s
  for Lachmann 281
  for Saunders (1983) 236, 236n, 243, 243(n1), 253s, 257–9, 261
  for Shackle (1972) 201s, 201n, 202, 231
  for Shackle (prospective 90th anniversary of birth) 340s
  Shackle memorial (2000) 348, 348(n1)
financial
  journalism 124
  policy 200
  sector 344
financial Times 120n, 311
financial World (1998–) 56(n1)
finanztheoretische Untersuchungen 88
fire 346, 346n, 347
'first Thoughts on Convertibility' (Scammell, 1959) 105s, 105n
flims 122n
florence 104
food A334, A335, A336
forecasts 198
Foreign Office 80
Framework of International Banking (Frowen, 1979) 218s, 218n
France 280
Frankfurt 138, 168, 201s
Frankfurt University 138, 316
  Frowen awarded a Chair (1987) 221n
Frankfurter Allgemeine Zeitung **181–4s**
Friends of Royal Academy 245s, 247
friendship xii, xiii; 2, 39, 59n, 113s, 118, 157–8, 173, 185–6, 216, 248, 294s, 305s, 330, 330(n1–2), 331, 333, 338s, 348
future xviii(n9); A333

garden 336s
G.A.T.T. (General Agreement on Tariffs and Trade) 95
'G.A.T.T. at Cross-Roads' (Morgan, 1954) 78, 78(n2)
General Certificate of Education (G.C.E.), Advanced Level 124, 172, 174, 177s, 203, 314n

General Theory of Employment, Interest and Money (Keynes, 1936) 183
'General Thought-Schemes and the Economist' (Shackle, Woolwich lecture, 1964) 139s, 140, 146, 147–8, 148n, 149, 152–3, 155
Genoa University 8, 109, 126n
George Shackle Foundation 316
German Economic Society 327s
Germany (Federal Republic) xi; 3, 7, 14, 68, 138, 150n, 161, 201s, 247, 248s, 259, 292, 302, 309s, 315s, 317, 329s, 346n; A340
  bank balance-sheet picture (1954) 64
  currency reform (1948) 45, 48, 49
  demand for money 203n, 209
  economic affairs 172, 174, 175
  Frowen lecture tours 122s, 123, 124, 167s, 168, 170s, 171, 174s, 175, 177s, 181, 182s, 264s, 265, 316
  high-investment free enterprise economy 64
  recent financial history 200
G.H. Lee Ltd (Liverpool) 120
gifts
  Clapham/Ferneyhau-Frowen (2003) 186n, 268n
  Frowein-Shackle 13, 13n, 20, 81
  Frowein-Shackle and wife (1953) 20, 55
  Frowen-Shackle 106, 142–3, 163, 185–6, 186n, 211, 212, 216, 225, 229, 305s
  Frowen-Shackle and first wife (1957) 96
  Frowen-Shackle and second wife (1986) 285
  Shackle (C.)-Frowen (1993) 350
  Shackle (G.)-Frowein (1951) 1, 1n
  Shackle-Frowen 138s, 182s, 183, 232–3
  Shackle-Michael Frowen 10, 104, 104(n1), 122s, 181
  Shackle-Tatiana Frowen 92, 101–2, 104, 105, 110, 112, 122, 123, 133, 136s, 137, 144, 149, 164, 165, 170s, 180
  Shackle-Tatiana Frowen (wedding to Richard Hosburn, 1974) 206, 208, 209, 210s
  Shackle and second wife–Frowen and wife 245–6
god-fatherhood (Shackle to Tatiana Frowen) xiii; **86–8**, 90, **101–6**, **110–14**, 120, 122–4, 133–8, 143, 144, 149, 150, 164, 165, 170s, 180, 206, 208, 227n, 283s
Goethe Society 335s
Gold Coast 13
government 164, 212
government debt 215
Granham Hill A331
Great Japan Exhibition 245, 246
Greece 185
Grindlays Bank 14n
Guildford 188, 190, 197, 214, 221, 222, 254, 258s, 261
Guildford Educational Press 218n
Gulf War (1991) 332

Hamburg University 181
Hampstead 172, 180s, 231, 264
  Frowen family's 'new house' (1956) 90, 92
Hampstead: American School 327
Hampstead: Parish Church of St. John (Anglican) 315, 315n, 317s, 319s, 327
Hampstead: St. Mary's Town & Country School 92
Hampstead: University College School 92, 122s, 125s, 138s, 164s
handwriting xi, xii; 35–6, 94, 194, 219, 263s, 267s, 269s, 299, 313, 350n; A328, A340
happiness 79, 112, 171–2, 185, 205, 215, 216, 219, 222, 240, 242, 250
'Harrod as Economist' (Shackle) 275, **277–9**, 284, 286s, 287; A338
Heffers (Cambridge) 144s, 149
Heligoland 327s, 329s
Herencia de Keynes (1988) 303
Highgate Public School 92
history 85s, 227, 272
History of Economic Thought Study Group 241
holidays/vacations 32, 33, 90–1, 100s, 104, 122n, 124s, 143, 162, 163–4, 167s, 169, 170, 184, 208, 288, 290s, 301s
House of Hohenzollern 309s

Human Freedom after Darwin (Watkins) A337
Human Mystery (Eccles) A328–A329
Hungary 335s

I.C.F.C. 120n
I.C.I. (Imperial Chemical Industries) 124
ideas xvi; 186s; A332–3
  history of 208
  heretical/heterodox 219s, 231
  new 344
ill-health/illness 2(n1), 6s, 17, 85, 121s, 153, 154, 170, 196, 210, 211s, 245s, 262s, 281, 283s, 285, 292, 297s, 317, 334s, 335s, 336, 341–2, 346–7
  arthritis 327, 329s, 335s
  cancer 80, 336s
  coronary 283s
  depression 118, 172
  emergency operation 195
  eyesight xvi; 253s, 263s, 267s, 273, 299, 327, 329s, 335s, 336, 339s, 345
  focal Jacksonian epilepsy 301s
  hospitalisation 191, 218s, 296s, 320s, 327, 331, 339, 343, 346n
  influenza 23, 265, 267s, 268
  leukaemia 138
  macular degeneration 327
  old age 354s
  overwork/strain 53, 136s, 172, 204s, 258s
  pancreatitis 195
  skin disease 335s, 336s
  tonsillitis 170s
  tuberculosis xii; 2, 2(n1), 14
imagination xv; 227, 272, 274s; A336
Imagination and the Nature of Choice (Shackle, 1979) xv, xviii(n9); 291; A330, A338
'Imagination, Unknowledge and Choice' (Shackle) 269
imports A335
Impressions that Remained (Smyth) 331
income 322
Incomes Policy (Hawtrey, 1965) 164s, 169
Independent, The 311s, 340s, 340n; **A338–A339**
indexing A330
Industrial and Commercial finance Corporation Ltd ICFC 120(n)(later 3i)
  Economic Adviser (Frowen) 110s, 118, 118n, 120(n)
industrialists 138, 150n
'infinite divisibility' 19
inflation 209
Institute of Bankers 110s
intellect/intellectuals 178, 179, 320s
interest 322
interest rates 215, 231, 256
'Interest Rates and Investment Decisions' (paper by Frowen, 1984/1990) 247, 247(n2)
International Banking Summer Course 258s
international:
  borrowings 171
  economics 172, 177, 185s
  organisations 53
International Economics series (University of Surrey) 178–80, 193
'International Liquidity' (Hawtrey) 178–80
International Monetary Fund (I.M.F.) 129
International Textbook Company 209n
internationalisation 344
interviews 46, 47–9, 56, 127, 128, 141, 145, 161, 195s
investment: effect of interest rate changes 256
'Investment by Nationalised Industries' (Please, 1954) 77, 77(n2)
Ipswich Hospital 339
Ireland 169s
Iron and Steel Board 110s
Ironic German, The (Heller) 289s
Isle of Wight 31, 32, 33, 90, 91
isolationism A335
Italy 109, 167s, 259, 288, 312s

JAI Press 275, 279, 284, 286s, 287
Japan: industrial and monetary problems (Allen) 80
Johannesburg University 253s
Journal of Economic Studies 279, 280
Journal of Economics (German) 327s
Journal of Institute of Bankers 56(n1)
journals 5, 6s

Kennet valley A331
Kenya A331
'Keynes: Meeting Point of History and Thought' (paper by Shackle) 271
French translation (by Poulon) 291
Keynes centenary (1983) 231, 236, 244s
Keynes Lecture (1976) A339
'Keynes and the Swedes' (lecture by Shackle) 32, 33
Keynesian economics 306s; A334
Keynesian Kaleidics (Shackle) 209
Kiel 64, 306s
Kiel: *Institut für Weltwirtschaft* 309
Kilimanjaro 327s
Kluwer Academic Publishers A332n
knowledge xvi; 186s; A332
theory of xviii(n9)
Königstein 168
Kredit und Kapital: Volume 9, Number 3 (1976) 216(n1)
Kyklos 88, 89, 243(n1), 258, 258(n2)

labour 289s
Lake District 325
Lancaster University A337(n4)
Lancing College 283n, 314n
language 137, 328, 333
English ('finest vehicle for economic thought') xi-xii, xiv; 59n, 179, 305s; A342
French 182s; A338
German 11, 21, 29, 137, 175, 182
Greek 305s, 337
influence on economists 49
Latin 137, 182s, 336; A338
Spanish 137, 346s
Wicksell's mastery of German 11
see also translation
Lavenham 282s, 336s
lectures 2, 6s, 48, 79, 82, 103, 109, 122s, 126, 139s, 160s, 172, 184, 190, 222s, 284
Black 196s
Hurwicz 143s
Shackle 202, 222s, 252, 266
lectureships 86s, 122s, 125, 126, 127, 128, 139, 156, 160, 161, 164s, 167, 170s
principal 149
senior 149, 221s, 221n
lecturing 204s, 219s, 261
Leeds 1, 2, 38s, 39, 46, 48–52s, 74–5, 80s, 103, 113s, 299, 325; A339
Leeds: St. Anne's Cathedral xiii
Leeds College of Technology 14s
Leeds University xii; 6s, 14(n3), 45, 76, 174, 175s, 185, 248; A340
Leipzig 327s
Leiston A331
Leontief's system 32
'Levels of Simplicity in Keynes's Theory of Money and Employment' (Shackle) 236
Leverhulme Fellowship 201, 203
'Liberal Tradition in Economics' (Shackle, 1954) **78–80**, 89
Life of John Maynard Keynes (Harrod, 1951) 2s, 2n
Life of Wicksell (Ga[o]rdlund) 106, 106n, 107
Liverpool 38s, 48, 50, 57, 81s, 84–5, 113s, 122, 126, 155, 177
Liverpool Economic and Statistical Society 122n, 125
Liverpool University xii; 6s, 8, 182s, 231, 252, 348s
Bookshop 156s
Brunner Chair of Economic Science A339
Economics Department **74–6**, 77, 94, 107n
German Department 76, 80s
Library 184
Staff House 82
vacancy for Assistant Lecturer (1954) **74–6**
Liverpool University Press 63, 67
vacancy for Secretary (1954) 76
Lloyds Bank 14(n2), 100s
Locarno 335s
logic A342
London 14s, 21, 33n, 74, 82, 85, 101, 110s, 138, 154, 161, 167s, 172, 181, 183, 184s, 185, 186n, 190, 193, 199, 203, 204s, 205, 209s, 210, 212, 217, 247, 254, 259, 270s, 281, 282s, 288, 302, 307, 310s, 319s, 327, 334s, 335s, 336s, 338s
Frowen house 'nearing completion' (1985) 268
London: Dean Trench Street 124
London: Goldsmith College 205s

London: Highgate Cemetery 315s
London: Houghton Street 169
London: Imperial College 253s
London: Moorfields Eye Hospital 327
London: National Hospital, Queen Square 301s
London: Polytechnic, Regent Street (later University of Westminster)
  Frowen applies for lectureship (1962) 125s, 127, 127n, 128
  Frowen part-time lecturer (1961) at 123
London: University College (U.C.L.) ix; 125s, 138s, 145, **156–61**, 164s, 180s, 316
  Department of Economics 139s
  Department of Political Economy 43
  German Department 41, 122s
  vacancy for Assistant Lecturer or Lecturer in Banking (1953) **41–9**, 51, 53
London Airport 192s, 327
London School of Economics (L.S.E.) 32, 53, 78, 80, 111, 116s, 124(n1), 138s, 141, 144, 175s, 218s, 283s; A332
  doctoral research by Frowen 156
  Economic Club 79
  Economics Research Division 45
  German Conversation Classes (1953) 52s
  Hayek Seminar 114, 124, 234s
  Library 327s, 332
London University 125s, 131s, 201s; A338
London University: Royal Holloway College 314n
loneliness A328
Longman 126, 127, 129, 131s
Longmans, Green & Co. 130, 135
Loughborough University 190s, 192, 193s, 194s, 195s
Lübeck: Buddenbrook-Haus 307
Lucca 104
Lund 309s

Macmillan (later Palgrave Macmillan) ix–x, xv; 56(n1), 209, 236, 243, 253, 254, 255s, 269s, 275, 281, 291, 300, 302, 308, 319
  'honourable embodiment of economists' work' 293s
  publicity department 311
macro-economics 128, 174, 177, 180, 185
Madrid 266, 269s, 280, 343
Malvern 325; *see also* conferences
Manchester 101, 171, 196, 209
Manchester Guardian 82s
Manchester School 225
Manchester Statistical Society 64
Manchester University: vacant Lectureship in Banking and finance (1962) 127
Manila 78
Mannheim 298
Mansfield Park (Austen, 1814) A328
'Marginal Revolution' (Shackle, early 1970s) 252
Marlborough A330–A331
marriage 139, 351s, 353; A332
Married to Single Life (Blunt, 1983) 245s, 245(n1)
mass production A335
mathematical analysis 180
mathematical models xvi; 186, 196
mathematicians 75, 76, 198
mathematics 170s, 174, 175s, 178s, 180, 339; A340
Mathematics at fireside (Shackle, 1952) 104s, 104(n1), 122s, 181; A338, A342
  French edition (1967) A342
  possible new edition 243, 244s
'Means and Meaning in Economic Theory' (Shackle) 233, 272
Mechanism of Economic Systems (Tushin) 75
medical research prize 315
medical school 14
'Medium and Long-Term finance for Small Businesses' (Frowen, 1960) 120, 120n
memorial service (for G.L.S Shackle) 348, 349; **A340–343**
memory (faculty) 317s
Merry Wives of Windsor (Shakespeare) 335s
'Method in Economic Theory' (Shackle) 287, 289–90
Mexico City 136s
Michael Frowen Foundation 13n
Michael Frowen Memorial Fund 315

micro-economics 185s, 335
microfilms 309s
Middlesex Polytechnic 234, 238
Midland Bank Intelligence Department 40, 42, 44, 44n
Minnesänger (book) 13, 15
'Minnow on the Say' (Pearce) 144s
Modern Economic Thought 254
monetary
  affairs 219s
  economics 94, 156, 160s, 161, 170s, 174, 175, 218s
  institutions 135
  policy 182s, 202
  system 171
  theorists/theory 45, 49, 94, 177, 182s, 199, 201s, 202, 209
  thought 309, 313
Monetary Policy and Economic Activity in West Germany (Frowen, Courakis and Miller, 1977) 203n, 209n
'Monetary Policy and Investors' (Frowein, 1955) 85s, 85n
Monetary Theory and Monetary Policy: New Tracks for the 1990s (Frowen, 1993) 301n
money 95n, 128, 135s, 164s, 182s, 204, 209, 215, 276
money study group 221
money supply theory 182s
Monopolies and Mergers Commission 136n
moon voyages 337
moral theology xvi
mountain scenery 288
multipliers 75, 215
Münster University 316
music 219, 312, 333, 335, 337, 339; A334
  Aldeburgh Festival 185, 203
  Bach Choir 219, 336s
  Britten record 237
  Death in Venice (Britten) 203
  Glyndebourne 306
  Midsummer Night's Dream (Britten video) 306s
  Prince Louis Ferdinand 309s
Muzot Castle 339s

Namur University 258s
National Economic Development Office 164s
national income 95s, 215
National Institute of Economic and Social Research (N.I.E.S.R., London) 125n, 127, 129, 164s; A334
  Research Officer (Frowen) 121, 121n, 124
National Liberal Club 110s
naturalisation xiii; 14, 14n, 53, 88n
Nature of Business Success (ed. Shackle, 1969) 176, 182s, 183
Nature of Economic Thought (Shackle, 1966) 113n, 267s
'Nature, Notion et Notation de l'Incertitude' (Shackle paper in translation) 303
'Nature of Profit' (Shackle, Woolwich lecture 1967) xviii(n6); 177s, 178, 247(n1)
neo-classical theory A333
Nervi 109
New Dictionary of National Biography **351, 353**
New Forest A329
New Prospect of Economics (eds. Hyde and Shackle, 1958) 104, 104(n2), 107, 107n
New York 302
New York: Columbia University 100
New York University Press 281, 307s, 311
'News from Sweden' (Shackle) 269, 271
newspapers 85s, 155s, 182s, 186s
Nieuwe Amsterdam (Dutch vessel) 109
North London Collegiate 138
North Wales 353
North-Western Polytechnic 172, 174
Northanger Abbey (Austen, 1818) A328
Nottingham 176

Observer, The 124, 124(n2)
'observership' A330
occupation A334
O.E.C.D. (Organisation for Economic Cooperation and Development) 216
O.E.E.C. (Organisation for European Economic Cooperation) 64, 65
O.E.R.G. (Oxford Economists' Research Group) 114
Oldenburg 329s

'Optimal Choice of Monetary Policy Instruments: The U.K. Case' (Arestis) 211
originality of mind 201s
'Origination of Choice' (Shackle) 269, 271
Oslo University Institute of Social Economy 37, 38s
Oslo "Institute of Economics" 32
output 289s, 290
overseas trade 121
Oxford 206, 211, 228, 239s, 241, 280, 350; A330–A331
Oxford: Institute of Statistics 42
Oxford: Brasenose College 227s, 228
Oxford: Nuffield College 81s
Oxford: St. Catherine's College 283n
Oxford: Worcester College 125s
Oxford English Dictionary–A New English Dictionary on Historical Principles 350, 350n
Oxford University 42, 47, 76, 331, 335s; A338

Paris 266, 303, 339s
Pennsylvania University 104
Perugia 104
Peter Rabbit (Potter, 1900) 110
Pewsey A330–A331
philosophers/philosophy A330, A337
 see also economics/philosophical aspect
photography 90, 101, 124, 169s, 221, 228, 237, 245s, 261, 292
Pioneers of Modern Economics in Britain (O'Brien and Presley, 1981) 243(n2), 269
Pisa 104
Pittsburgh University 176
poetry 135s, 339, 349; A337(n7), A342
 see also Rilke Society
policy: 'expectational basis and meaning' 290
'Policy, Poetry and Success' (Shackle, 1966) 174s, 174(n2), 183, 183n
Policy Studies A337(n4)
Policy Studies Institute (UK) A333, A337(n4)
politics/politicians 124, 178s, 195s
Portrait of Friendship, Drawn from New Letters of James Russell Lowell to Sybella Lady Lyttelton, 1881–1891 (ed. Hayter, 1990) 330, 330(n1), 331
possessions, hand-made A335
'Possibility: Interpretation, Inverse Measure, Marginal Comparison' (Shackle) 298s
post-war era (1945–) xi; 329s
power 177
'Pressures in Macro- and Micro-economics' (Frowen paper, 1991) 335
price/price level 164s, 182s, 215, 322
Pride and Prejudice (Austen, 1813) 2
Principles of Economics (Marshall, 1890) 272, 328
probability xviii(n9); A338
professorships 130, 146, 177, 180s, 190s, 192, 193s, 194s, 195s, 217s, 218s, 221(n2), 231, 285
 emeritus 182s; A339
 personal chairs 221s
 visiting 190s, 226s
'Profit, on the Mature' (Shackle, Woolwich lecture, 1967) xviii(n6); 177s, 178, 247(nl)
profit **322**
prose 339; A338
protectionism A334, A335
psychiatrists 245s
Public finance 216, 216(n2)
public works 212
publisher's reader 191
publishing delays 98

qualifications 157s
quantity theory 186s
Quaritch 348s
Quarterly Review (Banca Nazionale del Lavoro) 241, 241(n2)
Quellenhof (Hotel) 327, 335s
'questions for G.L.S. Shackle' **A336**

Radcliffe Committee 120n
rail travel 188s, 191, 221s, 260; A331
 Euston (London) 50, 83, 113s, 140, 141
 Liverpool Street (London) 191s, 192, 214, 237, 249, 258s, 299
 Paddington (London) A330
 model railway 133

rational expectations **A333**, A337(n2–3)
readerships (university) 218s, 221s
Reading A330–A331
reading aloud xiv; 110s, 136, 165s, 194, 219, 280, 289, 294s, 295, 318, 320, 322, 328, 337, 339, 345, 347s; A328–A329
Reading University 145, 216
Reason in Human Affairs (Shackle) 303
referees 41, 125s, 128, 164s, 167, 172s, 175, 192
  see also testimonials
Reform Club 141, 167s, 177s, 180s, 183, 188s, 189, 190, 192s, 197, 199, 203, 205–7, 209, 211, 218, 243, 282s, 302
'Relative Strength of Pound and Dollar' (Hawtrey, 7.1954) 68, 68(n2)
'rent' 18s, 21
reputation 75, 116, 121s, 143, 194
research 13, 125, 156s, 177, 203, 203n, 218s, 221
  quantitative 215s
research fellowships 194s, 195s
Review of Austrian Economics A332n
Review of Economic Studies A339
Review of Political Economy 316, 340s; A342(n1)
reviewers A330
Richard Cantillon: Entrepreneur and Economist (Murphy): review-article by Shackle 298
Rilke Society 309s, 339s
risk xvi
Risk, Uncertainty and Profit (Knight) 308s, 311, 312
'Roaring 40' 149
Robbins Report 145, 146s
'Rôle of Economist in Official Employment' 31
rôle models xii, xvii
  Phelps Brown xvii; 47
  Shackle xvii; 125s
Roman Catholicism xiii
Rome 144
Rotterdam 109
Royal Academy: Private Views 245s, 247, 248
Royal Air Force xiii
Royal College of Music 335s
Royal Economic Society 140, 166, 167s, 169, 183, 184
  Newsletter 239s
Royal Free Hospital 283s, 315
Royal Free Hospital School of Medicine 315
rush of events 64, 203
Russia 80
Rutgers University: Frowen Visiting Professor at (1981) 226s

sabbaticals/study leave 195s, 196, 221s, 227s, 228
St. Andrews University A338
St. Gallen 31, 283s, 335s, 336
St. Paul's (school) 92
salary 46, 47, 52s, 74, 75, 116s, 156s, 160s, 167s
Salisbury A331
Samaritans 298
Saxmundham A331
Scheme of Economic Theory (Shackle, 1965) 167s, 170s, 171, 172; A341
school reports 91
science/scientists 146s, 180s; A329, A335
Scottish Economic Society 252
Scottish Journal of Political Economy 253s, 271
Second World War xii, xiii; 178, 317; A338
security 46
seminars/tutorials xii; 128, 146, 160s, 172, 211
Shackle bibliography xviii(n7); 251s, 252, **263–9**, 279–80, 291, 298, 299s, 302, 303, 310s, 319s
Shackle Prize (projected) 300
Shamley Green: Mulberry Croft (Frowen's residence, 1967–1990) 177s, 178, 180s, 228, 231, 247, 258s, 319
Sheffield 32, 38, 40, 56, 231
Shelford 144
Sicily 205
silver/silversmiths 96, 186n
Slow on the Feather. Further Autobiography 1938–1959 (Blunt, 1986) 245s, 245(n2), 285, 285n, 292s
small business 120n
Snape 285

snobbishness 135
snow A331
Soil Association 320s
solitude 339s
'Some investigations of demand and supply functions for money in Federal Republic of Germany, 1965 to 1974' (Frowen, 1976) 203n
Sotheby's 334s
South African Journal of Economics 234, 271
South Hampstead High School for Girls 174, 180s
South Wales A331
Southampton University 40, 170s, 171
Southwold 85s
Spain 256, 260–1
special deposits 103, 104s
speculative opinions 165
spring 336s
'stabilisation' measures 212
statistics 75, 215
steel industry 110s
'Stephen Frowen: Editor of *Bankers' Magazine 1955–60*' (Shackle, 1960) **117–19**
sterling 68, 171
sterling convertibility 105s, 105n
Stern Scholarship 171
Stockholm 103
Strathclyde University 265, 302, 351
Strutt & Parker 336s
'A Student's Pilgrimage' (Shackle, 1983) 241, 241(n2), 294s, 318s; A342
students 99, 108, 123, 124, 125, 131, 135, 136s, 136n, 148, 164s, 172, 186s, 196; A339
  mature 180s
  overseas 133
  postgraduate 177, 180, 183, 187s, 189, 195, 203, 209; A340
  reading lists 201s, 205
  turned away by universities 167s
  undergraduates 177, 180, 180s, 183
subjectivism 234s, 239s; A338, A341
Suffolk 85
  see also Aldeburgh
Sunday Times, The 56(n2)
Surrey 177s, 218s
Surrey Papers in Economics 193, 194, 195, 222s
Surrey University 192, 201s, 221s, 221(n1–2), 241, 243, 253s, 254, 279
  administration 178, 221(n1)
  appointment of Professor of Economics 177, 180s
  committee work 221(n1)
  conference (1974) 209, 209n
  conference in honour of Shackle (1984) xv; *see also* conferences/Shackle Conference
  Department of Humanities 180s
  Department of Linguistics and International Studies 216, 221s
  Department of Linguistics and Regional Studies 172, 174, 175, 177, 180s
  Frowen an Associate Lecturer (1967) **172–5**
  Frowen a Senior Lecturer (originally Lecturer) in Monetary Economics and German Economic Affairs (1967–87) xv; **174–7**, 221n
  Guildford campus (under construction) 174, 180s
  lacks economics department (1968) 180s
  Michael Frowen reading for M.Sc. in Economics 203
  paper read by Hawtrey (1967) 178
  postgraduate seminar programme (Shackle contribution, 1969) **185s-9**, 193, 194, 195
  public lectures in economics 195s, 200
  research programme (1979) 221
  Sub-Department of International Economics 172, 174, 175, 177, 180s
  'things have improved greatly' 190s
  undergraduate course in economics (intention to start) 177
Surrey University Press 209n
survival of fittest 317s
Sussex University (Brighton) 125s, 130
Swansea 204s
Sweden 75s, 77, 309s
Swindon A331
Switzerland 96, 122n, 162, 164, 167s, 209, 210, 247, 248s, 283s, 312s, 335s, 339s
Sylt 306s, 338s

Taunus 168
tax reform 121
teaching 108, 125, 131, 146, 165, 172, 174, 177, 180, 183, 197, 201s, 203, 246; A339
Technical Adviser to German Government (M.J. Bonn) 166n
technical colleges 144, 172s
technological progress/technology 289s; A335
telephone calls 45, 68, 82, 113s, 128, 230, 264, 266–7, 271–3, 275–6, 281, 292, 294s, 302s, 305, 310s, 311, 332, 341, 346–7, 351s
testimonials 44, 116, 130, 131, 140, 185, 186, 203
  see also referees
textbooks 39–40, 41s, 42s, 82, 107n, 108, 130, 248, 333
Thames Papers 246–7, 296
Thames Polytechnic 211
Thames River A331
theatre A334
theologians 335
theory of firm (*Expectation, Enterprise and Profit*, Shackle 1970) 191s
Theory of Profit (Lamberton, 1963) 311
T.H.E.S. 311
thought 36, 110s, 165, 183, 272, 274s; A336
  freedom of A337
  schemes of 146
  successful transmission 333
Ticino 335s
time xii, xvi; 2, 13, 23, 25, 36, 37, 38, 41, 42s, 44, 62, 65, 66s, 76, 95, 110s, 118, 127, 128s, 131, 145, 147, 165s, 199, 201s, 209s, 211, 221, 234, 246, 271, 272, 273, 274, 292s, 318; A338
  for preparation of lectures 175s
  for research 156s, 175s
Time in Economics: Decision, Order and Time in Human Affairs (Shackle, 1951) 318s; A338
Time, Expectations and Uncertainty in Economics: Selected Essays of G.L.S. Shackle (ed. Ford, 1990) 344, 344n, 345
Times, The 6s, 41, 74–5, 91, 120, 120n, 121, 202, 314, 332; A332
Times Literary Supplement, The 291s, 311
Torquay 125s
tourism A335
Towards Rescue of Sterling (Hawtrey) 68, 68(n1)
tragedy
  nature 180s
  personal xvii
training A335
translation 16, 42s, 75s, 335s; A338
  English-Czech A338, A342
  English-French 291s; A342
  English-German **3–8**, 166n
  English-Italian 8, 267s
  English-Spanish 282, 291s, 303
  Frowein (of works by W.G. Jöhr) 31
  German-English 181–4; A343(n11)
  Italian-English 39–40, 41s, 42s, 60
  'most exacting and difficult' 184s
  problems xiv
  put on hold (by Frowein) 48, 49
  see also languages; *Value, Capital and Rent*
Treago Castle (Herefordshire) 331
Treasury Bill rate 215
Treatise on Money (Keynes, 1930) 49
'Treatise, Theory and Time' (paper by Shackle) 271
  Spanish translation (by Beltrán) 282, 291s, 303

Über Wert, Kapital und Rente (Wicksell, 1893), *see Value, Capital and Rent*
U.C.L. *see* London: University College
uncaused cause 227; A341
uncertainty xvi; 61s, 227, 318s; A338, A341
  see also 'unknowledge'
Uncertainty and Business Decisions (eds. Carter, Meredith and Shackle)
  review by Frowein (*BM* 5.1954) **63–7**
Uncertainty in Economics and Other Reflections (Shackle, 1955) 267s; A342
Uncertainty and Expectations in Economics. Essays in Honour of G.L.S. Shackle (eds. Carter and Ford, 1972) 201s, 201n, 202, 231
United Kingdom/Britain 126, 127, 135, 138, 164s, 209, 215, 302; **A334–A335**

United Kingdom/Britain *continued*
England xi, xii; 64, 116, 125s, 144, 177s, 185, 280
Scotland 169, 184
Wales 202
United Kingdom: Government Economic Service A337(n2)
United Kingdom: H.M. Treasury A337(n2)
United States of America 80, 81s, 82s, 128, 135, 177, 203, 221s, 302
Congress: Joint Economic Committee 105s
dollar 68
Trade Expansion Act 139s
universities 129, 136s, 139s, 145, 167s, 283n
new (UK) 164s, 177
University College of North Wales 105
University of Constance 201s
University of Kent at Canterbury 164s, 165, 167, 244s
university teachers 99s
'unknowledge' xvi; 227; A341
Unknowledge and Choice in Economics: Proceedings of a Conference in Honour of G.L.S. Shackle (ed. Frowen, 1990) xv, xviii(n7); 247(n2), 310s, 311, 315s, 316s, **319–22**
dust cover 302, 320
preface by Frowen 320
introduction by Harcourt 320
nunc dimittis for Shackle 320
speech by Shackle xviii(n7); 262–5
see also Shackle bibliography
'Unquiet Market' (section of paper by Shackle, 1982) 252, 269s
Uppsala 75s, 103

Value and Capital (Hicks) 3
Value, Capital and Rent (Wicksell, translated by Frowein, 1954) xiv, xviii(n4); 9, **11–12**, 14s, **16–19**, **21–38**, 62, 65, 75s, 76s, 79, 80, 81, 211
bibliography of Wicksell works (Amundsen) 37, 38s, 58, 64
'excellent translation' 82s, 88
introduction by Shackle xiv; 9n, **26–8**, **30–8**, 51, 58, 59n, 61, 269
proofs 36, 51–2, 54, 61, 64
reviews 77, 77(n1), 78, 82s, 88, 89
'Translator's Note' (Frowein) xiv, xviii(n4); 58–9, 60
Venice Exhibition 245s
Vierwaldstätter Lake 162s
viva voce examinations 214, 215, 244s, 335s

wage behaviour 164s
Wannsee 301s
Warwick University 172, 177s, 178s, 180, 181, 185s, 187s, 194
Washington 116
Waterlow & Son Ltd 56, 74, 116s
weddings:
daughter of Norbert Kloten 309s
Richard Hosburn–Tatiana Frowen (1974) 205s-10s, 227n
G.L.S. Shackle–Catherine Squarey Gibb (1979) A330
Weimar 327s, 335s
Weltwirtschaftliches Archiv 203n, 306s, 309
'Kiel journal' 64
West Country 353
West Kirby 85, 353
Westminster Cathedral 320s
'What Did the General Theory Do?' (Shackle paper) 298
'What Makes an Economist' (Shackle lecture) 139s
Wind in Willows (Grahame, 1908) 136s
Windermere 312s, 325
Windsor Castle 335, 336
Wm. Brandt and Sons Ltd (variously styled) 14s, 14n, 16, 42, 54
Wonersh 178
Woolwich Economic Lectures (annually, 1963–) xiv; 164s, 166, 167s
Shackle (1964) 139s, 146, 147–8, 148n, 149, 152–3, 155
Woolwich Economic Papers xv; 166, 169, 246–7, 252
No 2, *General Thought-Schemes and the Economist* (Shackle, 1964) xviii(n6); 137, 148–54, 156s, 162, 164s, 165, 247(n1)
proofs 152–4
No 13, *Nature of Profit* (Shackle, 1967) xviii(n6); 177s, 178, 247(n1)

Woolwich Polytechnic (later University of Greenwich) xiv–xv; 138, 139s, 141, 145, 151s, 155–6, 160s, 175s, 178
aspires to university status 135s, 145, 164s, 167s
difficulty in attracting students 164s, 167s
first Annual Dinner (1965) 166
Frowen's application for lectureship (1962) 128, 129, 132
seventy-fifth anniversary celebrations (1965) 164s, 167s
Woolwich Polytechnic: Economics Department 139s, 164
Woolwich Polytechnic: Lecturer in Monetary Theory and International Trade (Frowen, 1962–7) xiv; 131, 133, 135
'considerable attractions' 158s
teaching load 135s, 136s, 140, 163
'Word-Efficiency and Economist' (Shackle) 333
World Bank 146
World Economy 311
'world of George Shackle' **A337**
Wreck of ABERGAVENNY: One of Britain's Greatest Maritime Disasters and its Links to Literary Genius (Hayter, 2002) 352, 352n
writer's art 305, 341; A340, A342
writing (scholarly) 174, 183, 218s, 219, 285, 289s, 290s, 310, 310n; A336, A342
Würzburg 181, 217s, 327s

Years of High Theory: Invention and Tradition in Economic Thought 1926–1939 (Shackle, 1967) 174s, 174(n1); A339, A341
Italian translation (*Anni dell'Alta Teoria*, 1984) 267s
York 233n, 252

Zürich 192